Interviewing Children About Sexual Abuse

Interviewing Children About Sexual Abuse

CONTROVERSIES AND BEST PRACTICE

Kathleen Coulborn Faller

OXFORD
UNIVERSITY PRESS
2007

OXFORD
UNIVERSITY PRESS

Oxford University Press, Inc., publishes works that further
Oxford University's objective of excellence
in research, scholarship, and education.

Oxford   New York
Auckland   Cape Town   Dar es Salaam   Hong Kong   Karachi
Kuala Lumpur   Madrid   Melbourne   Mexico City   Nairobi
New Delhi   Shanghai   Taipei   Toronto

With offices in
Argentina   Austria   Brazil   Chile   Czech Republic   France   Greece
Guatemala   Hungary   Italy   Japan   Poland   Portugal   Singapore
South Korea   Switzerland   Thailand   Turkey   Ukraine   Vietnam

Published by Oxford University Press, Inc.
198 Madison Avenue, New York, New York 10016

www.oup.com

Oxford is a registered trademark of Oxford University Press

Library of Congress Cataloging-in-Publication Data
Faller, Kathleen Coulborn.
Interviewing children about sexual abuse : controversies and best practice /
Kathleen Coulborn Faller.
p.   cm.
Includes bibliographical references and index.
ISBN-13 978-0-19-531177-8
ISBN 0-19-531177-9
1. Child sexual abuse—Investigation—United States.   2. Interviewing in
child abuse—United States.   3. Sexually abused children—United States.   I. Title.
HV8079.C48F37   2007
362.76'565—dc22   2006016751

9   8   7   6   5   4   3   2   1

Printed in the United States of America
on acid-free paper

We dedicate *Interviewing Children About Sexual Abuse* to our much-missed colleague, William N. Friedrich, better known as Bill. He was a personal and professional inspiration to us all. He had an extraordinary impact upon the field of child sexual abuse assessment and treatment.

Preface

Child sexual abuse is a hotly contested societal issue. Sexual abuse engenders controversy because both believing and disbelieving sexual abuse reports have grave and far-reaching consequences for the children, adults, and institutions involved in such allegations. For example, disbelieving an accurate child disclosure can leave the victim in dire jeopardy. On the other hand, incorrectly believing a child has been sexually abused can have devastating effects, principally on the accused. And perhaps even more fraught are decisions that must be made by childcaring and other institutions when sexual abuse allegations arise. These institutions face competing concerns and priorities, for instance, providing protection for children, supporting and standing by staff, and preserving the institution's good name. The stakes are very high, and emotional reactions can be overwhelming.

Among the sexual abuse issues in dispute are the extent of the problem, the accuracy of child and adult accounts of sexual abuse, the techniques and strategies used by professionals assessing and investigating allegations of sexual abuse, methods for decision-making about the probability of sexual abuse, appropriate interventions in sexual abuse cases, and the impact of sexual abuse on its victims. This book cannot address the full spectrum of contested issues. It focuses on child assessment and sexual abuse decision-making, which are related to the issue of children's accuracy in their reports of sexual abuse. It addresses these issues by focusing on knowledge rather than on emotions.

The primary objective of the book is to acquaint professionals with salient issues in substantive areas related to interviewing children about allegations of sexual abuse. The book does this by critically evaluating the research studies, best practice guidelines, and the conceptual, clinical, and opinion-based writings about interviewing and assessing suspected child sexual abuse. This knowledge will inform readers about how to conduct an adequate assessment of sexual abuse and, using this knowledge, prepare them to defend evaluation procedures in the court and other arenas.

Interviewing Children covers 17 knowledge areas, one topic per chapter, all of which are very relevant to assessing children for possible sexual abuse. The rationale for each chapter and knowledge area is described briefly below.

Interviewing children about possible sexual abuse occurs in both forensic (legal) and clinical (therapeutic) domains. The first chapter, by Kathleen Coulborn Faller, describes the differentiation between forensic and clinical work but also notes the variability of practice in each domain and the overlapping nature of forensic and clinical work.

Central to interviewing children about possible sexual abuse are concerns about their memory and suggestibility. There is a substantial body of research addressing accuracy of children's accounts of past experiences. In chapter 2, Erna Olafson examines the sources of information about children's memory and suggestibility and different types of memory and recall. In addition, she describes age differences, individual differences, the impact of trauma, and the research that compares the accuracy of children with and without an abuse history.

Professionals must decide whom to see in what configurations, when assessing for sexual abuse, and be able to provide a rationale for the model of assessment they employed. In chapter 3, Faller conceptualizes current practice as four overlapping models for conducting assessments for possible sexual abuse. The chapter also guides the reader through the research and opinion about models for assessment.

Current policy is to advise professionals interviewing for sexual abuse that they should take a neutral stance, that is, with no vested interest in finding or not finding evidence of sexual abuse. Faller covers etiology of the admonition for interviewer neutrality and its utility in chapter 4. In addition, research demonstrating that interviewer characteristics, such as gender and profession, predict whether interviewers are more likely to believe or disbelieve children's reports, is discussed.

Child welfare resources typically dictate the number of interviews children receive before a decision is made about the likelihood of sexual abuse, usually one interview. Relevant research, which suggests that the number of interviews should vary depending upon where the child is in the disclosure process, whether the assessor is trying only to determine abuse or has additional goals, whether the child is safe, how old the child is, and whether the child has mental health problems form the substance of chapter 5.

The documentation debate revolves around whether or not to video record child assessment interviews. In the 1980s, a videotape of the child's interview promised to be a solution to the documentation dilemma and a substitute for child testimony in court. Videos have not been entirely satisfactory in meeting either goal. Chapter 6 covers various forms of documentation, the professional debate about documentation, and advantages and disadvantages of videotaping and offers suggestions about how to and whether to videotape.

The phases or stages of the child interview are the subject of numerous guidelines, some informative research, and a great deal of opinion. Employing an interview structure that is evidence based, comports with best practice, and yet accommodates the needs of the individual child is a challenge. In chapter 7, Faller conceptualizes interview structures along a continuum of prescriptiveness. Taking into account both the research and practice literature, the chapter discusses the chronology of an interview, describing components that are recommended at various phases of the interview and their empirical support. Finally, the chapter presents advantages and disadvantages of structured interview protocols.

Perhaps the most hotly debated aspect of the child interview is the questions employed by the interviewer (e.g., Faller, 2003; Poole & Lindsay, 2002; Poole & Lamb, 1998; A. G. Walker, 1999, 2001). The core of the debate is whether or not a particular type of question elicits accurate information from the child. A great deal of research has been undertaken on questioning procedures, although most of this is analogue research. To assist readers, in chapter 8, question types are divided into three general categories: preferred, less preferred, and least preferred. Each type of question is described and illustrated, and differing opinions about the appropriateness of each type of question are discussed. Additional questioning controversies are also addressed.

Another contested issue is the use of media, props, tools, or aids, as means of communication about abuse. The controversy over media originated with the use of anatomical dolls, that is, dolls with private parts (Faller, 2003). The research and practice on anatomical dolls, anatomical drawings, and free drawing are covered in chapter 9 (Everson & Boat, 2002). Interviewers may employ other media, but other media lack an empirical base. Indeed, most of the research is on the use of anatomical dolls, which have been the subject of more than 100 written works.

Preschool children pose a special challenge in sexual abuse assessment because of their limited communication skills and increased suggestibility compared with older children (e.g., Ceci & Bruck, 1993). In chapter 10, Faller and Sandra K. Hewitt provide guidelines for both very young children, ages 18 months to 3 years, and older preschoolers. The chapter describes the unique developmental considerations and data-gathering methods for preschool children when there are sexual abuse concerns.

Children with special needs because of developmental and/or physical disabilities also require special interview skills. In chapter 11, Faller and Deborah Davies discuss research on children with disabilities, which includes their increased risk for abuse and greater dependency on potential abusers. Preinterview data gathering and adapting the interview structure to the child's abilities are also covered.

Professionals who interview children for possible sexual abuse tend to be white and middle class (e.g., Child Welfare League of America, 2002). At the same time, children and families who require assessment for sexual abuse are increasingly diverse. Professionals need to develop special skills to interview cross-culturally (Fontes, 1995, 2005b). Faller and Lisa Fontes, in chapter 12, describe the need for interviewers to take into account race, class, culture, subculture, religious, and language differences when interviewing children. How these differences can pose barriers for evaluators and strategies for enhancing agency and professional cultural competence are covered.

Nondisclosing children continue to challenge interviewers of sexual abuse cases, but there has been less progress in developing techniques for assisting them than there has been for disclosing children, in part because constructing appropriate research paradigms is so difficult. Chapter 13 covers research from several domains that yields an estimate of the extent of nondisclosure. The chapter also provides advice from research and practice on techniques that may be useful with children who are reluctant to talk about sexual abuse.

Both professionals and the public are attentive to and, in some instances, preoccupied with the possibility that sexual abuse allegation might be false. Chapter 14 first differentiates between false and unsubstantiated reports. Then the chapter addresses the obstacle of knowing with certainty that an allegation of sexual abuse is false, pointing out that the criterion employed in most research is the opinion of the researcher, or a group of researchers. The chapter then focuses on evidence—what is known from research about the extent and source of false reports of sexual abuse. The research suggests that consciously made false reports occur infrequently, and they are more likely to be made by adults than by children.

The use of standardized tests and measures can supplement information obtained from interviewing the child. In chapter 15, based upon a substantial body of research, Faller, Olafson, and William N. Friedrich provide information about instruments for both children and adolescents. The chapter covers instruments developed specifically to gather data on possible indicators of sexual abuse and trauma and to measure the impact of sexual abuse. Data from generic tests that have been employed with sexually abused children and adolescents are presented.

Once the professional has conducted interviews with the child and gathered other data, how then does he/she decide about the likelihood of sexual abuse? Faller begins chapter 16 by reviewing the literature on decision-making protocols and notes commonalities and differences. This review is followed by a framework and a process for decision-making. This framework allows professionals to document all of the information, from both the child interview(s) and other sources, on a single instrument to propose a range of explanations for each finding, to select the explanation most consistent with other facts and findings, and to determine the weight to place on each finding.

The final chapter guides the reader through the literature on conclusions about abuse and potential errors in forming conclusions. Readers are advised to consider multiple hypotheses and avoid focusing only on information confirmatory of sexual abuse. Chapter 17 provides a framework for considering the degree of certainty about sexual abuse and discusses how this framework interfaces with the legal system.

Some of these topics have a large literature and have been researched fairly extensively, resulting in longer chapters. Other topics have a more modest empirical base. All of the topics, however, are central to evaluating children for sexual abuse.

Contents

Contributors   xv

1. Forensic and Clinical Interviewer Roles in Child
   Sexual Abuse   3
   Kathleen Coulborn Faller

2. Children's Memory and Suggestibility   10
   Erna Olafson

3. Models for Assessing Child Sexual Abuse   35
   Kathleen Coulborn Faller

4. Interviewer Objectivity and Allegations of
   Sexual Abuse   44
   Kathleen Coulborn Faller

5. Number of Child Interviews   50
   Kathleen Coulborn Faller

6. Documentation of the Interview   58
   Kathleen Coulborn Faller

7. Interview Structure, Protocol, and Guidelines   66
   Kathleen Coulborn Faller

8. Questioning Techniques   90
   Kathleen Coulborn Faller

9. Media for Interviewing Children   110
   Kathleen Coulborn Faller

10. Special Considerations for Cases Involving
    Young Children   142
    Kathleen Coulborn Faller and Sandra K. Hewitt

11. Interviewing Children With Special Needs   152
    Deborah Davies and Kathleen Coulborn Faller

12. Conducting Culturally Competent Sexual Abuse
    Interviews With Children From Diverse Racial,
    Cultural, and Socioeconomic Backgrounds   164
    Lisa A. Fontes and Kathleen Coulborn Faller

13. Children Who Do Not Want to Disclose   175
    Kathleen Coulborn Faller

14. False Allegations of Sexual Abuse   191
    Kathleen Coulborn Faller

15. Standardized Tests and Measures   207
    *William N. Friedrich, Erna Olafson,
    and Kathleen Coulborn Faller*

16. Criteria for Deciding About the Likelihood
    of Sexual Abuse   226
    Kathleen Coulborn Faller

17. Formulating Conclusions About Sexual Abuse   245
    Kathleen Coulborn Faller

    References   255
    Index   299

Contributors

Kathleen May Lawton Coulborn Faller, Ph.D., A.C.S.W., is Professor of Social Work and Director of the Family Assessment Clinic at the University of Michigan. She received her M.S.W. and Ph.D. from the University of Michigan. She is the author of seven books and more than 70 articles. Presently she is the Principal Investigator of the Program on the Recruitment and Retention of Child Welfare Workers, funded by the U.S. Children's Bureau, and Principal Investigator of the Hasbro Early Assessment Program. She served on the Board of Directors of the American Professional Society on the Abuse of Children for 7 years and the Executive Committee for 6 years. She was the recipient of the APSAC Outstanding Service Award in 1996.

Deborah Davies, L.I.C.S.W., is a licensed clinical social worker who has been conducting forensic interviews as a member of a multidisciplinary team since 1985. Deborah is the lead social worker in the Forensic and Medical Services Department at the Chadwick Center for Children and Families at Children's Hospital in San Diego. She received her M.S.W. from the University of Maryland and a Specialist Certificate in the Habilitation of Developmentally Disabled Citizens from the University of Maryland, Johns Hopkins Medical School, and the John F. Kennedy Institute. She has conducted numerous trainings on forensic interviewing, including the APSAC Forensic Interview Clinic and APSAC institutes, throughout California and the United States and has published on forensic interviewing.

Lisa Aronson Fontes, M.A., Ph.D., has dedicated more than 15 years to making the social service, mental health, and criminal justice systems more responsive to culturally diverse people affected by family violence. Her second book, *Child Abuse and Culture: Working With Diverse Families,* was published in 2005. She has worked as a family, individual, and group therapist in a variety of settings and with people from diverse backgrounds. She has conducted research in Santiago, Chile, and with Puerto Ricans, African Americans, and European Americans in the United States. She received an M.A. in journalism from Columbia University and a Ph.D. in psychology from University of Massachusetts. She is an accomplished educator, speaker, researcher, and trainer. She has served on the Board of Directors of the American Professional Society on the Abuse of Children and the APSAC Executive Committee.

William N. Friedrich, Ph.D., A.B.P.P., was a professor and consultant in the Department of Psychiatry and Psychology at the Mayo Clinic and Mayo Medical School in Rochester, Minnesota. He received his M.P.H. from the University of Texas School of Public Health in 1975 and his Ph.D. from the University of North Dakota in 1980. He authored several books on the treatment of sexually abused children and published numerous articles and chapters on the evaluation and treatment of maltreated children and their parents. He developed of the Child Sexual Behavior Inventory published by Psychological Assessment Resources, Inc. His book *Psychological Assessment of Sexually Abused Children and Their Families* was published in 2001, and his book *Treating Children With Sexual Behavior Problems* is in press. He held a Diplomate with the American Board of Professional Psychology in both clinical and family psychology. Also, Friedrich served on the Board of Directors of the American Professional Society on the Abuse of Children and was awarded an Outstanding Career Research Award by APSAC in 2001.

Sandra K. Hewitt, Ph.D., is a child psychologist in private practice in St. Paul, Minnesota. She received her Ph.D. in school psychology from the University of Minnesota and was instrumental in setting up the Midwest Children's Resource Center, a specialty child abuse service, at Children's Hospital in St. Paul. She lectures widely both nationally and internationally on allegations of sexual abuse involving preschool children. She is the author of *Assessing Allegations of Sexual Abuse in Preschool Children: Understanding Small Voices* (1998). She is the author and co-author of several research and practice articles that focus on the needs of preschool children who may have been sexually abused. Her clinical specialties include the reunification of preschool children after unsubstantiated abuse allegations, attachment issues in young children, and custody/access cases involving young children.

Erna Olafson, Ph.D., Psy.D., is Director of the Program on Child Abuse Forensic and Treatment Training and Associate Professor of Clinical Psychiatry and Pediatrics at the Childhood Trust, Cincinnati Children's Hospital Medical Center and the University of Cincinnati College of Medicine. Her presentations and publications focus on domestic violence, sexual assault, and child abuse. As part of a multidisciplinary forensic team, she has investigated and reviewed alleged sexual assault and child abuse cases in more than 20 states and federal jurisdictions and in Canada. She directs the Childhood Trust's trainings in forensic interviewing and has written training curricula for Illinois, Ohio, and Pennsylvania. The Forensic Institute directed by Dr. Olafson has trained more than 600 investigators on-site in Cincinnati and offsite in Wyoming, New York, Illinois, Indiana, Oklahoma, Missouri, Belize, and Washington, DC. She is a certified trainer for the Ohio Child Welfare Regional Training Centers, and is also Training Director of Cincinnati Children's Hospital Trauma Treatment Replication Center, a regional center for National Child Traumatic Stress Network funded by the U.S. Department of Health and Human Services, Substance Abuse and Mental Health Services Administration (SAMHSA). She is on the Advisory Board for the American Prosecutors Research Institute's Finding Words: Half a Nation by 2010 training program on investigative interviewing of children. She has been a consultant in child abuse and forensic investigation issues for the Centers for Disease Control and Prevention, the American Professional Society on the Abuse of Children, and the American Academy of Child and Adolescent Psychiatry. She has been Editor-in-Chief of the *APSAC Advisor*.

ROLE OF THE AMERICAN PROFESSIONAL SOCIETY ON THE ABUSE OF CHILDREN

All the authors have been active members of the American Professional Society on the Abuse of Children (APSAC), an interdisciplinary organization of professionals. APSAC both inspired this book and provided a venue for networking and productive relationships among the authors through its annual colloquium, forensic interview clinics, one-day institutes associated with other national conferences, and professional endeavors on behalf of abused and neglected children. Indeed, the first version of this book, published 10 years ago, was an APSAC publication.

Interviewing Children About Sexual Abuse

ONE

Forensic and Clinical Interviewer Roles in Child Sexual Abuse

Kathleen Coulborn Faller

This chapter contextually situates child interviewing about possible sexual abuse. It describes which professionals are likely to interview the child, as well as the education and employment settings of these professionals. An important issue is whether practice should differ based upon whether the professional's role is forensic or clinical. There are professional organizations and professionals who think forensic and clinical roles should be totally separate. The chapter defines differences between forensic and clinical practice but argues that these may not be clearly distinct roles, and professionals may move from forensic to clinical practice or from clinical to forensic practice with children with a possible history of sexual abuse, whether they intend to or not.

WHO INTERVIEWS FOR CHILD SEXUAL ABUSE?

Professionals from a range of disciplines and in a spectrum of work settings may need to determine whether or not a child has been sexually abused. Persons assessing children for possible sexual abuse may be health care professionals—such as physicians, nurses, and mental health professionals—but they are chiefly social workers, psychologists, psychiatrists, law enforcement professionals, sometimes lawyers (including prosecutors), and child welfare staff. These professionals vary in their educational backgrounds—for example, they may hold associate, R.N., bachelor, master, Ph.D., M.D., or J.D. degrees. These professionals may work in medical settings, mental health agencies, social services settings, police departments, child protection agencies, children's advocacy centers, or court settings. All of these professionals need to be familiar with the research, best practice guidelines, and opinion regarding how to interview children about possible sexual abuse.

FORENSIC VERSUS CLINICAL PRACTICE

"Forensic" means belonging to the courts or to be used in legal proceedings, a term derived from the adversarial nature of the court and legal proceedings (*Merriam-Webster Online Dictionary*, 2006a). "Clinical" is a term often employed to connote mental health or therapeutic intervention, for example, relating to or connected with a clinical setting (*Merriam-Webster Online Dictionary*, 2006b).[1] An issue of debate is whether professionals should wear forensic and clinical hats for the same case. This issue has been addressed in professional guidelines and the professional literature.

The American Professional Society on the Abuse of Children (APSAC) *Guidelines for Psychosocial Evaluation of Suspected Sexual Abuse in Children* state that the same professional can play both forensic and clinical roles for a case, although the guidelines state that the professional must be aware when switching roles (American Professional Society on the Abuse of Children, 1997). In contrast, the American Psychological Association (APA) "Guidelines for Child Custody Evaluations in Divorce Proceedings" (American Psychological Association, 1994) specifically caution psychologists against assuming multiple roles in the same case. This admonition seems mainly directed toward children's therapists who intend to move into the role of custody evaluator in a divorce and is not specific to sexual abuse cases. The position of the American Academy of Child and Adolescent Psychiatry (AACAP) is somewhat different. Its guidelines for the evaluation of child and adolescent sexual abuse (American Academy of Child and Adolescent Psychiatry, 1990, 1997b) state specifically that the evaluator, who should be available to testify in court, should not also be the child's therapist. Although the positions of the APA and AACAP are, in part, intended to prevent unintended professional bias, they are also protective of the professional. The impact on the child of having to be evaluated by a stranger, when the child is already seeing a clinician, does not seem to have been considered.

A number of professionals writing on assessments of sexual abuse have strongly cautioned against a blurring of roles because of the many differences between forensic and clinical work (Kuehnle, 1996; Poole & Lamb, 1998; Raskin and Esplin, 1991b; Wehrspann, Steinhauer, & Klajner-Diamond, 1987). Kuehnle (1996) describes as legitimate the criticisms that have been leveled against interviews that were conducted by clinicians in child sexual abuse cases. She focuses on the differences between the goals of forensic evaluators (neutrality) and psychotherapists (advocacy) and suggests that there may be a conflict of interest in engaging in both roles. She cites as support for a position that these roles should be separate and distinct the APA guidelines for custody evaluations (American Psychological Association, 1994) and

AACAP guidelines for sexual abuse evaluations (American Academy of Child and Adolescent Psychiatry, 1990, 1997b) described above. Wehrspann et al. (1987) state that it is counterproductive and undermines the therapeutic relationship if the clinician seeks to determine whether or not the child, who is the clinician's client, has been sexually abused.

Other professionals, most of whom do not interview children either clinically or forensically for possible sexual abuse, admonish clinicians not to involve themselves in the forensic arena (e.g., Ceci & Bruck, 1995; Poole & Lamb, 1998). The implication is that clinicians do not know how to do forensic work because their training does not prepare them for it.

There is a competing view (Faller & Everson, 2003; James, Everson, & Friedrich, n.d.). James et al. (n.d.), in describing a model for extended assessments of children, advise that the same clinician move from clinical to forensic mode, forensic questioning techniques being triggered by the child's disclosure of sexual abuse for which the clinician is providing treatment. In addition, historically, both clinicians and mandated investigators of sexual abuse (child protective services and law enforcement) have conducted interviews for child sexual abuse. In practice, clinicians and mandated professionals rely on one another and often work together closely on sexual abuse cases. Current best practice for interviewing for sexual abuse is based upon both the clinical and forensic traditions.

Table 1.1 depicts some of the dimensions along which forensic and clinical work is supposed to differ (Faller & Everson, 2003). The table is intended to assist readers in differentiating forensic from clinical practice and is based upon a collaboration between Faller and Everson

Table 1.1 Forensic Versus Clinical Practice

Dimensions	Forensic	Clinical
1. Client	Court	Child
2. Context	Legal	Therapeutic
3. Stance	Neutral	Supportive
4. Type of data	Just the facts	Subjective experience
5. Structure	More structure	Less structure
6. Data-gathering method	Nonleading	Some leading
7. Fantasy	Only the real	Some pretend
8. Documentation	Extensive; video	Less extensive; notes
9. Collateral contacts	Extensive	Some contacts
10. Length of involvement	1–3 sessions	Several/many
11. Product	Long report	Short report

(2003). See also Kuehnle (1996, p. 32) for a less elaborated version of this table.

The client in forensic work is usually the court or some other legal entity (Sattler, 1998). In sharp contrast is clinical intervention with children who may have been sexually abused; professionals regard the child as the client, although the child's family may be part of the client system. As indicated above, the essence of forensic work is that it is for the legal arena, whereas clinical work focuses on therapeutic intervention, even at the assessment phase (Sattler, 1998). This means that the forensic professional expects to provide court testimony, whereas the clinical professional does not anticipate going to court.

Another contrast is that a forensic professional is supposed to be neutral. In order to establish and maintain that neutrality, Kuehnle (1996) recommends the forensic interviewer seek a court order for appointment as the forensic interviewer.[2] Neutrality means that technically the professional has no vested interest in the outcome of his/her involvement, for example, whether the child is found to be sexually abused or not abused. Moreover, the forensic interviewer does not necessarily take information provided by the child as true (Poole & Lamb, 1998). On the other hand, the clinician is supportive of the child and usually takes the information provided by the child at face value (Faller & Everson, 2003; Poole & Lamb, 1998).

The forensic interviewer in child sexual abuse cases seeks the facts, that is, what happened, whereas the clinical interviewer is focused less on the facts and more on how the abuse and related events have affected the child (Kuehnle, 1996). Whereas the forensic professional often follows a structured assessment protocol, the clinical professional is more flexible, more focused on the needs of the child (Faller & Everson, 2003). The forensic professional will avoid leading questions and other leading methods of data gathering; the clinical professional will employ some techniques that might be considered leading. The forensic professional may specifically admonish the child to talk only about what really happened and will avoid interview strategies that might result in fantasy (e.g., Bourg et al., 1998, 1999; Lyon, 1996; Merchant & Toth, 2001; Sorenson, Bottoms, & Porona, 1997; State of Michigan, 2005). Not so the clinical professional, who will allow the child to talk about fantasy and wishes.

As a rule, forensic professionals carefully document the information they elicit (Sattler, 1998). The standard of practice in many communities involves videotaping child interviews (Myers, 1998). On the other hand, clinical professionals usually rely upon written notes made in the interview or directly afterward. Forensic professionals' involvement will typically be time limited and involve one to several sessions. Generally, the clinician will have a longer involvement, often several months. Although there are exceptions, the usual product for the forensic professional is a long report that addresses the likelihood of sexual abuse (Sattler,

1998). The clinician will generate a shorter report that focuses on the child's functioning and provides a diagnosis, such as posttraumatic stress disorder (Sattler, 1998).

EXCEPTIONS TO THE FORENSIC–CLINICAL DICHOTOMY

Because of the variability in forensic and clinical roles and the variety of ways in which service delivery is structured, there are exceptions to the differentiation described above; the most important of these are noted here. First, professionals involved in forensic assessments in civil damages cases may not be neutral. Typically, they are hired by one side in the legal case and are not the court's expert. They may be hired on behalf of the alleged victim or the alleged offender. In such cases, they may not be disinterested with regard to either their findings or the case outcome.

Second, forensic professionals may compromise their ability to gather accurate and complete information from the child, if they do not invest in developing a supportive and warm relationship with the child (C. Carter, Bottoms, & Levine, 1996; Goodman, Bottoms, Schwartz-Kennedy, & Rudy, 1991; Hershkowitz et al., 2006; A. G. Walker, 1999). Research suggests that young children, especially, may falsely deny experiences to interviewers who lack warmth.

Third, there is a fair amount of variability in documentation methods. Some forensic programs do not use videotape because of prosecutors' concerns that the videos will be employed by the defense to undermine the case (e.g., Veith, 1999). This issue is discussed in detail in chapter 6, which covers documentation. On the other hand, clinical programs may audio or videotape child interviews, often for use in supervision.

Fourth, because of the variety of professionals who conduct forensic interviews, there are exceptions to the described differences in products. Children's advocacy centers and other high-volume forensic interview centers may write briefer reports. In some programs, these reports do not provide a conclusion about whether or not the child was sexually abused; rather, the reports document the child's disclosures and allow the reader to infer whether or not sexual abuse has occurred (e.g., D. Davies et al., 1996). Similarly, reports from law enforcement typically document the findings from the investigation. The reports are then delivered to the prosecutor or district attorney's office for a decision about whether to file criminal charges.

THE SPECTRUM OF FORENSIC AND CLINICAL PRACTICE

Despite the pedagogical utility of posing the dichotomy between forensic and clinical practice, in the real world of service delivery there may be overlap and shifting between clinical and forensic roles. In addition, clinicians may be asked to perform forensic roles (Sattler, 1998). Moreover, a clinician may not intend to appear in court but nevertheless find him/herself embroiled in the legal process. Further, in some communities, there are not sufficient numbers of professionals with expertise in sexual abuse to split these roles. Finally, because it is not particularly in the child's interest to have a separate forensic interviewer and clinician, these roles may be blended (Faller & Everson, 2003).

There are many ways clinicians may end up in the legal arena when they did not intend to, some of which are described here. Child sexual abuse is by definition a forensic issue, because it is both a crime and a threat to child safety. First, a child may present to a clinician for problems unrelated to sexual abuse and disclose sexual abuse during assessment or treatment. Since the clinician is almost surely a mandated reporter, he/she at the very least must report the disclosure to child protective services. If there is a substantiation of the allegation and a child protection court case, the clinical professional may be subpoenaed to testify. If the police become involved, the clinician may be interviewed in the course of the investigation and might even be drawn into the criminal litigation, although this is fairly uncommon.

Second, when sexual abuse is suspected but not substantiated, often-used interventions are to refer the child for extended assessment or for treatment. During these interventions, the child may provide additional information that supports sexual abuse, which, again, must be reported to child protective services. As in the first circumstance, the clinician may become involved in the child protection or criminal case.

Third, a clinician may be providing treatment to a child with a history of sexual abuse, after case substantiation. Additional disclosures of sexual abuse in treatment that have a bearing on child safety and possible criminal prosecution may lead to forensic involvement. Moreover, if the case is already in the child protection court, the clinician's testimony regarding, for example, the child's progress in treatment or the advisability of family reunification may be required. Some clinicians providing treatment on substantiated sexual abuse cases have contracts with child welfare agencies and anticipate testifying, but others may be caught off guard by such a request.

In communities with limited sexual abuse resources, the same professionals may provide forensic and clinical services. They may even do so on the same case. In the latter instance, typically they begin their involvement conducting a forensic assessment and, after they have completed this work, move into therapeutic work with the child (American Professional Society on the Abuse of Children, 1997). For the child who has formed a relationship with a forensic professional, beginning again with a new professional who plays a clinical role may be problematic or even traumatic (Faller & Everson, 2003).

SUMMARY AND CONCLUSION

Professionals who interview children about possible sexual abuse vary in education, discipline, and work setting. Often a differentiation is made between forensic and clinical roles and domains in the sexual abuse field, and professionals performing clinical and forensic roles have different mandates. However, clear differentiations are not always found and may be more apparent than real, and professionals may move between forensic and clinical roles.

Because of the potential for clinicians to involve themselves in or be drawn into the court process, they should be cognizant of research and best practice about interviewing children and aware that their interview and assessment techniques may be scrutinized and held to a "forensic" standard. Despite the potential for dual roles, professionals should not compromise their clinical role with the child because of the possibility of being called into court. Rather, professionals in clinical roles should be prepared to describe and support their practices, should the need arise. Throughout this book, reference is made to practices undertaken for clinical and forensic reasons.

NOTES

1. That professionals working in the area of sexual abuse use the term "clinical" as they do is somewhat ironic because dictionaries and thesauruses propose as synonyms for "clinical" the words "analytic," "antiseptic," "cold," "detached," "disinterested," "emotionless," "impersonal," "objective," "scientific," and "unemotional."

2. Court appointment is possible in domestic relations cases and in child protection cases but is usually not in civil damages or criminal cases.

TWO

Children's Memory and Suggestibility

Erna Olafson

Underlying all of the guidance about child interviewing are concerns about children's memory and suggestibility and the ways in which the behaviors and questions of interviewers can affect children's statements. This chapter addresses these issues by providing a brief history of professional opinion about children's memory and suggestibility and then defining key terms, such as memory, suggestibility, and source monitoring. The chapter then describes sources of knowledge about children's memory and suggestibility, the issues related to children's memory and suggestibility about which there is consensus, and the circumstances and individual characteristics that can affect memory and suggestibility. Finally, the chapter discusses script memory, the effects of interview atmosphere, research about memory and suggestibility in maltreated versus nonmaltreated children, the effects of stress and trauma on memory, and the impact of other factors, such as embarrassment, on children's reports of experienced events.

BRIEF HISTORY

Throughout human history and for most of the twentieth century, mental health experts and legal professionals have expressed doubts about children's reliability as witnesses.[1] Historically, the witness capacity of females was also viewed as deficient, and in many parts of the world it still is. Because child sexual abuse is statistically most likely to involve an adult male assaulting a female child, prosecution and conviction rates for this crime historically have been very low, even in that minority of cases that are reported to the authorities (Myers, 2004). Despite two decades of publicity about child sexual abuse in the United States, retrospective surveys indicate that only about one-third of adults who were sexually abused as children revealed the abuse to anyone during childhood, and only 10–18% of these adult respondents recall that their cases were reported to the authorities (London, Bruck, Ceci, & Shuman, 2005; Lyon, in press; Olafson & Lederman, 2006; *Stogner v. California*, 2003).

In the past, when children made statements about being sexually assaulted, professionals argued and courts agreed that children had difficulty distinguishing between fantasy and reality, were prone to lying, or were extremely suggestible to adult influences (Lyon, 1999a). In the United States, renewed interest in prosecuting child sexual abuse cases, spurred by a revived feminist movement in the last third of the twentieth century, led to legal reforms that facilitated children's testimony (Lyon, 1999a; Myers, 2004; Olafson, Corwin, & Summit, 1993; Olafson, 2002).

Psychological researchers Gail Goodman and her colleagues pioneered analogue studies in the 1980s and 1990s that rehabilitated the child witness. They showed that, for the core aspects, the "gist" of emotionally significant or "salient" events in which children had participated, even very young children, was generally accurate and resistant to suggestive questioning (Goodman & Clarke-Stewart, 1991; Goodman & Reed, 1986; Goodman, Rudy, Bottoms, & Aman, 1990). In the 1990s, a new wave of memory researchers, led by psychologists Stephen J. Ceci and Maggie Bruck, challenged "first-wave" findings, based upon findings from a number of analogue studies that focused on young children's vulnerability to suggestion about the core aspects of emotionally significant events (Ceci, Crossman, Scullin, Gilstrap, & Huffman, 2002). In 1999, lawyer and psychologist Thomas D. Lyon published a balanced critical history of the two major schools of memory research (Lyon, 1999a). Lyon pointed out that, although areas of controversy remain, both first- and second-wave researchers agree that, when properly questioned, young children have good memories and can be competent witnesses. Areas of controversy and of consensus among researchers are explored in greater detail below.

DEFINITIONS

Explicit Versus Implicit Memory

As Daniel Siegel writes, "Memory is more than what we can consciously recall about events from the past . . . *memory is the way past events affect future function* [italics added]" (Siegel, 1999, p. 24). This broader definition encompasses both explicit and implicit memories.

Explicit memories are conscious, verbal, sequential, narrative descriptions of experienced past experiences. For children or adults to be competent witnesses who can recall and describe discrete experiences, they must be capable of reporting explicit memories. Indeed, in everyday usage, it is explicit memory that people generally mean when they talk about memory. When a child (or adult with disabilities) can describe a past event in terms of *who* participated, roughly *where* something happened, *what* was there, and *what happened*, this informant is a competent witness. For many such witnesses, interviewers may have to develop questioning strategies to obtain information about time, duration, and number (Hewitt, 1999; A. G. Walker, 1999; Weissman, 1991). Forensic linguist Anne Graffam Walker cautions against asking children younger than about 9 or 10 "when" something happened and recommends instead asking the child to tie the event being discussed to a familiar signpost such as breakfast time or what is on television. She also cautions against asking "how long" or "how many times" something happened and notes that even adults are often inaccurate in response to such questions.

A second kind of memory, *implicit memory*, is often described as somatic memory, habit memory, or unconscious memory. Adult humans, verbal and preverbal children, and animals all have implicit memories. Examples of implicit memories include the following:

- Pigeons classically conditioned to peck at a lever to receive grain remember implicitly what to do in order to get fed.
- Preverbal sexually abused children who act out sexually with adults and other children may be enacting their implicit memories of being sexually abused.
- A preverbal battered child who ducks fearfully when the therapist raises her hand to adjust the blinds has learned and remembers implicitly that an adult's raised hand will be followed by a painful blow.
- Implicit memory guides the habitual movement of the fingers on the keyboard by which these sentences are produced.

When "memory" is discussed in interviewer protocols and guidelines, it is generally explicit memory that is meant. Sandra Hewitt reminds us, however, that babies and toddlers have learned and remember much more than they can say (Hewitt, 1999). Indeed, the rehabilitation of the child witness formed only a small part of an exponential expansion in memory research in the past 20 years, much of which focused on preverbal memory. Studies now demonstrate that infants and preschoolers have extensive implicit memories that are behavioral, perceptual, and emotional long before they consciously remember or can put words to what they recall (Ornstein & Haden, 2002; Siegel, 1999). Much of this research has no forensic application. However, young children recall implicitly and enact both traumatic and nontraumatic experiences before they can provide complete verbal narratives about them. For this reason, interviewers must be alert to a child's nonverbal behaviors and emotional responses that reflect implicit memories. These behaviors and responses may offer information about aspects of a child's history that a child is unable or unwilling to disclose verbally. For information about the Child Sexual Behavior Inventory, a valid, reliable, caregiver measure about children's sexualized behaviors, see chapter 15 (Friedrich, 1997; Myers, 1998).

Memory Traces Versus Memory Constructions

In a century of debate about whether memories leave "traces" in the brain or are "constructed" each time they are recalled, there is now ample research evidence that the recall of an event is largely reconstructed rather than simply replayed like an audio or videotape. Ornstein and Haden (2002) discuss memory in terms of four general themes: (1) not everything gets into memory, (2) what gets into memory may vary in strength, (3) the status of information in memory changes over time, and (4) retrieval is not perfect. It is because memory is reconstructive that retrieval is imperfect (Brown, Scheflin, & Hammond, 1998). A reconstructed memory may contain elements not present in the original experience and its encoding, so accessing a memory is not like accessing a file on a computer or replaying a tape. Because retrieval is reconstructive, misleading questions by interviewers and other influences during retrieval can affect what children recall or report. Memory in both adults and children is malleable and variable, although its malleability should not be overstated (Marxsen, Yuille, & Nisbet, 1995).

Free Recall, Cued Recall, and Recognition

Free recall is defined as a memory retrieval process in response to general or open questions. Cued recall prompts recollection with a variety of verbal and nonverbal cues. Recognition memory is a form of cued recall in which the respondent picks from among various alternatives, including the correct one. Police lineups, yes/no questions, and multiple-choice questions are examples of recognition memory prompts.

Suggestibility

Exactly what is suggestibility? The definition matters, because academic researchers use at least three definitions when they discuss children's suggestibility, and researchers are not always explicit about which operational definition of suggestibility they are using.

a. In its narrowest definition, suggestibility is defined as the degree to which postevent influences alter memory for an event (Gudjonsson, 1987).

b. A broader definition also confines suggestibility to memory but broadens the time frame, such that suggestibility concerns all the influences on the encoding, storage, and retrieval of events (Ceci & Bruck, 1995). In this definition, suggestibility begins with the event itself, rather than with the first interviewer question. A child molester at bath time vigorously fingering the inside of a child's vagina or anus while explaining, "I'm making sure you get good and clean inside and out," is suggesting a particular (distorted) encoding of this event to the child. Skillful molesters often act in ways to distort children's original perceptions and thus their memories and reports of being sexually abused.

c. The broadest definition of suggestibility is "the degree to which encoding, storage, retrieval, *and reporting* of events can be influenced by a range of internal and external factors" (Ceci & Bruck, 1995, p. 44, emphasis added). This definition expands suggestibility beyond memory and implies that individuals can make statements that they know to be untrue under real or imagined pressure from someone else. As Scullin, Kanaya, and Ceci (2002) explain this expanded conceptualization of suggestibility, it "goes beyond coping strategies to include conscious acquiescence and lying as well as destructive updating of memory due to incorporation of misinformation into the memory trace" (p. 2). The argument here is that children, who are dependent upon adults, are more vulnerable to this form of suggestibility than are most adults (with the exception of battered women, prisoners of war, torture victims, adults with disabilities, and other adults in dependent circumstances). They do not have "false memories"; these children, like battered women, hostages, and other adults who are constrained by terror or dependence, know that what they are saying is untrue.

When researchers argue about the suggestibility of adolescents, they are often actually arguing about their definitions of suggestibility. If suggestibility is about memory alone, researchers have shown that there are very few differences between developmentally average children about 10–12 years old and adults (Cole & Loftus, 1987; Myers, 1998; Warren & Marsil, 2002). However, when the dependence of children is factored in—that is, when researchers study false *statements* rather than false memories—then even adolescents are somewhat more "suggestible" than adults, especially for plausible experiences or when lied to by their mothers rather than by researchers (Warren, Hulse-Trotter, & Tubbs, 1991; Warren & Marsil, 2002).

For children who appear to have acquired inaccurate memories, it is not always clear in the analogue studies whether they are recalling what they report or simply being sociable or agreeable with the adults in charge (Huffman, Crossman, & Ceci, 1997). The issue of dependence is complex, because children are often compliant and submissive to adults, and children are often aware of the authority of adults who question them. It can be nearly impossible to sort out children's false statements from false recollections.

It is significant that most of those researchers who have expanded the definition of "suggestibility" from memory alone to include children's knowingly false statements made under a variety of pressures from adults belong, for the most part, to the second wave. Using this expanded definition enables these memory skeptics to argue that children are more "suggestible" even into adolescence than they could argue if they limited their definition of suggestibility to memory alone. It should be noted that it is more consistent with general linguistic usage to limit the definition of suggestibility to memory alone.

Scullin and Ceci (2001) have used their expansive definition of suggestibility to modify a scale first developed by Gudjonsson (1984, 1987) for use with adolescents and adults. The Gudjonsson Suggestibility Scale measures suggestibility in two ways: "Yield," in which the subject is asked 20 questions about an audiotape they have just heard, 15 of which are inaccurate leading questions; and "Shift," during which the interviewer tells the subject, "You made some errors so I'm going to read the questions again." Shift measures the number of answers to the inaccurate leading questions the subject changed in response to negative feedback. Total Suggestibility is made up of the Yield and Shift subscores. Scullin and Ceci (2001) adapted the test for children, which they call the Video Suggestibility Scale for Children (VSSC). They show their child subjects a videotape rather than have them listen to an audiotape. Interrogative suggestibility can theoretically be caused by two kinds of interviewer errors: by asking misleading questions or by giving negative feedback to a subject's answers. It seems clear that the broadest definition of suggestibility is being assessed here, that is, the definition that includes not only memory but also reporting. In addition, one can question the ecological validity of applying suggestibility studies about children's memories of watching brief videotapes, which are nonparticipant events, to children's memories of sexual abuse experiences, which are participant events.

"Source monitoring" is defined as a person's awareness of the sources of a memory. An example of a source monitoring error would be a child's false belief that something their parents had discussed as having happened to the child (e.g., sexual abuse) was an event the child had actually experienced.

SOURCES OF KNOWLEDGE ABOUT CHILDREN'S MEMORY AND SUGGESTIBILITY

Studies of High-Certainty Cases

When the details of assaults upon children are known, either through offender confession or because offenders photographed, videotaped, or audiotaped the sexual abuse, many children respond to questioning by saying nothing or omitting many details about what happened to them (Bidrose & Goodman, 2000). It is not clear whether this is because of faulty memories for the assaults or unwillingness to talk about them. A Swedish case involving 10 children (nine boys, one girl; mean age, 5.9 years at the time of the sexual assaults) illustrates this dilemma. Police questioned these children (none of whom had previously disclosed) after they discovered videotapes made by the offender of 102 incidents of sexual assault. Five of these children, including the child most severely abused for the longest period of time (60 incidents), disclosed nothing about the abuse during police interviews; two others minimized the abuse, and only three children's accounts fully matched those documented by the videotapes. One of the three full disclosures took place only after the police used a leading question (Sjoberg & Lindblad, 2002). Although some of the children stated they could not remember the abuse, others stated that they had tried hard to forget the abuse or did not want to talk about it. No child disclosed any sexual behavior not documented on the videotapes.

There are also studies of children with sexually transmitted diseases or other external evidence of abuse who do not disclose when asked about the abuse. Lyon has summarized the rate of disclosure in 21 studies published between 1965 and 1993 of children diagnosed with gonorrhea and found a disclosure rate of 43%; Lawson and Chaffin (1992), in a similar study, also found a disclosure rate of 43%. These studies do not clarify whether children cannot recall or simply will not say what happened. It is clear that maternal support enhances sustained disclosure, and maternal skepticism impedes it, but maternal support could influence either memory or disclosure readiness (Elliott & Briere, 1994; Lawson & Chaffin, 1992; Lyon, in press; Olafson & Lederman, 2006; *Stogner v. California*, 2003). In subsequent research on their sample, Chaffin, Lawson, Selby, and Wherry (1997) found that four of the originally nondisclosing children (all of whom had had gonorrhea) tested three times higher on dissociative symptoms than did the disclosing children, suggesting a possible link between dissociation and nondisclosure among sexually abused children. Children's false denials of sexual abuse constitute an ongoing problem for child protection and prosecution of offenders.

Analogue or Laboratory Research

By far, the largest body of research devoted to children's memory and suggestibility consists of analogue studies. Because researchers cannot and would not sexually assault children and then question them about their memories, researchers stage analogue experiences, record carefully what transpired, and question children about these experiences. In some studies, efforts are made to contaminate children's accounts by providing inaccurate information (lying to them) before, during, or after staged events (Faller, 1996a&b). Variables studied have included time elapsed between staged event and interview, developmental stage of the child, supportive versus nonsupportive interviewer manner, and the impact of interview aids such as drawings or dolls (Faller, 1996a).

A second form of analogue research interviews children about stressful, embarrassing, and intrusive medical procedures to their private parts, such as the voiding cystoureothrogram fluoroscopy (VCUG) (Goodman, Quas, Batterman-Faunce, Riddlesberger, & Kuhn, 1994; Pipe et al., 1997). There have been a number of studies of children's memories for this procedure; see the section on stress, trauma, and memory below.

Are these two forms of analogue study ecologically valid? There are at least two aspects to ecological validity. The first is whether the staged events or medical procedures studied are comparable to child sexual abuse. With preschoolers, for example, it has been established that both memory and resistance to suggestion are better for the core aspects of emotionally significant (especially negative), personally experienced events than for routine events, observed events, and peripheral details of all events (Ceci, Loftus, Leichtman, & Bruck, 1994; Goodman & Clarke-Stewart, 1991; Rudy & Goodman, 1991; Saywitz, Goodman, & Lyon, 2002; Saywitz & Lyon, 2002). Analogue studies have greater validity when they approximate these conditions, as with medical procedures such as the VCUG.

The second is whether the questioning strategies employed during analogue studies resemble methods actually used by interviewers (Faller, 1996b). In one analogue study, for example, interviewers lied to preschoolers for 11 consecutive interviews about events that had not happened to them (Ceci, Loftus, et al., 1994). In a study by Finnila, Mahlberg, Santtila, Sandnabba, and Niemi (2003), children were asked leading questions following a staged event, such as, "He took your clothes off, didn't he?" and a subset of children were told before questioning, "I have already spoken to the big kids and they told me that he did some bad things that he shouldn't have done. Now I would like to know if you also have such a good memory and can help me, because I really need your help to find out what happened. I am going to ask you some questions" (p. 42). In many of these analogue studies, questions such as these deliberately resemble some of those asked during the notorious multiple-alleged-victim preschool cases of the 1980s (Lamb & Thierry, 2005). Although interview transcripts from these cases are still widely cited in the media and academic publications to give the impression that repeated misleading and coercive forensic questioning of children is the current child forensic interviewing norm, much has changed in child forensic interviewing training and practice since the mistakes of a generation ago. In addition, as Lyon (1999b) points out, the great majority of child sexual abuse investigations are about single-victim cases.

Indeed, the typical abuse investigation does not involve notorious multivictim cases, coercive questioning, and repeated interviews (Lyon, 1999a&b). In current practice, child protection and law enforcement usually interview children only one time. Even with the six-session extended interview protocol developed by the National Child Advocacy Center in Huntsville, Alabama, for reticent children, care is taken to avoid suggestive questions and possible contamination of the child's statements (Carnes, Nelson-Gardell, Wilson, & Orgassa, 2001; Carnes, Wilson, & Nelson-Gardell, 1999). Analogue studies where adults lie to children for 11 consecutive weeks or pressure children by telling them what other children allegedly said lack ecological validity when applied to most current child interviewing practice. However, current research on interviewing practices in four countries do show that even well-trained interviewers ask too few of the open questions that would invite free recall and could offer children the opportunity to be most complete and accurate. Instead, research on actual practice shows that interviewers still tend to rely heavily on the closed, recognition, option-posing questions that can inhibit narratives from witnesses and possibly introduce errors into their responses (Lamb & Thierry, 2005).

Every study of children's memory and suggestibility needs to be scrutinized with care, keeping all aspects about ecological validity in mind. (For further discussion of laboratory studies vs. actual interview practice, see Veith, 2002.)

CHILDREN'S MEMORY AND SUGGESTIBILITY: CONSENSUS ISSUES

In spite of ongoing controversies, there are areas of agreement between the two broad schools of memory researchers.

Even Very Young Children Can Have Accurate Memories

Goodman and her colleagues showed that even very young children can remember large amounts of accurate information about salient, personally experienced events and that even when very young, children can give "temporally organized and coherent narratives" (Pipe, Lamb, Orbach, & Esplin, 2004, p. 442). Robyn Fivush and her colleagues demonstrated that children as young as 3 can retain these accurate memories over several years (Fivush, Peterson, & Schwarzmueller, 2002). Second-wave researchers, who tend to focus on children's vulnerabilities, have reached similar conclusions. Thus, Ceci and colleagues wrote in 1994 that preschoolers, if properly questioned, can recollect "large amounts of forensically accurate information when the adults who have access to them have not engaged in repeated erroneous suggestions"

(Ceci, Huffman, Smith, & Loftus, 1994, p. 388), and again in 2002, "Under optimal conditions, children's memory can be highly accurate . . . a single leading question by an otherwise neutral interviewer is not usually sufficient to produce an inaccurate response from a child witness" (Scullin et al., 2002, p. 234).

In experimental studies, children as young as 3 or 4 are seldom misled when questioned falsely about actions that are very different from what they had actually seen or experienced.

Questioning Strategies That Mislead Children

Both very young and older children are more easily misled when the false questions introduce details or actions they had experienced at other times or that are congruent with what they experienced or saw (Pipe et al., 2004). Analogue studies in which mothers are instructed to lie to children show that even children 9–12 years old are somewhat more suggestible than adults when the events suggested are plausible, such as having become lost at a shopping mall, although not for implausible events such as experiencing a painful enema (Pezdek & Hinz, 2002).

Age-Related Differences

There is also agreement that there are clear age-related differences in memory performance by children, such that older children are generally better at monitoring the sources of their memories and resisting suggestive or misleading questioning. Older children generally forget less, remember in greater detail, and employ superior retrieval strategies (Ceci & Bruck, 1993; Ornstein & Haden, 2002; Pipe et al., 2004; Poole & Lindsay, 2002). Both children and adults are generally less accurate about peripheral details than about central events (Steward, Bussey, Goodman, & Saywitz, 1993). When children of school age and older are advised at the outset to report only about what they actually experienced, suggestibility is reduced (Poole & Lindsay, 1996).

It is also generally agreed that even adults can be suggestible under certain circumstances (Loftus & Pickrell, 1995).

Children may try to respond to questions even when they do not understand them, because children learn very early that cooperative conversations require answers to questions, a form of suggestibility that has more to do with false statements than with false recollections (Warren & McCloskey, 1997; A. H. Waterman, Blades, & Spencer, 2002). If an adult communicates to a child that an event happened or did not happen in a particular way, through the kinds of questions asked or even through nonverbal cues, younger children are more inclined to be influenced than are older children, but again, it is not clear the degree to which memory is implicated in these false statements (Saywitz et al., 2002). Children are also more suggestible when questioned by adults than when questioned by other children (Saywitz & Lyon, 2002).

By the time developmentally average children are about 10–12 years old, the average age for child witnesses in sexual abuse cases (Veith, 2002), they generally show only very small differences from average adults in terms of suggestibility, when suggestibility is defined in terms of memory alone (Cole & Loftus, 1987; Myers, 1998; Warren & Marsil, 2002). Because of this developmental reality, interviewers should avoid making assertions about "children's" suggestibility, and they must challenge fact finders or experts who make assertions about children in general. Much of the analogue memory research focuses on the very young and so has only limited applicability to school-age children and adolescents.

Findings Related to Preschoolers

Although preschooler testimony is rarely used in criminal cases, it is nevertheless crucial for protection. How suggestible are preschoolers? Three factors make these youngest children on average more vulnerable to suggestive interviewing than older children or adults (Saywitz & Lyon, 2002):

1. Young children find free recall considerably more difficult than cued recall and recognition. Preschoolers are less likely to make source errors when asked open (free recall) rather than specific (recognition) questions, although their accounts are likely to be sparse and to lack detail (Roberts, 2002; Roberts & Powell, 2006).
2. *Deference to adults*: Young children are particularly deferential to adults' beliefs.
3. *Source monitoring*: Young children—especially those younger than 5—are more likely than older children and adults to confuse what they have been told with what they have experienced. A relationship between source monitoring abilities and suggestibility has been established in children (Leichtman, Morse, Dixon, & Wilch-Ross, 2000; Roberts & Blades, 2000; Saywitz et al., 2002).

How easy is it to plant false beliefs in preschoolers? It depends on the age of the preschooler and the nature of the memory being implanted. Source monitoring improves dramatically between the ages of 3 and 5 for developmentally average children (Gopnik & Graf, 1988; Leichtman et al., 2000; Saywitz et al., 2002; Saywitz & Lyon, 2002). Five-year-olds are also far less likely than 3-year-olds to falsely assent to yes/no questions (Saywitz et al., 2002; Saywitz & Lyon, 2002). With children older than 3 or 4, teaching them to monitor the sources of their memories and to distinguish between events that they actually experienced versus events about which they had been told decreases errors and increases resistance to misleading questions (Roberts & Blades, 2000; Roberts, 2002). However, this source monitoring task is not effective for the 3- and 4-year-olds.

Source Misattribution Errors

Ceci and his colleagues have conducted a number of studies about source misattribution error designed to plant false beliefs in children about the core aspects of personally experienced, emotionally significant events, the constellation of characteristics for which Goodman had rehabilitated the child witness (Lyon, 1999a). In the first of these, often referred to as the "mousetrap" study, children 3–6 years old were asked about events and were asked to think real hard about them, while also being instructed that these events may or may not have happened to them. Ninety-six children were interviewed 7–10 times (Ceci, Huffman et al., 1994). The final interview in all cases was 10 weeks after the initial interview. The two false events about which children were interviewed were (1) having caught their hand in a mousetrap and going to the hospital to get it removed and (2) taking a hot air balloon ride with classmates. Children were also asked about two true events that had happened to them within the past 12 months, using information supplied to the researchers by parents. Results showed that true events were nearly always recalled accurately with little variation from week to week. For the false events, 34% of children falsely assented in the first session, and 34% of the children falsely assented in the seventh session, an unexpected average finding of no change with repeated interviewing. However, the 3- to 4-year-olds moved from more to fewer false assents as time went on, and the 5- to 6-year-olds moved from fewer to more false assents over time.

Readers may recall John Stossel's inaccurate reporting of this research on a *20/20* segment in which he argued that "most" of the children came to believe falsely that these events had happened to them. In actuality, Ceci and colleagues' research demonstrated that 66% percent of these preschool children resisted repeated questioning by researchers about negative and positive fictional events over 7–10 interviews.

Once false assents or false beliefs have been obtained from preschoolers, do they persist over time? Can a planted false story become part of a child's autobiographical memory narrative? To explore this question, Ceci's Cornell team of researchers interviewed 22 young children from the mousetrap study 2 years later and found that the children recanted 77% of their false consents, while remaining accurate 78% of the time in their recall of the true events they had described in the earlier study (Ceci, Huffman, et al., 1994). Among the later recanters was the famous boy interviewed by John Stossel on *20/20* at the time of the original study, a child who not only described in emotionally convincing detail having caught his finger in a mousetrap (negative participant event) but also resisted efforts by his parents and Stossel to disabuse him of this false account. Two years later, the boy explained to the researchers that he had told the mousetrap story to his family and on television but stated that it was "just a story" and that he was sure it had not happened (Huffman et al., 1997, p. 488).

In the published paper about this mousetrap study, Ceci and colleagues did not separate out the negative from the positive personally experienced events, a difference that became significant in a second study (Ceci, Loftus, et al., 1994). Twenty preschool children with a mean age of 3 years 5 months and 20 children with a mean age of 5 years 5 months completed the study. Researchers interviewed the children 11 times at approximately 1-week intervals about eight events, four of which the children had experienced and four of which the interviewers made up. The negative fictional event involved falling off a tricycle and getting stitches in the leg, and the positive fictional event was again a hot air balloon ride with classmates. The neutral fictional event dealt with waiting for a bus, and the neutral nonparticipant event involved observing another child waiting for the bus.

Interviewers instructed children that they were going to play a "picture in the head" game, and they had the children practice using mental images, saying such things as, "Let's try to think what Cinderella was wearing. I see an apron around her waist. Do you see it, too?" (Ceci et al., 1994, p. 310). Interviewers then lied to children by telling them that they were going to read some things that happened to them when they were little and that they had put together the list by talking to the children's mothers. They asked children to think real hard about each event. "Try to make a picture of it in your head. What do you think you would have been wearing when it happened? Who would have been with you? How do you think you would have felt?" (p. 309). Children were told not to worry if they could not remember.

In trainings, I present the research design to that point and ask trainees how many of the children aged 3 years 5 months falsely assented after 11 weeks of this "picture in the head" game that they had fallen off a tricycle and had to have stitches. The answer comes almost always in a unison chant, "All of them." From time to time, these child abuse and law enforcement investigators in training estimate lower percentages, from 50% to 80%.

The results are strikingly different. After 11 weeks of visualization practice about a fictional negative bodily experience, only 31% of the 3-year-olds in this Ceci study falsely assented, and 28% of the 5-year-olds did so. When in week 12 a different interviewer informed the children that the first interviewer had made errors, the percentages dropped to 28% and 23%, respectively. More than two-thirds of preschoolers in this study resisted 11 weeks of practicing visualization about fictional, negative, bodily experiences. When Ceci appeared on *Nightline* in 1996, he made a point of saying that he and his researchers have to work very hard to achieve these false assents in even the youngest children, and that most of the children resisted memory implantation.

However, for the fictional hot air balloon ride, the numbers were 59% false assents at week 11 and 54% at week 12 for the 3-year-olds, and 51% and 43% false assents for the 5-year-olds. This result suggests that it is easier to cause preschoolers to make source misattribution errors about positive events than about negative or painful ones.

When this source misattribution study by Ceci and his colleagues is cited in literature reviews, 43% is often cited as the percentage of preschoolers at ages 3 and 5 who persisted in false assents for all four types of fictional events by week 12 of this study, even after having been informed that the previous interviewer had made errors. It should be noted, however, that this percentage may be artificially inflated because of the presence of a flawed component in this research design. The neutral nonparticipant event chosen was having observed a child waiting for a bus, to which a majority of children allegedly assented falsely even at week 12. Were these false assents? Can any parent or any researcher state with certainty that these children had never seen another child waiting for a bus? The percentage of false assents at week 12 falls to 36% when this flawed component is extracted from the study.

As for the ecological validity of this study, most forensic interviewers do not lie to children for 11 weeks, do not tell children that they should use a "picture in the head" game, and do not have children practice visualization by using fantasy characters such as Cinderella. It can also be argued that most (although not all) child sexual abuse is experienced as a negative bodily event. Therefore, it is likely that even the rate of 31% false assents by the youngest participants in this study overestimates preschooler suggestibility during forensic interviews about alleged child sexual abuse.

Event Plausibility

Psychologist Kathy Pezdek and her colleagues have tested the hypothesis that false events can be implanted in memory "to the degree that . . . plausible and script relevant knowledge exists in memory" (Pezdek, Finger, & Hodge, 1997; Pezdek & Hinz, 2002; Pezdek & Hodge, 1999). In Pezdek and colleagues' research, the plausible false event selected was that the child had become lost while with her or his family at a shopping mall, and the implausible false even was that the child had once received a rectal enema. Both events could be described as "negative participant events." Parents or researchers with parents sitting nearby read four accounts of events that they told the child had happened when the child was 4. Two of these were the rectal enema and lost in the mall stories, and two were events that had really taken place. The sample consisted of 19 children 5–7 years old and 20 children 9–12 years old. Fifty-four percent of the children did not remember either false event. Three of the children in the younger age group stated that they remembered both false events, whereas none of the older children did so. Of the 15 children who remembered one false event on the second day of the study, 14 remembered the lost in the mall fiction and only one the more implausible rectal enema fiction, and this was a child from the 5–7 age group.

Pezdek and colleagues concluded that plausible false events appear more likely to be planted in memory than implausible false events, that prior knowledge of suggested events increases their likelihood of implantation, and that younger children are more suggestible than are older children. However, even the children 9–12 years old in this study are more suggestible than are adults for plausible events when these results are compared with "lost in the mall" studies upon adults (Pezdek & Hinz, 2002). Pezdek and colleagues' study is also significant because the research design involved having parents, rather than researchers, lie to the children. Because the experience of being lost from a parent, even briefly, is a very common one during childhood, it cannot be argued with certainty that some of the 14 "false" assents on the second day of the study were not instead partially accurate memories of past experiences.

A study by Scullin et al. (2002) challenges Pezdek and colleagues' assertion that it is harder to mislead children about implausible events than about plausible ones. This study, designed to test the construct validity of the Video Suggestibility Scale for Children (VSSC; Scullin & Ceci, 2001), showed that "some [children] came up with very elaborate accounts for unlikely events" (p. 12). The two events that these researchers describe as "implausible" are having helped a stranger find a lost stuffed or live monkey and having helped a stranger carry Play Doh down a hallway. It was suggested to the children that the stranger tripped, hurt her ankle, and had it bandaged by a nurse who happened to be there. Are these events "implausible" to children in the same way that a negative event to their own bodies—the fictional painful enema of Pezdek and colleagues' study—is implausible? It appears obvious which fictional event more closely resembles a child's experience of being sexually assaulted and therefore has greater ecological validity.

The ecological validity of the VSSC to test children's witness capacity about the core aspects of personally experienced, emotionally significant events such as, for example, most sexual abuse experiences, is also questionable. Children were questioned 1–4 days after witnessing a five-minute videotape titled "Billy's Birthday Party," first with open-ended questions and then with 18 specific questions based upon the VSSC, 14 of which are leading, to get Yield and then, after being told they had made a few mistakes, questioned again to get Shift. This video is a witnessed media event about strangers, not something that happened to their own bodies (Scullin et al., 2002), raising questions about its ecological validity.

CIRCUMSTANCES AND INDIVIDUAL CHARACTERISTICS THAT AFFECT MEMORY AND SUGGESTIBILITY

When an event was not recent or when children had little knowledge or understanding about it, children's recall is less complete, source monitoring is affected, and they are more vulnerable to suggestion (Lamb & Thierry, 2005; Pipe et al., 2004; Quas, Schaaf, Alexander, & Goodman, 2000).

Some adults and children are more suggestible than are others (Bruck, Ceci, & Melnyk, 1997; Quas, Qin, Schaaf, & Goodman, 1997). Adults with low intelligence demonstrate more interrogative suggestibility than do adults with I.Q. scores that are average or above, but the limited research about the relationship between intelligence and suggestibility in children is inconclusive (Bruck & Melnyk, 2004; Ceci et al., 2002; Gudjonsson, 1992; Quas et al., 1997; Scullin et al., 2002; Warren & Marsil, 2002). An analogue study shows that preschoolers and young school-age children with higher verbal intelligence recall more on free recall and are more resistant to suggestion than are children who have lower verbal I.Q. scores (Chae & Ceci, 2005). Overall memory function in children is also linked to socioeconomic status (SES) in a number of studies (Howe, Cicchetti, Toth, & Cerrito, 2004). Temperament, self-esteem, agreeableness, and self-confidence may also play roles in adult and childhood suggestibility, but here, the expanded definition of suggestibility that extends its meaning to false statements rather than false memories appears to be in play (Ceci et al., 2002; Pipe & Salmon, 2002; Warren & Marsil, 2002). Finally, in a review of 69 papers about the factors that affect children's suggestibility, Bruck and Melnyk (2004) conclude, "With the exception of children with MR [mental retardation], the scientific evidence suggests that one cannot, at present, identify individual children who are most at risk for heightened suggestibility" (p. 990).

Memory and suggestibility within any one individual can vary from time to time, depending on a number of physical and psychological factors and the nature of the suggestive influences (Warren & Marsil, 2002). The more children know about a topic, the more resistant they are to incongruent suggestions (Goodman, Quas et al., 1994, 1997). Stressful situations such as testifying in court have been correlated with impaired memory and heightened suggestibility in school-age children when compared with the control children in the same analogue study who were questioned in a familiar setting (Saywitz & Nathanson, 1993).

In this last-cited study, the children who reported that they felt most anxious about testifying in the mock court room performed less well in terms of free recall and were more suggestible to misleading questions than were children in the mock court group who reported feeling less anxious. This is important information for those who, in the post-*Crawford*[2] American courts, must prepare children to testify in criminal courts; asking children about their level of distress and working with them to manage it may well enhance their witness capacity.

It should again be emphasized that age remains the single best predictor of children's memory and suggestibility. Children 3–4 years of age are generally the most suggestible, and overall memory function gradually improves and suggestibility becomes less problematic as children develop and mature (Huffman et al., 1997).

MEMORY FOR REPEATED EVENTS AND SCRIPT MEMORY

When children or adults are asked to recall a single episode of events that have been repeated many times, they will have difficulty recalling the specific details of that one instance. Memories blur into a generic script, although features shared across these experiences are remembered better and these memories are more resistant to suggestion than are memories for single events. If you try to recall this morning brushing your teeth 2 weeks ago, for example, it is likely that you will be unable to recall that particular morning, but you can describe what you did that day because you clearly remember what you always do. This generalized description would not suffice for court testimony. On the other hand, if 2 weeks ago you were in a hotel, forgot your toothbrush, and had to send down to the front desk for one, then you may well recall that morning in some detail because the circumstances were unusual (Pipe et al., 2004). If asked about brushing your teeth this morning, you are also likely to be able to recall in detail because the event was very recent (Pipe et al., 2004).

This "script memory" problem is relevant in cases of ongoing abuse that was repeated dozens or even hundreds of times and may have occurred in a number of places (Myers, 1998). After obtaining a narrative description of the experience (which children often give in the present tense, as in, "And then he comes into the room . . ."), interviewers should ask the child if it happened one time or more than one time. It is not recommended to ask how many times the event happened, because even most adults cannot accurately give accounts from actual memory about repeated events, such as the number of times in their lives they have brushed their teeth (A. G. Walker, 1999). Children may try to please the interviewer by guessing and thus coming across as incompetent or noncredible. Avoid questions about how many times.

If the child states that it happened more than one time, interviewers are advised instead to seek information about specific events. Because an unusual event in a series of repeated events is recalled more clearly than are single events that are similar to the generalized script memory, the interviewer can ask first about an event that was "different" (Pipe et al., 2004). One can also ask about the most recent time it happened, the first time it happened, and the time the child remembers the most. In cases where police will be searching a crime scene for corroborative evidence, details from the most recent event are especially useful (Veith, 2002). Interviewers can also ask if there was a time that was worse in some way and ask for a description if the child says that there was. Infantile amnesia may prevent children maltreated from very early childhood from being able to answer questions about the first time.

Interviewers should be cautioned about this sequence of questions, in that both children and adults often blur differences between episodes and respond with script-related intrusions when trying to recall specific incidents (K. P. Roberts, 2002; Roberts & Powell, 2006; Powell & Thomson, 1997). Pipe et al. (2004, p. 445) argue that some confusion among occasions should not adversely affect perceptions of a witness's accuracy. However, as they conclude, "At present, we have to acknowledge . . . that the children who are abused repeatedly and are most in need of intervention may find it the hardest to provide the kinds of accounts required by the courts" (p. 446).

INTERVIEW ATMOSPHERE

A supportive context may be especially important in bolstering young children's resistance to suggestive misinformation about abuse (C. Carter, Bottoms, & Levine, 1996; Davis & Bottoms, 2002; Goodman, Bottoms, Schwartz-Kennedy, & Rudy, 1991; Saywitz et al., 2002). Research suggests that interviewers should be noncontingently warm, matter-of-fact, and neutral throughout their interviews with children, even when children are making outlandish statements (Saywitz et al., 2002). Although findings are somewhat mixed, the available studies indicate that moderate warmth and support lead to greater resistance rather than acquiescence by young children to misleading questions (Davis & Bottoms, 2002; Quas et al., 2000; Saywitz & Lyon, 2002). Intimidation can add to young children's suggestibility about abuse-related events, and younger children appear to be more easily intimidated than are older ones (Saywitz et al., 2002). Thus, interviewers should be noncontingently warm and supportive rather than authoritarian, cold, or condescending.

ARE ABUSED CHILDREN MORE SUGGESTIBLE THAN NONABUSED CHILDREN?

How does child maltreatment affect memory and suggestibility? Some studies show explicit memory decrements, whereas others suggest better recall, and it appears that variables such as the kind and degree of stress, social support, and individual differences in children may account for these diverse findings.

Eisen, Goodman, Qin, and Davis (1998) studied 108 children who were hospitalized for assessment of abuse and neglect, of which 53% were classified as physically or sexually abused and 22% had no documented abuse or neglect history and served as a control group. Children were administered memory, dissociation, and intellectual functioning tests. They were also given anogenital examinations and, on the final day of hospitalization, a structured interview composed of specific, leading, and misleading questions about the anogenital examination from 3 days before. Preliminary analyses indicated few differences between the maltreated and nonmaltreated children. Age progression analyses showed that 11- to 15-year-olds resisted misleading questions 91% of the time, 6- to 10-year-olds 83% of the time, and 3- to 5-year-olds 63% of the time.

In a comparison study of 159 middle and lower SES-status children 5–12 years old, Howe et al. (2004) found no positive or negative effects on basic recall and recognition memory processes between maltreated and the nonmaltreated children. The maltreated children had experienced child sexual abuse, neglect, child physical abuse, and/or emotional maltreatment. The authors write, "Specifically, these results agree with the study by Eisen, Goodman, Qin, & Davis (1998), who found that maltreated children were no more or less susceptible to suggestion and misleading information than nonmaltreated children" (p. 1412). Howe et al. did find differences in overall memory function as a function of SES, and they argue that SES differences in memory are "reasonably well established" (p. 1412).

STRESS, TRAUMA, AND MEMORY

The acts that constitute child sexual abuse vary from traumatizing, violent rape to nonviolent genital fondling. As a consequence, research about the impact of stress and trauma applies to some, but not to all, child sexual abuse cases.

For penetrating sexual abuse, studies of children's memories for a painful, genitally invasive, embarrassing medical procedure used to identify urinary tract problems, VCUG, appear to be the most ecologically valid. In this procedure, a child's urinary tract is catheterized, the bladder is filled to a degree that creates discomfort, and the child has to urinate on the table in front of the assembled treatment professionals. Children find this experience extremely aversive. Merritt, Ornstein, and Spicker (1994) found that children 3.5 to just over 7 years old demonstrated high recall immediately after the VCUG test, showed little forgetting at 6-week follow-up, and demonstrated surprisingly few age differences. Goodman, Quas, Batterman-Faunce, Riddelsberger, and Kuhn (1994, 1997) in a study of 46 children 3–10 years old who underwent VCUG found that younger children (3 and 4 years old) recalled less and made more commission and omission errors than did older children. Children in the Goodman et al. study whose mothers were not sympathetic and physically comforting after the VCUG were more inaccurate during free recall and made more commission errors in response to misleading questions. There were also more commission errors among children whose mothers did not discuss or explain VCUG to their children. Children's emotional responses also affected accuracy. Children who expressed positive emotions (not embarrassed, proud of themselves) were more accurate. Children who expressed sadness were accurate on free recall but made commission errors to direct questions. The four children who displayed subsequent posttraumatic symptoms made more commission errors in response to both open and direct questions. Long-term memory for this traumatic medical procedure was studied by Pipe et al. (1997), who interviewed children at intervals ranging from 9 months to 8 years after the procedure. The delay between the procedure and children's memory of it did not predict how much accurate detail was recalled, but children who were younger than 4 at the time of the VCUG in some cases did not remember it at all and in other cases were less accurate in their recall than were the older children.

Other research indicates that children (and adults) may remember core aspects of events better when they experience moderate distress during encoding than when they are not distressed (Eisen et al., 1998). However, research results about the relationship between stress and memory are mixed (Saywitz et al., 2002), and some researchers argue that stress debilitates memory (Ceci & Bruck, 1993). Studies more specifically focused on memory of details that pertain to the gist of the event have shown that moderate arousal enhances recall (Engelberg & Christianson, 2002). Specifically, details that are central or critical to the cause of the stress are better retained in memory than are details that are peripheral or that were stressful in ways not connected with the event being encoded (Engelberg & Christianson, 2002).

Extreme stress such as overwhelming trauma that involves terror, helplessness, horror, fear of obliteration, and extreme arousal, as in violent, aggressive, or penetrating child sexual assault, combat, or torture, appears to debilitate rather than enhance memory (Pezdek & Taylor, 2002). Partial or total amnesia, on the one hand, and hyperamnesia in the form of flashbacks and nightmares, on the other, are part of the posttraumatic symptom pattern for survivors of traumatic events. Memories for traumatic events may be fragmentary or partial sensorimotor or emotional fragments not organized into coherent narratives (van der Kolk, 1999). Hyperamnesias and amnesias occur in a minority of sexual abuse cases, and interviewers need to adjust interview techniques to take them into account. Interviewing children about child sexual abuse stresses them—there is no way to avoid this. Washing and stitching a wound can also cause a patient pain as a necessary precursor to healing. However, if an interview becomes traumatizing for a child, the interview should be stopped and resumed later, in some cases only after psychiatric or psychological evaluation and possible treatment.

Some severely traumatized children incorporate fantastic elements into their abuse narratives when questioned about their experiences (Everson, 1997). In a review of a random sample of 800 videotaped interviews from a San Diego child protection facility, psychologist Constance J. Dalenberg and her associates found that among children 4–9 years old whose child sexual abuse was independently confirmed by offender confession and physical findings, more than 15% of children in cases of severe, traumatizing sexual assault incorporated bizarre and impossible details into their abuse accounts (Dalenberg, 1996; Dalenberg, Hyland, & Cuevas, 2002). For children from this sample whose sexual abuse was classified as "mild," rates of fantastic or implausible details were less than 4% (Dalenberg et al., 2002). The authors apply reality monitoring theory to consider how an abuse context affects children's ability to distinguish between internally generated and externally perceived events (Dalenberg et al., 2002).

EMBARRASSMENT, MODESTY, AND OMISSION ERRORS

Children who expressed embarrassment about the VCUG gave less correct information during free recall (Goodman et al., 1997). This result is consistent with the Saywitz, Goodman, Nicholas, and Moan (1991) study of girls who were questioned about genital touching following a pediatric examination; a majority of the girls did not disclose the touching in response to open questions and did so only when asked directly, "Did the doctor touch you there?" Although it has been suggested that schemata about pediatric examinations may have inhibited disclosure, the fact that more 7-year-olds than 5-year-olds failed to disclose the genital and anal touching suggests that modesty, rather than schemata, silenced these girls. However, because memories for events are enhanced by recalling them and describing them, embarrassed avoidance of certain events may over time affect how well they can be remembered.

SUMMARY AND CONCLUSIONS

Researchers on all sides of current memory and suggestibility controversies agree that even young children, if properly questioned, can provide accurate information about core aspects of personally experienced, emotionally significant events, especially negative ones (Berliner, 1997a; Ceci & Bruck, 1995; Ornstein & Haden, 2002). "The surprising sophistication of young children's memory, on the one hand, and clear age-related differences in performance, on the other, represent two themes that characterize our current understanding of the development of memory" (Ornstein & Haden, 2002, p. 29).

Proper questioning includes both interviewer attitude and the specific questions used. Because children often believe that adults already know the answers to the questions they ask them, they may defer to what they assume to be the more accurate adult viewpoint, unless questions are very carefully and neutrally phrased (Saywitz & Lyon, 2002). To obtain complete, accurate reports from children (and adults), it is recommended that interviewers ask questions designed to elicit what the witness remembers. The most effective way for interviewers to avoid imposing their own beliefs on the child's statements is to keep quiet while listening, preserve an open mind, and avoid prejudging the facts of a case (Saywitz & Lyon, 2002). Initial questions that invite free recall narratives should be attempted with children of all ages, even preschoolers. When specific, recognition, option-posing, multiple choice, or yes/no questions become necessary, they should generally be followed by open prompts such as "Tell me about it." Because some recognition questions may be necessary in almost every interview, pairing such questions with free recall follow-ups can invite fuller responses from those being questioned. Narrative inviting questions have two advantages over more closed questions: children generally give more details, and their responses are more accurate (Lamb et al., 2003).

Free recall questions also make child interviews more defendable in a forensic arena where many have become overly skeptical about children's witness capacity. Widespread media distortions about human memory and children's suggestibility, such as John Stossel's *20/20* report on Ceci's research or the PBS series "Divided Memories," on memory, both aired in the 1990s, now influence the general public from whom fact finders are drawn. Marxsen et al. (1995) frame the issue thus:

> That young children are more suggestible than adults is well established. That does not mean that the investigative interviewing of children is impossible, only that it requires skill and care. However, the literature's overemphasis on suggestibility can give the police, the judiciary, the media, and the general public the mistaken impression that children are inherently unreliable. This is an issue of considerable moment because such an impression can be the basis for societal decisions with far-reaching consequences. . . . The suggestibility problem is a complex one, but the literature [gives] the impression that children are simply untrustworthy witnesses. This is simply not true. (p. 451)

Poor questioning of children, and the consequences in courtrooms, costs lives. Alejandro Avila, who in July 2002 dragged 5-year-old Samantha Runnion kicking and screaming from her front yard and raped and murdered her, had been acquitted of child sexual abuse less than 2 years previously by a California jury. His ex-girlfriend's daughter and her niece, both 9 years old, testified against him in this earlier case, despite Avila's alleged threats to one of the girls that he would kill her or her mother if she talked (ABC News, 2003). Following this acquittal, one juror explained that the children "weren't consistent on their story. Everything was yes, yes, yes." The same juror explained, "We all 12 walked out of there 100 percent feeling we did justice. We let an innocent man go" (Lyon, 2002a).

THE BOTTOM LINE

Although all human beings can be suggestible, children are not highly suggestible. Statements such as this one by UCLA professor Daniel Siegel in his widely read primer on cognitive development, "The human mind is extremely suggestible throughout life, particularly in childhood," overstate the problem of suggestibility, ignore developmental differences in children, and could mislead interviewers and fact finders to be unduly skeptical about victim and witness statements by children (Siegel, 1999, p. 55).

1. The media, even listener-supported public media, are unreliable sources of information about children's and adult's memory and suggestibility. Many judges and juries have been educated primarily by sensationalistic, anecdotal media portrayals of memory and suggestibility issues.

2. When examining analogue studies, readers should check whether the conditions of the experiment approximate conditions experienced by children when they are being sexually abused, keeping in mind that sexually abusive acts vary greatly.

3. When examining analogue studies, readers should check whether the conditions of interviewing approximate current child forensic interviewing practice.

4. Children and adults generally have better recall for the core aspects of emotionally significant events that they personally experienced and worse recall about peripheral details. This is especially true for negative events.

5. Although moderate stress during encoding appears generally to enhance recall, being traumatized by terrifying and overwhelming events such as violent, aggressive, prolonged, and painful child sexual abuse can interfere with memory.

6. Developmental level is the best predictor of memory and suggestibility, but there are also individual differences.

7. Individuals vary in both memory and suggestibility, depending on levels of fatigue and stress during retrieval, as well as other factors.

8. Whereas moderate stress appears to enhance encoding during an event, the situation appears to be reversed during retrieval. Some studies indicate that stress appears to diminish recall and increase suggestibility during retrieval.

9. A noncontingently warm (but not overly familiar) interview manner improves children's recall and makes them less suggestible to misleading questions than does a cold, authoritarian, or condescending manner.

10. Research on preschoolers has limited applicability to school-age children or adolescents and should not be applied to them in the clinic, the interview room, or the courtroom.

11. Recommendations for interviewers to employ predominantly invitational, narrative-inviting, open questions and limit their use of closed, option-posing, suggestive questions are grounded in extensive memory research about the greater accuracy and completeness of free recall versus recognition memory in humans of all ages, but especially in children.

NOTES

1. The concepts of "validity" and "reliability" are referred to throughout this book, but especially in this chapter on children's memory and suggestibility, chapter 13 on nondisclosing children, and chapter 15 on standardized tests. The concepts of validity and reliability are important in assessing measures used in research and standardized tests. In both research and testing, instruments are used to collect data. In both instances, the data are only as good as the instruments employed to collect them.

Validity refers to whether the instrument employed measures what it is intended or said to measure. A new instrument is often tested against other instruments that measure similar concepts. This endeavor determines if the instrument has *concurrent validity*. For example, the Trauma Symptom Checklist for Children, a relatively new instrument, was cross-validated with other instruments that measure posttraumatic stress disorder.

Ecological validity is a concept that is frequently used in discussing analogue studies related to children's memory and suggestibility. Ecological validity refers both to whether or not the events being studied contain elements that are like sexual abuse, and to whether the questioning and other data-gathering techniques reflect the methods used by actual interviewers. The reader will note that in chapters 2 and 13, challenges are raised to the ecological validity of analogue studies. These challenges include whether children watching a video is like children being sexually abused, and whether researchers programming children over 11 sessions is similar to interviewers questioning children about sexual abuse.

In chapter 15 on standardized tests, the concept of *predictive validity* is discussed in reference to the use of psychological tests and screeners versus interviews. For example, what is a better predictor of future dangerousness, a standardized test or an interview with the possibly dangerous person? As noted in chapter 15, standardized measures have better predictive validity than do interviews.

Reliability refers to whether scores on research or testing measures are consistent across observations. One of the subcategories is *test–retest reliability.* That is, whether an individual will respond approximately the same each time he/she completes the measure. For example, if someone takes an I.Q. test at two different points in time, will their I.Q. be approximately the same both times?

Another important subcategory of reliability is *interrater reliability.* This refers to whether two researchers or experts code responses from a test or research instrument approximately the same.

2. *Crawford v. Washington* is a Supreme Court case which upheld the right of those accused of a crime to confront their accuser (under the 6th Amendment to the U.S. Constitution). In the *Crawford* case, the witness was the accused spouse, but the court decision has been construed as also applying to child witnesses. The Court's opinion can be accessed on the Web at http://www.supremecourtus.gov/opinions/03pdf/029410.pdf#search=%22Crawford%20 supreme%20court%20decision%22.

THREE

Models for Assessing Child Sexual Abuse

Kathleen Coulborn Faller

Effective approaches to assessment of physical abuse and neglect, which rely on medical evidence, the child's physical condition, and the family's living conditions, are not very useful in sexual abuse cases. Medical evidence of sexual abuse is usually not present on exam (Bays & Chadwick, 1993), and even when there is physical evidence, it is generally transitory (McCann, Voris, & Simon, 1992). As a rule, injuries from sexual abuse quickly resolve. Professionals, therefore, resorted to interviewing family members in order to determine the probability of sexual abuse (Faller, 1984) and ultimately came to view the child interview as the most viable and valuable source of information about the likelihood of sexual abuse (Conte, Sorenson, Fogarty, & Dalla Rosa, 1991; Hibbard & Hartmann, 1993; Morgan, 1995).

However, in the past 20 years, several factors have resulted in the evolution of varied approaches to assessing allegations of sexual abuse. First, some professionals have raised concerns about relying too heavily on a child interview because of questions about the accuracy of children's reports. Second, there has been a social policy shift toward greater priority on handling sexual abuse as a crime, rather than a mental health problem. This shift is reflected in states amending their child abuse statutes to require or allow for greater collaboration between child protective services (CPS) and law enforcement in the investigation of sexual abuse (Faller, 2000a; National Center for the Prosecution of Child Abuse, 1997). Third, mental health professionals with a spectrum of expertise brought their knowledge to bear on the sexual abuse assessment process.

In this chapter, current practice is conceptualized into four overlapping but somewhat distinct models for assessing allegations of sexual abuse (Everson, 1992b; Everson & Faller, 1999): the child interview model, the joint investigation model, the parent–child interaction model, and the comprehensive assessment model. However, others have conceptualized models for assessment somewhat differently (California Attorney General's Office, 1994; Everson, 1996; Kuehnle, 1996). The characteristics, origins, relevant research, and assumptions of each model are discussed. Few professionals describe the theory that underlies their approach to assessing sexual abuse allegations; consequently, the observations about assumptions are based upon practice experience (Everson & Faller, 1999).

CHILD INTERVIEW MODEL

The essential component of the child interview model is the interview with the suspected victim. In most agencies and programs, this is a single interview (e.g., Bourg et al., 1999; D. Davies et al., 1996; Merchant & Toth, 2001). Since most children do not come to an evaluation on their own, usually the accompanying adult is also interviewed, not to assess the adult's functioning but to gather information about the child and the allegation. When conducted in medical settings, an additional component of the child interview model is a medical examination of the child (e.g., D. Davies et al., 1996).

The child interview model has its origins in CPS investigations of complaints of possible sexual abuse. It also became the model of preference at most children's advocacy centers (Carnes & LeDuc, 1998), at other high-volume programs (e.g., Bourg et al., 1999; D. Davies et al., 1996; McDermott-Steinmetz-Lane, 1997), and in some law enforcement agencies (Morgan, 1995). However, as discussed below, when joint investigation by CPS and law enforcement is mandated, the child interview model tends to be superseded by the joint investigation model.

Some programs employing the child interview model (e.g., children's advocacy centers) forbid the alleged offender from coming to the facility because it is felt that his/her presence will prevent the child from believing the facility is a "safe place" to disclose, if there is anything to disclose (Center for Child Protection, 1992). Moreover, most adherents of this model assume that conjoint interviews of victims and alleged offenders are both counterproductive to disclosure and an additional betrayal of the child's trust, this time by the interviewer (Faller, Froning, & Lipovsky, 1991).

Research findings support the efficacy of the child interview model. Its use results in disclosures by about two-thirds to three-fourths of children who are interviewed in studies (Bradley & Wood, 1996; Cantlon, Payne, & Erbaugh, 1996; Carnes, Wilson, & Nelson-Gardell, 1999, 2000; Hershkowitz, Horowitz, & Lamb, 2005; Lamb & Sternberg, 1999; Sternberg, Lamb, Orbach, Esplin, & Mitchell, 2000). A single interview is effective with children who have already disclosed sexual abuse (e.g., Bradley & Wood), children who are older, and children who were abused by a nonparental figure (Hershkowitz et al., 2005).

This is the most parsimonious of models and the most widely employed. This model is applicable to most extrafamilial sexual abuse cases and to many intrafamilial cases (see Conte et al., 1991; Hibbard & Hartman, 1993). The practical reality is that the volume of referrals to many agencies using this model is too high for most cases to receive a more involved or complex assessment.

Some of the assumptions inherent in this model are that children are usually reliable when they give accounts of their sexual abuse and that they rarely make false allegations (Everson, 1996). Furthermore, if children deny that they have been sexually abused, this statement is taken at face value as well. That is, interviewers then tend to assume no abuse took place (Haskett, Wayland, Hutcheson, & Tavana, 1995).

In contrast, it is assumed that offenders and nonoffending parents (in intrafamilial abuse cases) may have vested interests in concealing the sexual abuse (Faller, 1984, 1988a). The child interview model also assumes that there is no single offender profile and that many offenders cannot be differentiated easily from individuals who do not sexually victimize children (Everson, 1996).

THE JOINT INVESTIGATION MODEL

The joint investigation model involves collaborative investigation by CPS and law enforcement, and sometimes others (e.g., the prosecutor). As noted above, in the mid-1980s most states amended their child protection statutes to require greater collaboration between CPS and law enforcement (National Center for the Prosecution of Child Abuse, 1997). Currently, at least 33 states and the District of Columbia have statutes requiring joint CPS/law enforcement investigation of some types of child abuse cases (U.S. Department of Justice, 1993). These statutory changes are both the cause and effect of a shift in social policy to criminalization of child abuse, especially sexual abuse.[1] In response to changes in mandates, four offices of the federal government held a symposium in June 1992 on joint investigations. From this meeting came a research report describing the state of joint investigative practice and making a series of recommendations to enhance joint investigations (U.S. Department of Justice, 1993). Joint investigation by CPS and law enforcement of child sexual abuse cases has thus become an important model for investigation (Pence & Wilson, 1994).

The joint investigation model is implemented in a variety of ways. It may involve a conjoint interview of the child by law enforcement and CPS. When the interview is conjoint, there may be a primary and a secondary interviewer, with the secondary interviewer taking notes and asking additional questions after the primary interviewer has exhausted his/her inquiry. In other instances, one professional is behind the one-way mirror while the other interviews the child. Some communities employ a separate forensic interviewer, who talks to the child while both CPS and law enforcement (and, in some communities, the prosecutor) are behind the one-way mirror. The interviewer may employ a "bug-in-the-ear" so that those behind the mirror can influence the direction of the interview,[2] usually by suggesting questions or a line of inquiry. The goal of such collaborations is to minimize the number of interviews by gathering information necessary for both protection and prosecution in the same interview.

However, in joint investigation, data gathering is not limited to the child interview. Other parties, including the suspect, the nonsuspected parent(s), and other potential witnesses are interviewed. How these responsibilities are divided between law enforcement and CPS varies by local practice, but a common division of labor is to have the police interview the suspect and CPS interview the nonsuspected caretaker(s). Law enforcement also has responsibility for collecting and preserving physical evidence. Some types of evidence are obtained from the crime scene, and others collected by a health care professional during the physical exam. In the latter instance, the health care professional collects and preserves specimens using a rape kit, which is then turned over to police for analysis at a crime lab.

Early research on joint investigation documents how difficult it was for child welfare and law enforcement professionals to work together (Pence & Wilson, 1994). A more recent study demonstrates that joint investigation can be very successful in eliciting confessions from suspects, obtaining pleas, and avoiding child testimony at trial (Faller & Henry, 2000). This study does not document what proportion of children were successfully interviewed, however.

An assumption of the joint investigation model is that the most positive case outcome is successful criminal prosecution. When evidence will not support criminal prosecution, which, as a rule, requires child testimony and evidence to meet the standard of proof, "beyond a reasonable doubt,"[3] law enforcement usually closes its case. This decision may leave the child protection case in jeopardy. CPS may doubt the other confirming evidence and may not substantiate the case (Faller, 1997).

PARENT–CHILD INTERACTION MODEL

The parent–child interaction model has two origins in mental health practice. In the 1970s and 1980s, some clinicians, trying to understand the causes of child maltreatment, came to the conclusion that maltreatment represented distortions in the bonding between parent and child. These distortions were asserted to manifest in the way parents interacted with their children (Steele & Pollock, 1974), a theory especially applied to children with failure to thrive and battered child syndrome. For example, clinicians reported parents whose children failed to thrive did not engage in eye contact with the child, did not hold the child in the *en face* position (so the parent could look into the child's eyes), and failed to vocalize (e.g., by making cooing noises to the child) (Steele & Pollock, 1974). Battered children were often described as hypervigilant and avoidant of eye contact with the parent. The parents were noted to speak in a negative tone of voice to their children and to handle them roughly (Haynes-Seman & Hart, 1988). Important is the fact that, because of their young age, these children did not have the language needed for an interview.

The second source of this model derives from divorce cases. Often, evaluators attempt to assess the quality of parent–child relationships in divorce when there are custody and visitation disputes (i.e., mental health evaluators use various methods to ascertain who is the child's primary or psychological parent when recommending custody to one parent or the other). Similarly, they assess parent–child attachment when deciding if and how much contact the child should have with the noncustodial parent. Although evaluators using this model may use additional means to understand the nature of the child's relationship with the parent, the primary method is by having a parent–child session, which is observed by the evaluator, who may be in the interview room or behind a one-way mirror (e.g., Bricklin, 1995; Stahl, 1994).

When clinicians applied this model to sexual abuse, they assumed victims and offenders would engage in sexualized interaction while being observed and/or the child would show fear of or avoid contact with the sexually abusive parent. In addition, a number of writers (Gardner, 1992; Green, 1986; Wehrspann, Steinhauer, & Klajner-Diamond, 1987) have suggested that observing how the child behaves both with the accused and nonaccused parent will be instructive in differentiating true from false allegations. Writers disagree about the significance and meaning of various reactions of the suspected victim to face-to-face contact with the suspected offender (Benedek & Schetky, 1987a; Gardner, 1992; Green, 1986) and the other parent. But it is assumed by those using this model that parent–child interactions will be readily interpretable by skilled mental health professionals (Haynes-Seman & Hart, 1988; Haynes-Seman & Krugman, 1989). There are concerns, however, about both the utility and the ethics of an assessment model that includes such a session (American Academy of Child and Adolescent Psychiatry, 1997b; American Professional Society on the Abuse of Children, 1997; Faller et al., 1991). In terms of utility, the concern is whether mental health professionals can reliably detect sexually abusive and nonabusive relationships. With regard to ethics, the concern is the impact of these parent–child encounters on the child, especially if the child has been sexually abused.

As noted above, clinicians employing the parent–child interaction model generally use data-gathering methods in addition to the parent–child interview. An evaluation of this sort would usually include review of background material, an interview with each parent, and interview with the child, as well as an observation of the interaction between the child and each parent. An unusual version of this model is that advocated by Haynes-Seman and Hart (1988), which actually has the child present during the assessment of each parent, in addition to a parent–child session with the interviewer absent. Some clinicians allow the accused parent to confront the child regarding the allegations of abuse (Gardner, 1992; Kaplan & Kaplan, 1981), or the clinician asks the child about the allegation in the presence of the accused parent (Benedek & Schetky, 1987b). This model assumes that there is an accusing and an accused parent and has been used primarily when allegations of abuse are made in the context of a divorce.

Although some research has been conducted to ascertain clinicians' ability to differentiate abusive from nonabusive relationships, the findings are not entirely supportive of this model. In a study involving 23 mental health professionals (with an average of 15 years of experience) and 45 psychology undergraduates, Starr (1987) found that both groups could differentiate only at chance levels (50% of the time) between abusive and nonabusive parent–child dyads involved in free play situations. A comparable study of 52 child welfare workers conducted by Deitrich-MacLean and Walden (1988) found them somewhat more skilled, being able to classify correctly mother–child dyads involved in a task 76% of the time. However, only one case in these two studies involved sexual abuse.

In contrast, researchers employing standardized measures have been more successful in differentiating abusive from nonabusive parent–child interactions (Cerezo & D'Ocon, 1999; Cerezo, D'Ocon, & Dolz, 1996; Madonna, Van Scoyk, & Jones, 1991). The study by Cerezo and colleagues (Cerezo & D'Ocon, 1999; Cerezo et al., 1996) involved mothers and children with a history of physical, not sexual, victimization. In-home observations were coded using the Standardized Observation Codes III and later analyzed. Patterns of responses for the abusive and nonabusive mothers to children's aversive behavior could be differentiated, but this analysis requires painstaking coding of parent–child sequential interactions and therefore is not feasible for clinical work.

In a study of 30 incest families and 30 families with a child referred to a psychiatric clinic, Madonna et al. (1991) were able to differentiate incest from nonincest families in ratings on the Beavers-Timberlawn Family Evaluation Scale, an instrument that taps family competency along 13 dimensions. The incest families were significantly more dysfunctional overall and rated more pathological on 12 of the 13 dimensions. None of the dimensions relates directly to sexually abusive behavior, and, at this point, the Beavers-Timberlawn is not structured in such a way as to guide the decision-making of mental health staff, CPS, or law enforcement.

An assumption of the parent–child interaction model is that "actions speak louder than words," that is, that more can be learned about sexual abuse allegations from observing the parent–child interaction than from the children's statements. Their statements about sexual abuse cannot be relied upon, because children can be coached or may lie about sexual abuse, and many allegations are false (Everson & Faller, 1999). A further assumption is that children will not be traumatized unduly by confrontation from the accused parent. Finally, the model assumes that mental health professionals have the skill to differentiate sexually abusive from nonabusive parent–child relationships. Because overt sexual behavior is uncommon, professionals must interpret correctly more subtle interactions.

This model is not widely espoused by clinicians evaluating sexual abuse allegations. For example, Conte et al. (1991) found that 96% of sexual abuse experts responding to their study did not interview the child in the presence of the offender. Similarly, sexual abuse evaluation guidelines from both the American Professional Society on the Abuse of Children (1990, 1997) and the American Academy of Child and Adolescent Psychiatry (1997b) do not recommend a suspect–child interview. However, a model that includes observation of the parent–child interaction is both appropriate and widely employed in making decisions about custody and visitation in divorce when there are no allegations of maltreatment (American Academy of Child and Adolescent Psychiatry, 1997a; Stahl, 1994).

COMPREHENSIVE ASSESSMENT MODEL

To a considerable extent, the comprehensive evaluation model has evolved because of criticisms, especially in court, of simpler models (American Academy of Child and Adolescent Psychiatry, 1997b; Cohen-Lieberman, 1999; Kuehnle, 1996). However, it also has its origins in a tradition of comprehensive family evaluations used in the mental health and child welfare fields.

Although models involving a single professional who gathers information from a variety of sources are described in the literature (American Academy of Child and Adolescent Psychiatry, 1997b; Hoorwitz, 1992; Kuehnle, 1996), comprehensive assessments are also conducted by multidisciplinary teams (California Attorney General's Office, 1994; Hibbard & Hartmann, 1993; Rosenberg & Gary, 1988). The teams consist of physicians, social workers, psychologists, and sometimes nurses, psychiatrists, and lawyers. Some team members may be experts in child interviewing and child development and others in adult assessment and sex offenders. Medical exams of alleged victims, psychological testing, and interviews are all generally employed. The team reads and integrates background information, for example, the family's protective services history or past allegations and investigations of abuse by other agencies. Cases are often referred to a multidisciplinary team by mandated agencies (i.e., protective services, law enforcement, and the courts), and collaboration is sought with them and community professionals who have been involved with the family. Professionals conducting comprehensive assessments expect to provide expert testimony in court (Faller, 2003).[4]

In addition to those involved directly in the allegations of sexual abuse, siblings not alleged to have been victimized and others (e.g., grandparents, stepparents, and foster parents) may be interviewed. In cases where it is deemed essential to answering the questions posed, parent–child and family interactions may be undertaken (e.g., Kuehnle, 1996). However, such sessions will not be central to decision-making about the likelihood of sexual abuse.

It is evident from the description that this model is suited to allegations of intrafamilial sexual abuse, and not necessary for most allegations of extrafamilial sexual abuse. Its scope makes it useful for complex cases, where there may be allegations of multiple offenders and/or victims, where the family dysfunction includes other problems such as substance abuse and domestic violence, and where there may have been prior assessments that were inconclusive or with disputed conclusions.

Moreover, the model is used to answer questions in addition to "has the child been sexually abused?" Typically, it can address issues such as the type of treatment needed for the offender and nonoffending parent and their prognoses, the victim's treatment and placement needs, the advisability of ultimate family reunification, and the impact and possible success of criminal prosecution. The drawbacks to this model are the time it takes, its cost, and its intrusiveness into family life.

A number of studies support the utility of the comprehensive assessment model (California Attorney General's Office, 1994; Hibbard & Hartmann, 1993). Moreover, a study by Kaufman, Jones, Steiglitz, Vitulano, and Mannarino (1994) demonstrates its efficacy with sexual abuse cases previously unsubstantiated. Cases involving 56 children were referred to an intervention/research project. The professionals examined information from child protection workers, parents, medical records, and observations of parent–child interactions. Of the 13 children in this study who were substantiated as sexually abused, five had not been so identified before referral to the research/intervention project (Kaufman et al., 1994).

This model assumes that the child interview is only one of several types of information that need to be considered. However, the child interview is usually regarded as the most important part of the assessment, and usually the child is interviewed more than once. The model's hall-mark, however, is extensive data gathering from a variety of sources and a careful review of past history and reports.

SUMMARY AND CONCLUSION

Child interviews for sexual abuse usually occur within a context of information gathering. Current practice is conceptualized into four models: the child interview model, the joint investigation model, the parent–child interaction model, and the comprehensive assessment model. While these are described as discrete models, in practice they may be overlapping, and components attributed to a particular model may be employed by professionals using another approach or model. Although the parent–child interaction model has serious drawbacks as a method for determining sexual abuse, all of these models have utility. Professionals need to be aware of the spectrum of approaches and models as they select an approach that is appropriate for their work set-ting, educational background, or the particular case they are assessing.

NOTES

1. Of course, sexual abuse was already a crime, but before this shift, it was more likely to be treated as a mental health problem or sickness.

2. Ear bugs may be employed in other models, as well.

3. See chapter 17 for a discussion of standards of proof.

4. Other models involve court testimony but not necessarily expert testimony.

Interviewer Objectivity and Allegations of Sexual Abuse

Kathleen Coulborn Faller

An important issue is how professionals should approach an allegation of sexual abuse. In part, stance toward an allegation is influenced by the professional's role, for example, whether the role is primarily forensic or clinical (for a discussion of these roles, see chapter 1).

The current, prevailing view is that interviewers should be neutral toward an allegation of sexual abuse and entertain multiple hypotheses that might explain an allegation (e.g., American Academy of Child and Adolescent Psychiatry, 1997b; American Professional Society on the Abuse of Children, 1997; Kuehnle, 1996; Ney, 1995). This admonition derives, in part, from the criticism that professionals interviewing children about possible sexual abuse have confirmatory bias (e.g., Ceci, Bruck, & Rosenthal, 1995; Gardner, 1991; Ney, 1995). This means that professionals attend to and put weight on information supportive of sexual abuse and ignore or discount information that does not support the allegation. Its opposite is disconfirmatory bias, that is, privileging information that does not support sexual abuse and disregarding information that supports sexual abuse.

Without regard to challenges of interviewer bias, there are good reasons for considering multiple hypotheses when addressing an allegation of sexual abuse. The world has changed in many ways in the last 25 years that make it even more important to consider alternative explanations for concerns about sexual abuse, as described below.

First, children's social world has changed substantially. Today, advanced sexual knowledge, which is often the source of concern about possible sexual abuse, is more easily obtainable from nonabusive experiences than in the past. These include sex education, sexual abuse prevention programs, pornographic videos or television, and sexually explicit material on the Internet (Finkelhor, Mitchell, & Wolak, 2000). In addition, research suggests that the most common way children obtain advanced sexual knowledge, which they may then imitate, is by observing people engaged in sexual activity (Boat & Everson, 1994; Everson & Boat, 1990). Moreover, through the media and other sources, children may come to know that people sometimes make false allegations of sexual abuse, which might increase the likelihood that some children will make them.

Second, general awareness of the problem of sexual abuse has increased. Professionals, parents, and the general public are more knowledgeable about the existence, signs, and symptoms of sexual abuse, which likely results in more ready consideration of sexual abuse as a possible explanation when children display signs and symptoms. In addition, information about the array of interventions when sexual abuse is alleged or substantiated could spur not only reports of genuine concerns but also false reports.

The current adherence to "neutrality," however, should be placed in both a historical and gendered context. History documents the rise and fall of belief in the veracity of children's allegations of sexual abuse by adults (e.g., Masson, 1984; Mildred, 2003; Myers, 1998). Moreover, because most offenders are men and most victims are children, more often female children, belief in and support of victims of sexual abuse challenge the prevailing social order (Herman, 2000; Rush, 1980; Russell & Bolen, 2000, Ward, 1985). Asserting that there is a serious problem of child sexual abuse inspires retaliation and backlash against the believers and supporters both because of society's inability to sustain a focus on child sexual abuse (Finkelhor, 1994; Myers, 1994) and because the accused hold substantially more power than their accusers (Herman, 2000; Russell & Bolen, 2000).

In this chapter, information about three different stances toward an allegation of sexual abuse—believing, neutral, and skeptical—are described. In addition, the research on professional biases in sexual abuse is discussed and practical considerations related to the particular allegation are covered.

A Believing Stance

Child sexual abuse was "rediscovered" in the late 1970s and early 1980s. At that time, several influential professionals argued for a believing stance toward sexual abuse allegations. Sgroi (1980), a pioneer in the sexual abuse field, wrote, "Recognition of sexual molestation in a child is entirely dependent on the individual's inherent willingness to entertain the possibility that the condition may exist" (p. 29). Herman (1981) and McCarty (1981) took an a priori position that most accounts are true. Drawing upon clinical experience and research, Faller (1984, 1988a) asserted that false allegations are quite rare and pointed out that children have little motivation for making a false accusation, but offenders have considerable motivation for persuading professionals that children are either lying, mistaken, or crazy. Similarly, in his conceptualization of the Child Sexual Abuse Accommodation Syndrome, Summit (1983) assumed that children were suffering because actual abuse but, because of their powerlessness, accommodated themselves to the abuse, delayed disclosing it, and sometimes recanted after disclosure.

A Neutral Stance

On the other hand, the guidelines of the American Academy of Child and Adolescent Psychiatry (1990, 1997b) advocate "emotional neutrality" and "an open mind." Similarly, White and Quinn (1988) argue for a neutral position, suggesting that any other might contaminate the content of the interview. Because of this concern, they recommend the interviewer have no information other than the child's name and age (White, Strom, Santilli, & Halpin, 1986) before interviewing the child. The concern that knowledge about the allegation corrupts the interview is more recently reflected in Idaho's use of a blind interview in children's advocacy centers (Cantlon, Payne, & Erbaugh, 1996; Hewitt, 1999). However, most writers advise gathering background information before conducting an interview with a child; such information can facilitate artful and thorough exploration for possible sexual abuse (Faller, 1988a; Morgan, 1995; Myers, 1992, 1998). Nevertheless, those favoring informed interviews admonish that interviewers should take care to ensure that knowledge about the allegation does not result in a leading interview (e.g., Faller, 2003; Myers, 1998; Poole & Lamb, 1998).

A Skeptical Stance

Still other writers (e.g., Gardner, 1992, 1995; Wakefield & Underwager, 1988) have asserted that one should be skeptical of children's statements about sexual abuse because a substantial proportion, in general or in certain contexts (e.g., divorce, daycare), are false. This perspective is supported by some analogue studies, which show that some children are inaccurate in their reports (e.g., Bruck, Ceci, & Francoeur, 2000; Bruck, Ceci, Francoeur, & Renick, 1995; Bruck, Ceci, & Hembrooke, 1998, 2002; Ceci, Bruck, & Rosenthal, 1995; Clarke-Stewart, Malloy, & Allhusen, 2004). The results of analogue studies and factors identified in studies that lead to inaccurate reports are discussed in chapter 2. Some who are skeptical hold the opinion that children frequently make false allegations because of some external influence, for example, a vindictive accusing parent (Benedek & Schetky, 1985) or an incompetent "validator" (a poorly trained child interviewer who has an agenda to find sexual abuse for personal or financial reasons) (Gardner, 1992). Others regard the defendant's rights as overriding and are less concerned with issues of protection of children and society from sex offenders (e.g., Bruck, Ceci, & Rosenthal, 1995; Wakefield & Underwager, 1988).

RESEARCH ON INTERVIEWER/
PROFESSIONAL STANCE

Research relevant to this issue suggests that true "neutrality" is elusive, but in part this is because "ground truth" (whether the vignette, behavioral indicator, or case in point involves sexual abuse or not) is difficult to establish. In four studies, researchers examined the impact of interviewer characteristics on interviewer stance (Boat & Everson, 1989; Everson, Boat, & Robertson, 1992; Jackson & Nuttal, 1993; Kendall-Tackett & Watson, 1991). The important characteristics studied were the respondent's gender, profession, professional experience, and beliefs about the likelihood of sexual abuse.

The researchers vary somewhat in their approach. In their first study, Boat and Everson (1989) asked child protective services (CPS) workers what proportion of the cases they saw were false allegations and then conducted follow-up interviews with both those who reported no false allegations and those reporting false allegations. In their second study (Everson et al., 1992), the researchers asked the respondents about the likelihood that children of different ages and gender would be lying when reporting sexual abuse. Jackson and Nuttal (1993) used vignettes of possible sexual abuse, systematically varying race, victim characteristics, offender characteristics, and family characteristics. Kendall-Tackett and Watson (1991) asked professionals, whom they divided into two general categories (law enforcement and mental health personnel), whether they approached an allegation with a believing, neutral, or skeptical stance and then asked them to rate 14 indicators of possible sexual abuse for three different age groups.

On the whole, the research indicates that professionals are likely to believe children when they report sexual abuse. However, there are some variations based upon gender, profession, and abuse characteristics, and some inconsistencies among studies.

A fairly consistent observation is that female professionals are more likely to make a finding of sexual abuse than are male professionals, when presented with either vignettes or behavioral indicators. Everson et al. (1992) and Everson and Boat (1989), however, present no data on gender.

As mentioned above, Kendall-Tackett and Watson (1991) queried respondents about general stance and, predictably, found that respondents with a believing stance were more likely to rate the characteristics presented to them by researchers as indicative of sexual abuse. Boat and Everson (1989) found that workers who report they encountered false allegations, as compared to those who reported encountering none, were more likely to be skeptical about children's reports.

As a rule, legal professionals (law enforcement, judges, and attorneys) were more skeptical than were mental health professionals, and

Everson et al. (1992) found that a small but important minority (10%) of judges and law enforcement officers believed that substantial proportions of reports are untrue. In contrast, Kendall-Tackett and Watson (1991) found law enforcement personnel reporting smaller percentages of false accounts than mental health professionals. Law enforcement professionals were more persuaded by reenactments with anatomical dolls and by general symptoms (e.g., depression, aggression, and fear of the perpetrator) than are mental health personnel.

Everson et al. (1992) found that persons seeing more cases were less likely to think children's reports were false. However, Jackson and Nuttal (1993) found younger professionals (who probably had seen fewer cases) to be more likely to believe that the children in their vignettes had been sexually abused.

Among Everson and Boat's (1989) CPS sample, 54 respondents (of 88) reported having investigated no cases in the last year where children falsely alleged sexual abuse. Everson et al. (1992) also found that some respondents believe children "never lie" about sexual abuse (judges, 14%; law enforcement, 9%; mental health, 14%; CPS workers, 30%). It should be noted that these findings are more than a decade old and likely would not be replicated if the studies were repeated today.

Finally, with regard to victim characteristics, younger children generally were judged more believable than older ones, and Everson et al. (1992) found boys were more likely to be regarded as truthful. In their earlier study (Everson & Boat, 1989), in more than half the cases, one reason cited for believing the allegation false was the child's retraction.

PRACTICE OBSERVATIONS ABOUT INTERVIEWER/PROFESSIONAL STANCE

A potential influence on interviewer objectivity is the circumstance under which the assessment is conducted. Everson (1993) has noted that the relative amount of time the interviewer spends with the child and the alleged offender may influence the opinion. In addition, who is paying for the evaluation and whom the interviewer sees first can affect objectivity, often without conscious awareness (Everson, 1993). Although nothing has been written directly about a related issue, it is clear from a review of the literature that professionals who routinely are retained by the accused (e.g., Gardner, 1992, 1995; Wakefield & Underwager, 1988) are much more skeptical than those who conduct evaluations for CPS or law enforcement (e.g., Everson et al., 1992; Faller, 1988a; Sgroi, 1982).

Other potential influences are the amount of information about the case and sources of information. For instance, if the interviewer receives volumes of background information related to the victim and nothing about the offender, this may influence the interviewer's stance.

The known facts of the case at hand will and should affect the interviewer's stance. For example, if there is a positive finding for venereal disease or evidence of vaginal penetration, the interviewer will likely approach the assessment thinking that the child has been sexually abused. On the other hand, if the child has made a false allegation in the past and/or the allegation is vague, greater skepticism will be warranted.

The research on false allegations and the context in which they are likely to be made are relevant here. This research and its limitations are covered in some detail in chapter 13. However, the research suggests that false allegations of sexual abuse by children are uncommon, representing 1–10% of reports by children (e.g., Berliner, 1988; Faller, 1988a; Horowitz, Salt, & Gomez-Schwartz, 1984; Jones & McGraw, 1987; Oates et al., 2000). As discussed at greater length later, there are certain situations in which the probability may be higher (e.g., with older children, with children who have been previously sexually abused, and in divorce situations).

CONCLUSION

To conclude a consideration of interviewer objectivity, what the term "objectivity" really means must be defined. An objective professional approaches a case with an open mind but with an appreciation of the research findings on false allegations by children, a recognition of the importance of allowing the facts of the case, as they become known, to determine the interviewer's level of belief or skepticism, and an awareness that the circumstances of the assessment and the professional's personal characteristics can influence her/his reactions to cases in potentially problematic ways. Professionals should employ strategies to guard against an inappropriate stance based upon the latter.

FIVE

Number of Child Interviews

Kathleen Coulborn Faller

Prevailing practice, when interviewing for possible sexual abuse, is to conduct a single child interview before coming to a decision about the likelihood of sexual abuse (e.g., Bourg et al., 1999; Carnes & LeDuc, 1998; Carnes, Nelson-Gardell, Wilson, & Orgassa, 2001; Carnes, Wilson, & Nelson-Gardell, 2000; D. Davies et al., 1996; Lamb & Sternberg, 1999; McDermott-Steinmetz-Lane, 1997; Merchant & Toth, 2001). Nevertheless, most professionals appreciate that a single interview may be inadequate for the investigation of many cases (American Academy of Child and Adolescent Psychiatry, 1997b; American Professional Society on the Abuse of Children, 1990, 1997, 2002; Carnes et al., 2000, 2001; Hershkowitz et al., 2006).

In this chapter, issues germane to the appropriate number of interviews and relevant research and practice literature are discussed. These issues are multiple interviews versus multiple interviewers, the competing concerns that a single interview may not be sufficient to allow for disclosure versus multiple interviews may result in programming or contamination of the child's account, possible reasons for more than one interview, individual case differences that might affect interview number, and extended assessments.

SINGLE VERSUS MULTIPLE INTERVIEWERS

Professionals from a number of agencies need to know information about a child's sexual abuse. This need often results in children being interviewed by several different interviewers. For example, Conte, Sorenson, Fogarty, and Dalla Rosa (1991) conducted a national survey of approximately 200 sexual abuse experts. They found that, on average, children had talked to 2.3 persons about their sexual abuse before seeing the expert who participated in the study. The potential traumatic impact of having to repeat a description of sexual victimization to several different people was one concern that inspired the National Children's Advocacy Center (NCAC), founded in 1985 in Huntsville, Alabama (National Children's Advocacy Center, 1985; National Children's Alliance, 2006). Potential trauma derives, in part, from the fact these persons are strangers and therefore children may feel psychologically exposed by the requirement that they repeat their disclosure (California Attorney General's Office, 1994; Hibbard & Hartmann, 1993; National Children's Alliance, 2006; Sgroi, 1982). An additional concern is that some interviewers may not be supportive of the child.

Therefore, a goal in case management is to minimize the number of professionals who interview the child (California Attorney General's Office, 1994; National Children's Alliance, 2006). Children's advocacy centers, where children can be interviewed at the request of law enforcement, child protective services (CPS), and sometimes other agencies, intend to provide a single interview by a skilled interviewer in a child-friendly environment (National Children's Advocacy Center, 1985; National Children's Alliance, 2006). Other interventions, such as a medical examination and treatment, may be provided at the same location. Multidisciplinary teams with one skilled forensic interviewer who asks questions for all team members also are recommended to minimize the number of interviews (California Attorney General's Office, 1994; Hibbard & Hartmann, 1993). The State of California has demonstrated that such teams can reduce the number of interviews for children (California Attorney General's Office, 1994). Nevertheless, in many communities, children are still interviewed by at least two professionals because they first talk to a professional who refers them to a children's advocacy center or multidisciplinary team.

ONE VERSUS SEVERAL INTERVIEWS BY THE SAME PERSON

The appropriate or optimal number of interviews by a single evaluator has been the subject of writing, guidelines, and research. As noted above, writers have been concerned about the risks of both too few interviews to facilitate disclosure and too many interviews resulting in a false allegation. Resources also play an important role in the single interview preference. Substantial additional resources would be required to handle the volume of reports, if more than one interview were routine or required.

Many of the written guidelines for interviewing children suspected of sexual abuse recommend more than one interview (American Academy of Child and Adolescent Psychiatry, 1997b; American Professional Society on the Abuse of Children, 1990, 1997, 2002; Faller, 1988a; White, Strom, & Quinn, n.d.). There are a number of reasons an interviewer might conduct more than one interview. First, the professional may want to conduct more than one interview before deciding the child *has not been* sexually abused (Faller, 1988a; Hershkowitz et al., 2006). Second, White et al. (n.d.) advise more than one before deciding the child *has been* sexually abused. Third, in cases with extensive abuse, professionals may need multiple interviews before concluding that they understand the full extent of sexual abuse (American Professional Society on the Abuse of Children, 1990, 1997; Carnes et al., 2001). Fourth, interviewers may stop an interview and schedule a second because the child appears upset by the interview (Faller, 2003) or is uncooperative (Hershkowitz et al., 2006). Fifth, more than one interview will likely be needed to assess the child's overall functioning and developmental status, as well as possible sexual abuse (American Academy of Child and Adolescent Psychiatry, 1997b; American Professional Society on the Abuse of Children, 1990, 1997). Getting to know the child over the course of interviews can greatly enhance an understanding of the needs of the child (Faller, 2003).

Finally, logistical considerations may affect a decision about the number of interviews; the child or family may have to come a considerable distance for the assessment, or there may be other logistical difficulties in getting professional and child together. In these instances, a single session may well be preferable. Generally, in cases where a single interview is planned, the session should be longer. Thus, instead of scheduling 30- or 45-minute sessions, the interviewer plans for an hour or two, or even as much as a half day. This time can be broken up by snacks, lunch, or "breathers." Alternatively, the interviewer can stop talking about the sexual abuse and engage in other activities with the child and later return to the topic of sexual abuse (Faller, 1988a).

Some writers who support more than one interview recommend using the first interview to get to know the child and asking about sexual abuse only during the second interview (Carnes et al., 2001). Others recommend using a second interview to check for consistency in the child's report and gather additional details (Faller & DeVoe, 1995b; White et al., n.d.). Interviewers may use different methods of data gathering over two interviews. For example, they might rely primarily on verbal communication during the first interview and introduce media such as drawings during the second to check for consistency across media and to gather additional details (Faller, 2003). See chapter 9 for a discussion of the use of media. Interviewers also may use a second interview to gather information about certain details they neglected to ask about in the first.

The American Professional Society on the Abuse of Children (1990, 1997) guidelines suggest two or more interviews in part to allow the opportunity for a full psychosocial assessment, not just a determination of sexual abuse. Morgan (1995) recommends two interviews or more, a few days apart, because most children are not able to reveal everything in a single interview. In addition, support for a recommendation of more than one interview can be found in the research by T. Sorenson and Snow (1991), described below.

On the other hand, the American Academy of Child and Adolescent Psychiatry (1990) guidelines caution against too many interviews, advising, "Keep the number of interviews to a minimum. Multiple interviews may encourage confabulation" (American Academy of Child and Adolescent Psychiatry, 1997, p. 19). These guidelines also raise concerns that repeated interviews may cause the child unnecessary stress and lead the child to believe she/he has not provided enough information, thereby engendering a false allegation.

In a case involving alleged multiple victims who lived in a trailer park in Jordan, Minnesota (Humphrey, 1985), and in the McMartin preschool case in Manhatten Beach, California (Wilkinson & Rainey, 1989), concerns about the impact of multiple interviews played a role in the failure to convict alleged offenders.[1] Moreover, analogue studies inform forensic interviewers about the potential problematic impact of multiple interviews. Multiple interviews, coupled with leading, suggestive, and misleading questions, can result in young children (ages 3–5) falsely affirming experiences they have not had and even providing some details (Bruck, Ceci, & 2002; Ceci, Huffman, Smith, & Loftus, 1994; Ceci, Loftus, Leichtman, & Bruck, 1994). On the other hand, when children are questioned over several sessions in a nonleading manner, their accounts generally remain accurate (Poole & White, 1991, 1993, 1995). Moreover, Lyon (1999a) in his review of the research on the effects of repeated interviews concludes that repeated, less suggestive questioning not only does not contaminate children's accounts but also improves memory of events. Therefore, it appears that it is not the number of interviews but what happens in them that is most important.

As already noted, the majority of sexual abuse investigations consist of one interview. More than one interview is resorted to only when the first interview is inconclusive. The practice of a single interview is characteristic not only of child protection investigations but also of some of the foremost diagnostic programs in the country, for example, the Chadwick Center for Child Protection at Children's Hospital and Health Center in San Diego (D. Davies et al., 1996), the CARES Program at Emmanuel Hospital in Portland, Oregon, (*Guidelines for the Social Work Interview*, n.d.) and the Corner House model (Bourg et al., 1999). However, the goal of these programs is to determine whether or not children have been sexually abused. They generally do not assess children's overall functioning and do a limited assessment of developmental level and competency. Thus, their goals may be more circumscribed than programs conducting multiple interviews. Also, it should be noted that interview programs in Western Europe routinely involve more than a single interview (e.g., Keary & Fitzpatrick, 1994; Sternberg, Lamb, Davies, & Wescott, 2001).

INDIVIDUAL CASE DIFFERENCES

Best practice suggests that factors related to the child also should determine the number of interviews. These include the child's age, the child's functioning, the relationship of the child to the suspect, whether there has been a prior disclosure, and safety and logistical issues (Goodman-Brown, Edelstein, Goodman, Jones, & Gordon, 2003).

Research and practice suggest that younger children may require a greater number of interviews of shorter duration (Hershkowitz, Horowitz, & Lamb, 2005; Hewitt, 1999; Keary & Fitzpatrick, 1994). See chapter 10 for guidance on interviewing young children. In addition, children who are mentally ill, developmentally delayed or have some other emotional or behavioral disturbance may be more difficult to interview or have difficulty communicating. As a consequence, these children may need more sessions (Baladerian, 1991). See chapter 11 for detailed discussion of interviewing special needs children. Furthermore, interviewers may want more sessions with young and challenged children before they feel comfortable ruling in or ruling out child sexual abuse.

In addition, practice and research suggest that children may need more time to disclose and therefore more interviews, if they are close to or respect the person who is their abuser (Carnes et al., 2001; Faller, 1988a; Hershkowitz et al., 2005). For example, Hershkowitz et al. (2005) describe the results of a review of 26,446 forensic interviews conducted by Israeli youth investigators for physical and sexual abuse over a 5-year time frame. Among their important findings are differences based upon whether the alleged offender was a parent or nonparent figure. Although close to two-thirds of the alleged offenders were parent figures, disclosures of abuse occurred in only 20.9% of parent cases compared to 89.3% of nonparent cases.

Whether children have disclosed previously and/or whether they intend to do so when interviewed should affect the number of interviews. Research to date suggests that a minority of children tell about abuse right after it occurs (e.g., Sas & Cunningham, 1995; T. Sorenson & Snow, 1991). It is important for interviewers to appreciate that the majority of children who are reported to CPS and police probably have already told a parent, friend, or teacher.

Factors of intention and prior disclosure, in part, explain discrepant findings of two studies, T. Sorenson and Snow (1991) and Bradley and Wood (1996), both studies involving high-certainty cases. Sorenson and Snow examined cases involving children seen at a mental health center, three-fourths of whom did not intend to disclose, and Bradley and Wood reviewed case records of substantiated cases reported to CPS.

Sorenson and Snow describe a disclosure process that occurred over several interview sessions, in 116 cases with other corroborating evidence. Initially most children denied sexual abuse, but then tentatively disclosed. Moreover, 22% recanted after active disclosure, and then later reaffirmed sexual victimization. Older children were more likely to disclose intentionally and younger children accidentally. See chapter 13 on nondisclosing children for additional discussion of this study and challenges to its efficacy. Similar findings were noted in a case record review of 72 children conducted by Campis, Hebden-Curtis, and Demaso (1993).

In contrast to the findings of these two studies are those of Bradley and Wood (1996), whose sample consisted of 221 substantiated CPS cases of sexual abuse with corroborating evidence, 72% of whom had made a disclosure before their CPS interview. In this sample, children made full disclosures mostly without initial denial, tentative disclosure, or recantation. However, these researchers studied only substantiated CPS cases. Thus, their sample consisted of cases where children were probably prepared to and did disclose to CPS, usually in a single interview. These differences in findings suggest that interviewers should anticipate needing more interviews in cases where children have not disclosed previously and/or do not intend to do so. As noted, children who do not disclose and strategies for interviewing them are discussed in greater detail in chapter 13.

Safety issues also should be considered in determining the number of interviews needed before an opinion about the abuse is rendered. If the child is in a situation of possible ongoing sexual abuse, the practice of routinely conducting two or more confirming interviews before forming an opinion is ethically and practically questionable. Similarly, if the parent is allowing the assessment only reluctantly and is not compelled by court order to cooperate, taking the time to conduct two or more interviews may result in inability to complete the assessment. In contrast, if the child is already in foster care or is with a parent who is supportive of the assessment and protective of the child, then two or more interviews are appropriate.

EXTENDED EVALUATIONS

Extended evaluations may be recommended when results of the first interview(s) are inconclusive (Boat & Everson, 1988b; Carnes et al., 2000; James, Everson, & Friedrich, n.d.) and in cases where the children are 3 and younger (Everson, 1992a; Hewitt, 1991, 1999). In the latter instance, the children have short attention spans and limited capacity to communicate directly. One extended assessment model involving very young children allows time (about 6 months) for the child's communication skills to develop over the course of professional involvement with the child (James, Everson, & Friedrich, n.d.).

Research conducted by the NCAC adds to our knowledge about both the level of need and the structure for extended evaluations (Carnes &

LeDuc, 1998; Carnes, Wilson, & Nelson-Gardell, 1999; Carnes et al., 2000, 2001). Children's advocacy centers generally employ a single interview model, but data from the NCAC indicate that about 25% of cases coming to such programs cannot be resolved during a single interview (Carnes & LeDuc, 1998; Carnes et al., 1999). These researchers designated three situations that are appropriate for extended assessments: (1) cases in which the child makes no disclosure but there is serious cause for concern about sexual abuse based on other information, (2) cases in which the likelihood of abuse is unclear after a single interview, and (3) situations in which the full extent of the sexual abuse cannot be resolved in a single interview.

Initially, the NCAC developed a 12-session extended assessment protocol (Carnes & LeDuc, 1998; Carnes et al., 1999). Using this protocol, they found that about 75% of cases could be resolved, but most disclosures were made before the ninth session. Next, they conducted a pilot of an eight-interview extended assessment (Carnes & LeDuc, 1998; Carnes et al., 1999, 2000). Of the 41 cases involved in the pilot, about half were resolved by a substantiation of sexual abuse, about a fourth with a conclusion of no sexual abuse, and a fourth remained uncertain. These researchers then conducted an experiment involving 20 interview sites, in which cases not resolved in a single interview were assigned randomly to four or eight sessions (Carnes & LeDuc, 1998). The eight-interview protocol proved superior in resolving cases. However, in the eight-interview protocol, most children who disclosed sexual abuse did so by the sixth session. In all of the NCAC extended assessment models, the initial interview is with a caretaker, not the child. The second session is a rapport-building session with the child, and thereafter the number of abuse-focused sessions varies depending on the total number of sessions planned (Carnes & LeDuc, 1998). An extended evaluation composed of six sessions, which is consistent with NCAC research findings, is also consistent with recommendations made based upon practice experience (Faller, 2003).

SUMMARY AND CONCLUSIONS

It is important to differentiate the issue of multiple interviews by different professionals, which is not recommended, from more than one interview by the same professional, which is appropriate in a substantial proportion of cases. In deciding about the number of interviews necessary, the interviewer should consider several issues, including the purpose of the assessment/investigation (i.e., whether its goal is to solely to explore possible sexual abuse, or whether overall functioning is also being determined); the functioning and needs of the individual child, including any intentions related to disclosure; the child's age, anxiety, and activity level; issues of child safety and support; and practical aspects of conducting the assessment. Interviewers should be sensitive to the risks of too many interviews, both real and perceived. There is now a modest body of research supporting the structure and efficacy of an extended assessment for children for whom concerns about sexual abuse cannot be resolved by a single interview.

NOTE

1. In the Jordan, Minnesota, case, one offender confessed and was sentenced.

SIX

Documentation of the Interview

Kathleen Coulborn Faller

Child interviews related to possible sexual abuse, regardless of whether they are conducted for forensic or clinical purposes, require careful and complete documentation. In this chapter, methods used to document child interviews and advantages and disadvantages of videotaping interviews are discussed. In addition, relevant research and guidelines related to videotaping, including informing the child, are described.

METHOD OF DOCUMENTATION

There is universal agreement that investigators and clinicians interviewing children about sexual abuse need to employ some method of documentation (American Academy of Child and Adolescent Psychiatry, 1990, 1997b; American Professional Society on the Abuse of Children, 1990, 1997; Morgan, 1995; Myers, 1992, 1998). Although ideally there should be a good record of the entire interview, most important is the abuse-related portion. This should include not only the information provided by the child but also the questions and other methods used by the interviewer to elicit the information. In their pioneering study of sexual abuse assessment professionals, Conte, Sorenson, Fogarty, and Dalla Rosa (1991) queried respondents regarding means they used. Almost everyone (94%) made notes, but many used other methods, as well. Close to a third of the respondents videotaped (30%) and/or audiotaped (29%). In addition, 8% had another professional record from behind a one-way mirror, and 14% used a professional as a recorder in the room. It is likely that the proportion of interviewers working in forensic settings who videotape has increased since their study 15 years ago.

The American Professional Society on the Abuse of Children (APSAC) guidelines (American Professional Society on the Abuse of Children,

1990, 1997) indicate that, at minimum, there should be written notes and state that the use of video or audiotape should be determined by professional preference, logistics, and clinical considerations. Morgan's (1995) position is quite similar. Bourg et al. (1999) state that use of video, audio, or notes should be at the discretion of the individual program, citing the importance of political and legal considerations in making a decision about how to document. The American Academy of Child and Adolescent Psychiatry (AACAP) guidelines take a stronger position in favor of videotaping, describing its various uses, but note that it may have some disadvantages and risks, as well (American Academy of Child and Adolescent Psychiatry, 1990, 1997b).

Note Taking

Taking notes during the interview, immediately after the interview, or both is the minimum requirement for professionals interviewing children about sexual abuse (American Professional Society on the Abuse of Children, 1990, 1997). Note-taking probably remains the most widely employed method of documentation for law enforcement and child protective services workers because they work in such a variety of venues. For example, child protection workers may have to interview in schools, where obtaining permission even to interview children must be negotiated. Sometimes law enforcement officers have to talk to children in their cars.

To increase accuracy in note-taking, one practice involves one professional interviewing the child and a second taking notes. As Conte et al. (1991) observed from their survey, the note-taker may be in the room or behind a one-way mirror observing and listening to the interview (see also Bourg et al., 1999). In a study in the State of Washington, the note-taker used a laptop computer to document both the interviewer's questions and the child's answers (Berliner, 1997b, 2000, 2001). Results of this study are described below. But note-taking challenges include trying to make them truly "verbatim" and therefore accurate (Berliner, 1997b, 2001). The closer the notes are made to the interview and the more skilled the interviewer at taking verbatim notes, the more accurate they will be (Berliner, 2001). A second challenge is that interviewers are often concerned that note-taking during the interview will negatively affect rapport with the child and will interfere with the interviewer's concentration on the content and process of the interview (Wallen, 1998).

Often, law enforcement and sometimes child protection services workers destroy their hand-written notes after they create an official report (e.g., Faller & Plummer, 1996; Wallen, 1998). This practice can exacerbate speculation about what precisely took place in the interview (Wallen, 1998). Given this concern, in cases of sexual abuse, it is advisable to retain hand-written notes.

Audiotaping

A feasible alternative to note-taking is audiotaping child interviews. Audio recorders are small, portable, and easily employed in most interview venues. It is important that interviewers have good-quality audio recorders and know how to use them properly (Berliner, 2001).

There are some disadvantages of audiotaping. Interviewers may be worried that use of audiotapes will inhibit the child's willingness to be candid (Berliner, 2001). Second, although note-taking after the interview, and even during the interview, takes time, more time is needed to listen to and transcribe an audiotape. Berliner found that on average it took 116 minutes to transcribe a tape of a child interview. Thus, taping and transcription likely at least triples the time needed for an interview. Moreover, although the transcription is useful for writing a report of the interview, it cannot substitute for the report. Sometimes the interviewer can reduce the time needed by taking a few notes during or directly after the interview and then listening to and transcribing sections directly related to the abuse allegations. The sooner after the interview this tape review is done, the easier and less time it will take because the interviewer will have a better memory of where in the interview abusive material will be found.

Videotaping

Videotaping provides the most complete, although not perfect, record of the child interview. It provides both verbatim audio and visual record of everything that happens during the time the child and the interviewer are in video range. Although some professionals who employ videotape actually take a camera with them to various venues where child interviews are conducted (J. Henry, 1999), usually videotapes of interviews are made at sites set up specifically for videotaping. These vary in their technological sophistication, from situations where there is merely a video camera that is turned on by the interviewer to interview rooms with several cameras that can capture what takes place in the interview from more than one angle. Professional perspectives, advantages, and disadvantages of videotaping and guidelines for videotaping are discussed in this section.

The Videotaping Controversy

Videotaping provides a superior record to audiotaping and note-taking. Nevertheless, historically, videotaping child interviews has been the subject of debate and some controversy (Berliner, Stern, & Stephenson, 1992; Faller, 2003; Myers, 1993, 1998; Veith, 1999). In the mid-1980s, videotaping child interviews was regarded as a virtual panacea that would address many problems of investigating and litigating child sexual abuse (Colby & Colby, 1987a, 1987b). There were expectations that videotapes would relieve the child of multiple interviews, would persuade offenders to confess, and could be used in lieu of child testimony in court. The majority of states passed laws allowing for the use of videotapes in investigation and litigation (American Bar Association, 1985; National Center for the Prosecution of Child Abuse, 1997).

Although videotaped interviews can fulfill all of these expectations in particular situations, this is by no means always the case. Moreover, there are unanticipated potential disadvantages of videotapes, most important, defense's use of the tapes to impeach the victim and to attack the interviewer. Because of the risks of videotaping, some programs that previously videotaped gave up the practice in the late 1980s (e.g., the National Children's Advocacy Center in Huntsville, AL), and some law enforcement professionals and prosecutors actively opposed videotaping (e.g., N. Diehl, Wayne County Sex Crimes Unit, Detroit, MI, personal communication, June 1988; Veith, 1999; W. Walsh, personal communication, January 26, 2000). Furthermore, some professionals have had reservations about a requirement of videotaping forensic interviews for fear this requirement would be extended to clinical assessments and treatment (Berliner, 2000).

Advantages of Videotaping

Myers (1992, 1998) has elaborated on the advantages and disadvantages of videotaping. He notes the following advantages. Videotaping may decrease the number of interviews or the number of interviewers. It provides complete documentation of what is said by the child and the interviewer, which may ensure proper interview techniques (Berliner, 2001) and eliminate challenges regarding techniques. The videotape could be used to persuade a disbelieving nonabusive parent of the sexual victimization or the offender to confess or plead. For the victim, the tape may decrease the probability of recantation, can refresh the child's recollection before going to court (California Attorney General's Office, 1994), or can substitute for the child's testimony (Faller, 2003; Whitcomb, 1993).[1] In addition, an expert witness may view the tape in order to form an opinion about sexual abuse. The AACAP guidelines (American Academy of Child and Adolescent Psychiatry, 1997b) also mention that a videotape preserves the child's initial statement (assuming the tape is of the initial statement), and it can be used for interviewer supervision. Moreover, in situations in court where hearsay is allowed, the child's videotaped interview may be more persuasive to jurors than the interviewer testifying about what the child said in the interview (Redlich, Myers, & Goodman, 2002).

There are additional advantages of videotaping. Videotaping an interview demonstrates the interviewer's willingness to allow the information used in arriving at an opinion to be reviewed by others (Faller, 2003). It also provides the interviewer as complete a record as is feasible from which to draw conclusions. In addition to employing the tape to persuade a caretaker, it may be used to persuade other professionals (e.g., the police or the prosecutor) of the strength or vulnerabilities of the case. Moreover, a videotape can be much more compelling in capturing and communicating the child's affect during the interview than an audiotape, notes, or a written report. Finally, the tape may used to refresh the interviewer's recollection before a court appearance (California Attorney General's Office, 1994).

Disadvantages of Videotaping

Disadvantages of videotaping are also described by Myers (1992, 1998). The child can be subject to attack because of minor inconsistencies in the child's account. Similarly, because disclosure is often gradual, there may be inconsistencies among videotaped sessions. In addition, only some of the sessions are videotaped, and these are not the persuasive ones. The technique of the interviewer may become the focus of attack for how the questions were asked. In addition, videotaping may make the child (or interviewer) uncomfortable. The poor quality of the tape may obscure the data. Finally, tapes may be obtained by persons who have no regard for confidentiality. The AACAP guidelines (American Academy of Child and Adolescent Psychiatry, 1990) are more emphatic than Myers on this final point, noting that "videos may be shown out of context or fall into the hands of those who have no professional obligations of confidentiality or concern for the child's best interest" (p. 12). The AACAP guidelines also note that a videotape can be used to harass a child on cross-examination.

There are additional possible disadvantages of videotaping. First, the act of taping may not merely make the child uncomfortable but may also prevent disclosure, although this appears to be a less frequent problem than many interviewers have anticipated (Berliner, 2001; Faller, 2003). Second, the child may behave in ways that result in challenges, for example, acting silly or indicating positive feelings about the accused (Faller, 2003). Third, the camera captures only what is in range. Behaviors and demonstrations may occur out of camera range, or information may be disclosed in the hall, in the waiting room, or when the interviewer takes the child to the bathroom. Fourth, the existence of a videotape may result in the focus of the case becoming entirely interviewer technique, with little regard to what the child may have disclosed. Fifth, the evaluator may need to spend not only additional time reviewing tapes in preparation for court but sometimes hours on the witness stand responding to questions about the tape. Finally, although the AACAP guidelines and some analogue research (Swim, Borgida, & McCoy, 1993) suggest that the child's statement may be given more credence because it is on videotape, in fact, in court, a videotape may be less persuasive than live testimony from the child (Faller, 1996a).

RESEARCH ON DOCUMENTATION

There are two studies that compare methods of documentation. The first was undertaken subsequent to questions about the competency of child interviewers in a multioffender–multivictim case in Wenachee, Washington. This case resulted in a great deal if controversy and an external review of the child interviews. The review was inconclusive because of inconsistent and inadequate documentation of the child interviews (Wallen, 1998). One outcome of the review was a study that compared three different methods of documentation used at three separate sites: (1) "near verbatim notes" taken on a computer, (2) audio-taped interviews that were then transcribed, and (3) videotapes done at a child advocacy center that were also transcribed. Since the different techniques for documentation were used on different cases, a direct comparison of the efficacy of the three documentation methods could not be made. However, audio- and videotaped interviews contained almost five times as many interviewer questions than did the "near verbatim notes," and the questions employed in the audio- and video-taped interviews were more open-ended (Berliner, 2000; Berliner, 2001). Children were slightly more anxious in the video and audio interviews than in the "near verbatim notes" interviews. However, the researchers also found that in many instances a second interviewer was not available to take notes and concluded that this method of documentation is not feasible (Berliner, 2000, 2001).

The second study, by Lamb, Orbach, Sternberg, Hershkowitz, and Horowitz (2000), compared the "verbatim" notes of 20 interviewers to the audiotapes of the interviews. Interviewers' "verbatim" accounts underreported interviewers' utterances by more than half and details provided by children by one-fourth. Interviewers also tended to attribute children's responses to more open-ended interviewer probes than the interviewers actually used.

Findings from these two studies indicate that "verbatim" accounts are less than verbatim. The findings suggest that an electronic record of the interview is superior to notes.

There is also some research supporting the efficacy of videotaping for case outcomes. In multidisciplinary pilot projects in the State of California, videotaping child interviews was rated by professionals involved in the pilots as their most successful component, and the vast majority of respondents supported routine videotaping of child interviews (California Attorney General's Office, 1994). J. Henry (1999) conducted an exploratory study comparing cases involving videotaped child interviews with those not videotaped. He found that, in the videotaped cases, children were subjected to fewer interviews and had to testify less frequently. Moreover, offenders in the videotaped cases were more likely to plead to criminal charges, and the overwhelming majority of children in the videotaped cases reported taping was either helpful or had no effect on them. Similarly, Faller and Henry (2000) report descriptive findings from a study of 323 criminal court cases in a county that videotapes child interviews. If the child makes a disclosure of sexual abuse during the interview, the county's protocol requires law enforcement contact the suspect for an interview, show the videotape to the suspect, and attempt to obtain a confession. Over a 10-year period, 64% of suspects confessed, usually before arraignment, and a 77% pleaded to a sex crime when the case got to court. These examples suggest that videotaping does not hinder successful criminal prosecution; rather, it appears to help. Finally, in a study of a case involving 122 alleged victims at a church, Faller and Plummer (1996) found that a decision *not* to videotape allowed the defense to generate a scenario of coercive interviewing by law enforcement, which played a role in an acquittal of the accused.

GUIDELINES FOR VIDEOTAPING

When videotaping first began to be employed in sexual abuse cases, professionals proposed guidelines for videotaping (e.g., Colby & Colby, 1987b; DeLipsey & James, 1988; Slicner, 1989). Colby and Colby (1987a, 1987b), who described the experience with videotaping legislation in the State of Texas, also proposed guidelines for other state legislatures for creating statutory provisions for videotaping.

More recently, the APSAC has developed guidelines on the areas to be covered for professionals who are videotaping: (1) purposes of videotaping, (2) clients and interviewers who will be involved in videotaping, (3) technical considerations, and (4) polices related to videotaping. These guidelines are a product of a task force APSAC had for 3 years on videotaping. The fact that the task force could not reach a consensus on the advisability of videotaping speaks to the fact that videotaping remains a contested issue in forensic interviewing (American Professional Society on the Abuse of Children, 2000).

If the interviewer determines that videotaping will be useful, the reason for videotaping should control the specifics of the videotaping process. In situations where videos are to be made so that others can evaluate the data used in arriving at conclusions, it is advisable to tape all sessions. If the videotape is to be used to persuade others, the professional may choose to gather information from the child and then make a videotaped deposition. Interviewers should appreciate that they may be more likely to ask close-ended questions, if they already know the child's response, and guard against this tendency. If the goal is to use the tape in litigation, the interviewer should consult state statutes regarding the use of videotape in court. Generally, there are requirements for the tape's admissibility (National Center for the Prosecution

of Child Abuse, 1997; Whitcomb, 1993). These may include a stipula-
tion about who can be the interviewer (e.g., a law enforcement officer,
the prosecutor, or a designated child interview specialist), a requirement
for a court ruling before a video can be substituted for live testimony
(e.g., a finding that the child is "unavailable" to testify), provisions for
chain of custody of the videotape, limitations regarding the type of
hearings at which a tape can be shown, requirements of notice to all
parties (e.g., the defense) so that they can be present for the videotaping, and provisions for cross-examination of the child (National Center
for the Prosecution of Child Abuse, 1997).

INFORMING THE CHILD

Regardless of method of documentation employed, the child should be
informed about documentation (American Academy of Child and Adolescent Psychiatry, 1990; American Professional Society on the Abuse of
Children, 1990, 1997). The interviewer can explain the reason for taking
notes, videotaping, or audiotaping as she discusses the purpose of the interview. If video- and audiotaping, the evaluator can demonstrate the
equipment for the child. If the interviewer is using a one-way mirror, it is
advisable to introduce the child to the people behind the mirror and explain their function (American Professional Society on the Abuse of Children, 1997; Faller, 2003). Explanations and their completeness should vary
depending upon the child's developmental stage and specifics of the case.

SUMMARY AND CONCLUSIONS

Documentation of the child interview is a central component of assessing an allegation of sexual abuse. Without adequate documentation,
information may be lost or forgotten, findings may be consciously
or unconsciously distorted, and peer and professional review will be
difficult. The three methods of documentation described, note-taking,
audiotaping, and videotaping, each has advantages and disadvantages.
Research to date suggests that note-taking either by the interviewer or
someone else is less complete than either audio- or videotaping. Controversy remains, nevertheless, about the best method of documentation, even though a video record is the most complete.

NOTE

1. Because of the Sixth Amendment to the Constitution, which provides the
accused with the right to confront witnesses against him/her, the use of a
videotape as a substitute for child testimony is circumscribed, especially in
criminal cases and during the adjudicatory stage of the legal process (Faller,
2003; Whitcomb, 1993).

SEVEN

Interview Structure, Protocol, and Guidelines

Kathleen Coulborn Faller

Professionals who interview children about possible sexual abuse come from a variety of professions with different training about how to structure an interview (e.g., M. Aldridge & Wood, 1988; Ginsburg, 1997; Inbau, 2001; Kadushin & Kadushin, 1997; Sattler, 1998; Wilson & Powell, 2001; Zweirs, 1999). Moreover, interviews of children about possible sexual abuse have been the subject of criticism and debate (e.g., Ceci & Bruck, 1995; Garven, Wood, & Malpass, 2000; N. Walker, 1997; Warren & Marsil, 2002; K. Wood & Garven, 2000). Both of these issues have influenced the development of proposed sequencing of stages in interviews. This sequencing is variously referred to as "interview structure" (e.g., Orbach, Hershkowitz, Lamb, Esplin, & Horowitz, 2000) or "interview protocol" (e.g., Carnes & LeDuc, 1998; Lyon, 2002b; State of Michigan, 1998, 2005; Yuille, 2002). Some professionals, who worry that a protocol is too rigid, use the term "interview guidelines" (American Professional Society on the Abuse of Children, 2002; Bourg et al., 1998; Broderick, personal communication, July 2002). More than a dozen such interview structures are in circulation, and most are based upon a combination of practice experience and research. In this chapter, we cover the general components of interview structure with examples, the phases found in interview various structures, the advantages of having such a structure or protocol, and the limitations of interview structures/protocols.

COMPONENTS OF INTERVIEW STRUCTURE/PROTOCOL

Most interview structures call for a phased interview (e.g., Bourg et al., 1998; Hindman, 1987; Home Office, 1992; Lamb & Sternberg, 1999; Lyon, 2002b; Orbach et al., 2000; Sorenson, Bottoms, & Perona, 1997; State of Michigan, 1998, 2005; Sternberg, Lamb, Esplin, & Baradaran, 1999; Yuille, 2002). The number of phases in these interview structures ranges from three (Faller, 2003; McDermott-Steinmetz-Lane, 1997) to nine (Poole & Lamb, 1998; State of Michigan, 1998, 2005).

The simplest structure divides the interview into three phases. Illustrative is the one developed by McDermott-Steinmetz-Lane (1997):

1. Initial phase—rapport building
2. Information-gathering phase
3. Closure phase

An example of a multiphased interview is the Stepwise Interview (Yuille, 2002). It has seven steps, some of which have subcategories, and then optional steps:

1. The introduction: for the video, during which the interviewer indicates full names, date, time, and location, and identifies self and role.
2. Building rapport: to put the child at ease, to assess the child's language and memory skills, and to assess child's development.
3. The need to tell the truth (optional): establishing the need for the child to tell the truth.
4. Topic of concern: "Do you know why we're talking today?" If the child hasn't previously disclosed, use a different introduction.
5. The disclosure: This is the most important step.
   a. Free narrative: "Tell me everything you can remember." Don't interrupt the child during the narrative.
   b. Open questions: "Do you remember more?" "Who? What? When? Where?"
   c. Specific questions (optional): Avoid multiple choice questions. Never include information you have obtained from another source.
6. Clarification: Clarify problems and inconsistencies in the child's statement. Query inappropriate sexual knowledge for age. Give the child contact information.
7. Concluding the interview: Thank the child. Ask the child if he/she has any questions. Tell the child what will happen next.

Optional steps in the stepwise interview:

1. Use of interview aids—may be necessary with younger children. They should be used only when other steps in the interview are inadequate. In rare cases, anatomically detailed dolls may be required. Never use anatomical dolls to obtain a disclosure. Never use interview aids as a fun or play activity. (Media, including anatomical dolls, are discussed in detail in chapter 9.)

2. Leading questions or suggestion—should only be used as a last resort and may ruin the criminal case and may negatively affect civil court decisions. Younger children may be more susceptible to suggestion.
3. Requesting a repetition of the child's disclosures—may be helpful if the child's statement is in doubt.
4. Cognitive interview (described later in this chapter), which involves context reconstruction.

Another component of the Stepwise Interview is interview rules. These would not be appropriate for a preschooler (Yuille, 2002):

1. If I misunderstand something you say, please tell me. I want to get it right.
2. If you don't understand something I say, please tell me and I will try again.
3. If you feel uncomfortable at any time, please tell me or show me with the stop sign.
4. Even if you think I already know something, please tell me anyway.
5. If you are not sure about the answer, please do not guess, tell me you're not sure before you say it.
6. Please when you are describing something, I wasn't there.
7. Please remember that I will not get angry at you or upset with you.
8. Only talk about things that are true and really happened.

There are two reasons why interview structures vary in the number of phases or stages advised. First, some protocols attend to issues not addressed in others. For example, some protocols (e.g., Poole & Lamb, 1998; Yuille, 2002) specify a procedure for indicating the individuals present (child and interviewer), the time, the date, and the place of the interview—which are recorded on either an audio- or a videotape. Another issue unaddressed in some interview protocols is competency assessment, which usually involves ascertaining the child's capacity to differentiate the truth from a lie and obtaining a promise from the child to tell the truth during the interview. Competency assessment is not part of some interview structures (e.g., D. Davies et al., 1996; Faller, 2003) because there is no evidence that a child's capacity to differentiate the truth from a lie increases the accuracy of the child's report of abuse (Goodman, Aman, & Hirschman, 1987; Poole & Lamb, 1998). Similarly, the fact that the child makes a promise to tell the truth does not ensure the child will do so. Regardless of the interviewer's skill, the child's loyalty to or fear of the offender may be greater.

The second reason for variation in number of phases is that some writers combine several components into a single phase, whereas others separate them. For example, a protocol may specify the following goals for phase 1 of the interview: (1) introduction of the interviewer, (2) explaining the purpose of the interview, (3) rapport building, (4) developmental assessment, (5) assessment of overall functioning, and (6) providing the child with rules (e.g., Faller, 2003). Other protocols separate these goals into discrete phases, even though they may be overlapping, and more than one goal is addressed in a single activity. For example, rapport building, assessing the child's overall functioning, and conducting a developmental assessment can all be pursued with the same activities (e.g., Poole & Lamb, 1998; Yuille, 2002).

A related issue is that interview structures vary in their prescriptiveness. Interview protocols can be categorized as (1) scripted (e.g., Everson & McKnight, 2002; Lamb & Sternberg, 1999; Lyon, 2002b), (2) semistructured (e.g., Bourg et al., 1999; Broderick, personal communication, July 2002; Boychuk & Stellar, 1992; D. Davies et al., 1996; Merchant & Toth, 2001), and (3) flexible (e.g., Faller, 2003; State of Michigan, 2005; Steinmetz, 1997). In scripted protocols, the developers, as much as possible, attempt to specify not only the sequencing of phases but also the precise language to be used by the interviewer (e.g., Lamb & Sternberg, 1999; Lyon, 2002b). More prescriptive structures are more likely to be used in an interview intended for forensic purposes and less prescriptive ones for interviews intended for clinical purposes. But all interviews should be phased, and clinical interviews may be judged according to forensic standards.

PHASES THAT MAY BE INCLUDED IN INTERVIEW STRUCTURES

The list below incorporates the interview phases found in existing protocols and guidelines. Each is briefly described and referenced further below.

1. Documenting people, time, and place for the video
2. Informing the child about the interview
3. Competency assessment
4. Rapport building
5. Developmental assessment
6. Assessing overall functioning
7. Explaining the rules
8. Practice interview
9. Introducing the topic of concern
10. Obtaining a narrative account from the child
11. Obtaining additional details
12. Cognitive interview
13. Closure

Documenting People, Time, and Place for the Video

The interviewer identifies self, child, date, time, and place of the interview. Because this procedure may set a daunting tone to the interview, it is sometimes done before the child enters the interview room. This phase is more common in interviews by law enforcement (e.g., American Professional Society on the Abuse of Children, 2002; Merchant & Toth, 2001; Yuille, 2002).

Informing the Child About the Interview

a. Introducing the interviewer: The interviewer states his/her name.

b. Explaining the interviewer's role: The interviewer describes his/her role, such as "My job is to make sure kids are safe" or "I am a worry doctor."

c. Explaining purpose of the interview: The interviewer provides a brief description of why the child is being interviewed, which will vary depending upon the context of the interview. Many interviewers elaborate on the explanation of their role and tell the child that they will be asking lots of questions. Analogue studies indicate that children perform better if they understand the purpose of the interview (e.g., Saywitz, 1995; Saywitz & Snyder, 1993).

d. Introducing the videotape: If the interview is to be taped, as noted above, the child is informed. If there is a one-way mirror, the mirror is explained and usually the child is taken behind the mirror to meet the professionals who are observing (American Professional Society on the Abuse of Children, 2002; Faller, 2003; Yuille, 2002).

Competency Assessment

Competency assessment consists of determining both the child's ability to report events and the child's understanding of the difference between the truth and a lie. The first component of competency is defined by A. G. Walker (1999) as child's ability to observe, remember, and communicate. A somewhat different framework involves the interviewer's assessment of the child's ability to report information about his/her past history and environment, and the child's ability to communicate. Assessment of these competencies can be obtained from questions/probes asked during rapport building, such as, "Tell me all about your last birthday" (ability to observe and remember past history), "Tell me about school" (knowledge about environment and ability to communicate), and "Tell me all about your family" (knowledge about environment and ability to communicate).

Many interview protocols advise the interviewer to ascertain the child's ability to differentiate the truth from a lie and to obtain a promise from the child to tell the truth (e.g., American Professional Society on the Abuse of Children, 2002; Hindman, 1987; Merchant & Toth, 2001; State of Michigan, 1998; Yuille, 2002). This component takes a prominent place in many interview structures because if the child eventually testifies in court, he/she will probably have to promise to tell the truth.

A. G. Walker (1999) observes that by age 4 most children understand that a lie is a nonfact and something you can get punished for, but abstract concepts such as "the truth" come later. Research by Lyon, Saywitz, and colleagues tested the competency to take the oath of 96 children 4–7 years old who were in shelter care because of an action by the dependency court (Lyon, 1996; Lyon & Saywitz, 1999; Lyon, Saywitz, Kaplan, & Dorado, 2001). This study has advanced knowledge about children's capacities in understanding lies and truth and has influenced how many protocols handle this issue.

Children in the competency study were given three tasks: (1) they were asked to define the truth and a lie, (2) they were asked to tell the difference between a truth and a lie, and (3) they were given four examples and asked to tell the researcher whether each was the truth or a lie. The children did quite poorly at tasks 1 and 2. Not until 7 years of age could a substantial proportion of children in this study succeed at these first two tasks, and even then, only about half gave correct responses. In contrast, children ages 5–7 did quite well at accurately labeling the examples as truth or lie. Four-year-olds did well at labeling true statements but incorrectly labeled lies as true. Further research determined that the 4-year-olds did not want to tell adults (researchers) that they were lying (Lyon et al., 2001). Interviewers are therefore advised to say, "If *someone* tells you this is a pencil (while holding up a book), is that the truth or a lie?" rather than "If *I* tell you this is a pencil (while holding up a book), is that the truth or a lie?" Lyon and Saywitz (2000) have developed a series of pictured examples with accompanying text to use in competency assessment. These can be downloaded free of charge from University of Southern California Law School website (Lyon & Saywitz, 2000).

Some interview structures do not include a component focusing on the truth and lies and consequences of lying out of concern that it may add a negative valence to the interview, causing fear and possibly inhibiting the child's willingness to communicate (D. Davies et al., 1996; Faller, 2003). In addition, research does not support that the child's inability to differentiate truth from lies increases inaccurate information in interviews, or that the ability to make this differentiation and a promise to tell the truth increases accurate information (e.g., Goodman et al., 1987; Poole & Lamb, 1998).

Rapport Building

Most interview structures advise a period of rapport building in the beginning stages of the interview (e.g., Bourg et al., 1998, 1999; D. Davies et al., 1996; Jones, 1992; Merchant & Toth, 2001, 2002; Poole & Lamb, 1998; Sorenson, Bottoms, & Perona, 1997; K. Wood & Garven, 2000). During rapport building, the interviewer expresses interest in the child and usually asks questions about the child's life in order to develop a relationship with the child. Typically, interviewers ask questions about school, friends, and family. In Lyon's scripted protocol, children are asked to tell the interviewer about some things they like to do and then to tell about some things they don't like to do (Lyon, 2002b). In both analogue studies and research involving children suspected of abuse, Sternberg, Lamb, and colleagues (Roberts, Lamb, & Sternberg, 2004; Sternberg et al., 1997; Sternberg, Lamb, Orbach, Esplin, & Mitchell, 2000) tested the efficacy of asking open-ended questions during the rapport-building phase of the interview.

In an Israeli study of 51 children 3–12 years old suspected of being abused, during rapport building youth investigators asked either open-ended probes (e.g., "Tell me all about school") or close-ended ones (e.g., "Where do you go to school? "What grade are you in?"). Both groups then were asked an invitational probe at the beginning of the abuse-related phase of the interview: "I understand something may have happened to you. Please tell me everything that happened, from the very beginning to the very end, as best you can remember." Interviewers using open-ended probes during rapport building elicited 2.5 times the number of details and 60% more words than did those using close-ended probes.

In a more recent analogue study of 144 children 3–9 years old, Roberts, Lamb, and Sternberg (2004) tested the impact of open-ended rapport-building questions versus close-ended questions on children's later reports of a staged event involving a clown. The researchers found that the open-ended rapport building improved the accuracy but not the number of details children provided. On average, the rapport building in response to open-ended questions lasted 16 minutes, compared to 6 minutes in the direct question condition. The length of open-ended rapport building was more than twice as long as the 7 minutes of rapport building for both groups in the study of interviews conducted by Israeli youth investigators (Sternberg et al., 1997). Roberts and colleagues rightly point out that children may have become tired by such a long rapport-building phase in the open-ended condition and therefore were not as productive in the latter part of the interview.

Based upon the Israeli youth investigator study (Sternberg et al., 1997), some protocols (e.g., Merchant & Toth, 2001; National Institute of Child Health and Human Development, 1999; Poole & Lamb, 1998; State of Michigan, 2005) specifically advise the use of open-ended prompts and questions during rapport building. Taken together, these studies provide support for practicing responding to open-ended questions during the rapport-building stage but also suggest that the length of rapport building should be short. Rapport building should probably be less than 10 minutes and should vary in length and content based upon the child's age. Poole and Lamb (1998; see also State of Michigan, 2005) also advise the interviewer to show intense interest in the child's responses to rapport-building questions and encourage the child to say more.

Developmental Assessment

Some structures expect the interviewer to conduct a developmental assessment of the child (e.g., Carnes & LeDuc, 1998; Faller, 2003; Yuille, 2002). At minimum, the interviewer should determine the level of the child's communication (e.g., full sentences, two- to three-word phrases) and the extent of the child's vocabulary. Interviewers should tailor their verbal communication to the child's (American Professional Society on the Abuse of Children, 2002). That is, the interviewer's questions should contain about as many words as the child's responses. In addition, some protocols advise the interviewer to determine the child's understanding of prepositions and prepositional phrases (e.g., inside, beside, under, over, and on top of) (Faller & DeVoe, 1995b; Merchant & Toth, 2001; Yuille, 2002). The child's knowledge might be demonstrated by asking the child to place a piece of paper "on the floor" or "under the table." The purpose of determining the child's understanding of these terms is to assure that their responses to focused questions related to the specifics of the sexual activity are accurate. However, knowledge related to a piece of paper may not translate to knowledge about sexual activities. As a consequence, some protocols do not include routine determination of the child's knowledge about prepositions (Faller, 2003; Lamb & Sternberg, 1999).

Assessing Overall Functioning

Some interview structures include an assessment of the child's overall functioning (e.g., American Academy of Child and Adolescent Psychiatry, 1997b; Faller, 2003). The interviewer attends to the child's affects (e.g., angry, sad), behaviors (e.g., hyperactive), knowledge of their world, and level of cooperation. Children's capacity to describe people and places in their world will affect the level of confidence the interviewer has in abuse-related information provided by the child. The child's level of cooperation may affect the way the interviewer poses questions. If the child is oppositional, the interviewer will be more likely to use commands, such as "Tell me what happened." In contrast, if the child seems overly compliant, the interviewer may say, "Do you remember what happened?" (Faller, 2003). Questions used in interviews are discussed in detail in chapter 8.

Explaining the Rules

In most protocols, children are provided with rules for the interview to enhance their knowledge of what is required of them. As already noted, the Stepwise Interview provides the child with eight rules. Other protocols have fewer rules (e.g., Faller, 2003; Saywitz & Geiselman, 1998). An example of a less lengthy list of rules from Faller (2003) is the following:

1. "If you know the answer to a question, tell me the answer, but if you don't know, say 'I don't know.' "
2. "If you don't understand a question, tell me, and I'll try to ask it in a better way."
3. "Only talk about what really happened."

A very useful rule that is part of the cognitive interview (Saywitz & Geiselman, 1998) is, "I may ask the same question more than once; that doesn't mean your answer was wrong." This rule can inoculate the children against changing a response because they think the initial one was incorrect or to please the interviewer. Similarly, A. G. Walker (2001) points out that young children usually assume adults already know what happened and suggests that the interviewer tell the child, "I wasn't there, so . . . Even if you think I know it, tell me anyway. Even if you think it doesn't matter, tell me anyway," during the rule-setting phase.

An analogue study with 40 boys and girls 3–6 years old (Cordon, Saetermoe, & Goodman, 2005) employed either three "conversational rules," (1) to say "I don't know" if the child doesn't know the answer, (2) the interviewer wasn't there and can't help the child with the answer, and (3) the interviewer may try to trick the child; or three "placebo rules," (1) "We take turns," (2) "We look at each other," and (3) "We stay in our place." Each child was involved in a staged play activity and then questioned afterward in neutral, repetitive, or accusatory style. The conversational rules were effective in reducing the number of incorrect responses children made, regardless of interview condition.

A concern with having too many rules is that the child may not be able to remember all of them. However, as described in the next section, there are ways to assist the child in remembering the rules.

Practice Interview

Some protocols use practice exercises to increase the child's competence during the abuse-related parts of the interview.

Practicing the Rules

In order to increase the likelihood that the child will follow the rules, the protocol may call for practicing them (Lamb & Sternberg, 1999; Lyon, 2002b; Merchant & Toth, 2001; Poole & Lamb, 1998; Reed, 1996).

After each rule, the interviewer gives an example and asks the child to respond. For example, after the child is told not to guess, the interviewer might say, "So what is my dog's name?" The child is praised if he/she says, "I don't know" but is admonished not to guess if he/she tries to guess the dog's name.

Roberts and Lamb (1999) report a study that illustrates the importance of a rule that children should correct the interviewer if he/she makes a mistake and of giving an opportunity to practice the rule. They examined 68 interviews of children 3–14 years old that were to follow the Memorandum of Good Practice,[1] an interview structure developed for use by law enforcement in the United Kingdom when videotaping a child's statement for potential use in trial. The researchers found 140 interviewer distortions of child disclosures. Children corrected the interviewer only one-third of the time. Children were more likely to correct the distortion if the interviewer made a simple statement and if the mistake related to an aspect of someone's identity.

Practicing Responding to Open-Ended Questions

Much of adult communication with children involves adults doing most of the talking and children providing short responses. Therefore, providing narrative accounts in response to open-ended questions may be an unusual experience for many children. They may need to practice this kind of communication.

The research described above by Sternberg et al. (1997, 2000) supports the efficacy of providing practice opportunities. Moreover, it indicates that it is useful to ask open-ended, invitational questions in the rapport-building phase to determine the child's narrative capacity. Even if these questions do not elicit narrative responses, they inform the interviewer about the types of questions that may be needed to obtain information during the abuse-related portion of the interview.

Testing the Child's Suggestibility

Some protocols (e.g., American Professional Society on the Abuse of Children, 2002; Reed, 1996) advise the interviewer to test the child's suggestibility by deliberately misstating something the child has reported, such as, "Now you said you have a little sister," when the child has said she has a little brother, to see if the child corrects the interviewer or accepts the interviewer's misstatement. If this testing is used, the interviewer is advised not to use it about abuse-related disclosures. Misleading questions/probes are discussed in more detail in chapter 8.

Introducing the Topic of Concern

Most protocols provide interviewers with a strategy or strategies for introducing the abuse in an open-ended way. Some protocols suggest the interviewer precede the introduction with a statement such as, "Now that we've gotten to know each other" (Home Office, 1992; Poole & Lamb, 1998). Approaches vary, and should vary, depending upon the role of the interviewer and whether the child has already made a disclosure.

For example, the National Institute of Child Health and Human Development (NICHD) Investigative Interview Protocol,[2] a widely used protocol developed by researchers at the NICHD, is structured for situations in which the child has already made a disclosure. It gives the interviewer nine methods of introducing the topic of concern. The interviewer is advised to start with the first, which is the most open-ended, and move to subsequent probes if the more open-ended ones do not resolve the issue of sexual abuse (e.g., Lamb & Sternberg, 1999; Sternberg et al., 2000):

> Tell me why you came to talk to me. Tell me everything about that from the beginning to the end.
>
> It is important that I understand why you came.
>
> I hear you saw (professional). Tell me what you talked about.
>
> Tell me why you think (transporter) brought you here today.
>
> Is (caretaker) worried that something may have happened to you?
>
> I heard someone has been bothering you.
>
> I heard someone may have done something to you that wasn't right.
>
> I heard something may have happened to you at (location, time).
>
> I heard someone may have (allegation).

Lamb and Sternberg (1999; Sternberg et al., 2000) report that most children who described sexual abuse disclosed to the first probe. They also describe the last probe as a last resort.

As Yuille (2002) notes, a different type of introduction is needed when children have not disclosed previously. Focused questions that turn the child's attention to important people in their lives, to body parts, and to the possible context of abuse are appropriate (Carnes & LeDuc, 1998; Faller, 1993). The practice of educating the child about "good touch," "bad touch," and "confusing touch" is another way to introducing the topic of concern when children have not disclosed (e.g., Carnes & LeDuc, 1998; Hindman, 1987). Carnes, Wilson, and Nelson-Gardell (1999) noted that in the 12-session model of the National Children's Advocacy Center's extended assessment, most of the children who disclosed did so in the "Touch Continuum" portion of the extended assessment model. Although this finding may speak to the efficacy of the "Touch Continuum," it may also be a function of where in the model the "Touch Continuum" was placed (before the use of focused questions) (Carnes et al., 1999).

Introducing the topic of concern is addressed again in chapter 8.

Obtaining a Narrative Account From the Child

It is optimal for the child to provide a narrative about the abuse in response to an open-ended probe (e.g., Merchant & Toth, 2001; Poole & Lamb, 1998; State of Michigan, 2005; Yuille, 2002). In addition, interviewers are advised not to interrupt the child to ask for clarification or ask a follow-up question until the child has stopped talking. The Memorandum of Good Practice (Home Office, 1992, 2002) advises interviewers to use "wait time," that is, to allow silence after the child stops speaking, to ensure that interviewers do not interrupt and in case the child has something to add spontaneously.

Obtaining Additional Details

Specific questioning methods are discussed in chapter 8. However, a number of general methods are advised for eliciting additional information about the details of abuse.

Who, What, Where, When, How

The interviewer must gather data about the "wh" aspects of the abuse (e.g., A. G. Walker, 2001; Yuille, 2002) and may ask focused questions about these aspects of the sexual victimization, such as "Where was your mother when the man grabbed you?"

Segmentation

Another strategy for gathering more details is to segment the event. For example, the interviewer might ask the child to tell about everything that happened before they went into the bedroom, and then everything the child can remember that happened in the bedroom (Merchant & Toth, 2001; Poole & Lamb, 1998; Sternberg, 2001). Young children, however, have difficulty providing accurate responses to "before" questions but are more successful in responding to what happened next or "after" (D. Davies & Lyon, 2006; State of Michigan, 2005). Children do not have a good understanding of "yesterday," "not today," "before," and "after" until after age 7 (e.g., State of Michigan, 2005).

Narrative Elaboration

Saywitz and colleagues developed a strategy for gathering detail called narrative elaboration. It has been employed in analogue studies with children ages 6–11 and has been used clinically on a pilot basis (Saywitz, Nathanson, Snyder, & Lamphear, 1993; Saywitz & Geiselman, 1998). In narrative elaboration, the interviewer uses cue cards to remind the child of various aspects of the event. The cue cards are simple, nonsuggestive pictures to represent participants, actions/affective states, and resolutions.

Narrative elaboration has been compared to cognitive interview strategies (described next) and standard interview techniques in several analogue studies (Bowen & Howie, 2002; Brown & Pipe, 2003; Camparo, Wagner, & Saywitz, 2001; Dorado & Saywitz, 2001). These studies involve both preschoolers (Bowen & Howie, 2002; Dorado & Saywitz, 2001) and elementary-age children (Brown & Pipe, 2003; Camparo et al., 2001). Analogue studies demonstrate that narrative elaboration techniques increase the number of details children provide and do not increase inaccuracies, even when the study asks children to report a nonexperienced event (Camparo et al., 2001). Narrative elaboration, however, did not prove more effective than components of the cognitive interview (Brown & Pipe, 2003), and middle-class children performed better (Dorado & Saywitz, 2001). The use of narrative elaboration attenuated the impact of lower I.Q. scores on children's ability to provide details in one study (Brown & Pipe, 2003).

Cognitive Interview

Some protocols suggest using the cognitive interview (American Professional Society on the Abuse of Children, 2002; Carnes & LeDuc, 1998; Yuille, 2002), although the cognitive interview is an interview protocol in its own right (Fisher & Geiselman, 1992; Saywitz & Geiselman, 1998). Originally, it was used with adult witnesses and victims of crime and has been demonstrated to increase the amount of information the witness/victim recalls (Fisher, Brennan, & McCauley, 2002; Fisher & Geiselman, 1992; Milne & Bull, 2003; Milne, Bull, Koehnken, & Memon, 1995). More recently, the cognitive interview has been used with child victim/witnesses, in both analogue and actual case studies (Fisher et al., 2002; Hershkowitz, Lamb, Sternberg, & Horowitz, 2002; Saywitz, Geiselman, & Bornstein, 1992).

The central feature of the cognitive interview is the use of context reconstruction, that is, having the child either "make a picture in your head" of the place where the abuse took place or describe the place out loud (Saywitz & Geiselman, 1998). Clinicians who have used this method in practice sometimes have the child draw a picture of the place on a piece of paper (Faller, 2003) or use a dollhouse (Faller, 1993) to recreate the context. The child is then asked to report everything that happened, starting at the beginning, then the middle, then the end, reporting even details that do not seem important. Questions such as, "Do you remember any smells?" and "Who were the people there?" are used to elicit additional details.

When the cognitive interview is used with adults, they may be asked to take the perspective of someone other than themselves and describe events from that person's perspective. Also, adults may be asked to recount events backward, from the end, to the middle, to the beginning.

Both techniques are designed to increase the number of details the adult recalls. These two techniques may be less useful with children. The younger the child, the less capable the child will be of taking someone else's perspective, and temporal sequencing is difficult for children.

Studies using the cognitive interview in analogue and real-world research indicate that it can improve the amount of information children provide when compared to traditional interviews (Akehurst, Milne, & Kohnken, 2003; Milne & Bull, 2003). In analogue studies, the cognitive interview also can increase children's resistance to suggestive questions and postevent misinformation (Holliday, 2003a, 2003b; Milne & Bull, 2003). The analogue research includes research using detectives as interviewers (Saywitz et al., 1992). The cognitive interview's effects, however, are not as powerful with children as with adults (Geiselman & Padilla, 1988; Geiselman, Saywitz, & Bornstein, 1993; Saywitz et al., 1992).

Hershkowitz, Lamb, Sternberg, and Horowitz (2002) studied forensic interviews with 142 children who were allegedly sexually abused, comparing physical context reinstatement (taking the child to the crime scene), mental context reinstatement in an office interview (the cognitive interview), and an office interview without context reinstatement. They found that mental context reinstatement yielded more details in response to the main and an initial invitational probe than either physical context reinstatement or regular in-office interviews.

Closure

There are a number of strategies recommended for use during the ending phase of the interview (e.g., Home Office, 1992, 2002; Poole & Lamb, 1998; State of Michigan, 1998, 2005).

Recapitulating the Child's Account Using the Child's Words

The interviewer may summarize what the child disclosed at the beginning of closure. Best practice is to use the same words the child used to avoid subtle distortions of the child's information and to assure accurate communication with the child (American Academy of Child and Adolescent Psychiatry, 1997b; Home Office, 1992, 2002).

Asking About Other Abuse

Interviewers are advised to ask about any other person who may have sexually abused the child (Faller, 2003; State of Michigan, 1998, 2005). Some children are victims of multiple offenders. In addition, often a challenge to interview findings is that the child was sexually abused but by someone other than the person named. If another individual has actually been named, some guidelines advise asking directly about that person (Faller, 2003).

Switching to a Neutral or Positive Topic

Several interview structures (Bourg et al., 1998; Home Office, 1992; Merchant & Toth, 2001; Poole & Lamb, 1998) advise changing the subject to a neutral or positive topic, such as what the child will do after he/she leaves, as a way of calming the child and signaling that the interview is drawing to a close.

Helping the Child Reestablish Equilibrium

Some protocols recognize the forensic interview may trigger strong emotions. This is why protocols suggest reverting to a neutral topic at the end of the interview. However, merely talking about a neutral topic may not be sufficient for some children, and the interviewer needs to employ other methods to help the child cope with his/her emotions (Faller, 2003). These methods might include offering support or reconnecting the child with the accompanying caretaker.

Explaining What Will Happen Next

Often, information divulged during interviews has life-changing consequences for the child. On the other hand, the interviewer may not know what the long-term changes in the child's life will be. The interviewer, however, usually can tell the child what will happen in the near future. Examples are that the interviewer will be talking to the parent, or that the child will be staying in a foster home, at least for now. Protocols may admonish the interviewer not to make promises that cannot be assured, such as everything will turn out fine, or the offender is going to jail (Bourg et al., 1998; Faller, 2003; Merchant & Toth, 2001; State of Michigan, 2005).

Thanking the Child

Some protocols call for the interviewer to thank the child during the closure phase of the interview (e.g., Merchant & Toth, 2001; Poole & Lamb, 1998; State of Michigan, 2005; Yuille, 2002). If this is part of the protocol, the child should be thanked regardless of whether the child describes abuse. Merchant and Toth (2001), whose Child Interview Guide serves as the basis for training mandated for investigators in the State of Washington, emphasize the importance for thanking the child for participation, not for the disclosure the child provided.

Giving the Child the Interviewer's Card or Contact Information

If the child is old enough, the interviewer is advised to provide the child with a way to get in touch with him/her should the child feel the need (Lamb & Sternberg, 1999; Poole & Lamb, 1998). In some cases, especially those involving younger children, it will be more appropriate to help the child identify an adult who can be a resource (this might be a parent, a teacher, or some other trusted adult).

UTILITY OF INTERVIEW STRUCTURES

For several reasons, the development of interview protocols represents a significant advance in the endeavor of interviewing children about possible sexual abuse. As protocols are refined, they will be even more useful.

Interview Structures Provide Guidance Where It Is Needed

Prior to the development of protocols, many interviewers followed their intuition, or they based their practice upon interview strategies that they found compatible personally (Faller, 1996b). Moreover, research indicates that interviews often lacked a consistent method for data gathering, and interviewers often jump from topic to topic (Lamb & Sternberg, 1999; Poole & Lamb, 1998). Interview structures enhance both the uniformity and quality of interviews (Sternberg et al., 2000). Most protocols represent some level of consensus among professionals, and all have some empirical base.

Interview Structures Compensate for Insufficient Professional Training

Because interviewing children about possible sexual abuse may not be the subject of professional training, these protocols provide much needed guidance, even for trained professionals. Mental health training will involve instruction in assessment but may not cover information gathering using nonleading techniques. Similarly, health care professionals in their training learn how to take a medical history but usually not how to conduct a forensic interview. Law enforcement personnel are more likely to be trained in interrogation of adults than interviewing of children (Inbau, 2001; W. Walsh, personal communication, July 2001).

Interview Protocols Are Especially Needed by Professionals Who Conduct the Vast Majority of Child Interviews

Interview structures are especially needed by the professionals who do most of the interviews, child protection services (CPS) workers and law enforcement professionals. They often lack generic training in working with children. Moreover, there is a high turnover rate among CPS workers (General Accounting Office, 2003), and although police officers do not turn over at the same rate, they have multiple roles, not merely talking to and interviewing children. In fact, they are likely to get more training in interrogating suspects than in interviewing child victims (Inbau, 2001; W. Walsh, personal communication, July 2001). Techniques appropriate for interrogating suspects are the antithesis of those appropriate for interviewing child victims of sexual abuse, because the former may involve leading and suggestive questions, coercive questions, and sometimes deception and manipulation of the interviewee.

Therefore, for somewhat different reasons, CPS workers and law enforcement officers have particular need for the guidance that interview structures offer.

Interview Protocols Help With Especially Difficult Aspects of the Interview

There are specific aspects of the interview with which protocols can be helpful. Three of these are rapport building, transitioning to discussion of sexual abuse, and closure techniques. Observation of interview practice indicates that without specific guidance to include rapport building and closure, these stages are often not present (Lamb & Sternberg, 1999). Similarly, without model open-ended questions about abuse, interviewers may resort too quickly to direct questions, which may result in a legal challenge that the interviewer led the child (Merchant & Toth, 2001).

Most protocols specify the development of rapport before dealing with the emotionally fraught topic of sexual abuse, and many provide techniques for building rapport. Clinical practice indicates that building rapport will make it easier to discuss a sensitive topic. In addition, there is research that suggests that rapport building fosters greater cooperation and hence elicits more information (Lamb & Sternberg, 1999). Advice about questions that transition to discussion of abuse are discussed in the chapter 8 (see also the list of nine possible probes above, proposed by Lamb & Sternberg, 1999). Finally, the advice to assess the child's state of mind at closure and switch to a neutral topic or help the child reestablish equilibrium can ensure that interviews do not end abruptly or with the child feeling distraught.

Interview Protocols Can Reduce Interviewer Anxiety

Protocols help interviewers deal with the anxiety of conducting an interview about sexual abuse. Anxiety may derive from not knowing how to conduct such an interview, the task of asking about sexual abuse, or the fear of doing "something wrong" that may undermine the sexual abuse disclosure. Specific instructions about what to do and what not to do can reduce interviewer anxiety. Some protocols actually include a card that summarizes the "dos" and "don'ts" that the interviewer can refer to during the course of the session (Merchant & Toth, 2001; State of Michigan, 1998, 2005).

Interview Protocols Can Reduce the Interview's Vulnerability to Challenge

Finally, interview practices are often challenged. If interviewers have a protocol they are following, especially if it is one that is research based (e.g., National Institute of Child Health and Human Development, 1999), published (e.g., D. Davies et al., 1996), or endorsed by a professional group (e.g., American Academy of Child and Adolescent Psychiatry, 1997b; American Professional Society on the Abuse of Children, 1997, 2002; Bourg et al., 1999), interviewers will be in an excellent position to defend their practice. An example of the last situation is the Corner House interview protocol, which is used by the National Center for the Prosecution of Child Abuse (NCPCA) in their forensic interview training, Finding Words (Holmes & Veith, 2003). The NCPCA's use of the Corner House protocol adds credibility to the Finding Words training and to interviews by those who have received the training. Even without a published or endorsed interview structure, if interviewers have structures or practices that they routinely use, again, especially if they are evidence based, they will be able to justify and defend their work.

CAUTIONARY COMMENTS ABOUT PROTOCOLS

Despite the considerable advantages of interview structures, they do have some shortcomings.

Interview Structures Have Difficulty Accommodating Case-Based Differences

It is difficult for protocols to take into account the full spectrum of unique circumstances of all sexual abuse cases. Case-based variability can be categorized into demographic differences, sexual abuse specific differences, and systemic differences.

Demographic differences that need to be taken into account in the interview are child age, gender, and race. Although some interview structures call for a developmental assessment of the child, it is hard to take the child's age into account in the interview structure. Structured interviews are not very useful with preschoolers (Hershkowitz, Horowitz, & Lamb, 2005; Hewitt, 1999; Keary & Fitzpatrick, 1994). These children rarely can provide a narrative account, which is designated as the optimal communication mode in many protocols. In addition, most interview structures do not take into account the circumstances of the adolescent victim. For example, competency assessment may be experienced as silly by adolescents. In fact, most interview protocols are best suited to children ages 6–10. Research on incidence of sexual abuse, however, suggests that cases are fairly evenly distributed across the age span (U.S. Department of Health and Human Services, 2001). A very useful guide to children's linguistic abilities at different develop mental stages is A. G. Walker's *Handbook on Questioning Children* (1999).

As more has become known about child sexual abuse, evidence indicates boys represent about a third of victims (Finkelhor, 1979; U.S. Department of Health and Human Services, 2001). Research and practice suggest that boys may be more reluctant to disclose and experience sexual abuse differently than do girls (e.g., Finkelhor, 1979; Johnson & Shrier, 1985; Paine & Hansen, 2002; Welbourne, 2002). These differences might argue for different interview strategies. Moreover, the interaction of child and interviewer gender may either facilitate or inhibit disclosure of sexual abuse. Predicting how gender will operate in an individual interview is difficult. Nevertheless, it is a factor in a substantial portion of cases and is not an issue addressed in interview structures. In a study by Lamb and Garretson (2003), female forensic interviewers were found to vary their interview questions based upon child gender, but male interviewers did not. Although the authors concluded that women did less well on their criterion, following the NICHD scripted interview protocol (National Institute of Child Health and Human Development, 1999), another possible interpretation is that women took into account gender in question choice.

Perhaps of greater concern is the impact of race and ethnicity. As the child population in the United States becomes increasingly multicultural (Faller, 2000a), it becomes more important to consider race and ethnicity in child interviewing. Incidence data indicate that children of color, especially African-American and Native-American children, are reported to the child protection system at much higher rates than their rates in the general population (National Child Abuse and Neglect Data System, 2005a&b). Moreover, being a member of an oppressed minority and bilingual are both barriers to disclosure of sexual abuse (Dunkerley & Dalenberg, 2000; Fontes, 1993, 1995). Chapter 12 addresses interviewing children from different cultures.

Differences in sexual abuse experiences that are not, but perhaps should be, considered in interview structures are the type of sexual abuse suspected, offender–victim relationship, the methods the offender employed to engage the child and to prevent disclosure, and the child's cognitions related to the sexual abuse. Research indicates that children are less responsive to structured interview protocols when they have a closer relationship to the alleged offender (Hershkowitz, Horowitz, & Lamb, 2005). Some protocols address the issues of frequency and duration of the sexual abuse but not these other aspects of sexual abuse. In fact, some protocols advise the interviewer against mentioning the name of the suspect (Poole & Lamb, 1998).

System differences that need to be considered include for what agency the interviewer works, for example, law enforcement, a health care agency, or CPS; when in the process of disclosure and investigation the interview takes place (see chapter 13 for a discussion of the disclosure process); and the child and family's view of the agency and professional helpers. Many families in which there is intrafamilial sexual abuse have cautioned their children against talking to law enforcement and CPS.

The relative lack of capacity of existing interview structures to take individual circumstances into account is something that likely will change. Researchers and interviewers will develop interview protocols that take these differences into account (Poole & Dickinson, 2005).

Following the Child May Be Incompatible With Following the Protocol

Most protocols advise the interviewer to follow the child's lead but tend not to elaborate on what is meant by following the child. Lamb and colleagues do, however, and admonish interviewers to follow the child's disclosures with additional probes on the topic and not to jump from topic to topic (Lamb & Sternberg, 1999; Sternberg et al., 2000).

The more prescriptive the protocol, the more difficult it is to follow the child's lead. Moreover, the purpose of the interview may be incompatible with following the child. Clinical experience indicates that most children do not like to focus on unpleasant experiences and will avoid discussion of sexual abuse (e.g., Berliner, 1997a; Faller, 2003). A structured protocol may make it more difficult for interviewers to steer the discussion to sexual abuse in a nonthreatening manner. For related discussion, under the topic of coercion and coercive questions, refer to chapter 8.

Most Interview Structures Are Designed for Children Who Have Already Disclosed

Existing interview structures are better suited for children who have already disclosed sexual abuse (e.g., DeVoe & Faller, 1999; Keary & Fitzpatrick, 1994; London, Bruck, Ceci, & Shuman, 2005; Welbourne, 2002). For instance, initial probes usually assume there has been a recent outcry by the child. Examples are "I understand something may have happened to you; tell me about it as best you can" (Boychuk & Stellar, 1992), "Do you know why you came to talk to me?" and "I understand someone may have been bothering you" (Lamb & Sternberg, 1999). Welbourne (2002) examined videotapes of 36 Memorandum of Good Practice interviews. Twenty-three children had made a prior disclosure of sexual abuse. Of those, 19 girls reported sexual abuse during their videotaped interviews. No child who had not previously disclosed did so, and no boys disclosed. Her conclusion was the most important predictor of disclosure during the Memorandum of Good Practice interview was having previously disclosed.

Probably in most cases reported to CPS and law enforcement, children recently have told someone, but some reports involve symptomatic children who have not been questioned or who adamantly deny sexual abuse (Lyon, 2002b). There are also cases where, based upon referral information, the interviewer is suspicious that the allegation may be false. Starting with a query that suggests something has happened may not be advised.

Interview Structures Are Designed for Children Who Are Willing to Talk

Most interview structures assume that children are willing to talk about sexual abuse and that the main challenge is to assure that the interviewer does not ask leading or suggestive questions, thereby possibly contaminating the data or causing a false allegation. Research to date, however, suggests false negatives are a much greater problem than false positives. This research includes studies of adult survivors of sexual abuse who did not tell as children (Bagley & Ramsey, 1986; Finkelhor, Hotaling, Lewis, & Smith, 1990; Lyon, 2002b; Russell, 1986; Russell & Bolen, 2000), research on high-certainty allegations of sexual abuse (Bidrose & Goodman, 2000; Lawson & Chaffin, 1992; Terry, 1991), and analogue studies involving private parts touch (Saywitz, Goodman, Nicholas, & Moan, 1991; Steward et al., 1996). These findings are discussed in greater detail in chapters 8 and 9. The discussion above about "following the child's lead" is also relevant.

Limitations to Databases Used to Guide Interview Structure Development

There are some concerns about the databases relied upon in developing interview structures. Although protocols incorporate research findings, the research relied upon most heavily derives from analogue studies and findings about normal child development, rather than research on children with a history of possible sexual abuse (e.g., Poole & Lamb, 1998). Knowledge about the functioning of sexually abused children raises concerns about the ecological validity of this research for the target population (Lyon, 1996; Lyon & Saywitz, 1999). In their research on children's competency, Lyon, Saywitz, and colleagues administered to the 96 children in the study the Peabody Picture Vocabulary Test, which was used to screen for language comprehension, and found them on average 1.5 years behind (Lyon, 1996; Lyon & Saywitz, 1999).

In addition, interview structures are guided by legal considerations, which may bear no relationship to eliciting accurate information from children. For example, the protocol may admonish the interviewer not to use terms such as "pretend" or "play" or "hurt" (Merchant & Toth, 2001; State of Michigan, 1998) because then any disclosures the child makes may be challenged as representing fantasy. Similarly, the primary reason that competency assessments are part of interview structures is legal.

Finally, some protocol components have no empirical basis. For example, there is no research to support advising law enforcement not to wear their uniforms when interviewing children (American Professional Society on the Abuse of Children, 2002; State of Michigan, 2005).

Interviewers May Not Be Able to Follow the Linear Structure of the Protocol

Most protocols assume that an interview is linear, that the interviewer can proceed through the series of phases in the order they are prescribed (e.g., Merchant & Toth, 2001; Yuille, 2002). For example, protocols assume rapport building is achieved in the first phase of the interview, and thereafter it is in place for the entirety of the interview. In fact, the interviewer must attend to his/her relationship with the child throughout the interview. The task of eliciting information about sexual abuse may undermine the rapport the interviewer has established with the child. A sensitive interviewer will respond to the child's hostility or distress and digress from the interview protocol to reestablish rapport, thereby deviating from the protocol.

Other events can also disrupt the sequencing of the phases. Many protocols (e.g., Faller, 2003; State of Michigan, 1998, 2005) call for the interviewer to ask the child toward the end of the interview if there were any other sexual acts and if anyone else has sexually abused the child. Positive responses to these questions will cause the interviewer to move from closure back to the abuse-related phase(s) of the interview.

Similarly, many children who are referred for interviews about sexual abuse also experience other traumatic and salient experiences. These events are very important to understanding the child and the child's needs. Nevertheless, gathering data about these events and their effects usually will cause the interviewer to deviate from the interview structure.

Interviewers May Fail to Follow the Protocol

Although a protocol can offer useful guidance to interviewers, it can also be used to attack interviewers if they fail to follow it. As noted above, interviewers usually have competing agendas, to follow the protocol and to follow the child, and it may be difficult to do both. Failure to follow the child may result in inability to determine whether or not the child has been sexually abused. Failure to follow the protocol may result in the interview being challenged, especially in court. The more prescriptive the protocol, the more opportunities for the interviewer to deviate from it. Research to date indicates that interviewers have difficulty following protocols, even when they have been trained on them (Freeman & Morris, 1999; Sternberg, Lamb, Davies, & Wescott, 2001). Interviewers also may have difficulty maintaining new skills over time (Freeman & Morris, 1999; Lamb & Sternberg, 1999; Lamb et al., 2002). Moreover, research on the Memorandum of Good Practice indicates that interviewers may believe they are following the protocol when they are not (Lamb & Sternberg; Sternberg et al., 2001). Lamb, Sternberg, and colleagues have found that regular feedback on their interviews improves interviewers' ability to follow the protocol, but this research involved transcription of the interviews and their review by an expert in the NICHD protocol prior to feedback (Lamb et al., 2002). Most high-volume interviewing programs will likely have difficulty finding resources for such procedures for supervision.

In studies that document failure to follow the protocol, it is assumed to be a consequence of the inadequacy of the interviewer rather than the inadequacy of the interview structure (Sternberg et al., 2001). However, given some of the limitations of protocols, it may be the protocol that is at fault.

SUMMARY AND CONCLUSIONS

Considerable progress has been made in developing guidance for interviewers in how to structure interviews. Although these structures vary, there is also uniformity in these structures. There is consistency in advising a phased interview, which begins with an orientation of the child to the interview and allows the interviewer to gather information about the child and the child's functioning. The next phase focuses on the abuse or abuses experienced by the child. The final phase allows for closure for the interview and for the child. Guidance offered by these structures can assist interviewers, especially those who are mandated interviewers, CPS staff and law enforcement personnel.

Interviewers are cautioned, however, that these structures are best suited to children who are latency-aged, who have already disclosed, and who are willing to disclose. Furthermore, these structures are designed to avoid interviewers eliciting false positives, which appear to be a lesser problem than false negatives. More work is needed to address demographic differences in children, such as age, gender, and culture, in developing child-sensitive interview structures. Finally, research to date demonstrates that interviewers deviate from the structures they intend to follow.

NOTES

1. The Memorandum of Good Practice (Home Office, 1992, 2002; Welbourne, 2002) is an interview structure developed for law enforcement videotaping children's evidentiary statements about abuse. The structure involves four phases, (1) rapport building, (2) free narrative, (3) gathering details, and (4) closure, with additional specification about how to conduct each of these phases. Children's videotapes may be used in lieu of direct examination in a criminal proceeding but do not substitute for cross-examination (Home Office, 2002; Welbourne, 2002).

2. The National Institute of Child Health and Human Development is one of the U.S. National Institutes of Health. Under the leadership of Michael Lamb, Ph.D., and the late Kathleen Sternberg, Ph.D., NICHD has partnered with

several frontline investigative programs around the world, for example, in the United Kingdom (e.g., Sternberg et al., 2001), Israel (e.g., Hershkowitz et al., 2005; Sternberg et al., 1997), and Salt Lake City in the United States (e.g., Lamb et al., 2002). The researchers at NICHD have applied knowledge from developmental psychology to investigative interviewing of children who may have been abused and developed a scripted protocol titled the NICHD Investigative Interview Protocol (Orbach et al., 2000; Sternberg, Lamb, Orbach et al., 2001). Data have been systematically collected and analyzed on most aspects of this protocol. These findings have greatly enhanced professional knowledge about how to elicit accurate and detailed information from children who may have been maltreated and have informed most of the interview structures employed in forensic interviews of children.

EIGHT

Questioning Techniques

Kathleen Coulborn Faller

The manner in which children are questioned about possible sexual abuse has received a great deal of attention. Although a primary issue is concern that interviewers may employ leading questions that result in false allegations (e.g., Benedek & Schetky, 1987a&b; Ney, 1995; Sattler, 1998; State of Michigan, 1998, 2005), a more important and related issue is how to question children in a way that will elicit the most accurate and complete information about possible sexual abuse (Lamb, 1994; Lamb & Sternberg, 1999; Sternberg et al., 1997; Sternberg, Lamb, Esplin, & Baradaran, 1999). In this chapter, the research and practice bases used to derive advice about questions in interviews about sexual abuse are covered; the concept of a continuum of questions, beginning with preferred questions and ending with least preferred questions, is discussed; and additional questioning controversies are described.

BASES OF ADVICE ABOUT QUESTIONING TECHNIQUES

Much of the research that has been conducted on questioning techniques and leading questions consists of laboratory or analogue studies (e.g., Bruck, Ceci, & Hembrooke, 2002; Bruck, Ceci, & Rosenthal, 1995; Carter, Bottoms, & Levine, 1996; Ceci, Bruck, & Francoeur, 2000; Ceci, Huffman, Smith, & Loftus, 1994; Ceci & Leichtman, 1995; Ceci, Loftus, Leichtman, & Bruck, 1994; Clarke-Stewart, Thompson, & Lepore, 1989; Finnila, Mahlberg, Santtila, Sandnabba, & Niemi, 2003; Goodman, Bottoms, Schwartz-Kennedy, & Rudy, 1991; Goodman & Clarke-Stewart, 1991; Lepore & Sesco, 1994; C. Peterson & Bell, 1996; Pezdek, Finger, & Hodge, 1997). These studies involve naturally occurring events in children's lives, such as going to the doctor, or staged events, for example, going into a trailer with a "stranger." After the event, children are interviewed by researchers and asked to describe their experiences. In the questioning component of these studies, researchers use various types of questions, including open-ended, direct, leading, misleading, and suggestive questions. This research is discussed in detail in chapter 2, which covers the topics of children's memory and suggestibility.

Some important field studies involving the professionals mandated to interview for sexual abuse and children with a possible history of abuse have been undertaken by Lamb, Sternberg, and colleagues at the National Institute of Child Health and Human Development, one of the U.S. National Institutes of Health. This field research is conducted in collaboration with colleagues in England (e.g., Sternberg, Lamb, Davies, & Wescott, 2001), Israel (e.g., Sternberg et al., 1997), Sweden (Cederborg, Orbach, & Sternberg, 2000), and the United States (e.g., Lamb & Sternberg, 1999; Sternberg et al., 1999). Similar research has been conducted at the University of Southern California (Lyon, 2002b). These studies apply analogue research findings and knowledge about child development to the real world of forensic interviewing. The research is especially useful in providing information about what types of questions yield narrative responses and details from children with a reported history of sexual abuse. To date, this research has focused primarily on children who disclose in response to these interview techniques and not on those children who fail to disclose, but see chapter 13 for some research on children who did not disclose.

In addition, several authors have proposed guidelines for questioning relying upon practice experience and, to some extent, research (Boat & Everson, 1988a; Bourg et al., 1998, 1999; Boychuk & Stellar, 1992; Center for Child Protection, 1992; Faller, 1993, 2003; Hindman, 1987; Hoorwitz, 1992; Kuehnle, 1998; McDermott-Steinmetz-Lane, 1997; Morgan, 1995; Myers, 1992, 1998; Sorenson, Bottoms, & Perona, 1997; White & Quinn, 1988). There is a slight disjuncture between the analogue study research findings and the guidelines proposed, in that practitioners generally advise interviewers to be more conservative than the analogue research suggests they need be. This conservative advice is based in part upon legal considerations, that is, fear that questions employed in the interview will be challenged and that there will be a negative outcome in court.

USE OF A CONTINUUM OF QUESTIONS/PROBES

Most of the writings about questions to be used in child interviews indicate that some are appropriate for use and others are either less appropriate or not appropriate (e.g., Bourg et al., 1999; Merchant & Toth, 2001; Poole & Lamb, 1998; Sorenson et al., 1997; State of Michigan, 2005). Faller (1993, 2003) proposes a continuum of questions from open-ended to close-ended, suggesting that the interviewer should have more confidence in the child's responses to the open-ended questions (see also Bourg et al., 1998, 1999). This suggestion is consistent with the research findings that children's responses to open-ended questions are likely to be more accurate than their responses to more close-ended ones (e.g., Lamb, 1994; Lamb & Sternberg, 1999; Orbach, Hershkowitz, Lamb, Esplin, & Horowitz, 2000). Further, Faller (1993, 2003) advises a strategy that employs the most open-ended questions that elicit information, resorting to more close-ended ones only when open-ended ones are unproductive, and reverting to more open-ended questions when the child provides information in response to a close-ended question. This approach appears to be accepted by most professionals writing about questioning techniques (e.g., Bourg et al., 1999; Lamb & Sternberg, 1999; Merchant & Toth, 2001; State of Michigan, 2005), with some notable exceptions (Gardner, 1995, 1998). The strategy of proceeding from open-ended to close-ended questions and probes is called a "funnel approach." The terms "hourglass approach" and "paired questions" have been used for the process of reverting back to an open-ended question when a close-ended one produces information (e.g., Merchant & Toth, 2001; Sternberg, Lamb, Orbach, Esplin, & Mitchell, 2000).

Similar admonitions about the desirability of open-ended questions are provided in guidelines for interviewing (American Professional Society on the Abuse of Children, 1997; Boat & Everson, 1988a; Boychuk & Stellar, 1992; Home Office, 1992; Myers, 1992, 1998; Stellar & Boychuk, 1992; Yuille, 2002). Interviewers are advised to be very self conscious about questions, to employ more open-ended questions before resorting to more close-ended ones, and to appreciate that responses to close-ended questions may be less accurate. More close-ended questions may also result in challenges to the admissibility of findings in court (Pence & Wilson, 1994; Yuille, 2002).

Nevertheless, there are differences of opinion about what questions are optimal and what questions are less than optimal. In addition to lack of consensus, writers may use different terms for the same type of sentence structure, for example, suggestive questions or close-ended questions. Moreover, Lamb, Hershkowitz, Sternberg, Boat, and Everson (1996) initially used the term "leading" for what they now call option-posing questions discussed below (Orbach et al., 2000).

In the section below, the general categories *preferred*, *less preferred*, and *least preferred* are employed in discussing the types of questions or probes an interviewer might use (see table 8.1) and the spectrum of views about the relative appropriateness of different types of questions. Labels for types of questions/probes, definitions, and examples are provided. An attempt is made to include all the labels found in the literature for each question/probe. These are listed and described in order from what appear to be the most open-ended to the most close-ended. The reader will note that sometimes these different types of questions/ probes are slightly overlapping, because the continuum attempts to

Table 8.1 A Continuum of Questions to Be Used When Interviewing Children: From Open-Ended Questions (More Confidence in Child's Response) to Close-Ended Questions (Less Confidence in Child's Response).

Question/Probe Type	Definition	Examples
Preferred Questions/Probes		
General question	Open-ended inquiry about the child's well-being or salient issues; it does not assume abuse may have occurred.	How can I help you? How are you doing today?
Open abuse-related question, directive question	Open-ended inquiry that assumes there may be abuse or trauma.	Do you know why you came to see me today? Now that I know we know each other a little better, I want to talk about the reason you are here today. Tell me the reason you came to talk to me today (State of Michigan, 2005). I understand something may have happened to you. Tell me about it as best you can (Boychuk & Stellar, 1992).
Invitation or invitational question	Utterances that invite free recall and a narrative.	Can you tell me everything you can remember? Tell me all about what happened, from the beginning to the middle to the end (Lamb & Sternberg, 1999).
Facilitative cue, narrative cue, facilitators	Interviewer gesture or utterance aimed at encouraging more narration.	Un Huh (affirmative) Okay Anything else? What happened next?
Focused question, focused probe	A probe that focuses the child on a particular topic, place, or person but refrains from providing information about the subject (Myers, Goodman, & Saywitz, 1996).	Tell me about daycare. Can you tell me about your dad?

continued

Table 8.1 continued

Question/Probe Type	Definition	Examples
"Wh" questions, cued invitations	Inquiry to gather contextual and specific detail about the child's experience: Who, what, when, where.	When did this happen? Where were you? Where was your mom?
Less Preferred Questions/Probes		
Multiple choice question, option posing, forced choice, restricted choice (A. G. Walker, 1999)	A question that presents the child with a number of alternative responses from which to choose.	Did he do it one time or more than one time? Did the abuse happen in the daytime, night, or both?
Direct question, specific question, option posing	A direct inquiry about abuse or abuse related details.	Did John hurt your peepee? Did he put his finger inside you? Was your father the one who poked your butt? Was he wearing his pajamas, too?
Least Preferred Question/Probes		
Leading question, tag question	A statement the child is asked to affirm.	Isn't it true that your brother put his penis in your mouth? Chester was really cleaning, wasn't he? (Clarke-Stuart, Thompson, & Lepore, 1989)
Coercion, coercive question	Use of inappropriate inducements to gain cooperation or to elicit information from the child.	If you tell me what your father did, we can go for ice cream. Don't tell my boss that I was playing (and gives child a piece of candy) (Clarke-Stuart, Thompson, & Lepore, 1989).

address both the structure and the purpose of the interviewer utterance. For example, a question such as "What do you do at daycare?" could be regarded as a focused question, because it focuses the child's attention on daycare, and also an open-ended "wh" question," because it begins with "what."

Preferred Questions/Probes

Many writers advise starting the abuse-related portion of the interview with an open-ended, abuse-related question (Lamb & Sternberg, 1999; Merchant & Toth, 2001) or a directive question (Boychuk & Stellar, 1992), for example, "Do you know why we're talking today?" (Sorenson et al., 1997; Yuille, 2002) or "Tell me the reason you came to talk to me today" (Hindman, 1987; Lamb & Sternberg, 1999; see also Merchant & Toth, 2001; State of Michigan, 1998, 2005). Note that the first question may result in a yes/no or substantive response, whereas the second demands substantive information. Another, slightly more close-ended preferred question is, "I understand something may have happened to you. Tell me as best you can about it" (Boychuk & Stellar, 1992; Stellar & Boychuk, 1992; see also Poole & Lamb, 1998; State of Michigan, 1998, 2005) or "Now that we understand each other a little better, I want to talk to you about the reason you're here today. I understand something may have happened to you. Please tell me everything that happened; every detail, from the beginning to the very end" (Sternberg et al., 1997).

Interviewers attempt to elicit a narrative from the child. If the child does not provide one, the interviewer may use an invitation, such as, "Tell me everything you can remember about what happened." These preferred questions assume a salient experience of sexual abuse and/or a recent disclosure of sexual abuse.

The interviewer is advised to wait until the child has stopped talking (Home Office, 2002; A. G. Walker, 1999) and then to follow up the narrative with facilitative or narrative cues (Faller, 2003) or facilitators (Orbach et al., 2000). Examples include "Tell me more," "Anything else?" or "What happened next?" Another type of facilitative cue is a nod, saying "uh huh," or "okay," during the narrative or when the child pauses. These cues communicate to the child that the interviewer is tracking the child's responses but do not disrupt the child's account. Yet a third type of facilitative cue is repeating the child's previous statement as an invitation to say more or actually asking, after the repetition, "Then what?" or "Anything else you can remember?"

Although this open-ended form on inquiry is a preferred initial approach, A. G. Walker (1999) points out that it is unrealistic to expect children to provide detailed responses to nonspecific questions, such as "What happened?" She advises that children do not have "story models" that can help them organize their accounts into "who, what, when, and where" and require more scaffolding or close-ended probes from their questioners so that they know what information to provide.

A different approach to introducing the topic of concern is usually needed when the child hasn't been told why he/she is being interviewed, when it is less clear that the child has been abused, when the abuse may not be particularly salient to the child, and when the child has not disclosed (Faller, 2003; Yuille, 2002). Much less is written about these types of cases. Especially challenging are cases in which the child has not disclosed but is engaging in sexualized behavior. These situations are challenging because if the interviewer focuses on the sexualized behavior, the child is likely to believe he/she is the wrong-doer. Not only will there be risk of traumatizing the child further by focusing on the sexualized behavior rather than its etiology, but also the child may be more reluctant to tell. Nondisclosing children are discussed in detail in chapter 13.

The interviewer can begin inquiry in the four situations noted in the preceding paragraph with general probes or questions, such as "Tell me how things have been going," or "Do you have any worries?" (Faller, 2003; see also Bourg et al., 1998, 1999). (In the latter instance, the interviewer will have told the child at the beginning of the session that this is a place where kids talk about worries. Thus, there will be a prior referent.) It is uncommon for general questions to elicit a disclosure of sexual abuse (DeVoe & Faller, 1999, 2002; A. G. Walker, 1999). Indeed, the interviewer may try several of these probes without understanding whether or not the child has been abused (DeVoe & Faller, 2002).

When preferred general questions do not resolve concerns about sexual abuse, the evaluator may move to focused questions, using background information about the child or the abuse concerns (Bourg et al., 1998, 1999; Merchant & Toth, 2001). A focused question, as defined by Myers, Goodman, and Saywitz (1996), is a question "that focuses the child on a particular topic, place, or person but refrains from providing information about the subject" (p. 15). Focused questions can be more or less open-ended depending upon the explicitness of their content (Myers, 1998).

Faller (2003) described focused questions referring to people, body parts, and the context of the abuse. Boat and Everson (1988), writing about the use of anatomical dolls, differentiate among three types of focused questions, defining those related to critical events as the most open-ended, followed by person focused (critical individuals focus), and body parts questions (direct general inquiry) as the most close-ended.

When interviewers use person-focused questions, they should ask these questions about a range of important people in the child's life and not merely the person thought to be an abuser. Examples include, "Tell me all about your dad." The interviewer may follow this question with more close-ended focused questions: "What things do you like about him?" "Are there things you don't like about him?"[1] (Faller, 2003).

Questions and probes that focus the child on a place usually refer to the place the interviewer thinks the abuse occurred, for example, "Tell me all about daycare." Sometimes the interviewer has no specific information related to the abuse concern and may focus on topics or activities that may be contexts for abuse. Topic-focused questions may be about private parts and may be posed in the context of a body parts inventory. After having the child identify the names of all the body parts, using some kind of body map (e.g., anatomical doll, anatomical drawing), the evaluator asks focused questions such as, "Has anything ever happened to your peepee?" or "Has something happened to your peepee?" (A. G. Walker, 1999). Similarly, the evaluator may focus questions on bedtime or bath time or other times when there is risk of sexual abuse (Carnes & LeDuc, 1998). Other focused questions may be about secrets or games played with an adult, because sometimes abusive acts are defined or disguised as secrets or games (Faller, 1993, 2003).

If focused questions elicit a positive response, the evaluator uses an invitational question/probe, such as "Tell me all about what happened to your peepee." These may be followed by narrative cues, such as, "Is there anything else you remember?"

Another class of question that falls into the preferred category for many writers (Bourg et al., 1999; Faller, 1993, 2003; McDermott-Steinmetz-Lane, 1997) are cued invitations (Lamb & Sternberg, 1999) or "wh" questions. These are questions that ask who, what, where, when, and how, such as "How did he get you into the room?" "Wh" questions are used primarily after the child has indicated something has happened to gather specific information. For example, if the child said someone hurt her peepee, the evaluator might has, "Who was the person?" or "What is the person's name?" When and where questions address contextual issues about the abuse.

All of the "wh" questions are highly relevant forensically because they elicit information about the specifics of any abuse (American Professional Society on the Abuse of Children, 2002; Pence & Wilson, 1994). Lyon (1999b), in a comprehensive review of the analogue research on questioning children, notes that "wh" questions can be more or less open-ended. For example, "What happened at Mr. Jones' house?" is more open-ended than "What color was Mr. Jones' shirt?" although both are "what" questions. Children are able to answer the "who," "what," and "where" questions at an earlier age than "when" questions (State of Michigan, 2005).

Whether to use "wh" questions or narrative cues first is an area of disagreement among experts. Some writers (e.g., Lamb & Sternberg, 1999) are concerned that the demand characteristics of "wh" questions may elicit false details. They prefer to ask the child repeatedly if he/she can remember anything else about the abuse (Poole & Lamb, 1998). Boychuk and Stellar (1992) call "wh" questions direct questions and regard them as questions of last resort. Other writers (e.g., Faller, 2003) think that there are demand characteristics in repeatedly saying to the child, "Tell me more" (Merchant & Toth, 2001). Practice experience shows that repeated demands for more information may cause creative children to generate false details. In addition, thinking their initial response must be wrong, some children change their accounts when asked the same question repeatedly. Lyon (1999a&b) in his review of the research "wh" questions and C. Peterson and colleagues (Peterson & Bell, 1996; Peterson & Biggs, 1997), in their study of children 2–13 years old who were injured and went to a hospital emergency room, report that "wh" questions substantially increase the amount of information children provide with very little compromise of accuracy.

Less Preferred Questions

Two types of questions that most writers put into the category of less preferred are multiple choice (forced or restricted choice) and yes/no (direct, specific) questions about the abuse and related details. These questions are less preferred because they are more close-ended. They violate a forensic interview principle of gathering information from the child. Rather, the questions provide information and ask the child either to select a correct response, in the case of multiple choice questions, or affirm or deny, in the case of yes/no questions. Lyon (1999b) concludes from his review of the research that both multiple choice and yes/no questions result in more errors than do more open-ended questions, including "wh" questions. Interviewers are advised to attempt more open-ended questions before resorting to these less preferred questions.

White and Quinn (1988) admonish interviewers against the use of multiple choice and yes/no questions, defining both types of questions as leading. See also E. Sorenson et al. (1997), who are concerned about the suggestiveness of these types of questions in forensic interviews. Morgan (1995) makes similar points but also says sometimes these questions are necessary to elicit needed information. The United Kingdom's Home Office (1992) suggests these be used only after focused questions.

Lamb, Sternberg, and colleagues (Lamb & Sternberg, 1999; Sternberg et al., 1997, 2000, 2001) use the term "option-posing questions" for both multiple choice and yes/no questions and regard them as less preferred. In research documenting information elicited by different types of questions, option-posing probes elicit significantly fewer details and shorter responses than do invitations and cue questions (Sternberg et al., 1997, 2000, 2001). Despite the general advice against multiple choice questions, Lamb and Sternberg (1999) advise the use of a multiple choice question to determine the frequency of the abuse—"Did it happen one time or more than one time?"—because a more open-ended alternative ("How many times did he abuse you?") is beyond the capacity of young children and, indeed, of most children if the abuse happened many times.

Faller (2003) recommends the following limitations on the use of multiple choice questions. First, they should usually be preceded by a focused question to which the child fails to respond or says "I don't know" or "I don't remember." For example, after a child has said, "Jimmy hurt my peepee with his peepee," the evaluator might ask "Where were you when Jimmy hurt your peepee?" If the child does not answer, the interviewer might ask, "Were you indoors or outdoors?" Second, Faller advises that the evaluator take care to include the correct answer among the alternatives. Thus, instead of saying, "Did he hurt your peepee in the bathroom or the bedroom?" it is better to say "Did he hurt your peepee in the bathroom or the bedroom, or someplace else?" in case the correct response is neither of the rooms named (see also Lyon, 1999b; Merchant & Toth, 2001; A. G. Walker, 1999). Finally, Faller (2003) suggests limiting multiple choice questions to the context of the abuse or "where" and "when" and not using such questions when inquiring about "who" did it and "what" sexual acts. The rationale for this recommendation is that incorrect responses to context questions have lessened potential for life-altering consequences. A. G. Walker (1999) adds that if multiple choice questions are employed, they should be limited to three choices, the last being the "or something else" option.

Yes/no questions, direct, or specific questions are less preferred because of concerns they may elicit social desirability responses. Specifically, young children may say "yes" to please the interviewer when they do not understand the question or when they do not know the answer. On the other hand, children who are avoidant or resistant to disclosing sexual abuse will probably be no more forthcoming in response to a direct question than to a more open-ended one (Faller, 2003).

Boat and Everson (1988) state that yes/no questions (direct inquiry about specific individuals—"Has daddy ever touched your dingdong?") are potentially leading and suggestive, especially with 2- and 3-year olds. Boat and Everson state that yes/no questions should be used only when there is good cause for concern about sexual abuse but no disclosure. In such instances, they can be effective in "opening the door" and facilitating disclosure.

Although there are concerns about social desirability responses to yes/no question from young children, in analogue studies the evidence to date does not indicate that young children have a "yes" bias, but rather that they give less accurate answers to yes/no questions than to "wh" questions (Lyon, 1999b; C. Peterson & Bell, 1996; C. Peterson, Dowden, & Tobin, 1999). However, as discussed below, when yes/no questions are combined with coercion, they can result in false positives (e.g., Garven, Wood, & Malpass, 2000).

Moreover, as noted in chapter 14, in some analogue studies the number of false affirmations to yes/no questions about private parts touch is small compared to false negatives when interviewers fail to ask directly about this issue (Saywitz, Goodman, Nicholas, & Moan, 1991; Steward et al., 1996). As a consequence, many guidelines (e.g., American Professional Society on the Abuse of Children, 1997, 2002) advise asking directly about sexual abuse if indirect methods do not resolve the interviewer's concerns. Research from analogue studies supports this direct inquiry because accuracy in response to yes/no questions about central events is greater than to yes/no questions about peripheral events (Lyon, 1999b).

Furthermore, in some circumstances yes/no questions may be less suggestive or presumptive than an invitational probe or a "wh" question (Everson, 1999). For example, the interviewer might ask a direct question, "Was anyone else there?" rather than "Who else was there?" especially in circumstances when it is unknown if someone else was there. In addition, even when a fact is known, an interviewer might introduce a discussion of that factual situation by a direct question as a signal to the child that the interviewer is changing the subject. For example, in a case where the child has both a father and a stepfather, the interviewer might introduce the topic of the stepfather by saying, "Do you have another dad?" (Yes) "What do you call him?" before asking the child to tell about this dad. Similarly, A. G. Walker (1999) advises interviewers to contexualize their questions and probes to assist children in giving accurate responses.

As noted in chapter 7, Lamb, Sternberg, and colleagues (Lamb & Sternberg, 1999; Orbach et al., 2000) have provided a list of nine questions and probes to introduce the topic of concern, starting with most preferred. Thus, more close-ended probes, such as, "I heard someone may have done something to you that wasn't right," "I heard something may have happened to you at (location, time)," and "I heard someone may have (allegation)" fall into the less preferred category in their scripted interview. These probes illustrate, however, that like "wh" questions, yes/no questions can be more or less open-ended. The first and second of these probes do not mention either the alleged abuser or the abusive act. The third probe may do so. Interviewers, if they decide they need to ask direct questions, are advised to try to craft these questions in the most open-ended manner they can, and resort to more specific question content only when vaguer questions do not resolve concerns about victimization or the details of what happened.

The Protocol for Evidentiary Interviews from the Chadwick Center for Child Protection (D. Davies et al., 1996) advises using focused but not leading questions. However, the questions the center defines as focused fall into the direct question and multiple choice question categories. In addition, the center asks about a full range of sexual activity: oral contact; digital contact; vaginal, penile, and anal contact; as well as pornography, something not specifically recommended by other writers. In order not to lead the child, the protocol advises phrasing the question "Was there any touching with mouths?" rather than, "Did his mouth touch your peepee?" Also, the protocol advises multiple choice questions to inquire about the identity of the offender, rather than asking directly whether it was, for example, the father.

Least-Preferred Questions

Two types of questions are in the least preferred category because most writers will define them as inappropriate, at least in most situations. These are leading and coercive questions (coercion). There are other question types that fall into the least preferred category but about which there is less consistent agreement.

Leading Questions

There is fairly universal agreement that interviewers should avoid the use of leading questions when assessing for possible sexual abuse (e.g., American Academy of Child and Adolescent Psychiatry, 1997b; American Professional Society on the Abuse of Children, 1997, 2002; Benedek & Schetky, 1987b; Bourg et al., 1998, 1999; Faller, 1993, 2003; Home Office, 1992; Merchant & Toth, 2001; Morgan, 1995; Poole & Lamb, 1998; Yuille, 2002).

To complicate matters, writers may not define or give examples of leading questions (e.g., Gardner, 1995; Yuille, 2002). When they do, there is lack of agreement about what sort of sentence structure is leading. For example, some writers define as direct a question such as, "Did your daddy touch your peepee?" (Morgan, 1995; Poole & Lamb, 1998; Sorenson et al., 1997) or a multiple choice question as leading (White & Quinn, 1988). Some argue that even mentioning why the child is being interviewed is leading (Gardner, 1995). Similarly, some protocols advise against the use of terms "hurt," "abuse," and "bad" because they are leading and may contaminate the interview findings (Poole & Lamb, 1998; State of Michigan, 2005). On the other hand, many writers reserve the term "leading question" for questions that would be considered leading in a legal proceeding (e.g., DeVoe & Faller, 2002; Faller, 2000c; A. G. Walker, 1999, 2001).

In 1995, the American Professional Society on the Abuse of Children held an open forum on leading questions, attended by many experts in interviewing children about sexual abuse, to address the lack of consensus on leading questions and different views about appropriate questions for an interview related to sexual abuse. Out of that forum came support that the legal definition should be used. These are also called "tag" questions because there is a phrase tagged onto either the beginning or the end of the sentence (Myers et al., 1996; A. G. Walker, 1999). To quote A. G. Walker, a leading or "tag question makes a statement and adds a short question which invites corroboration of its truth"; she adds that a tag question "is one of the most powerfully suggestive forms of speech in the English language" (A. G. Walker, 1999, p. 48). Questions such as "Isn't it true that Mr. Jones kissed your penis?" and

"Your grandfather touched your breast, didn't he?" fit this definition of leading or tag question.

Professionals oppose or advise avoiding leading questions for two reasons: (1) they are confusing and beyond the cognitive abilities of most children, and (2) they may result in children providing false affirmative responses.

A. G. Walker (1994, 1999) describes leading questions as requiring the child to engage in seven cognitive processes: (1) judge the answer to the tag, (2) translate the tag from its elliptical or abbreviated form by determining what event the tag refers to, (3) track the pronouns and their referents in the question, (4) learn that a positive statement can take a negative tag and visa versa, (5) learn that a negative tag does not negate the positive statement (e.g., "She was nice to you, wasn't she?"), (6) understand that the tag on the statement represents the opinion of the person asking the question and isn't necessarily true, and finally (7) learn how to disagree or support the questioners viewpoint (A. G. Walker, p. 49). Although Walker is making observations about questioning methods employed in court, especially on cross-examination, they also apply to the challenges children face when asked leading questions during interviews.

Most of the opinion about leading questions focuses on the fear that they will result in false positive replies. Analogue research on responses to leading questions suggests that most children do not falsely affirm an incorrect assertion, but younger preschoolers are more likely to do so (Bruck et al., 2000; Bruck, Ceci, Francoeur, & Renick, 1995; Saywitz et al., 1991; Steward et al., 1996). In addition, repeated leading and suggestive techniques over a period of several sessions are successful in eliciting false positives from some children (Ceci, Huffman et al., 1994; Ceci, Loftus et al., 1994). (See also chapter 2.) These techniques include asking the child to make a picture of the false event in his/her head and providing details about the false event. In addition, the two studies by Ceci and colleagues paired a false event with a true event, that is, an incident that the child had actually experienced. Nevertheless, children were least likely to affirm a false event that was negative, such as falling off a tricycle and needing stitches, and most likely to affirm a false, neutral, nonparticipatory event, seeing someone standing at a bus stop (Ceci, Loftus et al., 1994). In addition, as Lyon (1999b) observes based upon his careful review of these two studies, most of the effect derives from the leading and suggestive characteristics of the research rather than the repeated interviews.

Despite widespread concerns about leading questions, some guidelines note that there are times when they are appropriate. The Memorandum of Good Practice (Home Office, 1992, 2002) indicates that they are a last resort but also that some children need to be led. Similarly, Faller (2003) observes that a leading question may be appropriate when referring to a prior disclosure or an inconsistency in a child's account. For example, referring to information the child has already revealed, the interviewer might say, "Now you said he was wearing blue jeans, didn't you?" Finally, Myers (1998) points out that even a question that is leading can vary in the extent to which it is leading, for example, "Isn't it true that something happened?" versus "Isn't it true that Mr. Jones pinched your breast?"

Coercion and Coercive Questions

Writers caution interviewers not to use coercive questions or coercion when interviewing for sexual abuse (Benedek & Schetky, 1987a, 1987b; Faller, 1993, 2003; Myers, 1992, 1998; White & Quinn, 1988). Coercion involves compelling or bribing the child to cooperate with the interview or to provide information. Not only is most coercion aversive to the child, but also it may lead to inaccurate reports if the child has not been abused or does not know the answer to the interviewer's question.

Some writers regard coercion in forensic interviews as rampant. Coercive techniques they cite include admonishing the child with various degrees of forcefulness to tell the truth, offering tangible rewards for talking, repetitive questioning, threats, and setting limits, such as telling the child she/he cannot leave the interview to go to the bathroom until the child discloses (Benedek & Schetky, 1987a, 1987b; Ceci & Bruck, 1995; White & Quinn, 1988). Although there is little evidence that such techniques are widespread today, information from high-profile cases from the 1980s suggests that cajoling and coercion were methods employed by some interviewers in the past (e.g., E. Butler, Fukurai, Dimitrius, & Krooth, 2001; Garven et al., 2000; L. Mansell, 1990; Myers, 1995). These coercive techniques should be avoided.

Moreover, analogue studies have demonstrated that coercive techniques can increase children's false positive responses (Finnila et al., 2003; Garven et al., 2000). Garven and colleagues studied the impact of suggestive questions about fictitious acts and five coercive techniques on children's accounts of a visit by "Manny Morales" to their preschool classroom. The techniques employed were (1) telling children that other children had already reported the fictitious acts (co-witness information), (2) describing negative consequences for not affirming the fictitious acts, (3) describing positive consequences for affirming the fictitious acts, (4) repeating a question the child had already answered, and (5) inviting the child to speculate about fictitious acts. Each child was asked four leading correct questions and eight suggestive, misleading questions. Almost all the children accurately responded to the leading correct questions. The researchers demonstrated that the use of these coercive techniques, plus suggestive questions increased significantly the proportion of false affirmations. Fifty-eight percent of the responses to suggestive, misleading questions were false positives when coercion was employed compared to 17% of the responses to suggestive, misleading questions when these techniques were not. The most effective techniques for eliciting false positives were negative and positive reinforcement and co-witness information.

Based upon the above findings, Garven et al. (2000) conducted a second study with children ages 5–7. This study involved a similar research paradigm, except that the man who visited the classroom was named "Paco Perez," and it focused on the two most successful coercive techniques: use of reinforcement and co-witness information. In this study, children were asked 16 suggestive questions, including four correct ones. Again, children were accurate in response to the correct questions. In this study, the positive and negative reinforcement had a marked effect on producing false positive responses, but the use of co-witness information did not.

Building upon the research of Garven and colleagues, Finnish researchers (Finnila et al., 2003) studied the effects of high-pressure suggestive interviews versus suggestive interviews on preschool and school-age children who scored high and low on a standardized measure of suggestibility. The analogue about which children were questioned was being told a story and shown four colored pictures related to the story. In the high-pressure condition, interviewers used co-witness information, selective reinforcement, and repeated questioning. Children were asked 17 misleading questions. The researchers demonstrated that the impact of the interview was more important in eliciting false positives than were the children's scores on the suggestibility measure, although both had an effect. Nevertheless, when individual misleading questions are examined, no more than a fourth of children gave clear "yes" responses to any of them, in either the high-pressure or low-pressure interview conditions.

Finally, returning to actual interviews for sexual abuse, professionals conducting them should be mindful that interviews of children about possible sexual abuse can be structurally coercive. The interviewer is an adult and has a power advantage vis-à-vis the child. Moreover, few children look forward to the interview and talking about sexual abuse. In fact, the interview involves adults asking children to talk about a subject most children would like to avoid. Consequently, the child may respond to questions by saying, "I don't want to talk," or "Let's play, not talk." The interviewer may respond, "You need to tell me what happened," which may be experienced by the child as coercion. Alternatively, the interviewer may say, "After we talk, you can play," which may be interpreted as a bribe to report sexual abuse. There is no way to eliminate this coercive component for the interview situation; all the professional can do is be aware of it and try to mediate or diminish it. For example, the interviewer might allow the child to color while talking or might digress from discussion of possible abuse when the child objects to talking and return to the abuse topic later.

OTHER QUESTIONING CONTROVERSIES

The questioning controversies discussed in this section include issues related to question structure, use of information from other sources in questioning, repeated questions, and misleading questions. These are all issues about which there is disagreement among persons writing about interview questions used in sexual abuse assessments and investigations.

Structure of Questions and Probes

Writers disagree about whether evaluators should give the child an "out" by first asking a yes/no question or using a command. For example, should the interviewer pose a question, "Can you tell me what happened?" (Faller, 2003; Poole & Lamb, 1998; Yuille, 2002) or use a command, "Tell me what happened" (Lamb et al., 1999; Poole & Lamb, 1998; Merchant & Toth, 2001)? The former invites a yes/no response, with a yes followed by an invitation for a narrative, "Tell me all about that." However, it also risks a "no" response. The "Tell me what happened" format invites a narrative. Other types of questions that capture this interviewer dilemma are, "Do you remember where you were?" versus "Where were you?"; and "Do you know what he was wearing?" versus "What was he wearing?" On the one hand, assuming the child has the knowledge and demanding the information may decrease the likelihood the child will avoid responding by saying, "I don't remember" or "I don't want to talk about it." On the other hand, commands and questions that assume the child has the information may cause children to provide a response when they do not know the answer.

Faller (2003) suggests that the circumstances of the case should determine the demand characteristics of probes. For example, if, during the rapport-building phase of the interview, the evaluator determines the child is oppositional, commands and "wh" questions will likely be more appropriate. In contrast, if the evaluator finds the child to be compliant or suggestible, then probes that do not assume the child knows the answer may be better. Similarly, if the event happened some time in the past, a "Do you remember" question may more appropriate. If there is a genuine issue about whether the child has the information the evaluator is seeking, for example, what happened to the child's younger sister, then a "Do you know" question may be best.

A different position about what she calls "DUR-X" questions (do you remember or do you recall) is held by A. G. Walker (1994, 1999, 2001). She argues that such questions require too many cognitive processes for children. The child must first process the recall part of the question and then go to his/her long-term memory for the information, which then must be communicated to the interviewer in a comprehensible manner. These mental processes often occur in a stressful environment, further compromising the child's capacity to answer the question.

Externally Derived Questions

Another area of controversy is the use of questions based upon externally derived information or information obtained from a source other than the child interview. Boychuk and Stellar (1992) uses the term "cue question" for this type of probe. Most professionals agree that an evaluator who interviews a child more than once may rely on and repeat information obtained in a previous interview. The issue of controversy is whether the interviewer should use information obtained by or from someone else, for example, the child's mother, teacher, or a police officer. Some professionals oppose externally derived questions altogether (e.g., Merchant & Toth, 2001; Yuille, 2002), while others think such questions can be used judiciously (Boychuk & Stellar, 1992; D. Corwin, personal communication, January 1998; Faller, 2003; Stellar & Boychuk, 1992). Such questions may be necessary to avoid a situation of prior inconsistent statement (i.e., the child alleging certain acts at an earlier time but not mentioning them in the interview), a situation that could result in impeachment of the child. Alternatively, the information not mentioned may seem crucial to establishing the likelihood of abuse or protecting the child.

Externally derived questions can vary in their degree of open-endedness. For example, take a situation in which a child has previously indicated that fellatio was among the sexual acts, but fails to mention it response to a narrative cue, "Anything else?" The interviewer can ask if the child recalls "anything about mouths," rather than saying, "Didn't you tell the detective he put his penis in your mouth?"

Repeated Questions

Evaluators may be challenged in the legal arena for asking repeated questions. The implication is that they coerced or programmed the child by repeating the same question until they have obtained the desired response. Nevertheless, there can be acceptable reasons for repeating a question: to check for consistency in the child's response, to obtain a response if initially the child did not answer the question, and to check for the accuracy of the child's response (because the interviewer thinks the child's initial response was inaccurate). A fourth reason an interviewer may repeat the question is because he/she does not remember the child's answer or that the question has already been asked.

A concern about repeating questions is that children will think their correct initial responses were incorrect and will change their answers.

Some practitioners and analogue researchers inoculate children against changing their responses by telling them the same question may be asked more than once, but that does not mean the child's answer is wrong (e.g., Merchant & Toth, 2001; Saywitz, Geiselman, & Bornstein, 1992). Interviewers can also preface a repeated question by saying, "I just want to make sure I got it right," as a way of reassuring the child that the interviewer is not questioning the original response.

There is some analogue research indicating that children are more likely than adults to change a correct response to a yes/no question when repeated (Warren & Marsil, 2002). However, the general research findings from analogue studies are that repeated, neutral questions do not increase inaccuracy, may elicit more may enhance recollection (Lyon, 1999b; Poole & White, 1991, 1993, 1995). These benefits are stronger for within-session repeated questions.

When interviewers want to repeat a question that the child has not answered or a question thought to have been answered incorrectly, the best practice is to ask the question slightly differently. Initial failure to respond may be because the interviewer's question did not trigger the child's memory, or the child conceptualizes the event differently. For example, a question such as, "Did something happen to your peepee?" may not be a specific enough trigger, but "Did your peepee get hurt?" may trigger recollection. Illustrative of how conceptualization affects responses, Poole and Lamb (1998) cite court testimony in which a 5-year-old girl responded "no" when asked if she put her mouth on the offender's penis, but "yes" when asked if the offender put his penis in her mouth (pp. 163–164).

A child may have been unwilling to answer a particular question, for example, a question about abuse. Asking repeated questions in the hope the child will change the response is not advisable. If the child does eventually affirm abuse, the disclosure will be quite vulnerable to the challenge that the evaluator would not take "no" for an answer and coerced the child with repeated questions to change his/her response. Note also that in the analogue studies described above in the section on coercion, researchers repeated misleading questions in conjunction with other suggestive and coercive techniques and obtained a large proportion of false positives (Finnila et al., 2003; Garven et al., 2000).

There is a difference between repeating a question and asking numerous questions. Although it may be optimal to have the abuse-related phase consist of general or invitational questions with a few follow-up questions to gather details (Lamb, 1994; Yuille, 2002), in both analogue studies and research on actual cases, such patterns of disclosure are rare. It is usually necessary to ask many questions because considerable information is sought.

In an analogue study involving medical exams, Saywitz et al. (1991) provided children with 215 opportunities (with questions and anatomical dolls) in order to gather information about a single medical checkup. Similarly, Steward et al. (1996) employed about 100 questions to gather information about body touch during a single medical exam.

In sexual abuse cases, the interviewer may be gathering information about more than one event, and in some cases about sexual abuse that has persisted for years. Thus, one would anticipate needing many questions in real-world cases. In a study of actual sexual abuse cases by DeVoe and Faller (1999, 2002), it took children who revealed sexual abuse an average of 95 questions to disclose. Similarly, in research on interviews using the Memorandum of Good Practice (Home Office, 1992, 2002), Sternberg et al. (2001) found that interviewers made on average 207 "utterances," of which 145 were substantive.

Misleading Questions

A misleading question is a question that assumes a fact that is not true, which the child is explicitly or implicitly asked to confirm. Misleading questions are discussed in chapter 7 as a method of demonstrating the child's resistance to suggestion (Reed, 1996). They are also used extensively in analogue studies. Children are fairly resistant to isolated misleading questions, such as, "What color scarf was the nurse wearing?" (when she wasn't wearing one) (Goodman & Aman, 1990; Goodman et al., 1991; Rudy & Goodman, 1991; Saywitz et al., 1991). Repeated misleading and suggestive questioning, when coupled with other coercive techniques, can lead a substantial proportion of children to affirm false events (Ceci, Huffman et al., 1994; Finnila et al., 2003; Garven et al., 2000; Leichtman & Ceci, 1995).

Some professionals question the practice of asking children misleading questions in forensic interviews to check for suggestibility because children who have been sexually abused might associate this kind of "trickery" with their abuser's manipulations (Faller, 2003). In addition, although the interviewer may have gained an advantage in cases where children do not affirm a misleading question, they considerably disadvantage children who reply affirmatively. Analogue studies fail to find consistency in response to misleading questions unrelated to the target event and accuracy of their reports of target events (Reed, 1996).

SUMMARY AND CONCLUSION

Professionals writing about questioning techniques generally agree about the importance of using questions that are as open-ended as possible and resorting to more close-ended questions only as needed to gather information. Even within the preferred questions/probes, there is variability in question openness. In addition, the typologies of questions vary somewhat, as do opinions about particular types of questions.

Questioning strategies also need to vary depending upon whether the alleged abuse is recent or salient and whether the child has already disclosed. Appropriately interviewing children whose abuse is less salient, less certain, or undisclosed is more challenging and usually requires more close-ended questions.

Despite the level of consensus about acceptable and unacceptable questions, there are still many questioning issues where there is disagreement. Interviewers need to be mindful of these controversies as they interview children and be prepared to explain their choices about what questions they used.

Finally, Myers (1998) has challenged the categorization of particular questions as more or less preferred, rightly pointing out that the appropriateness of a particular question is dependent upon the larger context of the interview, especially on what content and disclosures preceded the question in point. For example, if the child has previously disclosed fondling, probing further by saying, "Now you told me he touched your penis, didn't you? (a leading question) Tell me more about that," would be an appropriate use of a leading question coupled with an invitation.

NOTE

1. Note that these two questions are called more close-ended focused questions, but their structure differs from "Tell me all about your dad." "What do you like about your dad?" is structurally a "wh" question, and "Are there any things you don't like?" is structurally a yes/no question. However, substantively they are questions that focus the child's attention on the father.

NINE

Media for Interviewing Children

Kathleen Coulborn Faller

In this chapter, media for communicating with children during interviews are discussed. The terms "tools," "props," and "interview
aids" are also used to refer to media. The advantages and disadvantages of using media are described, and relevant research and practice
related to anatomical dolls, anatomical drawings, and free drawings
are covered. These three are not the only media that professionals can
use. For example, interviewers may use dolls without private body
parts (Britton & O'Keefe, 1991; Samra & Yuille, 1996), a dollhouse
(Faller, 1993), or other props to facilitate communication with children.
Anatomical dolls, drawings, and free drawings appear to be used most
widely (e.g., Conte, Sorenson, Fogarty, & Dalla Rosa, 1991). Moreover,
there is research on both anatomical dolls and anatomical drawings
that professionals can use to guide practice. Although there is also
some research on free drawings, it is less directly relevant to interview practice.

ADVANTAGES AND DISADVANTAGES
OF USING MEDIA

In the 1980s and 1990s, professionals interviewing children for sexual
abuse commonly used media when interviewing children (Conte et al.,
1991), for example, anatomical dolls (e.g., Boat & Everson, 1988a, 1988b,
1993; Conte et al., 1991; Kendall-Tackett & Watson, 1991), puppets (e.g.,
Garven, Wood, & Malpass, 2000), and dollhouses (e.g., Faller, 2003). However, support for the use of media in child interviewing has declined,
and use of verbal communication with children has been emphasized.
This change is inspired mostly by challenges to anatomical dolls, especially in legal arenas.

Advantages of Media

There are a number of empirically and practically sound advantages of using media. First, young children may be more accomplished in communicating by demonstrations than in words. Most children manipulate objects and engage in play with objects before they are very verbal (Vizard & Trantner, 1988). Thus, media can serve as language substitutes (Thierry, Lamb, Orbach, & Pipe, 2005). Young children typically have more recessive language than active language (A. G. Walker, 1999). As a consequence, they may be able to understand a simple question and respond by showing on their own bodies or with media but incapable of providing a verbal response (Faller, 2003).

Second, use of media affords the interviewer two modes of communication, verbal and actions. When children both show and tell, interviewers often can place greater confidence in the information children provide (Faller, 2003). Similarly, if a child's verbal communication about an event is sparse or unclear, the interviewer may be able to clarify the verbal communication using media.

Third, use of media may allow the interviewer to collect detailed information using fewer questions; questions could potentially lead the child or contaminate the child's information. Thus, when gathering details about an abusive incident, the interviewer can ask the child to show with an appropriate medium what happened, rather than ask a series of close-ended questions (Thierry et al., 2005).

Fourth, certain media provide children cues needed to trigger their memories (G. M. Davies, 1991; Thierry et al., 2005). For example, a body map or anatomical drawing may be needed to trigger the child's recollection of details of an experience (American Professional Society on the Abuse of Children, 1995).

Fifth, media may overcome children's reluctance to disclose (Faller, 2003). This reluctance may derive from distress associated with speaking about the abuse, admonitions not to say "dirty words" needed to explain the abuse, or specific threats of consequences of telling. Some children take literally an instruction by the offender or others not to tell what happened and do not interpret this instruction as preventing them from showing or writing responses.

A sixth and related advantage is that, for some children, it may be less stressful to show than to tell what happened. However, balanced against this advantage is concern about traumatic reenactment. That is, by requiring the child to reenact the abusive experience, the interviewer may cause additional trauma.

Finally, if the interviewer has concerns about programming, media may be helpful in resolving this concern. If an adult has programmed a child or told the child to make a false allegation, very likely this instruction will have been given verbally. It would be highly unusual for an adult to obtain anatomical dolls or drawings and use them when programming a child (Faller, 2003, 2005). Thus, the lack of capacity to demonstrate abuse with a prop after a verbal disclosure may raise questions about the truth of the verbal disclosure.

Disadvantages of Media

There are disadvantages to using media. First, probably the most salient potential disadvantage for interviewers is a challenge in the legal arena. Concern about these challenges may be the rationale for admonitions in interview guides *not* to use media (Merchant & Toth, 2001) and cautionary statements about their use (Poole & Lamb, 1998; State of Michigan, 1998, 2005). In order to address challenges to the use of media, interviewers are advised to acquaint themselves with research relevant to the medium being used, to follow any relevant practice guidelines, to know local practice, and to give forethought to decisions about when and which media to use. In addition, as noted below, there are issues regarding the use of media that need further research.

Second, in analogue studies, some media, such as doctor toys, can result in distortions and inaccuracies (Bruck, Ceci, & Francoeur, 2000; Bruck, Ceci, Francoeur, & Renick, 1995; Goodman & Aman, 1990; Goodman, Quas, Batterman-Faunce, Riddelsberger, & Kuhn, 1997; Salmon, Bidrose, & Pipe, 1995; Steward et al., 1996). These toys are usually presented to children along with anatomical dolls. Similarly, in analogue studies when these media are used with 2- to 4-year olds, in conjunction with leading and misleading questions, they may result in inaccurate reports (Bruck, Ceci, & Francoeur, 2000; Bruck, Ceci, Francoeur, & Renick, 1995).

A third and related disadvantage is that media may engender play or fantasy. This is not surprising, since children's prior experience with, for example, dolls or a dollhouse has been in play activities. Interviewers are advised to tell children, when presenting them with anatomical dolls, that "these are special dolls and not for play." However, practice suggests that this admonition is not always successful. Moreover, as discussed below, some uses of anatomical dolls, specifically as a memory stimulus and a screening tool, call for free play with the dolls.

Thierry et al. (2005) describe research involving a review of 178 videotapes of child protection services (CPS) interviews conducted from 1986 to 1994. In these interviews, anatomical dolls were employed and other toys were present. They note that fewer than 7% of children engaged in spontaneous play behavior (with the dolls or toys), but an additional 30% engaged in play behavior when invited to speculate about what may have happened to them. Because speculation may involve play or fantasy, it is not advised in eliciting information about possible sexual abuse, either with or without media.

Fourth, children and their caretakers may become upset by the use of media, such as anatomical dolls or drawings, because they depict private parts. Parents may argue that their children had heretofore never seen a male penis and should not have been exposed to penises during the interview. Research on the impact of anatomical dolls on children with (Cohn, 1991) and without (Boat, Everson, & Amaya-Jackson, 1996; Boat, Everson, & Holland, 1990; Simkins & Renier, 1996) a history of sexual abuse does not support this concern.

Finally, children age 3 and younger are usually not able to use dolls or anatomical drawings as representational objects (DeLoache, 1995; DeLoache & Marzolf, 1995; Hungerford, 2005; State of Michigan, 2005). Especially confusing for them is using a doll or drawing to represent themselves, because they are actually in the room. They are more likely to be able to show on their own bodies where they were touched and may be more capable in using a doll to represent someone not present, for example, the accused, than themselves. They understand the concept of two dolls doing something together before they grasp the concept of a doll representing a person (DeLoache & Marzolf, 1995).

Summary of Advantages and Disadvantages of Media Uses

To summarize, it appears that the advantages of using media outweigh the disadvantages. Nevertheless, interviewers should use media in a planned manner. Despite support for their use, there has been a decline in the use of media and an increased preference for reliance on verbal communication alone (e.g., Lamb, Hershkowitz, Sternberg, Boat, & Everson, 1996; Merchant & Toth, 2001; Poole & Lamb, 1998).

ANATOMICAL DOLLS: REVIEW AND CRITIQUE

Anatomical dolls have also been referred to as anatomically detailed (Morgan, 1995), anatomically or sexually correct (White, Strom, Santilli, & Halpin, 1986), anatomically explicit (Faller, 1993), anatomically complete (Morgan, 1995), and sexually anatomically correct (e.g., Cowling, 2006; Realmuto, Jensen, & Wescoe, 1990) dolls. Because the dolls usually have sewn-on eyes, navels, and nipples, terms implying that the dolls are "correct" and "complete" have been challenged (e.g., Wakefield & Underwager, 1988). Everson (e.g., Everson & Boat, 1997) has advocated for the uniform use of the term "anatomical dolls." Several different companies produce them commercially (e.g., Amamanta Family Dolls, Maple Hill, Migima Designs, Teach-A-Bodies), and some are home- and hand-made. These are cloth dolls, usually with mouth openings, private parts, anal openings, and secondary sex characteristics, as appropriate for the developmental stage, for example, breasts and pubic hair. The most widely used are Teach-A-Bodies (http://www.teach-a-bodies.com/), developed in 1981 for use in sex education of developmentally challenged children and adults. These dolls come in six developmental stages: (1) infant, (2) toddler, (3) school age, (4) adolescent, (5) adult, and (6) elder. They are male and female and are white, African American, and Hispanic. They come with clothing, including underwear, but no shoes.

In the late 1980s, Conte et al. (1991) conducted a survey of 212 sexual abuse experts. Among the experts, anatomical dolls were the most widely used medium (used by 92% of respondents) in interviews of children suspected of sexual abuse. Similarly, Kendall-Tackett and Watson (1991) reported that in a survey of 201 Boston area professionals conducting sexual abuse investigations, 80% of mental health professionals and 62% of law enforcement personnel indicated they employed anatomical dolls. In contrast is a more recent finding from the United Kingdom; Davey and Hill (1999) found in their survey of 60 investigative interviewers that only 36% used anatomical dolls. Similarly, in a study of 175 cases seen by 20 CPS workers from the states of Florida and North Carolina, Haskett, Wayland, Hutcheson, and Tavana (1995) reported that anatomical dolls were used in only 38 (21.7%) cases. These findings reflect a change in perspective about anatomical dolls.

There have been a number of challenges to the use of anatomical dolls. The most important is the criticism that anatomical dolls are suggestive because they have private parts; that is, they cause children who have not been sexually abused to say that they have. In part, their suggestiveness is asserted to be because they have disproportionately large private parts. Additional concerns are whether they elicit accurate information because they rely upon cued rather than free recall and whether there is "value added" by using anatomical dolls (Lamb et al., 1996; Poole & Lamb, 1998; Thierry et al., 2005). Finally, there have been concerns that they have not been used appropriately. When anatomical dolls first became widely used, professionals were concerned that anatomical dolls were being used as a substitute for a child-focused interview. That is, interviewers were merely presenting the child who may have been sexually abused with anatomical dolls and asking direct questions about sexual abuse. These challenges have been addressed in both research and practice guidelines.

Research and Guidelines

Despite change in attitude and practice related to anatomical dolls, of the various communication media, the dolls have the largest body of research. A literature search yields more than 100 citations related to "anatomically detailed dolls," most published in the last 15 years. Forty-three citations are data-based, peer-reviewed articles. These works involve studies of responses to the dolls by children without a sexual abuse history (Boat & Everson, 1994; de Marneff, 1997; Everson & Boat, 1994; Sivan, Schor, Koeppl, & Noble, 1988; Weill, Dawson, & Range,

1999), comparisons between children with and without a sexual abuse history (e.g., Cohn, 1991; Jampole & Webber, 1987; Kenyon-Jump, Burnette, & Robertson, 1991; Realmuto & Wescoe, 1992; White et al., 1986), and analogue research in which the dolls are used as anatomical models and communication aids (Bruck, Ceci, & Francoeur, 2000; Bruck, Ceci, Francoeur, & Renick, 1995; Goodman & Aman, 1990; Goodman, Quas, Batterman-Faunce, Riddelsberger, & Kuhn, 1994, 1997; Katz, Schoenfeld, Levanthal, & Cicchetti, 1995; Saywitz, Goodman, Nicholas, & Moan, 1991; Steward et al., 1996). Katz et al.'s (1995) study involved children with a history of sexual abuse, but the study tested the accuracy of their accounts of the sexual abuse medical exam using anatomical dolls. About a fourth of the children in the study by Steward et al. (1996) were seen at the child protection clinic, meaning they had a history of suspected abuse.

There are three field studies of how interviewers actually use anatomical dolls (Boat & Everson, 1996; Lamb et al., 1996; Thierry et al., 2005). In addition, there are six doctoral dissertations that focus on anatomical dolls (Bauer, 1994; Carlson, 1995; De Marneff, 1994; Geddie, 1994; Jedel, 1994; Moyer, 1994). There are also more than a dozen reviews of research (e.g., Bartlett-Simpson, Kneeshaw, & Schaffer, 1993; Boat & Everson, 1993; Ceci & Bruck, 1993; A. Elliott, O'Donohue, & Nickerson, 1993; Hungerford, 2005; Levy, Markovic, Kalinowski, & Ahart, 1995; Lie & Inman, 1991; Maan, 1991; Simkins & Renier, 1996; Skinner, 1996; Skinner & Berry, 1993; Vizard, 1991; Wolfner, Faust, & Dawes, 1994) and several commentaries on doll use (e.g., Everson & Boat, 1994, 1997, 2001; Faller, 2005).

Finally, several professional organizations (e.g., American Academy of Child and Adolescent Psychiatry, 1997b; American Psychological Association [Koocher, Goodman, White, & Friedrich, 1995]; American Professional Society on the Abuse of Children, 1995, 1997, 2002) have addressed the issue of use of anatomical dolls in sexual abuse assessments. The American Professional Society on the Abuse of Children (APSAC) is the professional organization that has addressed doll use most thoroughly and has developed guidelines specific to anatomical doll use (American Professional Society on the Abuse of Children, 1995).

To a considerable extent, research on anatomical dolls has been driven by challenges to the dolls. Moreover, research paradigms and interpretation of findings vary somewhat depending upon whether the researcher sees the dolls as a potentially useful medium for communicating with children (e.g., Goodman & Aman, 1990; Goodman et al., 1997; Saywitz et al., 1991; Steward et al., 1996) or a potentially dangerous source of false positive findings (e.g., Bruck, Ceci, & Francoeur, 2000; Bruck, Ceci, Francoeur, & Renick, 1995). Conclusions about the suggestiveness of anatomical dolls are drawn primarily from studies of the reactions of children with no history of sexual abuse to the dolls. These findings are complemented by those from comparative studies, involving children with and without a history of alleged sexual abuse and a study by Bays (1990) of the size of the genitalia and breasts of anatomical dolls. Most analogue studies find that use of anatomical dolls result in more information and more accurate information than relying on verbal communication alone. But anatomical dolls have not been shown to be superior to other media (Goodman, Quas et al., 1994, 1997; Saywitz et al., 1991; Steward et al., 1996).

The following sections cover research on the suggestibility of anatomical dolls and research comparing the effectiveness of anatomical dolls to other techniques.

Studies of Children With No Abuse History

Most of the research on the reactions of nonabused children to the dolls indicates that the dolls do not elicit sexual activity in the doll play of children with no prior sexual knowledge. However, children may be curious about the sexual parts of the dolls and insert fingers in the orifices (Everson & Boat, 1997, 2001).

Sivan et al. (1988) exposed 144 middle-class 3- to 8-year-olds from the Iowa City area to anatomical dolls. None of the children engaged in sexualized behavior with the dolls; only 2% of participants exhibited aggressive play with the dolls; and, as might be predicted, girls were more interested in the dolls than were boys. A more recent study (Dawson, Vaughan, & Wagner, 1992) with a smaller number of children (10 boys and 10 girls) reported no intercourse behavior demonstrated by the children, but higher percentages engaging in aggressive behavior than reported by Sivan and colleagues. Glaser and Collins (1998) describe a study in the United Kingdom involving 91 children, ages 3–6, who varied in ethnicity and socioeconomic status. Only five children engaged in play with sexual qualities, and in three cases, the source of the sexual knowledge could be identified. Three children engaged in aggression toward the dolls.

Everson and Boat (Boat & Everson, 1994; Boat et al., 1990, 1996; Everson & Boat, 1990, 1994, 1997) studied the reactions of a sample of 223 children 2–5 years old from Chapel Hill, North Carolina, who were varied demographically. In this study, children were given the instruction, "Show me what the dolls can do together," after the dolls were undressed. Six percent of Everson and Boat's subjects engaged in oral, anal, or genital intercourse using the dolls. None of the 2-year-olds demonstrated such behavior. On the other hand, older, black, and poor children had higher rates of sexual behavior. The rates for older, black, poor males were 27% (4 of 15) with the interviewer present and 22% (2 or 9) when the child was alone. This group was the only one to demonstrate sexualized behavior with the dolls in the presence of the interviewer. Everson and Boat (1997; Boat et al., 1990) interviewed the mothers of children demonstrating sexualized behavior and found most of them could offer relatively benign explanations for their children's sexual knowledge, usually having viewed pornography or observed adolescents involved in sexual activity.

Everson and Boat (1997) aggregated cases across studies to examine the rate of sexualized behavior among children, ages 2–8 years, without a history of sexual abuse. The total number of children is in excess of 550. The overall rate of sexualized behavior is 4%. They note that the frequency of sexualized behavior varies by culture and socioeconomic class, suggesting that both sexual knowledge and views about revealing that knowledge are influenced by demographics. They conclude, based upon their own research and that of others, that the dolls do not cause sexually naive children to act out sexually, but they do appear to provide sexually knowledgeable children a stimulus to engage in sexualized doll play.

Weill et al. (1999) compared responses of 16 children 3–6 years old with high scores on externalizing behaviors (acting out behaviors) to 44 children without externalizing behaviors. Both groups received structured interviews with anatomical dolls. Although the externalizing children demonstrated higher activity levels and more aggression toward the private body parts during the body parts inventory, they did not engage in sexual behaviors or verbalizations. These results suggest that the findings with anatomical dolls regarding children without a history of sexual abuse may also apply to aggressive children, but also see chapter 15 on rating of aggressive children with the Child Sexual Behavior Inventory.

In contrast, Bruck and colleagues (Bruck, Ceci, & Francoeur, 2000; Bruck, Ceci, Francoeur, & Renick, 1995) present findings from two analogue studies that they interpret as indicating anatomical dolls are suggestive, one with 3-year-olds and a second with 4-year-old boys and girls who received medical exams. Bruck and colleagues found that some children (they do not say how many) inserted fingers in the vaginal and anal openings of the anatomical dolls. Although this behavior is considered normal by interviewers and clinicians (e.g., Everson & Boat, 1994), these researchers thought the behavior would be viewed as suspicious of sexual abuse. Bruck and colleagues' studies are discussed in greater detail further below.

Comparisons of the Responses of Children With and Without a History of Sexual Abuse to Anatomical Dolls

Six studies compare the responses to anatomical dolls of children referred for sexual abuse assessment to those not so referred (August & Foreman, 1989; Cohn, 1991; Jampole & Webber, 1987; Kenyon-Jump et al., 1991; Realmuto & Wescoe, 1992; White et al., 1986). Altogether, about 200 children were involved in these studies, with Cohn's study having the largest number of children, 70. Thus, only a modest number of subjects have been involved in this sort of research. All but one study (Realmuto & Wesco, 1992) had equal numbers of children referred for sexual abuse and nonreferred children, and ages ranged from 2 to 8 years. Except for the research of August and Foreman (1989), which only included girls, the studies had both male and female subjects. The comparison children in these studies came from a variety of sources.

With the exception of the research of Cohn (1991) and Realmuto and Wesco (1992), studies found statistically significant and higher proportions of intercourse demonstration by children referred for sexual abuse evaluation. In order to arrive at this result, Kenyon-Jump et al. (1991) had to combine clear sexual behavior with suggestive behavior data, but there were only 18 children (nine with and nine without a history of abuse) altogether in their study. Cohn reported that 3% of subjects in both groups demonstrated intercourse with the dolls; however, the total exposure time of her children to the dolls was 11 minutes (in most other studies, it is about 30 minutes) (e.g., Boat & Everson, 1994; Everson & Boat, 1997; Sivan et al., 1988). Realmuto and Wesco's (1992) research involved having 14 clinicians rate whether 13 children had a history of sexual abuse and did not include any data analysis. They merely note that clinicians did better at rating children without a history than children with one and that the dolls did not elicit sexualized behavior from children without a history.

In all the studies, a substantial proportion of the children referred for sexual abuse did not demonstrate sexualized behavior with the dolls, the smallest proportion (10%) being found in the work of Jampole and Webber (1987), but they had only 10 children in each group. White et al. (1986), Realmuto and Wescoe (1992), and August and Foreman (1989) reported no sexual intercourse demonstrations among their nonreferred subjects.

Thus, it appears that sexually abused children are more likely to engage in sexualized behavior with anatomical dolls than are nonabused children. However, many abused children do not demonstrate sexual activity, and a small number of nonabused children do. The findings related to the comparison group research are consistent with the findings from the larger sample studies of children without a sexual abuse history. As noted above, the studies of normal populations find that dolls do not elicit sexual responses from children who are sexually naive, but can from children with sexual knowledge.

Genital Size on Anatomical Dolls

The final concern regarding anatomical doll suggestibility relates to their genitals. These have been asserted to be large relative to doll size (Gardner, 1992; Wakefield & Underwager, 1988). In addition, concerns have been raised that viewing the genitals is traumatic to interviewees (Naumann, 1985; Tylden, 1987). Research to date fails to support these assertions (e.g., Boat et al., 1996; Glaser & Collins, 1988).

Nevertheless, frustrated by such challenges, Bays (1990) set out to study size of genitalia with 17 adult male dolls and genitalia and breasts of 17 adult female dolls. She also reported on a preliminary study of nine pairs of male and female child dolls. Her findings were that the breasts and genitalia of adult dolls are either proportional or smaller than normal, except that with some penises it depends upon whether they are considered stretched or unstretched flaccid penises. With the child dolls, the vulvar openings were proportional to girls ages 4–10 and the penises proportional for boys ages 4–18. Bays admonishes doll manufacturers that they should make their juvenile penises the equivalent of those for boys 3 through 12.

With regard to the possible traumatic impact of exposure to anatomical dolls, Boat et al. (1991) followed up on 30 children 3–5 years old without a history of sexual abuse who participated in their anatomical doll study (Boat & Everson, 1994). The mothers of the children were interviewed to ascertain any negative impact of being exposed to unclothed dolls with genitals. The mothers did not perceive their children's participation in the study as having a negative impact. However, it did increase the children's awareness of private parts, with 50% of 3-year-olds and 75% of 4-year-olds being described as more sexually aware after being involved in the study.

Is There "Value Added" From Using Anatomical Dolls?

The initial response of interviewers and clinicians to anatomical dolls was that the dolls greatly enhanced their ability to obtain information about sexual abuse from children. The dolls were regarded as better than relying on verbal communication alone, and the dolls were thought to be superior to other media. The research findings, however, are not as supportive as practitioners would have anticipated (e.g., Bruck, Ceci, & Francoeur, 2000; Bruck, Ceci, Francoeur, & Renick, 1995; Saywitz et al., 1991; Steward et al., 1996; Thierry et al., 2005).

The research consists of both analogue and field studies. These studies compare children's reports assisted by anatomical dolls with reports relying solely on language or language and other media. Several analogue studies involve children receiving medical examinations (Bruck, Ceci, & Francoeur, 2000; Bruck, Ceci, Francoeur, & Renick, 1995; Goodman, Quas et al., 1994, 1997; Katz et al., 1995; Quas et al., 1999; Saywitz et al., 1991; Steward, 1989; Steward et al., 1996). There are also staged analogue studies in which anatomical dolls are employed to ask the child about the staged event (e.g., Aman & Goodman, 1990; Goodman & Aman, 1990). Six studies that can be used to explore the "value added" question involve children alleged to have been sexually abused (Britton & O'Keefe, 1991; Katz et al., 1995; Lamb et al., 1996; Leventhal, Hamilton, Rekedal, Tebano-Micci, & Eyster, 1989; Thierry et al., 2005). With notable exceptions (Bruck, Ceci, & Francoeur, 2000; Bruck, Ceci,

Francoeur, & Renick, 1995; Lamb et al., 1996; Thierry et al., 2005), these studies indicate that generally anatomical dolls improve children's responses to abuse-related queries when compared to questioning without props (Aman & Goodman, 1990; Katz et al., 1995; Leventhal et al., 1989; Steward, 1989; Steward et al., 1996) but that anatomical dolls are not superior to nonanatomical dolls (Aman & Goodman, 1990; Britton & O'Keefe, 1991; Samra & Yuille, 1996) or other media (Steward, 1989; Steward et al., 1996).

Analogue Studies

The medical exam studies by Saywitz et al. (1991) and Steward et al. (1996) both involve private parts touch and support the use of anatomical dolls. (These studies are described in greater detail in chapter 13.) Both of these studies found that a very small percentage of children provided information about private parts touch when interviewers rely on verbal communication that accesses free recall. However, if interviewers employed anatomical dolls and asked direct questions about private parts touch, a large percentage of children accurately indicate that the doctor (or nurse) touched their private parts. This procedure also resulted in a small increase in children falsely affirming private parts touch, with false positive findings higher for anal touch. Steward compared verbal communication only to verbal assisted by anatomical dolls, anatomical drawings, or a computer-assisted interview. In all of the assisted conditions, children revealed more and more accurate information, but dolls were not superior to drawings or the computer.

Goodman and colleagues (Goodman, Quas et al., 1994, 1997; Quas et al., 1999) conducted studies involving children's memory of voiding cystourethrogram fluoroscopy (VCUG). (These studies are described in chapter 2, which focuses on children's memory and suggestibility.) Because VCUG is an intrusive, painful, and humiliating procedure, it is a very good analogue for sexual abuse. In part of the research, anatomical dolls were used to gather information about the VCUG. In the doll use condition, children were given the dolls and doctor tools, some of which were used in the VCUG procedure and some of which were not. Thus, the study of the utility of anatomical dolls was confounded with other props. Despite this confounding of the doll condition, when the dolls were introduced, 70% of children reported the VCUG procedure, compared to 20% during free recall. The doctor tool props appeared to result in errors with 3- to 4-year-olds, but aided 5- to 6-year-olds and 7- to 10-year-olds.

As noted above, Bruck and colleagues (Bruck, Ceci, & Francoeur, 2000; Bruck, Ceci, Francoeur, & Renick, 1995) conducted two studies of private parts touch, one with 40 boys and girls 3 years old and one with 44 children 4 years old. The children were given a well-child exam, during which half of the children received a light touch on the genitals and buttocks. After the exam, first the children were asked direct questions about genital and anal touch with anatomical dolls ("Did Dr. F touch you here?" as the interviewer pointed to a private body part). Then they were asked leading or misleading (misleading if no such touch had occurred) questions, "Show on the doll how Dr. F touched your buttocks" (the child's name for the relevant body part was used). Finally, they were commanded to show on their own bodies how Dr. F touched their private parts (this probe was used only with children who had actually experienced the touch). These researchers found high rates of inaccuracy among both 3- and 4-year-olds interviewed within minutes of a medical exam, regardless of method of information gathering.

Both the 3- and 4-year-olds provided high rates of false negative responses (~50%) to these direct questions and commands, and the 3-year-old girls provided high rates of false positives (~50%) in all three questioning conditions (Bruck, Ceci, & Francoeur, 2000; Bruck, Ceci, Francoeur, & Renick, 1995). A response was scored incorrect if the child touched, for example, the anus instead of the vagina in response to a command to show on the doll or themselves how the doctor touched the vagina. In addition, apparently to support their hypothesis that the anatomical dolls are not useful, the researchers recoded behaviors with dolls, departing from their original definition of a correct response. Thus, initially any demonstration of touching, rubbing, or insertion to the correct private part was considered an acceptable response to the command, "Show me on the doll how Dr. F. touched your vagina/buttocks." However, since Dr. F. only lightly touched the relevant body part, anything other than a touch was recoded a false positive. As a result, the correct replies for the 3-year-old girls who received the private parts exam decreased from 71% to 38%.

Such high proportions of incorrect responses are not found in other doll studies, even those involving 3-year-olds (e.g., Goodman & Aman, 1990; Saywitz et al., 1991; Steward et al., 1996). Nevertheless, in part, the results may derive from the young age of the children. The mean age of children in the 3-year-olds study is 35 months, and that of the 4-year-olds is 49 months. Other research indicates that children 3 years of age have difficulty using dolls as representational objects (DeLoache, 1995; DeLoache & Marzolf, 1995). If this were the sole cause of the inaccuracies, one would expect the 4-year-olds to do better when asked to show on the doll, but the only statistically significant age difference was for 4- versus 3-year-olds who received no body touch, with the 4-year-olds being less likely to affirm falsely and demonstrate private parts touching using anatomical dolls.

More likely, the touching in these studies was not memorable— a light touch on private parts—when presumably many other parts of the body were handled. Young preschoolers are likely to remember salient and central, but not peripheral, events (Brainerd & Ornstein,

1991; Goodman & Clarke-Stewart, 1991; Lyon, 1999a). The light touches on private parts are arguably peripheral to the medical exam. Furthermore, these findings do not indicate that anatomical dolls create inaccuracies; the children were inaccurate in all three questioning conditions. A final confusing component of the study is that the researchers state that children in the no private parts touch condition were then reexamined so the physician could do the anal and genital exam (Bruck, Ceci, & Francoeur, 2000). However, such an exam should involve more than a light touch on the genitals and anus.

Goodman and Aman (1990; Aman & Goodman, 1990) conducted a staged analogue study in which anatomical dolls, dolls without private parts, and other props were employed to assist 3- and 5-year-old children in reporting an event. Children were asked a range of questions, including leading and misleading ones. The staged event was children going into a trailer with a stranger and engaging in a range of activities, including putting on dress-up clothes, being touched by the stranger on the nose, and having something to eat. Both anatomical dolls and dolls without private parts were useful in assisting children's reports. Since the event did not involve private parts, one would not expect anatomical dolls to be superior to dolls without private parts in helping children recount the event. The researchers also report that the anatomical dolls did not result in any false allegations of private parts touch.

Thus, in analogue studies, the anatomical dolls appear to elicit more information when the research involves memorable private parts touch. However, they may also elicit a very small amount of inaccurate information, especially from young preschool children.

Field Studies

There are two studies by Lamb and colleagues that take advantage of existing videotapes of CPS interviews (Lamb et al., 1996; Thierry et al., 2005). See also Boat and Everson (1996); discussed below. Because these studies involve actual interviews, they are very instructive, but when the interviews were conducted, there was no plan to use them in research on anatomical dolls. Consequently, there was no opportunity for experimental manipulation, for example, randomly assigning interviewers to use and not use anatomical dolls.

The 1996 study draws from 97 videotapes of child protection interviews (Boat & Everson, 1996). In eight of these interviews, the workers relied on verbal communication only. The Lamb et al. (1996) research matches these eight cases on demographics with twice the number in which dolls were used, yielding a total sample of 24. The study finds that doll interviews do not elicit more information than interviews without dolls, and that open-ended questions were the predictor of information from the child, not the use of dolls. The interview protocol called for introduction of the dolls after an attempt to elicit information verbally, and researchers note that children with whom the dolls were used were less verbally productive than those in the no-doll cases before introduction of the dolls, although this difference is not statistically significant.

The more recent study involves a larger sample size, 178 interviews of children 3–12 years old, and in all of them, anatomical dolls were employed (Thierry et al., 2005). Although the researchers do not report specifically on whether all of the interviews involve disclosure of sexual abuse, presumably they did. The researchers examined whether more information was elicited verbally or with dolls. In 87% of interviews, the dolls were introduced after an initial verbal disclosure. For the most part, results for younger (3–6 years) and older (7–12 years) children are reported separately. The researchers coded the following child utterances: (1) new details, (2) repeated details, (3) contradictory details, and (4) play with anatomical dolls versus other toys in the interview setting.

The proportion of new details out of total information provided by the child, relying on verbal communication alone, is higher than the proportion of new information with dolls. For the younger children, the proportion was 75% new details with verbal communication only and 59% with anatomical dolls. For older children, the proportion of new detail relying on verbal communication only was 85%, and that with anatomical dolls was 66%. There were no differences in the repeated details for younger children, with and without anatomical dolls (about one-fifth), but older children were less likely to repeat details in the verbal only parts of the interview (19% verbal vs. 27% anatomical dolls). These findings are difficult to interpret because, in most cases, dolls were introduced after some verbal disclosure, and the researchers do not control for the amount of time in the verbal and doll conditions. In addition, the type of question asked has to be taken into account, and, as might be expected, interviewers asked different types of questions with older (more open-ended) and younger (more close-ended) children. Interviewers asked fewer questions of all types when employing the dolls. For example, when using anatomical dolls, they asked on average 1.31 option-posing (multiple choice and yes/no) questions per interview, compared to 28.59 when relying on verbal communication.

However, when the number of questions without and with dolls is controlled for, children reported as many details in response to open-ended invitations (tell me), option-posing questions (yes/no and multiple choice), and directives ("wh" questions) with and without dolls. The proportion of contradictory details was 1% or less in all conditions. Both age groups were more likely to engage in play and ambiguous enactments in the doll condition than without dolls, but the proportion was higher for the younger children.

Although in both of these studies of CPS interviews the researchers question the "value added" from the introduction of anatomical dolls, professionals should be cautious about accepting this conclusion. Neither study was able to control whether, when, or how the dolls were used, for example, the length of interview time before the dolls were introduced or the extent of abuse disclosure before the dolls were introduced. In addition, in all interviews studied, CPS interview guidelines called for an initial attempt to elicit information verbally before the introduction of anatomical dolls. One would therefore not expect the use of dolls to elicit more information than verbal communication only, but rather to elicit additional, clarifying, and corroborating information.

Anatomical Doll Functions and Strategies for Using Them

As noted above, when anatomical dolls were first employed in sexual abuse interviews, there was a concern that they were being used as a substitute for a good interview. Thus, many writers warn that anatomical dolls should not be used by persons who are untrained in their use (e.g., American Professional Society on the Abuse of Children, 2002; State of Michigan, 1998). It is not clear, however, who should provide training, what it should consist of, and how much training is needed. Presently, the national programs that routinely offer training in the use of anatomical dolls are Finding Words sponsored by the American Prosecutors Research Institute (Walters, Holmes, Bauer, & Veith, 2003) and the Corner House Interagency Child Abuse Evaluation and Training Center (Ellefson, 2006). A second strategy for assuring proper use of anatomical dolls is the development of guidelines for their use (e.g., American Professional Society on the Abuse of Children, 1995). Guidelines describe the functions of anatomical dolls in the interview process and strategies for employing them.

Anatomical Dolls Functions

Everson and Boat (1994, 1997; see also American Professional Society on the Abuse of Children, 1995) found 20 sets of guidelines for using anatomical dolls. From these they derived six uses or functions for the dolls. The functions and, in parentheses, the number of guidelines endorsing them are as follows: a comforter (2), an ice breaker (5), an anatomical model (16), a demonstration aid (18), a memory stimulus (11), and screening tool (11). Thierry et al. (2005), in their study of anatomical doll use by CPS workers, described two functions, as a memory stimulus and a language substitution (demonstration aid). They found that older children were more likely to rely on them as a memory stimulus and younger children as a language substitution.

Boat and Everson's survey demonstrates convergence of views as well as some differences of opinion about how to use the dolls. There is universal support by professionals who see the dolls as having value (e.g., American Professional Society on the Abuse of Children, 1995; Everson & Boat, 1994, 1997; Faller, 2003) for the opinion that anatomical dolls are not a psychological test but a communication aid (American

Professional Society on the Abuse of Children, 1995, 1997; Everson & Boat, 1994, 1997; Faller, 2003; Koocher et al., 1995; Morgan, 1995; White et al., 1986). What this means is that the reaction of children to anatomical dolls, by itself, cannot be used to differentiate sexually abused from nonabused children. As the research comparing children with and without a sexual abuse history indicates, the fact that children fail to demonstrate sexual activity with dolls does not mean they have not been sexually abused. Conversely, as the research on children without a history of sexual abuse indicates, the fact that children do show sexual activity does not mean that they have been sexually abused, because sexual knowledge can come from sources other than sexual abuse.

Reviews of the anatomical doll literature that find the dolls lack psychometric properties have an expectation that they are a psychological test and that professionals should be able to tell whether children have been sexually abused merely by observing their interactions with the dolls (Elliott et al., 1993; Skinner & Berry, 1993; Wolfner et al., 1994). There are additional expectations that there should be a standardized method for doll presentation, which there is not, and a scoring system for children's responses. In addition, some of the dissertations addressing anatomical doll use make an assumption that there is an "anatomical doll test" (e.g., Bauer, 1994; Carlson, 1997; Moyer, 1994). Since these doctoral students have chosen to study an unendorsed function for the dolls, their research does not support the dolls' efficacy.

Most reviews of the research support their utility in communication with children, serving as an anatomical model and a demonstration aid in sexual abuse evaluations (e.g., Aldridge, 1998; Boat & Everson, 1993; Everson & Boat, 2001; Lie & Inman, 1991; Maan, 1991; Simkins & Renier, 1996). When the dolls are used an anatomical model, they used to conduct a "body parts inventory," that is, as a means for identifying the child's names for the private parts and discussing body part functions (e.g., American Professional Society on the Abuse of Children, 1995; Faller, 2003). When the dolls are used as a demonstration aid, they function as a medium for assisting the child in disclosure of sexual abuse (Boat & Everson, 1994; Ellefson, 2006; Everson & Boat, 1994; Faller, 2003). They may be used to (1) facilitate, (2) clarify, or (3) corroborate an abuse disclosure (Faller, 2003). As noted above, there is some research that indicates that the dolls (and other props) can facilitate disclosure of private parts touching.

In addition, a substantial number of guidelines support use of dolls as a screening tool (e.g., American Professional Society on the Abuse of Children, 1995; Everson & Boat, 1994). That is, a child's statements or demonstration of sexualized behavior with the dolls raises concern about possible sexual abuse. The interviewer then inquires about the behavior the child has demonstrated to determine the source of the child's statements and sexual knowledge.

There is support for use of anatomical dolls as a memory stimulus (Thierry et al., 2005). The sight of the private parts on the dolls may jog the child's memory and may result in a statement or demonstration that provides information about sexual activity. Research cited above comparing the effectiveness of anatomical dolls (or other aids) to mere questioning supports their use as a memory stimulus (e.g., Everson & Boat, 1997, 2002). The research on responses of children without a history of sexual abuse to anatomical dolls and the studies comparing the responses of children with and without a history of sexual abuse to the dolls rely on their functions as a screening tool and a memory stimulus. Nevertheless, that children's reactions should serve only as a screen is supported by the findings of Everson and Boat's (1994) research that nonabused, but sexually knowledgeable, children may be stimulated by the dolls to engage them in sexualized behavior.

Strategies for Using Anatomical Dolls

In part, because guidelines differ regarding what they describe as the dolls' primary functions, researchers differ in how they recommend the dolls be used. For example, writers differ in their advice about when the dolls should be presented. Some suggest that they should be presented during rapport building, before any questions are asked that might indicate possible sexual abuse (Boat & Everson, 1988a & b; White, Strom, & Quinn, n.d.). This is appropriate if the dolls are to be used as an anatomical model. Boat and Everson (1988a & b) suggest observing the child in free play with the dolls after they have been presented and before questions are asked. This strategy would allow for doll use as a screening tool and a memory stimulus.

Others suggest the dolls be presented later, after the child has begun to disclose, has made a verbal statement (American Professional Society on the Abuse of Children, 1995; Faller, 1993, 2003), or has exhausted verbal recall (J. Aldridge et al., 2004; Merchant & Toth, 2001; Yuille, 2002). In such cases, the dolls serve as a demonstration aid, that is, as a means of facilitating descriptive information from a child whose language skills are limited or who is reluctant to talk, as a medium for clarifying verbal statements, or as a way of corroborating disclosures (Faller, 2003). However, requiring verbal disclosure first would defeat the use of the dolls as a demonstration aid for children who are fearful or reluctant to disclose or as a memory stimulus and screening tool (American Professional Society on the Abuse of Children, 1995).

How many and what type of dolls the interviewer is advised to present vary depending upon their function. When describing dolls as an anatomical model, writers recommend two, three, or four. As an ice breaker, it might be useful to present four or more so the child becomes desensitized to the dolls and sees that the interviewer is comfortable talking about private parts, before any questions are asked about possible abuse. However, if the dolls are to be used as a demonstration aid, the interviewer might assist the child in choosing dolls of the same number, race, age, and gender as the people in the circumstance in which the child may have been sexually abused.

Guidelines advising the use of dolls as an anatomical model instruct the interviewer to assist the child in undressing them and to have the child identify the body parts and their functions, including the sexual ones. This is good practice because it assures accurate communication about private parts. In addition, it allows the interviewer to assess some aspects of competency (the child has names for body parts and knows their functions), and it can serve as a screening tool (if the child, in describing the functions of private parts, reveals advanced sexual knowledge). However, failure to present the dolls in this manner, or asking the child to identify the private parts because the interviewer is using the dolls only as a demonstration aid or a memory stimulus, does not invalidate the assessment.

White, Strom, and Quinn (n.d.) advocate use of dolls only as an anatomical model and provide 14 questions about body parts, with instructions that the interviewer should ask these about sexual and nonsexual parts. Their advice does not allow for other doll functions, nor does it allow the interviewer to vary doll use according to case circumstances.

Faller (1993) suggested three possible scenarios for doll use, which allow them to serve various functions, and stated these scenarios should not be considered inclusive. The scenarios are as follows. The child may spontaneously initiate interaction with the dolls because they are present in the room, and the interviewer facilitates their use. The interviewer introduces the dolls after the child has begun discussion of sexual abuse to facilitate, clarify, or corroborate disclosures. Finally, the interviewer presents the dolls without any cues from the child in order to initiate a discussion of body parts if other attempts to understand whether or not the child has been sexually abused are unsuccessful.

Morgan (1995) recommends caution in using anatomical dolls because they have been subject to legal challenges and suggests introducing them after the child has indicated sexual abuse has occurred. She says that dolls may be presented either clothed or unclothed, but clothing may need to be put on for the child to use them to demonstrate the abuse. Morgan recommends a period of unstructured exploration of the dolls after they have been introduced, and then a body parts inventory. The interviewer returns to a discussion of the child's prior disclosure after the inventory and asks the child to choose appropriate dolls and demonstrate what happened. Follow-up questions are employed.

Yuille (2002) is concerned about the dangers of using anatomical dolls. He includes their use under optional methods in the Stepwise Interview and advises relying on verbal disclosure whenever possible.

He states, however, that dolls may be needed with young children, but they should never be used to elicit a disclosure, only to clarify one.

Boat and Everson (1996) conducted a study to determine the extent to which child protection workers in a state that employed dolls extensively and videotapes their interviews used them according to the functions identified in guidelines. Altogether, Boat and Everson reviewed 97 videotapes representing 60% of the counties that videotape interviews. Anatomical dolls were used in more than 80% of the interviews in the study. They report findings separately for younger and older children. No uses of anatomical dolls that had not been identified in Boat and Everson's review of guidelines were identified in the videotapes. The most common use of the dolls was as an anatomical model (93% for 2- to 5-year-olds and 92% for 6- to 12-year-olds), followed by their use as a demonstration aid (71% for 2- to 5-year-olds and 89% for 6- to 12-year-olds). A primary focus of the study was to identify worker misuses of anatomical dolls. No serious misuses of the dolls, such as making them engage in sexual behavior or using them as a psychological test, were noted. The most common problem the researchers noted was the introduction of the dolls before the child had exhausted verbal recall.

Similarly, the study by Thierry et al. (2005) cited above examined use of anatomical dolls in 178 interviews, conducted from 1986 to 1994. They found that in 87% of cases, child protection workers introduced anatomical dolls after some initial verbal disclosure and in 62% of cases when the central details of the abuse had been provided. They state, however, that children had seldom exhausted their free recall abilities (they do not indicate how they knew this or what proportion of the children they represented).

Although Boat and Everson (1996) cite introduction of the dolls before free recall is complete as a problem, and Thierry et al. (2005) believe that interviewers should make sure the child has exhausted free recall before introduction of the dolls, this is a relatively recent view of the best way to gather information. This would not have been the dominant view when these interviews in either of these studies were conducted (e.g., Faller, 1993; Morgan, 1995).

Summary

The assertion that anatomical dolls cause nonabused children to state they have been abused is not supported by the existing research. Anatomical doll research on whether the dolls assist children in providing information about abuse is somewhat mixed, but generally supports their utility.

Professionals recommend using anatomical dolls in various ways, which vary depending upon their function. The greatest support is for their use as a demonstration aid, but they can also be used to conduct a body parts inventory, preparatory to invitational and focused questions about possible abuse. No specific way of using anatomical dolls has been empirically shown to be superior, but there is consensus among professionals that there is no "anatomical doll test" for sexual abuse.

Interviewers are probably safe in taking their cues from the child and varying their doll technique according to the function the dolls are serving and the circumstances of the case. However, the dolls should not be used in a leading manner, for example, asking the child to show with the dolls how or where the alleged perpetrator touched the child, when the child has not indicated there was any such activity (American Professional Society on the Abuse of Children, 1995; Bruck, Ceci, & Francoeur, 2000; Bruck, Ceci, Francoeur, & Renick, 1995). Given the current controversy over anatomical dolls, interviewers should be mindful that using dolls may result in greater challenges to the child's disclosures than if dolls were not used and should expect to provide a rationale for how anatomical dolls were employed.

ANATOMICAL DRAWINGS: REVIEW AND CRITIQUE

Anatomical drawings are so called because they are unclothed representations of the human body and provide details of the body parts, including the private parts. The first and most widely available version was developed by Groth and Stevenson (1990). Although they describe them as useful in the investigation and treatment of child sexual abuse (Groth & Stevenson, 1990), in reality they have been employed mostly in forensic interviews (e.g., State of Michigan, 2005). The Groth and Stevenson (1990) drawings come in five developmental stages: (1) preschooler, (2) school age, (3) adolescent, (4) adult, and (5) elder. The drawings are of both males and females, with front and back views, and African American and white. More recently, forensic interviewing programs have developed their own series of pictures (e.g., CARES Alaska, which has created pictures that can be used to represent Native Alaskan children and adults). In addition, for field studies conducted by the National Institute of Child Health and Human Development (NICHD) in collaboration with interview sites, a gender-neutral childlike drawing has been developed (J. Aldridge et al., 2004; Brown, Lamb, Pipe, Orbach, & Lewis, 2005).

Less has been written about the use of anatomical drawings in interviewing children thought to have been sexually abused than about anatomical dolls. However, Conte et al. (1991) reported that almost two-thirds of the experts responding to their survey used anatomical drawings, and Kendall-Tackett (1992), in a report from a survey of 201 Boston area professionals assessing sexual abuse, found that 47% employ anatomical drawings. Other, later surveys found smaller proportions of professionals using anatomical drawings. In Boat and Everson's (1996) study of CPS videotapes described in the preceding section, 10% of interviewers employed anatomical drawings. Similarly, in their report on 175 interviews conducted by 20 CPS workers, Haskett et al. (1995) found only 20 (11.4%) involved the use of anatomical drawings. In their research review related to dolls and anatomical drawings, Everson and Boat (2002) noted the paucity of research related to drawings, but since that time anatomical drawings have been the subject of analogue and field studies.

It appears, however, that some practitioners have turned to anatomical drawings as a substitute for anatomical dolls, because the drawings have not been attacked vigorously (Ellefson, 2006; Everson & Boat, 2002; State of Michigan, 2005). In addition, interviewers are employing a gingerbread-shaped drawing, which is a body outline with no private parts to avoid challenges that genitals on drawings are leading or traumatizing to children (Faller, 2003).

Research

A modest number of studies have examined the utility of anatomical drawings either compared to verbal communication only or compared to other media (J. Aldridge et al., 2004; Brown et al., 2005, Steward et al., 1996; Willcock, Morgan, & Hayne, 2003).

As noted above, Steward (1989; Steward et al., 1996) compared the amount and accuracy of information about medical procedures elicited using verbal communication only, anatomical drawings, anatomical dolls, and a computer-assisted interview with 3- to 6-year-olds. The anatomical drawings were found to be superior to verbal questioning, although not superior to other media.

More recently, Lamb, in collaboration with British colleagues (J. Aldridge et al., 2004), employed a human figure drawing in forensic interviews with 90 children 4–14 years old who may have been sexually abused. These children were interviewed by police officers, first using the NICHD protocol (e.g., Lamb & Sternberg, 1999; also see chapter 7). After the children had exhausted verbal recall, the interviewers showed them the childlike NICHD human figure drawing and asked a series of focused questions, which varied depending upon whether or not the children had disclosed abuse. On average, the drawing elicited 86 new forensically relevant details. The drawing was especially productive with children 4–7 years of age. It elicited, on average 94, new forensically relevant details from the younger children, 27% of the total information from them. Although the authors caution that the drawing information relied on recognition memory, rather than free recall memory (see chapter 2), which may be less accurate, the study demonstrates the efficacy of drawings when interviewing for sexual abuse.

Brown et al. (2005) used the NICHD interview protocol and childlike drawing to evaluate in 112 children 5 and 6 years old the accuracy of their memories of a staged event that occurred at school. The event involved a photographer who also touched the children in the process of taking pictures. Children were interviewed in three different conditions: (1) the NICHD drawing with a general question about touching and then specific questions about touching body parts (three correct and three incorrect queries; e.g., "Did the photographer touch your knees?"), (2) the NICHD drawing with feedback about the correctness of their information in response to a general question about touch, and then specific questions, and (3) general questions and then specific questions about touch, which could be made more specific if the first specific question resulted in no report. The findings are generally that although 60% of children reported new information in response to specific questions, a large proportion of it was inaccurate. There were large numbers of false negatives, 56% to specific questions, and there were also false positives, but a smaller proportion. The drawing did not provide improvement in the accuracy of children's responses. The researchers conclude that the touch part of the staged event with the photographer was not salient and therefore was not encoded.

Willcock et al. (2003) employed drawings of clothed children (even they call the drawings anatomically detailed) to test the accuracy of memories of 125 children 5 and 6 years old who varied by socioeconomic status. These children experienced a staged event as part of a visit to a fire station. A male confederate touched the children on the head, shoulders, and under the arms as he assisted them in putting on a firefighter's costume. A month later, children were interviewed and asked to use the drawing to indicate where the confederate touched them while helping them put on the costume. Overall, 32% of children failed the test by indicating they had been touched below the waist and 10% indicated genital touch. Children of lower socioeconomic status were more likely to make these errors. Thinking that the inaccurate responses might have been the result of the long delay and the lack of salience of the event, Willcock and colleagues repeated the costume-donning part of the study in a learning laboratory with 47 children. Children were interviewed immediately, 24 hours, and 1 month after the event. There were no errors regarding the places of touch immediately after the event, but 40% errors at 24 hours and 30% at 1 month. The researchers conclude that the children of lower socioeconomic status had difficulty using the drawings to represent themselves and that children could provide accurate responses immediately after the event.

The findings from the four studies are inconsistent. The most likely explanation is probably differences in the salience of the touch, with the touch of the last two studies not being a central part of the event. Even in Willcock et al.'s (2003) second experiment, the touching lacked salience because it was embedded in putting on the firefighter costume. Additional research needs to be undertaken, however, to understand more about the circumstances in which anatomical drawings can be helpful to children and elicit accurate information.

Practice

Anatomical drawings are employed extensively by medical staff conducting physical examinations of abused children to document injuries and their location. As noted, the first set of drawings to be used in interviews with children was developed by Groth and Stevenson (1990) for Forensic Mental Health Associates which published and marketed these drawings. In their directions for the use of his drawings, Groth and Stevenson suggest that the child be given a set of the drawings copied from the booklet and asked to choose the drawing that looks most like her/him and one that looks like the offender. The child is then asked to mark on the drawings where the offender touched/abused the child, or the child is asked multiple choice questions about the body parts ("Did he touch you on the penis, the buttocks, or somewhere else?"—the interviewer pointing to the parts on the drawing). If the child indicates she/he or the offender was clothed or partially clothed, clothing is to be drawn on the pictures. Groth and Stevenson also suggest that the drawings might be used to clarify something in a free drawing or as a prelude to the introduction of the anatomical dolls. Because of increased concerns about the suggestibility of multiple choice questions in the years since Groth and Stevenson's drawings were developed, probably interviewers should use more open-ended probes, such as "Show (or mark) where you were touched." There are no empirical data related to Groth and Stevenson's instructions for drawing use.

Anatomical drawings can serve many of the functions Everson and Boat (2002) describe for anatomical dolls. The drawings can be used as an icebreaker, an anatomical model, a demonstration aid, a memory stimulus, and a screening tool. The research of J. Aldridge et al. (2004) demonstrates their effectiveness, especially with young children, as an anatomical model, a demonstration aid, and a memory stimulus. Steward (1989; Steward et al., 1996) noted that drawings were less useful than anatomical dolls when children needed to show how they were genitally and anally touched, especially penetration. Similarly, Faller (1993) stated that it is more difficult for children to demonstrate interaction between two or more individuals with pictures than with dolls. Interviewers should also bear in mind the findings of Brown et al. (2005) and Willcock et al. (2003), which did not demonstrate any particular utility of drawings.

Some interviewers use anatomical drawings to conduct a body parts inventory during the rapport-building stage of the interview (e.g., Ellefson, 2006). Interviewers may then reintroduce the drawings and ask questions focused on body parts during the abuse-related stage of the interview. Other interviewers use drawings only in the abuse-related phase of the interview. For example, if other methods fail to resolve concerns about sexual abuse, the interviewer introduces the drawings, conducts a body parts inventory, and then might point to the vagina and, using the child's term for this private part, ask if "anything has ever happened to" or "something happened to" this part (Faller, 2003).

Anatomical drawings can be useful after a child has made a verbal disclosure to clarify or corroborate the child's verbal disclosure. When used to clarify or corroborate a disclosure, the interviewer and the child can choose appropriate drawings, usually ones representing the child and the offender. The interviewer then asks the child to mark each part of the child drawing where something happened. The interviewer then asks the child to say what happened to each part the child has marked. A similar process can be employed with the offender drawing. The child is asked to mark each part the offender used and then explain what the offender did with each part.

Anatomical drawings have an advantage over anatomical dolls in that the copies employed in the interview can become a part of the case record. The child or the interviewer, if the child is unable, can write on the relevant drawings the names the child gives for body parts, as the drawings are used as an anatomical model. Likewise, remarks the child makes as the drawings are used as a screening tool or a memory stimulus can be written on the drawings. Finally, when they are used as a demonstration aid, the interviewer can ask the child to indicate on the drawings whom they represent and what happened with body parts that were involved in any sexual touch or activity. As when the drawing serves other uses, if the child can write, the child can be instructed to write on the drawing. If not, the interviewer can record the child's statements on the drawing. It is also a good practice for the interviewer to write any questions she/he asked when using the drawings (Faller, 1993, 2003). As part of the case record, the drawings may be admissible under the business records exception to the hearsay rule in litigation and therefore become an exhibit for the fact-finder to review when arriving at a disposition.

Perhaps another advantage anatomical drawings have over anatomical dolls is that they have not been the subject of as much controversy.

PICTURE DRAWING: REVIEW AND CRITIQUE

Another medium that can be used to assess children and elicit information from them is picture drawing. The use of drawings in projective testing are described in greater detail in chapter 15. The focus in this chapter is on their use as a screening tool and a communication aid.

Conte et al. (1991) found that 87% of respondents from their study used free drawings when evaluating sexual abuse allegations. A smaller proportion of Kendall-Tackett's (1992) Boston-area respondents used drawings (fewer than half).

Although APSAC guidelines (American Professional Society on the Abuse of Children, 1997, 2002) mention drawing as one means of eliciting information about possible sexual abuse, the guidelines do not elaborate. In contrast, the American Academy of Child and Adolescent Psychiatry (1990) guidelines and practice parameters (American Academy of Child and Adolescent Psychiatry, 1997b) have separate sections on the use of children's drawings, with suggestions for drawing tasks and some guidelines regarding interpreting drawings.

Research and Opinion Writings

The literature contains articles supporting the use of children's drawings as screening tools and communication aids. A number of proposed uses of drawings build upon traditional or generic drawing tasks for children. Some of these writings present empirical data, and others offer advice and conclusions without presenting any research findings. In addition, there are some analogue studies that test the utility of drawings as communication aids.

Using Children's Drawings as a Screening Tool

A number of approaches have been taken in using children's drawings as a strategy to screen for a history of sexual abuse. These include examination of free drawings, using traditional drawing tasks to screen for sexual abuse, and a series of drawing tasks developed by Burgess, a pioneer in identification of child sexual abuse and adult rape victims.

Free Drawings

Some research and a number of articles attempt to differentiate characteristics of free drawings by sexually abused children from nonabused children. Several writers have focused on the sexual body parts in free drawings (Grobstein, 1997; Hagood, 1992, 1999; Riordan & Verdel, 1991; P. Sadowski & Loesch, 1993; Yates, Beutler, & Crago, 1985). Yates and colleagues used free drawings with 18 sexually abused girls and 17 disturbed nonabused girls, ranging in age from 3.5 to 17; they found that the sexually abused children were likely either to exaggerate and focus on the sexual parts of the body or to avoid them. P. Sadowski and Loesch (1993) made similar observations, although they report no data. Friedrich (1990) provided comparative data from parental responses to the Child Sexual Behavior Inventory. Parents of children referred for sexual abuse are more likely to report that their children include genitals in their drawings than are parents of children not referred for sexual abuse. However, Friedrich noted that some nonreferred children also were reported to draw genitalia.

Traditional Drawing Tasks

Writers examined content using traditional drawing tasks, such as House-Tree-Person (B. Kaufman & Wohl, 1992) or Human Figure Drawing (Grobstein, 1997; Hibbard, Roghmann, & Hoekelman, 1987; Miller, Veltkamp, & Janson, 1987; Sidun & Rosenthal, 1987; Verdun, 1988). In one study, Hibbard et al. (1987) found that 57 children 3–7 years old assessed for sexual abuse were six to eight times (the variation based upon whether they were suspected or confirmed cases) more likely to draw genitalia than were 55 nonabused children. However, the rates of genital drawings were quite low for both groups. In a later study by Hibbard and Hartmann (1990) with 65 victims and 64 nonvictims, only victims drew genitalia in their pictures, but the number was so small that differences were not statistically significant. Children without a sexual abuse history, however, may also draw genitals; Hagood (1999) scored 306 man, woman, and self drawings from 34 nonabused children 5–12 years old on Anatomical Sex Abuse Indicators and found that 23.5% of these children drew sexual parts, which were found on 6.2% of the drawings. The likelihood of drawing sex parts decreased with the child's age.

There also have been attempts to examine the affective content of drawings of children who may have been sexually abused. In a study that also involved the use of the Louisville Behavior Checklist (Tarte, Vernon, Luke, & Clark, 1982), Chantler, Pelco, and Mertin (1993) asked participants to "draw a whole person." Participants were sexually abused, clinic, and community samples. Their pictures were then scored according to Koppitz's 30 emotional indicators and six flag items for maladjustment (Koppitz, 1983). Although there were significant differences in findings on both measures by group, predictive validity was quite modest. The authors suggest caution in using this drawing task to decide whether children have been sexually abused.

A somewhat different approach is taken by B. Kaufman and Wohl (1992) in a book on drawings by sexually abused children. They scored the House-Tree-Person and Kinetic Family drawings on 86 items said to be indicative of Finkelhor's (1986) four categories of traumatagenic impact from sexual abuse: betrayal (24 items), traumatic sexualization (32 items), stigmatization (19 items), and powerlessness (11 items). Only a small number of these 86 items are described. Children from high-certainty sexual abuse cases were compared to clinic and community samples, with 18 children 5–10 years old in each group. There are some statistically significant differences among groups on total scores, but none on the items within the categories of betrayal and powerlessness and only one each on sexualization and stigmatization. Moreover, although no statistic is provided, the clinic sample is more a year older than the other two groups, and no post hoc tests to look at between-group differences were conducted after the ANOVAs. Thus, the approach developed by Kaufman and Wohl may have merit but cannot be evaluated as it was presented.

Burgess's Drawing Tasks

Another approach to the use of drawings is that developed by Burgess and colleagues (e.g., A. Burgess & Hartman, 1993; A. Burgess, McCausland, & Wolbert, 1981). They instruct interviewers to have children draw seven separate pictures: (1) your favorite weather, (2) your whole self as a younger child, (3) your whole self today, (4) the family doing something together (the Kinetic Family drawing), (5) what happened to you (i.e., the sexual abuse), (6) a house and a tree, and (7) your own drawing (free drawing). Burgess and Hartman describe each of these drawings and drawing tasks as having a specific function in the assessment process. They state that such drawings should be used as an "associative tool for memory" (screening tool) and caution that those interpreting drawings should be professionals trained in interpreting artwork.

Several studies have used this series of drawings. A. Burgess, Hartman, Wolbert, and Grant (1987) had 81 drawings by sexually abused children who testified in court rated by six clinicians skilled in the use of drawings with sexually abused children. They found indicators of numerous psychosocial sequelae of sexual abuse in the children's drawings (e.g., anxiety, insecurity, isolation, body image problems, regression, and repeated memories of the abuse).

E. Burgess (1988) also employed this schema in research with a sample of nine children sexually abused in daycare and eight comparison children. She examined 53 characteristics of these two sets of drawings and noted differences in percentages of such traits in the two groups. Because of the small number of cases and the large number of variables, no statistical analysis was possible. Nevertheless, she found that the drawings of sexually abused children depicted an avoidance of drawing the sexual abuse, omission and sexualization of body parts, sad and affectless mood, and anxiety. She also found evidence of the success of therapy in the abused children.

Finally, Burgess and colleagues (J. Howe, Burgess, & McCormack, 1987) had 124 runaway adolescents, 53 of whom reported sexual abuse, engage in this drawing exercise. Statistically significant differences were found in psychiatric diagnosis based upon the drawings, specifically psychotic, avoidant, anxious-avoidant, and anxious-aggressive. Nevertheless, because this drawing exercise has been interpreted in a variety of ways, the study's generalizability is limited.

The primary finding related to using drawings as a screening tool for sexual abuse is that sexually abused children may be more likely to focus on sexual parts in their drawings. However, drawing sexual parts in response to generic drawing tasks is a low-frequency behavior; thus, such drawing tasks may not be clinically useful. Second, sexually explicit drawings are cause for concern and further inquiry but not sufficient to form a conclusion about the presence (or absence) of sexual abuse (Friedrich, 1990; Hagood, 1999).

Indeed, several writers caution interviewers that the presence of concerning elements in drawings (e.g., genitals or a focus on the genital area) should not be used, by itself, as an indicator of sexual abuse (e.g., Cohen-Lieberman, 1999, 2003; Hagood, 1992; Riordan & Verdel, 1991). Hagood (1992) suggested that traditional projective drawing tasks no longer are valid because children are currently exposed to so much sexually explicit material in their everyday lives. M. Carter (1995), who studied the capacity of trained raters to classify correctly girls with a history of sexual abuse, girls faking an abuse history, and non-sexually abused girls, found a lack of ability to classify some cases and significant differences by rater. Veltman and Browne (2002), who systematically reviewed both practice and research related to children's drawings in cases of maltreatment, caution practitioners about making assumptions about the significance of drawing characteristics. Cohen-Lieberman (1999, 2003) advocates the use of drawings as one of several methods in a multidisciplinary response, but not as a sole indicator of sexual abuse.

Drawings as a Communication Aid

Drawing also may be a method employed to gather information from children about their experiences. The research in this area consists of analogue studies.

Analogue Studies

There is a modest number of analogue studies using drawings to elicit details about an event or as a communication aid. S. Butler, Gross, and Haynie (1995) used drawing an event as a way of enhancing the recall of children, ages 3–6, of a benign experience (e.g., a class trip to a fire station). The researchers reported that drawing resulted in twice the number of details when compared to merely telling about the event without any decrease in accuracy. Moreover, they report similar results when they followed up these children a year later (Gross & Haynie, 1999). In addition, Gross and Haynie (1998) used drawing as a strategy to facilitate talking about feelings (an event that made the child happy, sad, mad, or scared). They found not only that drawing increased the number of verbal details children provided, but also that more developmentally advanced drawings were associated with a greater number of details. Finally, they had parents assess the children's accounts for accuracy and found children to be very accurate. These three studies employ drawing as a communication aid, in the manner comparable to their most common use in sexual abuse interviews. As additional support for the utility of drawing to enhance children's disclosures, Gross and Haynie (1998) cite a study of children of substance abusers. The researchers found that when children, ages 5–9, were asked to draw their parent's most recent substance abusing episode, they gave three times the amount of information than if they were asked to describe it (Drucker, Grego-Vigorito, Moore-Russell, Alvaltroni, & Ryan, 1997, as cited in Gross & Haynie, 1998).

In contrast is a study by Bruck, Melnyk, and Ceci (2000) in which the goal was to examine the effect of drawing on suggestibility in 3- to 6-year-old children who participated in a staged event involving a magician. After the event, children were interviewed twice by a confederate who attempted to contaminate their recollection of the event. The confederate made both true and false assertions about the staged event with the magician. If the child stated the false component did not occur, the researcher told the child to pretend it did and draw it (or talk about it) anyway. Bruck and colleagues found that children in both the talking and drawing conditions had highly accurate recall before attempts to contaminate their recollection. In addition, they found that requiring the child to draw aspects of the event enhanced children's recall of true components but also of false components in a follow-up interview. This study has questionable ecological validity because the children were told to pretend and then to draw or talk about false components. Although it the past interviewers may have asked "what if" questions, these are not currently regarded as good practice. In addition, drawing was used with 3-year-olds, who are too young to draw.

Practice

From a practice perspective, many writers recommend the use of drawings (e.g., Ahlquist, 2002; Bourg et al., 1999; Faller, 1993, 2003; McDermott-Steinmetz-Lane, 1997; see also Everson & Boat, 2002) when interviewing children. Interviewers should be aware that guidance about using drawings is not research based but relies on practice experience.

Drawing is used as a rapport-building strategy (Ahlquist, 2002) and as a way of decreasing anxiety during the abuse-related portion of the interview (Faller, 2003). In addition, drawing is used as communication aid, that is, as a means for collecting information related to the abuse allegations.

Some practitioners have offered suggestions regarding generic drawing tasks that might elicit information relevant to sexual abuse. Children may first be asked to draw anything, and their choice of subject may be revealing (Faller, 1988a). They may be asked to draw themselves (Benedek & Schetky, 1987b; Faller, 1988; Friedrich, 1990) and then tell something about the picture, such as what makes them happy, sad, angry, and scared (Faller, 1993, 2003). They might also be asked to draw their family or the Kinetic Family Drawing, that is, their family doing something (American Academy of Child and Adolescent Psychiatry, 1990; Benedek & Schetky, 1987b; Faller, 1993; Friedrich, 1990). Any of these drawing exercises may yield information helpful in assessment for possible sexual abuse, but none of these drawing tasks is directly related to abuse allegations. The research and opinion literature cited in the previous section supports the limited utility of these generic drawing tasks.

There are drawing tasks that are more specific to sexual abuse and less open to a variety of interpretations. It may be advisable to precede one or more of these drawing tasks by asking the child to draw one of the generic drawings above (Faller, 2003). Possible abuse-specific drawing tasks are the following: (1) a picture of the alleged offender (Friedrich, 1990), (2) the place where the sexual abuse occurred (Faller, 2003; see also Saywitz, Geiselman, & Bornstein, 1992), (3) an instrument that might have been used in the abuse (Faller, 2003), or (4) the abusive act itself (Benedek & Schetky, 1987b; Faller, 1993; Friedrich, 1990).

Drawing tasks have been noted in practice to have the following advantages in interviewing: (1) they slow the pace of the interview so the child does not feel pressured, (2) they give the child control over part of the interview process, (3) they can help the interviewer gather details about the abuse, (4) they enhance the interviewer's visual comprehension of the abuse, and (5) they increase the interviewer's confidence in the disclosure because he/she has collected data in another medium (i.e., the drawing) (Ahlquist, 2002; Faller, 2003; Friedrich, 1990).

Although Benedek and Schetky (1987b) emphasize the importance of the affect in the picture (see also Chantler et al., 1993; B. Kauffman & Wohl, 1992), abuse-related details in the drawing may be more important (Faller, 1993, 2003). As with anatomical drawings, having the child write (or writing for the child) who and what is in pictures that portray aspects of the sexual abuse can render them pieces of evidence that are clinically and legally convincing. They may be admissible in court as a part of the business record (Faller, 1993, 2003).[1]

SUMMARY AND CONCLUSION

Media should be considered by interviewers as useful adjuncts to verbal communication with children who may have been sexually abused. For some children, demonstrations through media are a central method of disclosure.

Media have been explored in research on children without a history of sexual abuse, on children with a sexual abuse history, and in analogue studies. Despite the extent of this research, there are still many unanswered questions, in part because of the limitations of existing research. Everson and Boat (1997, 2001) have reviewed with great care the analogue research on anatomical dolls and anatomical drawings. They set out eight criteria that must be met for anatomical doll research to be forensically relevant (and ecologically valid) and therefore useful to interviewers:

1. The "to be remembered event" (the event the child will be asked to recount using the dolls) is salient.
2. The event's memorability is established in at least one condition in which the child is asked to report it (e.g., verbal, body demonstrations, anatomical dolls).
3. Accepted doll uses are tested (e.g., anatomical model, demonstration aid—doll uses are discussed in the next section).
4. Confounding the use of dolls with other props (e.g., a ribbon, a stick) is avoided.
5. Confounding the use of dolls with leading questions is avoided.
6. The forensic questioning is realistic (ecologically valid).
7. There is a realistic interval between the event and the doll interview.
8. The dolls are used to ask children to describe private parts touch.

These criteria can also be partially applied to the anatomical drawing analogue studies, for example, all but criterion 4. Most of the existing research does not satisfy these criteria. For example, Everson and Boat (1997, 2002) point out that both of the studies of the use of anatomical dolls with 3- and 4-year-olds by Bruck and colleagues (Bruck, Ceci, & Francoeur, 2000; Bruck, Ceci, Francoeur, & Renick, 1995) do not satisfy criteria 1, 2, 4, 5, 6, and 8. Indeed, only criterion 3 is satisfied, accepted use of anatomical dolls (as a demonstration aid). Comparable observations can be made about the anatomical drawing studies of Brown et al. (2005) and Willcock et al. (2003); specifically, the touch embedded in the staged events does not seem to have been salient. Interviewers are advised to give more weight to analogue studies that meet more of the Everson and Boat criteria, for example, the medical examination studies of Saywitz et al. (1991), Steward et al. (1996), and Goodman et al. (1994, 1997).

There are three field studies involving interviews by mandated professionals of children with a history of sexual abuse (J. Aldridge et al., 2004; Lamb et al., 1996; Thierry et al., 2005). On all of these studies, Lamb and colleagues were collaborators. Two explored the use of anatomical dolls, and one, anatomical drawings. The researchers reached somewhat different conclusions on the doll and drawing studies, even though the actual findings are similar. In all three studies, media resulted in more forensically relevant details about sexual abuse. That is the primary reason to use media; interviewers should not expect that media would produce more information than questions, but rather additional information to augment children's verbal communications. The results of these three field studies are consistent with the more ecologically valid analogue research (e.g., Goodman et al., 1994, 1997; Saywitz et al., 1991; Steward et al., 1996).

Communication methods, such as drawing and demonstrating, should continue to be part of the repertoire of professionals interviewing children about possible sexual abuse. What will assist children in accurately conveying experience should drive practice. Nonetheless, because interviews may take place in a forensic context, interviewers need to take into account the potential necessity of defending their methods in court in selecting methods. In providing a rationale for their use of media, interviewers should rely on research and views about best practice.

NOTES

1. There is no case law on the admissibility of anatomical drawings as part of the business record, but in practice drawings are reviewed and entered into the record in both child protection and criminal cases involving abuse allegations.

TEN

Special Considerations for Cases Involving Young Children

Kathleen Coulborn Faller & Sandra K. Hewitt

Both clinicians and researchers recognize that "young children" present particular challenges in assessment for possible sexual abuse. A number of professionals have written about the forensic interview dilemmas posed by these children (Bruck, Ceci, Francoeur, & Renick, 1995; Ceci & Bruck, 1993; Everson, 1991; Haynes-Seman & Baumgarten, 1994; Hewitt, 1993, 1999; Hewitt & Friedrich, 1991a, 1991b; James, 1989).

Young children have less general and sex-specific knowledge (Eisen & Goodman, 1998); they have less developed language with which to communicate; they have undeveloped free recall memory (e.g., Goodman & Aman, 1990; Hewitt, 1999); and they are more suggestible than older children (e.g., Ceci & Bruck, 1993, 1995). Interviewers have thus tried to rely on young children's demonstrations rather than words. Unfortunately, as noted in chapter 9, children younger than 3 years 7 months usually do not yet understand the concept of having a doll represent themselves (Deloache, 1995; Deloache & Marzolf, 1995). Despite this limitation, before children understand that a doll represents themselves, they may understand that a doll represents the offender, since he is not present. They may also be able to show on their own bodies where something has happened to them (Faller, 2003; Hewitt, 1999).

In addition to the just noted undeveloped abilities, young children are less capable of protecting themselves from sexual abuse than are older children, because they lack the capacity to flee and are even more lacking in physical strength than are older children. Moreover, young children are more dependent upon adults for their physical and psychological needs and, conversely, have fewer potential social supports than do older children. This set of characteristics poses a terrible dilemma for the interviewer: a highly vulnerable population with minimal communication skills that requires direct questions but whose responses to such questions are less likely to be accurate than those of older children.

In this chapter, various definitions of "young children" and their response to interviews are discussed, relevant research on the memory capacities for nontraumatic and traumatic events is described, and special assessment techniques for young children are covered. Assessment techniques involve gathering information from several sources, including the child's caretaker, employing standardized measures, interviewing the child several times, using different media from those that might be used with older children, employing different questioning strategies, and the integration of all sources of data in the decision-making process.

WHO IS A YOUNG CHILD?

It important to define "young children." Often professionals include all preschool children in this group, but analogue research has documented distinct differences between 3- and 4-year-olds versus 5 and 6-year-olds in their capacities (e.g., Goodman & Aman, 1990; Goodman, Quas et al., 1994, 1997; Quas et al., 1999; Saywitz, Goodman, Nicholas, & Moan, 1991; Steward et al., 1996). As children become older, even by weeks and months, their capabilities improve—their understanding of events, recall of experiences, and ability to resist suggestion (Hewitt, 1999).

In the practice world, "young children" may refer to 5-year-olds (Keary & Fitzpatrick, 1994) and "very young children" to those 3 years and younger (Everson, 1991; Haynes-Seman & Baumgarten, 1994; Hewitt, 1993, 1999; Hewitt & Friedrich, 1991a, 1991b; James, 1989). Research on disclosure of sexual abuse during forensic interviews indicates that there are significant differences in disclosure capacities for children 5 and younger, compared to children older than 5 (Cantlon, Payne, & Erbaugh, 1996; Hershkowitz, Horowitz, & Lamb, 2005; Keary & Fitzpatrick, 1994). For example, in Keary and Fitzpatrick's (1994) study of 250 children who were interviewed using a structured protocol, the disclosure rate for children older that 5 was about 60%; disclosure for children 5 and younger was 29%. In addition, among children who disclose abuse, there are differences in the amount of information children provide, with younger children providing less information than older ones (e.g., Lamb et al., 2003; Thierry, Lamb, Orbach, & Pipe, 2005).

Hewitt (1999) divides young children into three developmental stages, organized around developmental capacities. If a child is younger than 18 months, he/she cannot be evaluated for possible sexual abuse. For these "stage 1" children, sexual abuse can be determined only by physical findings, an eyewitness observer, or a confession. Children ages 18 months to age 3, or "stage 2" children, require a combination of careful history, current status, and detailed behavioral repertoire. For these children, their behaviors and spontaneous utterances, over time and across situations, provide the most powerful information about their possible abuse history (Hewitt, 1999). Hewitt further describes preschoolers of ages 3 and 4, who can respond to a somewhat structured interview, as "stage 3" children. They have intelligible speech, sufficiently developed language and concepts (who, what, where), an understanding of representation of self, narrative capacity, the ability to cooperate in an interview, and a level of competence. However, even with stage 3 children, the structure of the interview must be adapted to their developmental level (Hewitt, 1999).

As pointed out by Goodman and Reed (1986), however, developmental age is more important than chronological age. Moreover, research has documented the importance of individual differences in young children in both their memories and their suggestibility, independent of their age (Eisen & Goodman, 1998; Pipe & Salmon, 1999).

RESEARCH FINDINGS

Little research has been conducted on interviewing young children for sexual abuse. Much of the research that is relied upon in determining how to interview preschoolers derives from studies of normal child development and analogue research involving children without a possible history of sexual abuse (e.g., Eisen & Goodman, 1998). This research indicates that children as young as 3 can have well-organized memories of nontraumatic events (Eisen & Goodman, 1998; K. Nelson, 1986). As noted in chapter 8, children without a history of sexual abuse likely differ in their functioning from children with a history.

Relevant research in early childhood memory often divides children into two groups, children with procedural memory (memory for nonverbal events and skills) and children with explicit memory (ability to verbalize about events, people, places, etc.). Nonverbal memory operates before children are able to disclose verbally. Studies with nonabused children have shown that children as young as 13 months of age can recall three-step procedures with good accuracy after 8 months have passed (P. Bauer, Hertsgaard, & Dow, 1994). Although children 16 and 18 months cannot verbally report events they have experienced, they can reproduce elements of the event sequence. Children experiencing events at 22 months of age can recall and verbalize these events at age 4 (P. J. Bauer, 2002). Later ability to verbalize an early memory has been found to be related to the amount of language a child has at the time of the event occurrence (P. J. Bauer & Wewerka, 1995).

Traumatic memory in young children has not been well researched; however, several studies show an active presence of early traumatic experiences in memory. Terr's (1998) work with children who have experienced trauma has shown that memory for events experienced younger than 27 months of age is not recalled verbally but can be expressed behaviorally. Children 27–36 months at the time of trauma tend to recall and relate the event in verbal fragments, while children 36 months and older can provide narrative information. Sugar (1992) documented three case studies of trauma from age 16–28 months. He found that the earlier the trauma occurred, the less able the child is to organize it in narrative form. He suggested, therefore, that memories begin about the age that speech develops. Hewitt (1994) describes later verbal recall of two children experiencing sexual abuse at age 2. One child was 2 years 7 months when abused and 4 when she reported it. The other child was 2 years 1 month when victimized and 6 when she disclosed. Generally, studies of traumatic experiences indicate that memories of trauma are fragmented and disjointed (Eisen & Goodman, 1998; Foa, Steketee, & Rothbaum, 1989).

In terms of asking about trauma, children 3 and 4 years of age can respond to simple sentences, such as "show me," "tell me," and "correct me" (Hewitt, 1999). Interviewers should avoid complex and compound sentences (Carter, Bottoms, & Levine, 1996; Hewitt, 1999; A. G. Walker, 1999, 2001). Similarly, preschool children cannot process double negatives, and they are more likely to say no to questions including "any" (e.g., anywhere/anything) than to questions including "some" (someone/somewhere) (A. G. Walker, 1999, 2001). Finally, research indicates that young children are more accurate when interviewed by a supportive interviewer than by one who speaks in legal language (Carter et al., 1996; Goodman, Bottoms, Schwartz-Kennedy, & Rudy, 1991). Research on normal children indicates that the younger they are, the more suggestible they are (Ceci & Bruck, 1993).

These research findings support interviewer patience, use of simple questions, a warm and friendly demeanor, and avoidance, when possible, of direct and leading questions. As advised in chapter 8, when interviewers must use direct or suggestive questions, they should have less confidence in the child's responses.

PRACTICE RECOMMENDATIONS

In contrast to the sparse body of research on young sexually abused children, there is a modest body of practice literature on interviewing young children. Practices recommended differ somewhat from those for older children; they include heavy reliance of information from caretakers, use of standardized measures, several interviews, and the use of "scaffolding" when asking questions.

Information From Caretakers

The majority opinion is that evaluators should elicit and rely upon information from the child's caretaker, especially with young children (American Professional Society on the Abuse of Children, 2002; Everson,

1991; Hewitt, 1999; Hewitt & Friedrich, 1991a). This information includes that obtained with standardized measures, caretaker observations of specific behavioral patterns, and reports of the child's history and development.

Standardized Measures

These instruments are completed by the caretaker and are useful because they cover a spectrum of information that might be useful in determining the likelihood of abuse and they serve as a complement to the information the caretaker finds salient. Two commonly employed instruments are the Child Behavior Checklist, which has a version for 2-and 3-year-olds (Achenbach, Edelbrock, & Howell, 1987; Achenbach & Rescorla, 2000) and the Child Sexual Behavior Inventory (Friedrich, 1990, 1997, 2002), which is validated for children ages 2–12. These are described in chapter 15. Another instrument with efficacy is the Trauma Symptom Checklist for Young Children, a 90-item measure with a total score and eight subscales (Response Level, Atypical Response, Posttraumatic Stress, Sexual Concerns, Anxiety, Depression, Dissociation, and Anger/Aggression). The instrument is applicable to children ages 3–12 and is completed by the caretaker (Briere, 1999). Hewitt (1999) also recommends use of the 270-item Child Development Inventory, which elicits information about social behaviors, self-help skills, gross motor skills, fine motor skills, expressive language, comprehension of language, and skills in recognition of letters and numbers. The instrument yields findings related to these subscales and an overall score of development (Ireton, 1992). In one study, Hewitt and Friedrich (1991a) found significant differences in scores of 43 children 3 and younger who had probably been sexually abused and those who had probably not been sexually abused on the Child Sexual Behavior Inventory and sleep problems as rated on the Achenbach Child Behavior Checklist.

Caretaker Behavioral and Affective Observations

Although young children cannot give a narrative, young sexually abused children are more likely than children without a history to have unusual or sexualized play and increased levels of stress-related behaviors (separation anxiety, fears and phobias, and sleep difficulties) (Hewitt & Friedrich, 1991a). In addition, their spontaneous utterances often provide better information about their history than does an interview (Hewitt, 1999). Since children spend more time with caretakers than anyone else, caretakers are the best reporters of these indicators. Similarly, Hewitt, Friedrich, and Allen (1994) reported on 21 children 2 years old and attempted to differentiate between those who were sexually abused and those who were not. Hewitt and colleagues noted that all of those determined to have been sexually abused had elevated levels of sexualized play and sleep disturbance.

Child's History

A careful history of the child is taken from the caretaker. Hewitt (1999) recommends the evaluator plan for a 2-hour meeting with the caretaker before seeing the child. Hewitt states the caretaker interview should cover the following topics: child's developmental history, child's current living situation and relationships, past abuse history, associated risk and safety factors in the caretaker's history and current situation, causes and source of concerns about sexual abuse, and any observed sexualized behaviors. Indeed, most interviewers of young children emphasize the importance of caretaker observation of sexualized behavior, statements indicating sexual knowledge, and statements that might indicate sexual abuse. Trigger events (e.g., bath time, bedtime) and the place of these indicators in the larger context of the child's life are ascertained. In addition, associated behavior problems, such as sleep disturbance, tantrums, diapering refusal, fears, and skill regression are carefully documented (Everson, 1991; Hewitt, 1993, 1999).

Critical Assessment of Caretaker Information

Hewitt (1999) points out the vulnerability of reliance on the caretaker in that he/she may or may not be an accurate, unbiased historian/reporter. See also chapter 15 on standardized measures. A caretaker may have a vested interest in either believing or not believing abuse, which may influence whether the caretaker notes incidents and symptoms, the caretaker's interpretation of these, and whether she/her reports these to the interviewer.

In contrast to an approach that encourages reliance on information from the (nonaccused) caretaker is one advocated by Haynes-Seman and colleagues (Haynes-Seman & Hart, 1988; Haynes-Seman & Krugman, 1989). Haynes-Seman (1991) is skeptical of such information because of potential caretaker bias and believes that observing the interaction between the alleged abuser and the child can be the key to determining whether a young child, with limited verbal skills, has been sexually abused. Hewitt and Friedrich (1991b) challenged this contention, stating that "given the relative lack of autonomy in children of this age, face-to-face interaction of the child with a perpetrator may impair the evaluation process" (p. 3). Similarly, as noted in chapter 3 on interview models, use of alleged offender–child interaction to assess for sexual abuse is a controversial practice (Faller, 2003; Faller, Froning, & Lipovsky, 1991).

Assessment Format

Generally, writers on the subject of evaluations of young children suggest the use of several interviews (e.g., Everson, 1991; Hewitt, 1999). Hewitt and Friedrich (1991b) report an average of 3–6 hours of child contact and two to four appointments. Everson (1991) says that these children require six or more sessions of short duration before an opinion can be formed. An extended assessment (Carnes & LeDuc, 1998; Faller, 2003) that may be composed of six sessions is appropriate for young children. Hewitt (1999) suggests using the first child session to determine the child's capacity to be interviewed and assessed. She then recommends different assessment approaches depending upon the child's capacities.

Observation of the child is an important component of assessing young children. Children's memory precedes the time when they can communicate recollections verbally (Hewitt, 1993). The interviewer is alert to themes in the child's play with self, in interaction with the interviewer, and in the child's statements (Hewitt, 1999). These might occur when using a sand tray or dollhouse or with items resembling the alleged abuse situation (Everson, 1991). These themes may suggest possible sexual abuse or fears related to abuse. The interviewer may construct scenarios using a variety of media that may elicit themes that could reflect possible sexual abuse (Everson, 1991). It is important to appreciate the variety of possible meanings of the child's behavior and integrate observations with knowledge about the child's life and experiences from other sources.

As already noted, Hewitt (1999) recommends different formats for assessing young children of different ages. For children 18 months to 3 years, she advises a preinterview screen to determine their ability to form relationships, to use language, and to separate from a caretaker. The interviewer also observes the child's capacity to play and to use play objects representationally. If the preinterview screen indicates that the child has adequate abilities to be interviewed, Hewitt recommends a simple format involving a body parts inventory, follow-up questions, and observation of structured, abuse-related play for children who lack verbal capabilities to respond to follow-up questions.

With children ages 3–5, Hewitt (1999) describes the following capacities as ones that should be assessed initially: language (amount; articulation; vocabulary); concepts of who, what, and where; length of attention span; memory of past events; ability to engage in representational play; real or imaginary thinking; remembering or forgetting concepts; truth and lie understanding; source monitoring; and use of symbols (e.g., a dollhouse to represent the child's house). Hewitt also provides a critique of existing interview formats (e.g., the cognitive-graphic interview, the Stepwise Interview) as they relate to interviewing preschoolers.

Media That May Be Helpful With Young Children

As noted above, young children may have difficulty employing dolls, dollhouses, and other media to represent actual objects, but there may be other uses of media that can facilitate communication.

A potentially useful drawing task is one described by Hewitt and Arrowood (1994; Hewitt, 1999), called the Touch Continuum. It actually is two drawing tasks, and most of the drawing is done by the interviewer. Hewitt and Arrowood recommend this strategy for children 4–8 years old and noted findings on 42 children, whose drawing outputs were compared to clinical conclusions about sexual abuse. The first task involves dividing a piece of paper into four boxes and drawing faces in each to represent happy, sad, mad, and scared affects. The interviewer then encourages the child to label the emotion in each face. The second task begins with the interviewer dividing a piece of paper into six boxes. Stick figures that represent the child are drawn in each box, and the interviewer labels or has the child label the box hugging, tickling, spanking, kissing, hitting, and private parts touching. Each type of touch is discussed with the child in terms of the feelings it generates, the body parts involved, and the persons who touch the child in that way. This drawing task may elicit information about physical and sexual abuse. Hewitt and Arrowood present findings comparing touch continuum data to conclusions based upon a comprehensive assessment of possible sexual abuse. There were no false positives from the Touch Continuum data but a high rate of false negatives.

Scaffolding

Preschool children, especially those ages 3 and younger, perform poorly in response to the open-ended format of most forensic interview protocols. This may result in responses that make the child look incompetent. Asking questions more complex than young children can fully comprehend developmentally discriminates against them and may leave them exposed to additional harm.

Young children have less developed free recall memory and require more cuing by interviewers. Examples of inappropriate open-ended probes include, "I understand something may have happened to you; tell me every thing about it from the beginning, middle, and end" (Stellar & Boychuk, 1992); "Do you remember more about the touching?" (Lamb & Sternberg, 1999); and "Tell me everything that happened before you went into the bedroom" (Sternberg, Lamb, Orbach, Esplin, & Mitchell, 2000). The last question is inappropriate not only because it demands free recall but also because it assumes the ability to provide a sequential narrative, which is beyond the capacity of young preschoolers.

Children 3 and 4 years of age are able to respond to simple interview questions, but this capacity varies widely across these 2 years. Most of these children can offer simple narrative, and they have mastery of essential communication elements such as, "who," "what," "where," "show me," and "tell me." They often do not understand the more complex requests of "how many," "how long," and "what time" (Hewitt, 1999).

Interviewers must scaffold or cue the child. An example from the analogue research is as follows. The interviewer uses progression of questions, beginning with a scaffolding question, "Did you eat anything when you were there?" followed by "What did you eat?" and "Who went with you?" (Fivush & Hammond, 1990; Hewitt, 1999). In an interview, the professional may cue a young child that the discussion will be about daddy by beginning with a scaffolding question, "Do you have a daddy?" (a direct question requiring a yes/no response), followed by a question to clarify who is called daddy, "Does he have another name beside daddy? (another direct question requiring a yes/no response), and then, "What is his other name?" (a focused question). Then the interviewer may ask "What do you do with daddy?" "Does daddy do things you don't like?" Scaffolding questions are needed to contexualize the query and trigger the memory of young children.

Similarly, young children often require more structured interview strategies, needing to rely on the organization framework of the interviewer to access their knowledge, for example, "Where were you?" or "Who was there?" or "What did they do?" (Hewitt, 1999).

Of course, there is danger that the demand characteristics of the questions may elicit responses to please the interviewer or to avoid showing ignorance (see chapter 8), although the analogue research on young children does not show that they have a "yes" bias (Lyon, 1999b). Nevertheless, interviewers should place less weight on the responses to more close-ended questions than responses to more open-ended ones. To address this drawback, the professional interviews the child several times and observes for consistency over time. And, as discussed in the next section, the interviewer checks the disclosures against information from other sources.

The reader is referred to chapter 8 for additional discussion of questioning methods, to chapter 9 for a discussion of the use of media, including their use with young children, and to chapter 2 for the issues of children's memory and suggestibility.

Integration of Information From Several Sources

Although in all cases it is important to integrate information from several sources, this practice is especially important in cases involving young children. Hewitt (1999) advises against relying solely on the child interview. Interviewers should integrate findings from police, medical exams, standardized measures, caretakers, collateral contacts such as daycare providers and relatives, the child's play, and interviews over time to form a conclusion about the likelihood of sexual abuse. In most cases, the goal of assessment of young children is to provide safety, rather than pursue criminal prosecution. In addition, safety plans often "buy time" for young children until they are older and can provide a narrative about their experiences.

Hewitt (1999) cautions interviewers to entertain multiple hypotheses and to use a "rule out" approach when making decisions. These strategies are also discussed in chapter 13 regarding children who do not want to disclose, but they are especially important in cases involving young children. Because their capacity to communicate is limited, minimal information from the child may be misconstrued and misinterpreted.

SUMMARY AND CONCLUSION

Very young children pose a special challenge for interviewers, especially interviewers working in a forensic context. Very young children lack language to communicate, have greater difficulty using media, and are more suggestible than are older children. These characteristics coupled with their greater vulnerability make their assessment especially difficult for professionals.

Although there are challenges to assessing very young children for sexual abuse, there are some strategies interviewers can use. These include gathering data from a range of sources, taking time over several sessions to understand the child's communications, using developmentally appropriate questions and media, carefully considering all information during decision-making, and structuring safety plans for very young children.

Despite the fact that very young children less frequently disclose (Cantlon et al., 1996; Hershkowitz et al., 2005; Keary & Fitzpatrick, 1994) and provide fewer details when they do (e.g., Lamb et al., 2003; Thierry et al., 2005) compared with older children, there is evidence that they also are sexually abused (National Child Abuse and Neglect Data System, 2005a&b). Interviewers, therefore, are advised to use the special methods necessary with young children in order to provide them protection and justice.

ELEVEN

Interviewing Children With Special Needs

Deborah Davies & Kathleen Coulborn Faller

Professionals who interview for sexual abuse often encounter children with special needs because of developmental and physical challenges. In this chapter, definitions of special needs children are provided, sexual abuse risk for special needs children is discussed, barriers to sexual abuse disclosure are described, and strategies for the interview process are covered. The latter include preinterview data gathering, techniques for the initial stage of the interview, abuse-related data-gathering strategies, and forming conclusions about the likelihood of sexual abuse.

DEFINITIONS OF SPECIAL NEEDS CHILDREN

As the field of interviewing for sexual abuse has developed, professionals have acknowledged the unique challenges of interviewing children with special needs, especially children with developmental disabilities. A developmental disability may be caused by a mental and/or physical impairment, is defined by onset prior to age 22, and results in substantial limitations in two or more areas of life activities (American Psychiatric Association, 2000). These areas are social skills, communication skills, daily living skills, personal independence, and self-sufficiency (Gorman-Smith & Matson, 1992; Tharinger, Horton, & Millea, 1990). Developmental disabilities are life-long in duration. Common diagnoses found among the disabled children are autism; Asperger's syndrome, which is a form of autism characterized by high function; seizure disorders; severe learning disabilities; cerebral palsy; mental retardation; and sensory impairments (D. Davies, 2002). A child may have more than one type of disability. Developmental disabilities affect 1.9–4% of the general population (American Association on Mental Retardation, 1992).

Disabilities vary in severity, generally categorized as mild to profound, with an additional marker being the individual's capacity for self-care (American Association on Mental Retardation, 1992). The most common developmental disability diagnosis is that of mental retardation; not all children with a developmental disability, however, will have mental retardation. For example, an individual with cerebral palsy may have serious physical challenges but above normal cognitive skills.

Mental retardation is defined as having an intelligence quotient (I.Q.) below 70, an impairment in at least two adaptive skill domains, and the condition present/diagnosed during childhood. Mental retardation is further defined as mild, I.Q. 55–70 (~85% of the retarded population); moderate, I.Q. 40–55 (10% of the retarded population); severe, I.Q. 24–40 (3–4% of the retarded population), and profound, I.Q. below 25 (1–2% of the retarded population) (American Psychiatric Association, 2000).

RISK FOR SEXUAL ABUSE FOR SPECIAL NEEDS CHILDREN

Developmentally disabled children are at particular risk for abuse and neglect (e.g., Gorman-Smith & Matson, 1992). Findings from research on increased vulnerability for sexual abuse vary depending upon the research methodology employed, type of disabilities included, and population studied. Perlman and Ericson (1992) state that research indicates that one in three persons with developmental disabilities will be sexually abused before the age of 18. In a population-based study of reports of child maltreatment, children with moderate to severe learning disabilities were six times more likely to be reported for sexual abuse than the general child population (Spencer et al., 2004). A sexual abuse prevalence study, comparing children with and without disabilities, documents that children with disabilities are at 1.8 times greater risk for sexual abuse than nondisabled children (Crosse, Kaye, & Ratnofsky, 1993). Similarly, Strickler (2001) reports the rate of sexual abuse among the disabled to be at least 1.5 times that of nondisabled individuals. Kvam (2000) states disabled children are two to three times more likely to be sexually abused than children without disabilities. Illustrative of the greater risk are the findings from 43 institutionalized intellectually disabled children in England. About half had been sexually victimized (Balogh et al., 2001). Sullivan and Knutson (1994) examined all types of maltreatment and found that 6.2% of almost 3,000 abused children they studied were mentally handicapped, compared to 1.3% of a comparison group ($n = 880$) without an abuse history. Finally, in a more recent study (Sullivan & Knutson, 2000), these authors merged school databases with Central Registry, foster care, and police cases. Examining a sample of 50,278 children, they found an abuse prevalence rate of 9% for nondisabled children and 31% for disabled children.

Moreover, it also must be acknowledged that many children who are sexually abused have special needs, even though they do not have a diagnosable physical or mental disability (National Child Abuse and

Neglect Data System, 2005a&b). Illustrative of the special needs of the forensic interview population are the findings of Lyon and Saywitz (1999), who studied 96 children 4–7 years old in shelter care in Los Angeles County. These researchers used the Peabody Picture Vocabulary Test–Revised (PPVT-R) to screen for developmental status. Their findings were that half of the children scored below 70 on PPVT-R, and on average, the children were 1.5 years behind in vocabulary acquisition.

The literature reflects an awareness of the risk for maltreatment, including sexual abuse, of children with developmental disabilities (Baladerian, 1991a, 1991b, 1994; Crosse et al., 1993; Goldson, 2001; Gorman-Smith & Matson, 1992; Kvam, 2000; National Clearinghouse on Child Abuse and Neglect Information, 2003; Rappaport, Burkhardt, & Rotatori, 1997; Sgroi, Carey, & Wheaton, 1989; Tharinger et al., 1990; Wescott & Jones, 1999). Yet there is little research on the impact of sexual abuse on this population (S. Mansell, Sobsey, & Moskal, 1998; Tharinger et al., 1990). Moreover, the literature on how to interview children with developmental disabilities is modest (Bull, 1995; D. Davies, 2002; Dent, 1986; Ellis, McCartney, Ferretti, & Cavalier, 1977; Gorman-Smith & Matson, 1992; McCartney, 1987; Wang & Baron, 1997). Although some of the interviewing literature is based on data, much of it is practice based. There is also a 13-module Web-based child and adult maltreatment course developed by Virginia Commonwealth University Partnership for People With Disabilities (2005) titled *Abuse and Neglect of Children and Adults With Developmental Disabilities*.

Although some of the interviewing literature for special needs children is data based, much of it is practice based. The advice in this chapter on how to interview developmentally disabled children draws upon both research and practice.

BARRIERS TO IDENTIFICATION OF SEXUAL ABUSE IN SPECIAL NEEDS CHILDREN

Interviewers for sexual abuse must appreciate that there are unique barriers to sexual abuse identification in cases involving children with developmental disabilities. These barriers pertain to both the professionals and the children. The general consensus of researchers and practitioners is that sexual abuse of persons with developmental disabilities is seriously underreported (Gorman-Smith & Matson, 1992; Reynolds, 1997; Sobsey, 1994). Anecdotally, few multidisciplinary teams report a proportionally greater number of developmentally disabled clients in their caseloads. Similarly, Kvam (2000), in a survey of 26 Norwegian pediatric hospitals, found that developmentally disabled children were not brought for a medical exam in the numbers expected, given their increased risk for sexual abuse. However, when they were, there was a greater likelihood, based upon medical exam, that disabled children would be assessed as "probably assaulted" compared to "probably not assaulted" or "uncertain" compared with nondisabled children.

Professional Barriers

Barriers related to professional identification include what S. Mansell et al. (1998) call "diagnostic overshadowing," defined as a form of clinical bias that results in professionals assuming that symptoms of sexual abuse are caused by the child's developmental disability. S. Mansell and colleagues illustrate this phenomenon by noting that when developmentally disabled children engage in self-injurious behavior, the assumption is that it is because they are retarded, even though in the nonretarded population self-injurious behavior is a red flag for sexual victimization. Many writers cite as a barrier to identification an assumption by professionals that retarded children do not have the same level of sensibility and therefore are not as traumatized by sexual abuse as are children of normal intelligence (Baladerian, 1994; D. Davies, 2002; S. Mansell et al., 1998; Tharinger et al., 1990). Thus, professionals may underrespond to concerns about sexual abuse of disabled children (Cruz, 2000; Richards, Watson, & Bleich, 2000).

Professional barriers are not limited to the identification of child sexual abuse. In a forthcoming study of court files of 39 Swedish District Court cases involving children with disabilities, Cederborg and Lamb (2006) found deficits and inequity in case handling. Children's accounts were expected to comport with statement reality analysis and criterion-based content analysis[1] to be deemed credible. Many children did not receive expert assessments, and the experts who evaluated the children's cases often lacked expertise in evaluating developmentally disabled children. These experts often prepared poorly written reports. Finally, the judges tended to hold the children's accounts to the same high standards employed on cases of children without developmental disabilities.

Child Barriers

On the child's part, there are also a number of barriers. Lack of knowledge about sexuality and sexual abuse may be a barrier to identification of sexual victimization (Gorman-Smith & Matson, 1992; S. Mansell et al., 1998; Tharinger et al., 1990). Professionals who work with special needs children decry the fact that sex education is not routinely provided to this population (e.g., S. Mansell et al., 1998; Tharinger et al., 1990). This knowledge deficit may result in the child's failure to understand that he/she is being sexually abused. Special needs children may not even have the language for private parts and sexual acts.

Sexual abuse is often disguised as childcare. Since some special needs children are dependent upon others for their personal care, because they lack either the physical ability or the mental capacity to care for

themselves, they are accustomed to bodily intrusions. They may lack
the basis for differentiating appropriate from inappropriate touching
and intrusions. Because deficits in social judgment are often associated
with developmental disabilities, making these distinctions is especially
challenging.

Even if disabled children appreciate that the sexual abuse is wrong,
because of their dependence upon the offender, they often fail to report
it (Cruz, 2000; D. Davies, 2002; Gorman-Smith & Matson, 1992). They
may require the services of the offender for physical care and/or for
negotiating everyday living. Offenders are likely to be family members,
caregivers, and service providers (Balogh et al., 2001; Cederborg & Lamb,
2006; Marchetti & McCartney, 1990). Furthermore, developmentally
disabled children may experience social isolation, which increases their
vulnerability to abuse and decreases their capacity to disclose. In addition, the child may fear retribution, fear being separated from family, or
fear being blamed for the maltreatment (D. Davies, 2002). All of these
impediments to disclosure are found with children without disabilities
but may be even greater with children who are disabled because of
their stigmatization in society.

Lack of communication skills and language is likely to be a major
obstacle to reporting. This problem will vary based upon the child's disability. D. Davies (2002) describes language and communication problems of children with developmental disabilities:

> Almost all children with mental retardation have a language delay.
> The receptive language skills of many children exceed their expres-
> sive language skills. There also may be delays in understanding and
> processing language. Developmentally disabled children may have
> hypotonia, which is reduced muscle tone, or dystonias, which are
> involuntary muscle movements that the child is not able to control
> (for example because the child has cerebral palsy). This may affect
> muscles in the tongue and palate, which are used to produce speech.
> The child may have difficulty creating or linking the sounds that
> form words. Some children may not be able to communicate through
> spoken language. Children who rely on verbal communication often
> need to work very hard at articulation. This is above and beyond the
> tasks of memory search, retrieval, and communication. Often children
> with developmental disabilities that involve movement and speech
> disorders are adversely affected by feelings of stress and pressure,
> and it becomes more difficult for them to process and produce speech.
> They may not be able to respond to questions that would be within
> their ability when less stressed, or to repeat information they may
> have previously given. This is related to incapacity rather than in-
> consistency or oppositional behavior. As part of this issue, many of
> the disabled children that we interview may have articulation and

pronunciation errors that render their speech difficult to understand. Furthermore, the pace of processing language and speech production may be much slower than what the interviewer is used to. (p. 3)

Preinterview Data Gathering

Current best practice when interviewing any child about sexual abuse includes gathering information about the child and about the abuse concerns before interviewing the child (e.g., Bourg et al., 1999; Faller, 2003). Gathering information about the child and the allegation is even more important in cases involving children with developmental disabilities (D. Davies, 2002). The interviewer needs to know specific information about the child's disability and how it may affect the interview (American Professional Society on the Abuse of Children, 2002; Cruz, 2000; D. Davies, 2002). More important than an I.Q. score is obtaining information about the child's day-to-day functioning, the child's communication skills, and adaptive functioning. Interviewers must remain sensitive to the child as an individual and not as a diagnosis.

Children with developmental disabilities may have difficulties with maintaining and focusing their attention, with impulsivity, and with managing their own feelings and behavior. In the interview, the child may exhibit acting out behaviors that may include self-injurious behavior. Interviewers are advised to ascertain the behavior management plan that has been used at home and at school to manage these behaviors and to be prepared to implement this during the interview(s) (D. Davies, 2002). Participation in an interview may be stressful and anxiety producing for the child and consequently increase levels of acting out and stress-reducing problematic behaviors.

The interviewer may need the expertise of someone knowledgeable about the child's disability, either as a consultant or as an assistant helping with communication during the interview (Cruz, 2000; D. Davies, 2002). Some children employ devices such as a computer or a communication board to communicate with others, or they may use sign language. The child's communication method may require augmentation to include vocabulary specific to sexual abuse. Interviewers need to either familiarize themselves with these methods of communication or secure assistance. This assistance should be provided by a professional rather than a relative of or someone close to the child (D. Davies, 2002). This person needs to be neutral with regard to the allegations. Because at times these professionals may lack experience with interviews for sexual abuse and may have their own emotional reaction to the content of the interviews, they need special instruction (D. Davies, 2002). For example, they may require information about the allegations and terminology that may be used in the interview. There should be discussion about possible barriers to direct translation and how this may be managed during the interview.

Interviewers need to be aware that special needs children are usually abused by individuals responsible for their care (Baladerian, 1994; Balogh et al., 2001; Cruz, 2000; D. Davies, 2002; Tharinger et al., 1990). These may be professionals (Marchetti & McCartney, 1990) or relatives. Strickler (2001) divides these offenders into predatory caregivers, that is, individuals who seek out positions caring for the disabled with the conscious intention of sexually abusing them, and corrupted caregivers, who become offenders "accidentally" because of lack of training, lack of adequate supervision, and/or failure to adhere to appropriate boundaries between the child and the caregiver.

Because the very people from whom interviewers seek information are sometimes offenders, they may conceal or distort information. As noted above, an additional dilemma is that often others provide bodily care for the child, such as assistance with bathing and toileting. Developmentally disabled children are taught to be compliant and to tolerate intrusions into their physical privacy. Interviewers, therefore, need to gather information about the child and possible abuse from as many sources as they can (Cruz, 2000).

Initial Phase of the Interview

It is crucial for interviewers to learn about the strengths of the child to be interviewed, not merely weaknesses. As with other children, the establishment of rapport (Bull, 1995; D. Davies, 2002) and explaining to the child the interviewer's role and the purpose of the interview are important. Interviewers should relate to the child at the appropriate level, which requires taking into account both the child's chronological age and the child's mental age.

The initial phase of the interview is especially important for the interviewer as an opportunity to develop an understanding of the child's capacities. However, because, as a rule, developmentally disabled children will have reduced capacity to attend, the length of the initial phase of the interview may be shortened. The interviewer should be prepared to move quickly through rapport building into exploration of possible abuse. At the same time, the interviewer should be constantly assessing how the child is managing the interview and adapt the pace of the interview accordingly.

Interviewers may expect that children who have mild to moderate mental retardation will have the ability to participate in the interview, with language and/or augmentive means of communication. Children who fall within the severe to profound range of mental retardation typically are not appropriate candidates for a structured interview. This does not mean that they cannot provide information, although many cannot, but in these circumstances a language-based interview is not the best way to assess allegations of abuse.

Interviewers will often be told that a child has a "mental age" versus chronologic age. Interviewers should not assume that a child with the "mental age of 6" will actually have the language skills and social knowledge of a 6-year-old. Because the child may be socially isolated or has not been exposed to the same life experiences as the typical child, he/she may lack developmentally expected knowledge. Moreover, language acquisition may be a greater challenge for the developmentally challenged child than the typical 6-year-old.

Older children who are mildly retarded have an understanding of normal functioning, and these children long to fit in (D. Davies, 2002; Tharinger et al., 1990). They may try to present as having the expected understanding of their world, and they probably will have developed strategies to conceal deficits in their abilities. Interviewers need to probe beyond superficial responses to ascertain whether the children genuinely understand what has been said and what is reflected in their replies (D. Davies, 2002).

Interviewers should discuss a few, simple rules, such as "If you don't know the answer it's ok to say 'I don't know.' " Similar instructions may be given for situations when a child may not understand a question. It is recommended that the interviewer elicit the child's understanding of these rules by practicing them. The interviewer must remember that developmentally challenged children and adults have been socialized to be compliant and cooperative with authority figures. Therefore a victim with special needs may not be comfortable correcting the interviewer or providing clarification. See chapter 8 for a discussion of "rules" for children who do not have special needs.

Abuse-Related Data-Gathering Strategies

There is a modest body of knowledge related to information-gathering techniques with children with developmental disabilities (Bull, 1995; D. Davies, 2002; Dent, 1986, 1992; Sgroi et al., 1989). This knowledge derives from analogue research, research on children with developmental disabilities, and practice experience.

Dent (1986, 1992) conducted analogue studies with mildly mentally handicapped 8- to 11-year-olds and learning disabled 8- to 12-year-olds, comparing their capacities to those of children of normal intelligence and adults. The findings indicate that mentally retarded and learning disabled children's unprompted recall (answers to free recall questions) is the most reliable, but also the sparsest (Dent, 1986, 1992). Next most accurate are responses to "general questions," which Dent defines as "wh" questions that ask for descriptions, such as "What did the man look like?" These are differentiated from "specific questions," which are also "wh" questions but that pull for a particular piece of information, such as, "What color was the man's hair?" Specific questions elicited more information than general questions, but the responses to general questions were more accurate than answers to specific questions. Dent (1986, 1992) notes that responses were poorest to the most open-ended (less complete) and most close-ended questions (less accurate).

Patterns were similar in terms of accuracy and completeness among the other two groups, normal children and adults; however, generally both of these groups were more accurate and complete in their responses than the two groups of children with developmental disabilities. Dent recommends that interviewers start with free recall questions, but resort first to general questions and then to specific ones to obtain additional information.

Similar findings are reported in studies by Henry and Gudjonsson (1999, 2003, 2004; Gudjonsson & Henry, 2003), who compared reports from children with developmental disabilities about a staged event with those from children of the same chronological age, children of the same mental age, and adults. Compared to normal children of the same chronological age, developmentally delayed children have poorer memories and report fewer pieces of information than do normal comparisons (Gudjonsson & Henry, 2003; Henry & Gudjonsson, 2003). But their capacity depends upon the type of questions asked. Developmentally delayed children were more accurate in responses to free recall, general, and open-ended questions than to specific and leading questions (Henry & Gudjonsson, 1999, 2003, 2004). In a similar vein, D. Davies (2002) advises use of simple questions, such as "Who was there?" and "What were you wearing?"

Another questioning challenge is that a major vulnerability of developmentally disabled children is "yes saying" (Bull, 1995). Dent (1986) found study children particularly likely to provide false positives to questions whose response is yes or no. Because of the risk on inaccurate responses to yes/no questions, some professionals advise the use of forced choice questions (Bull, 1995). However, D. Davies (2002) points out the vulnerability of this population to the problems of recency (choosing the last option) and primacy (choosing the first option), a problem also identified by Sigelman, Budd, Spanhel, and Schoenbrock (1981). Nevertheless, Sigelman and colleagues found responses to either/or questions more accurate and consistent than responses to yes/no questions.

Because of the need for cues, a number of writers suggest the use of media, such as pictures, anatomical drawings, and photographs of important people in the child's life, including the alleged offender (Baladerian, 1991a; D. Davies, 2002), or dolls, either anatomical or without private parts (Bull, 1995), when interviewing children who are developmentally disabled. Sgroi et al. (1989) favor three-dimensional over two-dimensional media for communication because children can handle and manipulate the object. The interviewer needs to ensure, however, that the child has the capacity to use a drawing or doll as a representational object, a capacity nondisabled children attain at about age 3 years 6 months (DeLoache & Marzolf, 1995).

In a study with 30 mentally retarded adults, Valenti-Hein (2002) noted their difficulties using visual representations. These adults were asked to name the body part that had a sticker on it, using an anatomical doll, an anatomical drawing, or a live model, and place a sticker on their own body on the same body. Participants were more accurate when a live model was used than with either dolls or drawings, and not surprisingly, mildly mentally retarded individuals performed better than moderately mentally retarded ones.

Developmentally disabled children's receptive language is likely to be greater than their expressive language, another reason why media may be useful in communication. Similarly, Baladerian (1991a) remarked that interviewers should be comfortable with physical demonstration as a substitute to language. Many children with special needs find it easier to demonstrate what happened through pointing, gestures, and reenactment when other expressive communication modalities have been attempted or are not available.

Children with developmental disabilities may have difficulty with pronouns. They may confuse gender of pronouns, substituting he for she. Interviewers are advised as much as possible to avoid use of pronouns and to use individuals' names. This is not substantially different than what is recommended for conducting interviews with younger children.

Research on children with developmental disabilities indicates that they can be more suggestible than children with normal intelligence (e.g., Bull, 1995; Gudjonsson & Henry, 2003; Sigelman et al., 1981). These children have been socialized to be compliant and to cooperate with adults. Chong, Yu, Martin, Harapiak, and Garinger (2000) studied the propensity for response switching to repeated questions among young adults with developmental disabilities, finding 62% of participants changed their responses when questions were repeated. Participants in Chong and colleagues' study were especially likely to change answers when the question was repeated shortly after its initial presentation, but Henry and Gudjonsson (2003) also found response switching in a repeated interview.

Bull (1995) points out, however, that there is no research directly addressing developmentally delayed children's suggestibility regarding sexual abuse or analogous situations. Nevertheless, existing knowledge argues for interviewers to be aware of the vulnerability of special needs children to suggestion and to avoid repeating questions that have already been answered. Conversely, it may be necessary to repeat a question that is not answered to assess that the child understood what was asked. Interviewers should remember to inform children that questions may be repeated, but this does not mean the child's first answer was wrong.

REACHING CONCLUSIONS ABOUT THE LIKELIHOOD OF SEXUAL ABUSE

As a rule, interviewers should conduct more than a single interview before forming a conclusion about the likelihood of sexual abuse of a special needs child. Given the high risk of this population and the challenges special needs children must overcome to communicate their experiences, careful evaluation is required. Interviewers are encouraged to not "give up" after a difficult interview but to assess what went wrong. Are there ways to maximize the child's participation that were not utilized and that may be implemented in follow-up interviews? While children should not be badgered through repeated interviewing, a special needs child may require more than one short interview or even more than an extended evaluation (D. Davies, 2002).

Because of the challenges of communicating with children with special needs, interviewers may have greater difficulty forming conclusions about the likelihood of sexual abuse than with children without special needs. Interviewers should use the format described in chapter 16, which involves consideration of the level of confidence or certainty the interviewer has in the conclusions. In very few child sexual abuse cases, regardless of the child's level of functioning, will the interviewer be 100% certain abuse did or did not occur. A high degree of certainty is needed for criminal prosecution, but less is needed for protecting the child from future abuse. With special needs children, interviewers should consider child safety and protection as important as criminal prosecution.

SUMMARY AND CONCLUSIONS

"Special needs children" is a term used for children with a spectrum of physical and mental disabilities. These children are at greater risk for sexual abuse. With increasing frequency, professionals are being asked to interview special needs children for possible sexual abuse, although data suggest that there are still serious problems with under-identification. The failure to identify sexual abuse in special needs children derives from both professional inadequacies and victim disclosure barriers.

There are, however, information-gathering and interview strategies that can be useful in assessing children with disabilities for sexual abuse. These include preinterview data gathering about the child's disability and strengths, as well as specific information about why there are concerns about sexual abuse. Since special needs children are very likely to be sexually victimized by caretakers, information about their functioning and sexual abuse concerns should be gathered from a variety of sources. Several interviews with the child need to be undertaken, rather than a single interview.

Abuse-specific data-gathering techniques should take into account the child's particular limitations in communication. When questioning the child, the interviewer should be aware of increased suggestibility and "yes saying," if the child is developmentally disabled. The responses of special needs children to free recall questions will be most accurate, but often quite sparse. These responses should be followed up with simple "wh" questions. Forced choice questions may also be useful. Media may be appropriate with special needs children, but the interviewer must ensure that the child understands the use of a doll or drawing as a representational object. Many developmentally disabled children will be more competent at demonstrating on a body, including their own.

Reaching conclusions about the likelihood of sexual abuse in cases of special needs children may be more difficult because of barriers to communication and because of their suggestibility. There are interventions, however, that can protect these challenged children, even if the question of sexual abuse cannot be clearly answered.

NOTE

1. Statement validity analysis (SVA) and criterion-based content analysis (CBCA) have achieved wide acceptance in Germany, Sweden, and Holland. They are techniques for analyzing a child's statement regarding events. SVA & CBCA rely heavily on the child's verbal productivity and the linguistic complexity of the child's statement. SVA and CBCA are discussed in greater detail in chapter 16 on decision-making.

TWELVE

Conducting Culturally Competent Sexual Abuse Interviews With Children From Diverse Racial, Cultural, and Socioeconomic Backgrounds

Lisa A. Fontes & Kathleen Coulborn Faller

The child's race, culture, and socioeconomic situation need to be taken into account when interviewing about possible sexual abuse. Although race and culture do not appear to be risk factors for sexual abuse (Finkelhor, 1994; Wyatt, 1985), children's backgrounds may play a role in their and their families' reactions to sexual abuse and their willingness to speak about it (Fontes, 1993; Fontes, Cruz, & Tabachnick, 2001). Children's racial, ethnic, and social class backgrounds also influence how they are treated by professionals (McGoldrick, Giordano, & Garcia-Preto, 2005; D. Roberts, 2002). Research provides little support for a relationship between family income and prevalence of sexual abuse (Finkelhor, 1994). However, poverty increases the probability of being reported (Finkelhor & Baron, 1986; van der Kolk, Crozier, & Hopper, 2001), influences the responses of official agencies, and limits the kinds of resources that families can access. Poverty also increases children's vulnerability to commercial sexual exploitation, although the correlation is primarily found among children from the developing world (End Child Prostitution, Child Pornography, and Trafficking of Children for Sexual Purposes, 2005).

Interviewers in child sexual abuse cases are not nearly as diverse as the populations they serve (Child Welfare League of America, 2002). Interviewers are predominantly white, female, and middle class. It follows that such professionals must make special efforts to become competent to interview, assess, and work with children and families from racial, cultural, and socioeconomic groups that differ from their own.

This chapter covers the overrepresentation of children of color and children from diverse backgrounds among children reported for child abuse, describes barriers between these populations and interviewers, and provides strategies for overcoming these barriers so that children from diverse racial, cultural, and socioeconomic backgrounds can experience equity when there are concerns about their sexual abuse.

THE OVERREPRESENTATION OF CHILDREN FROM DIVERSE BACKGROUNDS IN THE CHILD WELFARE SYSTEM

African Americans and Native Americans are overrepresented in the child welfare system generally in the United States, in reported cases of child maltreatment, and in foster care, as compared to their percentages in the population at large, and even their representation among people of lower income (Chipungu & Bent-Goodley, 2003; National Child Abuse and Neglect Data System, 2005a&b; National Data Archive on Child Abuse and Neglect, 2003). Whites and Asian Americans, on the other hand, are underrepresented in the child welfare and foster care systems, as compared to their proportion of the U.S. population. In national reporting statistics (National Child Abuse and Neglect Data System, 2005a&b), African-American children comprised 26.1% of reported cases (they are 12% of the child population), Hispanic children 11% (they are 13% of the child population), Native-American and Alaskan Native children 1.8% (they are 0.7% of the child population), and Asian Pacific Islander children 0.9% (they are 4% of the child population). Although Asian-American children are underrepresented in national statistics, their representation varies with geographic area, and reporting rates vary by country of origin. The causes of these differences in representation are unclear. Possibilities include true differences in maltreatment levels because of increased risk factors, differences in poverty levels, community or cultural differences (Booth & Crouter, 2001), institutional racism including biases in the reporting, substantiating, and handling of suspected child abuse (Ards, Chung, & Myers, 1998), lack of social services and outreach in certain communities, and differences by race in the way placements are handled (Barth, 2004). Moreover, once racial and ethnic minority parents become involved in the child welfare system, interventions are more likely to be adversarial, as indicated by a greater number of civil and criminal court proceedings (Tjaden & Thoennes, 1992).

Similarly, poor children are overrepresented in the child welfare system, including in reports of child sexual abuse. Children in poverty are more likely to come under the scrutiny of professionals who are mandated to make reports, but also professionals may be more likely to be suspicious of poor families and believe reports of maltreatment that concern them. Institutional racism, which results in impaired economic well-being, is an important reason why poor children reported to the child welfare system are more likely to be African American, Native American, or Latino than their general proportion of the U.S. population.

In addition, in the last 20 years, new populations have immigrated to the United States, especially from Southeast Asia, Eastern Europe, Africa, and Central Asia, dispersing throughout the country and coming to the attention of child welfare professionals. Census data indicate that a language other that English is spoken in one-fifth of American households, although more than half of (adult) respondents whose first language is not English report that they speak English "very well" (Bergman, 2003). These immigrants add to the racial and cultural diversity of the population to be interviewed about possible sexual abuse.

CULTURAL, RACIAL, ETHNIC, AND SOCIOECONOMIC DIFFERENCES AND SEXUAL ABUSE

Despite the abundance of research and writing on interviewing, scant attention has been paid to cultural competence in child interviewing (exceptions are Fontes, 2005a, 2005b, 2005c; Sattler, 1998). Some research- and practice-based writing acknowledges or describes differences in patterns and impact of child sexual abuse for African Americans compared to Caucasians (Pierce & Pierce, 1984; Russell, Schurman, & Trocki, 1988; Thompson & Smith, 1993; Thornton & Carter, 1986; Wyatt, 1985; Wyatt & Mickey, 1988). There is also some literature on sexual abuse and other populations of color (I. Carter & Parker, 1991; Earle & Cross, 2001; Fontes, 1993, 1995). Cohen, Deblinger, Mannarino, and de Arellano (2001) have reviewed the literature on how culture affects symptom formation, treatment-seeking behaviors, treatment preference, and treatment outcomes and recommend improving cultural competence to strengthen treatment of sexually abused children. More recently, de Arellano et al. (2005) have described a program that provides treatment in the home and school for culturally diverse and underserved victims of trauma.

The forensic interview field is beginning to apply the findings from studies of the impact of culture and race on experiences of sexual abuse. Some interviewing guidelines urge the interviewer to take culture and language into account in interviewing (e.g., American Professional Society on the Abuse of Children, 2000), but so far, little information is provided about how this may be accomplished. Sattler (1998) does include some information on interviewing children and families from different ethnic groups. Fontes (National Children's Advocacy Center, 2005) developed a week-long training for Spanish language forensic interviewers, which she implemented through the National Children's Advocacy Centers. Moreover, Fontes (2005) includes a chapter on interviewing culturally diverse children. In 2004, the California Institute on Human Services produced a very thoughtful *Guide for Forensic Interviewing of Spanish-Speaking Children*. This guide is available in both English

and Spanish and addresses numerous important cross-cultural interviewing issues. These include strategies for determining whether the
child is more fluent in Spanish or English, techniques for working with
interpreters in interviews, cautions about literal translation of abuse-
related content from English to Spanish and visa versa, translation and
transcription of interviews that are in Spanglish (a combination of English and Spanish), and working with a multidisciplinary team.

The interviewing literature does not address the issue of how a child
and family's poverty might affect their participation in the interviewing process. However, most certainly it does. Interviewers will be challenged to understand the child's world.

POTENTIAL IMPEDIMENTS TO
COMMUNICATION AND DISCLOSURE

Cultural and socioeconomic differences between the interviewer and
child have the potential to hinder communication and disclosure. All
interviews involving children who may have been sexually abused
have built-in potential barriers to disclosure and communication, including threats to the child, fear, and the child's limited language ability.
Children of color and immigrant children may face additional pressures
not to disclose stemming from characteristics of the wider society
and characteristics of their race, ethnicity, or culture (Fontes, 1993,
2005a).

The next section describes some of the potential barriers to disclosure
and ways interviewers can overcome the specific barriers. In the following
section, strategies for increasing interviewer and agency cultural competency are discussed.

Family Structure

Contemporary family structures are not limited to the two-parent, intact family with a stay-at-home mother and a father who supports the
family. Official statistics indicate that the two-parent family represents
only 69% of families overall (and this statistic includes both families
with working and stay-at-home mothers); 23% of children live with a
single female and 4% with a single male. For African-American children,
39% live in a two-parent family (Child Trends Databank, 2002). These
statistics do not take into account the role of extended family members
(grandparents, aunts, etc.), who may be instrumental in childrearing.
More than half of marriages end in divorce in the United States, and
at least half of those marriages involve children (National Center on
Health Statistics, 2002). Reconstituted families (families with stepparents) comprise at least 15% of families. As a consequence, substantial
numbers of children live in families with stepparents and stepsiblings
or with a parent and the parent's new partner.

Interviewers need to ask questions in ways that acknowledge this diversity in family structures. These structures include single-parent families, reconstituted families, families with a mother and a series of male partners, families where grandparents play a major caretaking role, lesbian and gay families, informal adoptions, and structures where nonparental adults and sometimes older children have caretaking responsibilities. Interviewers who ask questions in ways that assume the child lives within a particular family structure may unwittingly insult children and therefore may be less likely to obtain complete and accurate information.

Socioeconomic Status

The interviewer's lack of knowledge about the living circumstance of poor children and families can impede communication. The interviewer may fail to understand information the child provides or fail to appreciate the predicaments in which low-income parents often find themselves. For instance, an interviewer may be puzzled by a mother's seeming lack of concern for a child's disclosure of nonpenetrative sexual abuse and therefore respond to the mother with a lack of respect. If the interviewer considers all the pressures that are sometimes associated with a low income—homelessness, ill health, poor salary, and poor schooling—the interviewer may understand better why the mother does not consider the abuse an "emergency."

Less frequently, interviewers encounter children who come from far more affluent circumstances than their own. In this situation, the interviewer may discount the need to involve authorities or may be intimidated by the family's ability to muster resources—private attorneys and therapists, for example—in their attempt to remain beyond the reach of child welfare authorities.

Interviewers may underestimate the degree of mistrust many low-income families and children have for people in positions of authority, including child welfare professionals and police. The interviewer is advised to do everything possible to put the child at ease, including deemphasizing his/her position of authority, being supportive of the child (American Professional Society on the Abuse of Children, 2002; Carter, Bottoms, & Levine, 1996; Reed, 1996), and using language which is appropriate for children (American Professional Society on the Abuse of Children, 2002; Fontes, 1995).

Race

Because of racial and ethnic discrimination, children of color and white children have markedly different life experiences. Experiences of racism affect children's view of the world and often limit children's willingness to trust professionals. In one study, Dunkerley and Dalenberg (2000) compared the willingness of white and African-American children to tell an interviewer about a staged transgression by an adult (stealing from a purse). For white children, the race of the interviewer did not affect the child's willingness to tell on the adult, but African-American children were reluctant to tell a white interviewer about the transgression. The "thief" was the same race as the child. Since this is a single analogue study, and since the interviewers were not trained to be culturally competent, findings must be interpreted with caution. They suggest, nonetheless, that some African-American children are more willing to disclose difficult secrets to adults of their race. This study also supports matching an African-American child with an African-American interviewer, when possible, to increase the number of accurate disclosures. Finally, this study also suggests the need for all interviewers to attend to issues of cultural competency.

Culture

Cultural as well as racial differences can form a barrier between the child and the interviewer. Especially in areas with large immigrant populations, interviewers are likely to interview children from cultures different from their own. Impediments to disclosure include differing definitions of the appropriateness of a given sexual activity, cultural practices that mimic maltreatment, different conventions for nonverbal communication, and the child's reluctance to disclose sexual abuse and other experiences to an authority or a cultural outsider. Moreover, some immigrant children may fear disclosure will affect their and their family's ability to remain in the country. These issues are discussed in greater depth in Fontes (2005a).

Occasionally, people accused of sexually abusing a child will assert that a given practice is acceptable in their country of origin. This justification may be used to explain a full range of sexual behaviors from publicly kissing a child's genitals once at a christening to nightly fondling to anal and vaginal rape. Interviewers should not take these explanations at face value, but rather should try to determine whether the acts are or are not consistent with cultural practice. They may need to consult with experts from the culture (while protecting the client's confidentiality). In many cases, interviewers will find that this cultural justification is an offender's attempt to escape responsibility for offending behaviors. Occasionally, however, a given behavior may have cultural roots, such as a Latino mother or father grabbing briefly at her/his toddler or preschool son's crotch in public and commenting on how he is going to "get the girls" when he grows up. It would be inappropriate to treat this kind of display as sexual abuse, but reasonable to caution a parent that such behaviors are frowned upon in the United States and could result in highly disruptive interventions by public agencies.

Invasive practices that may have a cultural origin—such as digital penetration for a "virginity check," genital cutting, or child marriage—are considered illegal in the United States and should be handled accordingly. Understanding the cultural roots of these practices may help shape interventions, but all children within the United States deserve the same protection from illegal acts.

Subcultures

Subcultures exist within cultural groups. People from outside the culture may not appreciate these important differences and may mistakenly assume that people from the same cultural group or national origin share most characteristics. For example, the category "Asians" includes people who speak dozens of languages, who practice widely different religions, and who have varying histories. Fontes (1997) refers to employing overly broad ethnic/racial categories as "ethnic lumping." Another example of subcultural differences might involve two African-American families who live in Detroit. One family may have been living in Detroit for several generations, and the other may have recently moved from Biloxi, Mississippi. Even though these two families have the same racial background and are living in the same city, and perhaps even in the same neighborhood, their different geographic origins result in subcultural differences. An interviewer should be aware of these differences, seek to understand them, and anticipate how they may affect reports of sexual abuse and child interviews.

Language

When the child's first language is different from the interviewer's, this difference can form a significant barrier to accurate communication. Even if the interviewer has studied the child's language in school, the interviewer's competence in the language may not be sufficient to conduct an interview. Moreover, language is in a constant state of evolution, incorporating slang and integrating new words. In many nations and even regions of nations, the same word can have a different meaning. For instance, in Ecuador the word *gua-gua* means baby, but in Puerto Rico it means bus, and in Honduras it means dog. (In each case, the word mimics that sound that might be made by a baby's cry, a bus's horn, and a dog's bark, respectively.) An interviewer who has learned a language in school or has learned one nation's version of a language may not be able to understand a child's spoken language or may not be able to communicate with the child in a way that feels comfortable, natural, and familiar to that child. Even native speakers of a language can find themselves stymied by words used by speakers of the same language from another nation. For instance, how many people who interview in English in the United States know that the word "fanny" means vagina and not backside in England? Similarly important differences exist in the use of other languages among various regions.

Religion

Religious misunderstandings can impede an interviewer's ability to gather information from a child in a variety of ways. For example, atheists, agnostics, and families who practice religions that are in a minority in the United States, such as Judaism, Mormonism, Islam, or Seventh Day Adventism (Taylor & Fontes, 1995), may feel ill at ease with persons practicing mainstream Christianity and hesitant to discuss their beliefs and practices. The interviewer represents an authority and is likely to be mistrusted as an outsider. In the case of Islam, sociopolitical events may make Muslims particularly hesitant to become involved with official systems in any way. Also, as with other interviewer–child differences, the interviewer's lack of knowledge about the child's world impedes sensitive interviewing. For example, an interviewer who casually asks a Jewish, Hindu, or Muslim child, "What did you do for Christmas?" may be immediately rejected by that child and seen as untrustworthy. In addition, if the individual who has abused the child has status in the child's religion, such as a priest, minister, rabbi, imam, or church elder, this circumstance likely will inhibit disclosure.

STRATEGIES FOR ACHIEVING CULTURAL COMPETENCE

Achieving cultural competence in interviewing for child sexual abuse is a challenge. The strategies described below can improve the chances of culturally sensitive interview and agency practice.

Integrate Agencies, Assessment, and Treatment Teams

Diversity within all levels of an agency is helpful, whether or not ethnic matching is used in interviews. In an ethnically diverse agency, colleagues educate and advise each other about cultural issues. This makes all staff more competent to work with people from a variety of cultures. Ethnic diversity among professionals helps assure that policies and procedures are fair to people from diverse groups. Professional diversity also helps clients feel comfortable when working with the agency and may help clients feel that the agency is *for* rather than *against* them.

Be Careful Using Interpreters

Interviewers may have difficult choices when they are unable to speak a child's first language. Sometimes the interviewer or the child speaks enough of the other's language that they can communicate, but this communication may not be accurate, comfortable, or complete. Lack of language competency can impede disclosure. Wherever possible, a bilingual interviewer or a professional interpreter should be called in. Family members and people close to the family cannot serve as unbiased and accurate interpreters. Even with a professional interpreter, it is important that the interpreter be familiar with issues of sexual abuse and translate the interviewer's questions so they are communicated accurately to the child. Sometimes interpreters translate questions or answers in a way that alters their meaning. Moreover, even professional interpreters sometimes introduce bias through their own feelings about, experiences with, or views of sexual abuse in their culture (Fontes, 2005a).

Learn About the Child's Culture

Interviewers need to educate themselves about ethnic and racial groups who are different from themselves and who are represented in their client population. This information may be obtained from readings (e.g., Fontes, 1995; McGoldrick, Giordano, & García-Preto, 2005), getting to know people from the culture, appreciating ethnic arts, literature, and food, and attending community events.

The interviewer also may want to ask the child questions about his or her background. These may be woven naturally into the introductory section of an interview. However, the interviewer must be careful not to make the child feel uncomfortable or feel like an anthropological subject. A general inquiry such as, "Tell me about what you did yesterday, on Sunday," may yield some cultural information and is likely to be better received than, "Tell me about being Black."

Interviewers who work with children from a different part of the world are encouraged to become acquainted with people from that part of the world, so they can become familiar with the mannerisms and words used by people from that culture. In addition, they may want to have an interview critiqued by someone from that region.

It is important for bilingual interviewers to receive supervision from a bilingual supervisor. For instance, many native speakers of Spanish from Puerto Rico regularly integrate English words into their Spanish. Children who have recently emigrated from Central or South America may simply not be able to understand an interviewer who integrates English into her Spanish. A Puerto Rican interviewer might not even notice this stumbling block until it is pointed out by a supervisor who is familiar with the child's Spanish.

Appreciate and Compensate for Your Limitations

Interviewers should feel free to admit the limits of their language ability. For instance, a Cantonese-speaking interviewer may need to stop an interview with a Mandarin-speaking child and call in an interviewer or interpreter who can communicate more adequately with the child. Or a Spanish-speaking interviewer may need to stop interviewing an Ecuadorian child who speaks Quechua fluently but little Spanish. And, most commonly, interviewers who begin interviews in English may discover that the child is less fluent in English than he or she first appears. An interpreter may be needed obtain accurate information.

Consider Matching Child and Interviewer on Race/Culture

Matching children with their interviewers on race, culture, or ethnicity may decrease impediments based upon difference. Matching may result in a more culturally sensitive interview and may lead to greater family acceptance of both the interview process and the interview findings.

Such matching is not a panacea, however, and is not always indicated. Because of limitations in staff composition, matching may not even be feasible. Moreover, sometimes children and families do not understand confidentiality and may fear an interviewer from their cultural group will tell others from the culture about sexual abuse allegations or other family problems. All of the possible ramifications of matching need to be considered when making this decision. Where all staff members are culturally competent, matching may not be necessary or advisable, as long as the interviewer speaks the child's first language.

Orient the Child to the Interview

In every interview, the professional should help the child understand the purpose and expectations of the interview. This process is even more important when the child comes from a nondominant cultural or racial group and who therefore may be less familiar with the dynamics of the interview and less comfortable in the setting. Children usually have concerns about speaking with any authority figure and, in particular, with a child welfare or law enforcement professional. A careful explanation of the purpose and process of the interview may yield more accurate and complete information from the child.

Gather Information About the Child's Life
and the Specifics of the Allegation

Interviewers should gather specific information about the child's life and situation before conducting an interview. One of the reasons that the preferred practice is to gather information about the child's background before talking to the child is that such a practice maximizes the likelihood of sensitive interviewing and accurately understanding disclosures the child may make related to abuse. This background knowledge can also prevent the interpretation of benign events as abusive.

SUMMARY AND CONCLUSION

As we live in an increasingly global and diverse society, professionals who work in child sexual abuse must learn how to interview children from cultures different from their own. While research on cultural issues in interviewing for sexual abuse is scant, cultural competency guidelines from other fields can apply to interviewing for sexual abuse. These guidelines include suggestions that professionals avoid overgeneralizing about people from specific ethnic groups, that they become familiar with the history and culture of the peoples in their catchment area, and that they use trained interpreters or bilingual interviewers to conduct interviews with children whose native language is not English.

Conducting a culturally competent and child-sensitive interview about possible sexual abuse is not necessarily easy or automatic. Agencies need to alter their environments, their staff, and their practices to become as welcoming as possible to people from the various cultures in their catchment area. A child who is interviewed by a culturally competent professional will feel more comfortable and trusting, and therefore will be more willing to speak. Through continually learning about diverse cultures, having meaningful contact with people from different cultural groups, and revising their practices in response to new knowledge, professionals can improve their ability to interview children from diverse racial, cultural, and socioeconomic backgrounds.

THIRTEEN

Children Who Do Not Want to Disclose

Kathleen Coulborn Faller

Although there is a fair amount of research that indicates many children do not disclose when they are sexually abused, there is little guidance either from research or from practice about how to address this problem. Further, as noted in chapter 7, which describes interview structures, protocols, and guidelines, most interview techniques are based upon the premise that interviewers must avoid strategies that might produce false allegations. Thus, these protocols require interviewers to rely heavily on open-ended questions and avoid direct and suggestive questions. These are the expectations for professionals, who are usually strangers to the children they interview, in a context where children may have very close relationships with offenders, who may have engaged in a range of strategies to prevent children from disclosing sexual abuse. Protocols that are structured to guard against false positives may foster false negatives.

This chapter covers research that can inform professionals about the extent of disclosure failures, correlates of failure to report sexual abuse, research findings suggesting disclosure is a process that may involve initial denial and recantation, and interview strategies to be employed with children who are reluctant to disclose.

RESEARCH ON DISCLOSURE FAILURES

How might professionals determine whether false negatives or nondisclosure of sexual abuse is serious problems? There are several bodies of research that address this question. These include studies of adults reporting sexual abuse as children, studies of children in high-certainty cases, and analogue studies.

Studies of Adults Reporting Sexual Abuse as Children

Studies of adults who describe a history of sexual abuse as children include large general population surveys and smaller samples, but all ask respondents whether they told about their sexual abuse during childhood. Nondisclosure rates for women reporting sexual abuse during childhood range from 33% to 92% (Bagley & Ramsey, 1986; Finkelhor, Hotaling, Lewis, & Smith, 1990; Lyon, 2002c; Palmer, Brown, Rae-Grant, & Loughlin, 1999; Russell, 1986; Russell & Bolen, 2000; Smith et al., 2000; Ullman, 2003). Similarly, for men, the nondisclosure rates range from 42% to 88% (Finkelhor, 1979; Finkelhor et al., 1990; Johnson & Shrier, 1985; Lyon, 2002c). More recently, London, Bruck, Ceci, and Schuman (2005) reviewed 11 surveys of adults that used a range of methodologies. These researchers determined that the majority of adult victims did not report their sexual abuse during childhood. When they exclude one study of 18-year-olds, which uses a very broad definition of sexual abuse (Fergusson, Horwood, & Woodward, 2000), the disclosure rate is 31%. Four of the studies in London et al.'s (2005) review reported the rates of official report (to law enforcement or child protective services), which averaged 13%.

These findings suggest that nondisclosure of sexual abuse is a very serious problem, characteristic of more than half of victims. Moreover, only a small minority of cases appear to come to the attention of professionals. These studies reflect victims' recollections and behavior at least a generation ago; both professional and public knowledge about child sexual abuse has advanced in the meantime. However, there is no evidence that the capacity of offenders to control their victims' responses has changed. Moreover, penalties for sexual abuse may be greater, which would argue for more offender pressure not to tell.

Disclosure of Sexual Abuse in High-Certainty Cases

Although London et al. (2005) conclude that, in the past, disclosure failures were prevalent, they argue that times have changed; professionals are now asking children about sexual abuse and children are telling. They argue that, in current samples, most children who do not disclose have not been sexually abused. A useful strategy for testing their argument is reviewing studies of high-certainty cases (high certainty because there was an offender confession, compelling medical evidence, a criminal conviction, or audiovisual evidence).

There is a modest but growing number of studies that fall into the high-certainty category. These studies reveal disclosure failures, partial disclosures, and disclosure as a process, at least for some children (e.g., Bidrose & Goodman, 2000; Faller, 1988b; Lawson & Chaffin, 1992; Lyon, in press; T. Sorenson & Snow, 1991; Terry, 1991). In addition, there are studies of children's disclosures and disclosure failures, which include a subset of high-certainty cases (clear medical evidence, offender confession, and/or audiovisual evidence) (Dubowitz, Black, & Harrington, 1992; Elliott & Briere, 1994; S. Gordon & Jaudes, 1996). Both of these bodies of research document that a substantial number of sexually abused children do not disclose sexual abuse, even when interviewed by professionals.

Medical Evidence Studies

Studies relying on medical evidence include a pioneering study by Lawson and Chaffin (1992). They reviewed 800 cases of children coming to an outpatient sexually transmitted disease (STD) clinic. Lawson and Chaffin selected a sample (28 children) who were not suspected of having been sexually abused but were discovered to be positive for STDs. Children who tested positive for STDs were brought back to the clinic for an interview by a professional skilled in child sexual abuse assessment. Fewer than half (43%) of the children revealed sexual abuse in this interview, the predictor of disclosure being having a supportive parent.

Muram and colleagues (Muram, 1989; Muram, Speck, & Gold, 1991) report results similar to those of Lawson and Chaffin (1992) from a sample of children with medical findings consistent with sexual abuse. Almost half failed to disclose sexual abuse.

More recently, Lyon (in press) reviewed 21 studies involving children with gonorrhea, which span a time frame of 1965–1993, altogether 579 children. Of these children, 250 (43%) provided some sort of disclosure. When cases involving children younger that 3 (and therefore unlikely to provide a verbal account) and studies where the child's age could not be determined were excluded, the disclosure rate from the remaining 16 studies is 42% (185 of 437). Lyon's landmark review of the literature on children with gonorrhea provides compelling support for professional concerns about nondisclosing children.

Audiovisual Evidence Research

There are beginning to be studies of disclosure patterns in cases involving pictures, audiotapes, and/or videotapes. Bidrose and Goodman (2000) relied on audiotapes and photographs from a case involving four female victims and eight male offenders. The review of the tapes and photographs supported 318 sexual and related acts involving these girls, 194 (61%) of which had been alleged by one or more of the victims. There were also an additional 52 (21%) acts described by the victims for which no audiotaped or photographic evidence was found. Most of these were coercive, not sexual acts. That there were some acts not captured on audiotape or in photographs does not mean they did not occur.

Sjoberg and Lindblad (2002) compared videotapes made by a single offender of his sexual abuse to videotapes of police interviews with 10 victims, nine boys and one girl. This abuse occurred over an 8-year period. No child disclosed sexual abuse before the police interview, and five denied the abuse when interviewed by the police. No child disclosed a sexually abusive act that was not on videotape. Altogether, the children who did report sexual abuse to the police revealed 102 incidents of sexual abuse, but there was a marked pattern of minimization of the victimization.

These two studies suggest that many children fail to disclose or do not disclose all of their sexual abuse when questioned by professionals.

Offender Confession Studies

Offender confession is not entirely independent of the child's disclosure but, nevertheless, is a useful index of high certainty of abuse. Faller (1988b) studied the interviews of 103 children whose offenders confessed. Only about 80% of children made disclosures of sexual abuse, younger children and boys being significantly less likely to tell. Terry (1991) interviewed 18 children of a single offender who sexually abused them in a daycare center. The offender confessed, but the children disclosed only 80% of the activities he described.

T. Sorenson and Snow (1991) supplemented offender confession (80%) with conviction in a criminal case (14%) and compelling medical evidence (6%) in their study of 116 cases of children referred to mental health services because of possible sexual abuse. These cases were chosen from a sample 630 cases, 80% of which were seen at public mental health clinics and 20% in the authors' private practices. The authors do not report how many of the 116 cases were from their private practices. They report that 72% of the children initially did not disclose sexual abuse, but that, over time, 96% of children did.

Their study has been the subject of challenge. Its critics raise questions about whether these children actually were sexually abused, the implication being that leading questions were employed with nonabused children that eventually led to a false allegation (London et al., 2005; Poole & Lamb, 1998). It is certainly true that T. Sorenson and Snow (1991) do not document the methods for eliciting information from children, but the criteria for inclusion in the study (confession, compelling medical evidence, or criminal conviction) would suggest that most of the children were abused. In addition, London et al. (2005) question how the 116 cases were selected from the 630, but the selection criteria are included in Sorenson and Snow's article. Moreover, London and colleagues opine that some of the children were not abused because they assume that some cases involved allegations of ritual abuse and believe that ritual abuse reports, by definition, are false.[1] London and colleagues base this assumption that there were ritual abuse cases in the sample on the fact that Sorenson and Snow had written an earlier article on ritual abuse (Snow & Sorenson, 1990). T. Sorenson and Snow (1991) do not indicate whether or not any ritual abuse cases are included in the 116 high-certainty cases.

The findings on cases corroborated by offender confession indicate higher child disclosure rates than those found in medical evidence and audiovisual corroboration studies. These differences may relate to greater interdependence between disclosure and confession than between disclosure and medical evidence or audiovisual evidence. Thus, when children disclose, offenders may be more likely to confess than when they do not, and law enforcement may interrogate suspects more vigorously. When offenders confess, children may feel freer to disclose, and child interviewers may persist in trying to obtain a disclosure. Alternatively, the interview processes (more than a single interview) in these three studies may have increased the probability of disclosure. Nevertheless, in the offender confession studies, nondisclosure constitutes a notable problem.

Analogue Studies

The final body of research that indicates nondisclosures should be a concern for sexual abuse interviewers consists of analogue studies. As noted in chapter 9 on media, some analogue research indicates that children may avoid admitting to private parts touch. In addition, analogue research suggests that children can be persuaded by "perpetrators" not to tell about bad acts.

Private Parts Touch Studies

Analogue studies that document children's reluctance to describe private parts touch involve medical exams. Saywitz, Goodman, Nicholas, and Moan (1991) questioned 72 girls, ages 5 and 7 years, half of whom had received a private parts exam as part of a well child checkup, and half of whom had received a scoliosis exam. In the free recall questioning condition, all of the children who received the scoliosis exam mentioned it, but of those who received the private parts exam, 78% of children failed to mention genital touch and 89% failed to mention anal touch. The children in the private parts condition required direct questions ("Did the doctor touch you here?") using anatomical dolls to disclose these touches. When this direct questioning method was employed, 89% mentioned genital touch and 69% anal touch. The same questions were asked of children in the scoliosis condition, resulting in three false positives, that is, children falsely affirming private parts touch to the direct questions while the interviewer pointed to the doll's private parts. Only one child, however, provided any detail.

Comparable findings are reported by Steward et al. (1996). Their study involved 130 children, ages 3–6, both boys and girls, who received on average almost 14 types of body touch during an outpatient medical visit. About a quarter of the children were seen in the child protection team clinic. The reports of the 130 children during free recall were quite accurate, 90–97% (the latter number being the accuracy rate for 3-year-olds). However the children reported only a small proportion of the touches they experienced, 17% (3-year-olds) to 37% (6-year-olds). Similar findings were reported for private parts touch during the medical exam. For example, only a quarter of the children who received genital touch reported it. No child who did not experience genital touch reported it, when asked a yes/no question. Only 6% of children who received anal touch reported it when asked a direct question, and there were no false positives.

As noted in chapter 9, Steward et al. (1996) employed "enhanced" interviews (asking with anatomical dolls, anatomical drawings, or a computer program). With the enhancements, about two-thirds of the children reported genital touch and about a third anal and buttocks touch. As with the study by Saywitz et al. (1991), enhanced interviews produced a small number of false positives.

Steward et al.'s (1996) study is one of the few to assess children's memories over time. They reinterviewed children 1 month and 6 months after the visit to the outpatient clinic. In the meantime, many children experienced other medical visits, both outpatient and inpatient. Children's memory of the outpatient visit being studied diminished over time.

Bruck and colleagues (Bruck, Ceci, & Francoeur, 2000; Bruck, Ceci, Francoeur, & Renick, 1995) emphasized the false positives they elicited using misleading questions in their studies involving 3- and 4-year-olds who experienced medical exams (discussed in greater detail in chapter 8). These researchers also elicited a high proportion of false negatives to commands to demonstrate with anatomical dolls or on children's bodies, direct questions, and leading questions (about 50% in all three questioning conditions—doll demonstrations, own body demonstrations, and questions).

Secret-Keeping Analogue Findings

Analogue studies demonstrate that children who were admonished not to tell about wrong-doing by an adult often protected the adult. These admonitions were effective when the adult was a stranger or a parent (Bottoms, Goodman, Schwartz-Kennedy, Sachsenmeier, & Thomas, 1990; Clarke-Stuart, Thompson, & Lepore, 1989; Dunkerley & Dalenberg, 2000; Goodman & Clarke-Stewart, 1991; Peters, 1991; Tye, Amato, Honts, Devitt, & Peters, 1999; Wilson & Pipe, 1994, 1998).

Illustrative is a study of interrogation of 5- and 6-year-olds by Clarke-Stewart et al. (1989). Individual children observed Chester, the janitor, who was supposed to be cleaning toys in a classroom. Chester's behavior with the toys was ambiguous, but his statements indicated he was either cleaning the toys or playing with them. In one of the conditions, his statements indicated he was playing, he asked the child not to tell about his playing, and he gave the child a piece of candy. More than 60% of children in this condition were either noncommittal or said Chester was cleaning the toys, not playing with them, when interrogated later by "Chester's boss."

Dunkerley and Dalenberg's (2000) analogue study is discussed, in part, in chapter 12. These researchers studied the impact of race on children's disclosure of adult good (giving a box of candy) and bad (taking a purse) behavior, when admonished not to tell. They found children were less forthcoming when the interviewer, who asked about the source of the box of candy or the whereabouts of the purse, was of a different race from the child. These findings were more marked for African-American children and for children who were scored at high risk for sexual abuse.

Wilson and Pipe (1994, 1998) had 6- and 10-year-old children participate in or observe interactions with a magician. During one of the magic tricks, the magician "accidentally" spilled black ink on the child's white magic gloves. The magician quickly took the gloves off and hid them, warning the child not to tell, that this was their secret. Children were interviewed twice. In their first interview, only 25% of the 6-year-olds reported the "accident" during free recall questioning about the interaction with the magician, and 60% acknowledged the "accident" when asked a direct question. Ten-year-olds were more likely to report the "accident" in both free recall (66%) and when asked directly (84%). Although older age predicted less obedience to the magician, substantial proportions of both older and younger children kept the magician's secret.

Since children not only usually know their abusers but often are groomed and manipulated by them, it is reasonable to anticipate that their abusers' admonitions not to tell will be much more effective than those in analogue studies involving someone the child has never met before. Some analogue studies support this conclusion.

In a series of experiments, Tye et al. (1999) compared disclosure rates of 6- to 10-year-old children of a book theft by a stranger (research assistant) versus a significant other. Eighty-one percent of the children who had witnessed the stranger take the book truthfully disclosed the theft when asked. In contrast, 56% of children who had witnessed their significant other stealing a book wrongfully implicated the stranger when asked.

Similarly, Bottoms et al. (1990; also cited in Lyon, 2002c) reported on an analogue study conducted with 49 children 3–6 years old and their mothers. In one condition, mothers and their children were specifically told not to play with the toys. But they did, and, during the play, the mother "accidentally" broke the head off a Barbie Doll. Mothers asked their children to keep this breakage a secret. When specifically asked, only one child betrayed her mother and told. All of the 5-year-olds refused to implicate their mothers, even when asked a leading question.

These studies with significant others and mothers demonstrate children's willingness to protect people close to them. Neither of these studies, however, involves protracted manipulations to secure a promise of secrecy or any negative consequences for the children, should they tell on the transgressor. Nevertheless, they offer further support for the proposition that many children, sexually victimized by individuals close to them, will fail to report their abuse when asked.

PREDICTORS OF REPORTING AND NOT REPORTING

The literature suggests that certain case characteristics predict reporting sexual abuse or failure to report. Severity of the sexual abuse (Arata, 1998; Paine & Hansen, 2002), closeness of the victim–offender relationship (Arata, 1998; Cantlon, Payne, & Erbaugh, 1996; Gries, Goh, & Cavanaugh, 1996; Hershkowitz, Horowitz, & Lamb, 2005; Paine & Hansen, 2002), young age of the victim (Cantlon et al., 1996; DiPietro, Runyon, & Fredrickson, 1997; Hershkowitz et al., 2005; Keary & Fitzpatrick, 1994; Lyon, 2002c; Paine & Hansen, 2002), being a male victim (Faller, 1988b; Hershkowitz et al., 2005; Paine & Hansen, 2002), and having a nonsupportive caretaker (Bolen & Lamb, 2002; Lawson & Chaffin, 1992) all may decrease the likelihood of reporting sexual abuse. The most consistent findings relate to previously having reported the victimization, having been abused by someone close, and having a supportive or nonsupportive caretaker.

Prior Disclosure Predicts Present Disclosure

Research indicates that the best predictor of telling about sexual abuse during a forensic or investigative interview is prior disclosure to someone, either a professional or someone close to the child (DeVoe & Faller, 1999; DiPietro et al., 1997; Gries et al., 1996; Keary & Fitzpatrick, 1994; Olafson & Lederman, 2006). Thus, cases in which the concern about sexual victimization does not derive from the child having told will be less likely to result in an account of sexual abuse during a formal interview.

Proximity of the Perpetrator–Child Relationship Predicts Nondisclosure

Research suggests that the closer the relationship between the child and the abuser, the less likely the child is to report (Berliner & Conte, 1995; Faller, 1990a; Goodman-Brown, Edelstein, Goodman, Jones, & Gordon, 2003; Hershkowitz, Horowitz, & Lamb, 2005; Lyon, in press; Olafson & Lederman, 2006; Paine & Hansen, 2002). Especially difficult for children is reporting a caretaker. In a study using a national data set of 26,408 sexual and physical abuse cases interviewed by Israeli youth investigators, Hershkowitz et al. (2005) found that about two-thirds of reports involved parental figures. Youth investigator interviews, however, resulted in a disproportionately low number of disclosures involving parent figure offenders. With regard to sexual abuse disclosures ($n = 7,812$), 8%

involved parent figures, whereas 92% involved nonparent figures. Hersh-kowitz and colleagues then examined a subset of the nondisclosing cases ($n = 373$), in which investigators thought the child had been abused, because there was either a witness to the abuse or a prior credible disclosure by the child to a disinterested party. Parents or parent figures were the alleged offenders in 85.5% of the nondisclosing sexual abuse cases.

Caretaker Support and Disclosure of Abuse

Another important factor that predicts disclosure is whether or not the child has a supportive caretaker. Caretakers are less supportive in situations of a close relationship between the alleged offender and the caretaker, situations of domestic violence, caretaker substance abuse, and caretaker history of child neglect (Olafson & Lederman, 2006; Paine & Hansen, 2002). As noted above, in Lawson and Chaffin's (1992) study of children with STDs, the only predictor of describing sexual abuse in the hospital-based interview was having a supportive caretaker. Of the 12 children who disclosed sexual abuse when interviewed, 10 had supportive caretakers.

Indirect support for this predictor is found in Hershkowitz et al. (2005) analysis of the Israeli youth investigator data. Children in non-parent abuser cases likely had supportive caretakers and therefore were more likely to report.

DOCUMENTATION THAT DISCLOSURE IS A PROCESS

In 1983, Roland Summit published a seminal article titled "The Child Sexual Abuse Accommodation Syndrome" that described a child's process of revealing sexual abuse—characterized by initially maintaining secrecy, feeling helpless and entrapped, delaying disclosure, providing an unconvincing account of abuse, and often subsequently retracting the allegation (see also Olafson, 2002). The process Summit described was based upon his clinical and consulting experience. Because this clinical description was consistent with the experience of practitioners, it was widely accepted and employed in many venues to explain children's behavior. Evidence of the child sexual abuse accommodation syndrome does not prove the child has been sexually abused, however. In only explains children's reactions to sexual victimization (Conte, 2002; Lyon, 2002c; Olafson & Lederman, 2006; Summit, 1992). Nevertheless, the research on cases of suspected sexual abuse supports a number of these characteristics (e.g., Lyon, 2002c).

The most clear-cut research support for the child sexual abuse accommodation syndrome derives from the study by T. Sorenson and Snow (1991) cited above. These researchers documented the process of disclosure over several treatment sessions in a mental health clinic. Sorenson and Snow categorize children's behavior as initial denial, then tentative disclosure, followed by full disclosure, next recantation, and finally reaffirmation of sexual abuse. They note that in this population only about one-fourth of children intended to tell; for the remainder of the children, disclosure was accidental. When interviewed, almost three-fourths of children initially denied sexual abuse, but 96% made a disclosure of sexual abuse over several sessions. Of those who made a report, 22% recanted their initial disclosure, but almost all of them reaffirmed sexual abuse.

There are additional studies of actual cases that document delays in reporting sexual abuse and recantation following a disclosure. This research draws upon current case files and follow-up inquiries.

Delay in Reporting

Several studies of cases coming to professional attention document that a substantial proportion of victims initially do not report their sexual victimization (e.g., Elliott & Briere, 1994; Olafson & Lederman, 2006; Sauzier, 1989). Elliott and Briere (1994) studied 336 children 8–15 years old who received forensic evaluations at Harbor-UCLA's Sexual Abuse Crisis Center. Among their findings were that 75% of children had failed to disclose their sexual victimization within the year after it occurred.

Similarly, Sauzier (1989), who collected data from a pioneering assessment and intervention program with sexually abused children at Tufts New England Medical Center, found that of the 156 children seen in the program, 17% delayed reporting more than a year. Thirty-nine percent told no one until they were actually evaluated at the intervention program. On the other hand, 24% of children reported within a week of the sexual abuse.

Follow-up studies of children after disclosure and litigation also support the observation that a substantial proportion of victims delay disclosure (Berliner & Conte, 1995; Goodman-Brown et al., 2003; Sas & Cunningham, 1995). Sas and Cunningham followed up more than 500 child victims who experienced criminal court litigation regarding sexual abuse. They asked 135 children about the disclosure process and criminal litigation and found that 40% of children had no idea the behavior was wrong when they were first sexually abused, decreasing the likelihood that children would disclose. Boys and victims of intrafamilial sexual abuse were more likely to lack knowledge about the inappropriateness of the behavior. In 50% of cases, children said they were admonished by the abuser not to tell. Forty-three percent never considered telling, and 12% consciously decided not to tell. Forty-four percent of children who didn't tell were reabused by the same person. One-third of the children in Sas and Cunningham's study knew the sexual abuse was wrong and told soon after the first incident.

Berliner and Conte (1995) followed up with 82 children and their families on an average of 3.5 years after sexual abuse was reported, collecting data from both the children and their caretakers. Berliner and Conte noted that only 43% of children in the study told their parents first and quote children's statements from reabused interviews regarding the difficulty of disclosure.

Goodman-Brown et al. (2003) conducted a study of 218 cases referred for criminal prosecution in a single jurisdiction over a 2-year time frame (~60% of all such cases). In this study, 58% of children failed to disclose within 48 hours of the abuse. Predictors of delayed disclosure were being older, being a victim of incest, feeling responsibility for the abuse, and fearing the consequences of telling.

Retraction or Recantation

Based upon current knowledge, recantation of a true allegation of sexual abuse cannot be easily differentiated from a retraction of a false one (Faller, 2003). Research, nevertheless, supports a conclusion that a substantial minority of children recant actual abuse after initially admitting (Elliott & Briere, 1994; Lyon, 2002; Malloy, Lyon, Quas, & Forman, 2005; T. Sorenson & Snow, 1991). Similarly, when children initially make a disclosure of sexual victimization to someone they know and trust, but fail to disclose when formally interviewed, often this nondisclosure is attributed to leading questions or premature conclusions of abuse by the trusted individual. An alternative interpretation of this disclosure failure is that it represents recantation as the child begins to experience the consequences of revealing the abuse (DeVoe & Faller, 1999; Keary & Fitzpatrick, 1994).

One of the earliest studies to examine the issue of recantation was that of Jones and McGraw (1987), who examined 576 cases reported to Denver County child protective services in 1983. The researchers' review of these cases resulted in a categorization of "substantiated" for 309 or 53% of the cases. Of these, 9% ($n = 52$) involved recantations. Since recantation often occurs after substantiation, Jones and McGraw regarded the recantation rate in their study as an underestimate.

As noted above, T. Sorenson and Snow (1991) report a recantation rate of 22%. Bradley and Wood (1996) indirectly challenge the Sorenson and Snow findings using a sample of substantiated child protection cases. Seventy-two percent of Bradley and Wood's sample had made a prior disclosure, and most were interviewed once. Bradley and Wood report that only 6% of the children in their study initially denied sexual abuse, when interviewed, and only 4% recanted. However, as Jones and McGraw (1987) point out and studies by T. Sorenson and Snow (1991) and Malloy et al. (2005) (described below) suggest, a single interview is insufficient for examining recantation, which is likely to occur over time.

Malloy et al. (2005) described the results of a case record review study of the disclosure process in 217 children (257 cases) randomly selected from substantiated sexual abuse cases from the Los Angeles Dependency Court (1999–2000). Ninety percent of the children were girls with a mean age of 10.4 years. Sexual penetration was reported in half the cases. Close to 70% of children reported sexual abuse by a parent or stepparent. On average, these children were interviewed 12 times. The researchers tracked the disclosure process over these interviews. Seventy-eight percent disclosed to someone prior to their first interview by child protective services or law enforcement. Nine percent initially denied in the mandated interview, and 73% expressed reluctance to talk about the abuse, but 98% disclosed in at least one interview. Of these children, one-third recanted during at least one interview; 23% fully recanted, and 11% partially recanted. Predictors of full recantation were younger victim age, closer relationship with the male perpetrator, and lack of maternal support. The predictor of partial recantation (minimization of the abuse) was more severe sexual abuse. Factors not associated with recantation were medical evidence, perpetrator confession, prior offending history of the perpetrator, and a custody battle.

Gordon and Jaudes (1996) conducted a chart review of 141 children who were examined in a hospital emergency department for sexual abuse. Although 103 revealed sexual abuse in the emergency department, 17 recanted during their investigative interview, including several children with STDs.

Elliott and Briere (1994) focused on recantation in cases with external evidence of sexual abuse. Eighteen children with external evidence in their sample of 336 recanted. There were additional recanters in their sample, but these either had no external evidence or did not provide an initial credible disclosure. Recantation was associated with lack of caretaker support.

PRACTICE TECHNIQUES USED WITH CHILDREN WHO ARE RELUCTANT TO DISCLOSE

There is little direct research on facilitating disclosure by children reluctant to reveal traumatic experiences. The exceptions are the research by Carnes and colleagues on the extended assessment described in chapter 5 (Carnes & LeDuc, 1998; Carnes, Nelson-Gardell, Wilson, & Orgassa, 2001; Carnes, Wilson, & Nelson-Gardell, 1999, 2000) and a study by Hershkowitz et al. (2006). Most of the advice on practice techniques derives from practitioners.

Field Research

Carnes and colleagues' research supports conducting several interviews for children who fail to disclose in an initial interview. Based upon their three studies of children who present at children's advocacy centers, a six-session extended assessment will yield disclosures in about half of children who initially do not describe sexual abuse. In addition, about a quarter of such cases will be determined not to involve sexual abuse (Carnes & LeDuc, 1998; Carnes et al., 1999, 2000, 2001). Professionals should bear in mind, however, that most children who are interviewed at children's advocacy centers will have made a prior disclosure.

Hershkowitz et al. (2006) examined interviews conducted by Israeli youth investigators that followed the National Institute of Child Health and Human Development protocol (Sternberg, Lamb, Esplin, & Baradaran, 1999). They matched 50 interviews of nondisclosing 4- to 13-year-old children where there was reasonable certainty that the children had been abused, with 50 disclosing children. From the very beginning of the interview, nondisclosers were somewhat uncooperative, provided fewer details, and gave more uninformative responses than did disclosers. Perhaps because of these behaviors, interviewers used fewer free recall prompts and made fewer supportive comments with the nondisclosing children in the abuse-related stages of the interview. Hershkowitz and colleagues recommend spending a longer time engaging in rapport building when children are uncooperative, and considering more than one interview. See also Olafson and Lederman (2006), who document the need to accommodate nondisclosing children.

Practice Advice

Practitioners suggest four general strategies to assist children who are reluctant to disclose: (1) preinterview strategies, (2) use of reasoning, (3) normalizing disclosure, and (4) decreasing the stress related to disclosure. All of these strategies except the first require that the interviewer have reason to believe that the child has been sexually abused. This belief can derive from something the child has said (e.g., the child saying, "I don't want to say what he did") or done (e.g., sucking a peer's penis), from physical findings, or from reports of witnesses or other victims.

Preinterview strategies that some professionals advise include having the child's caretaker prepare the child beforehand for the interview process by explaining the purpose of the interview (Eagleson, 2002). Although interviewers may be concerned that the caretaker may influence or contaminate the child's information, it is reasonable to expect that the caretaker will say something to prepare the child. Probably it is better that the interviewer script this preparation than to rely on the caretaker.

Another preinterview strategy is to have the child's caretaker give the child permission to talk freely during the interview or to tell the interviewer specifically about what happened (Eagleson, 2002). Again, some professionals may be concerned that specific reference to the abuse may contaminate the child's account. Whether this is an advisable strategy will depend upon the particulars of the case.

During the interview, when children indicate there has been abuse but are reluctant to talk, reasoning strategies may be useful. Reasoning strategies are advised for older children, that is, children who can understand reason. Children may be afraid to disclose because they are concerned about the consequences of disclosure, and sometimes the interviewer can assuage that fear. For example, children may be afraid they will be in trouble if they tell. On the other hand, interviewers should beware of the trap of telling children that "everything will be fine" if they tell, because probably the child's life will be chaotic and stressful for a time after disclosure.

A second reasoning strategy involves motivating children to disclose in order to make something happen. Examples are getting the abuse to stop, protecting younger siblings or children, and causing the offender to be held accountable. Care should be taken not to use these reasoning strategies coercively.

Normalizing strategies are somewhat related to reasoning strategies and include normalizing the abuse ("Things like what happened to you happen to lots of kids") and normalizing the interview process. The interviewer may say, "I talk to lots of children about things like this. That's my job." Normalizing strategies are appropriate only if the interviewer has good reason to suspect the child has been sexually abused.

Related to this approach, many interviewers attempt to set expectations for disclosure during the rapport-building part of the interview, rather than waiting until they encounter resistance to disclosure (Eagleson, 2002). The interviewer might state that "This is a place where kids can talk about troubles" or employ interview rules such as "I'm going to ask you lots of questions. If you know the answer, tell me the answer, but if you don't know the answer, say, 'I don't know' " (Faller, 2003).

Finally, there are techniques that interviewers can use in the abuse-related data gathering, when children are reluctant to disclose, to reduce the child's distress while talking about the victimization. These include switching media and gathering information about the abuse context first.

With regard to the first technique, children may be allowed to switch from talking about the abuse to demonstration with dolls, showing on an anatomical drawing, drawing a picture, or writing responses to the interviewer's questions. The professional may say, "It seems to be hard to talk about what happened. Maybe you can show me with dolls." Although this technique is referred to as switching to another medium, usually the child is also saying at least a few words, resulting in a combination of verbal and some other means of communication. Children may be reluctant to talk because they take literally the offender's admonition not to tell, but they often do not apply the admonition to other means of communication. This interpretation of the admonition is more characteristic of young children. Some children benefit from being given the choice of medium in which to communicate. The interviewer can say, "Would it be easier to show me with these dolls or maybe you can draw me a picture?"

The second technique suggested, gathering information about the context first, can be helpful because describing context may be less stressful than talking directly about abusive acts. Context information includes when the abuse happened, where it happened, where other people were, what clothing the child and the offender were wearing, what clothing was taken off, whether the offender said anything to the child, and if so, what. Once these pieces of information are gathered, the interviewer can say, "Now I know (repeats the information the child has revealed). But I'm still not sure exactly what he did" (Faller, 1988a). Interviewers sometimes combine this technique with switching to another medium, by asking the child to draw a picture of the place where the abuse occurred (see chapter 9).

None of strategies generated by practitioners for assisting nondisclosing children has been evaluated in terms of their effectiveness. And, as noted above, all strategies except for the first require the interviewer have some information that indicates the child has been sexually abused.

SUMMARY AND CONCLUSIONS

A review of the research on adults with sexual abuse histories as children, on high-certainty sexual abuse cases, and from analogue studies involving private parts touch and admonitions of secrecy supports a conclusion that there are substantial numbers of false negatives or disclosure failures in cases of actual sexual abuse. This conclusion is buttressed by research on case files and follow-up studies. Of particular concern are cases of children abused by someone close to them and cases in which children's caretakers are unsupportive; these cases seem to result in a very high number of disclosure failures. Since the studies of reports of sexual abuse involve only cases that have come to professional attention, the findings regarding disclosure failures probably represent an underidentification of the problem of children who do not tell.

In addition, there is some empirical support for the child sexual abuse accommodation syndrome (Summit, 1983). This research indicates that, for many children, disclosure is a process, which may involve initial denial of abuse and later retraction.

In contrast to the data on the problem of nondisclosure, there is a paucity of empirically based advice about what interviewers should do about nondisclosure. Carnes and colleagues' field research (Carnes & LeDuc, 1998; Carnes et al., 1999, 2000, 2001) provides support for extended assessments of children who have evidence of sexual abuse but who initially do not disclose abuse. Similarly, the interview analysis conducted by Hershkowitz et al. (2006) yields two suggestions. When children are nonresponsive during initial stages of the interview, the interviewer should extend rapport building, and in such cases, interviewers should consider more than one investigative interview.

Additional advice comes from practice experience (e.g., Eagleson, 2002; Faller, 2003). This advice includes assuring the child is prepared and has appropriate expectations for the interview and instructing the caretaker to give the child permission to talk freely. Further, when older children clearly indicate that they have been abused but decline to talk about it, interviewers may employ reasoning or try to normalize disclosure. Finally, practice-based strategies for making disclosure less stressful include gathering contextual information before asking about the specifics of the abuse and allowing the child to communicate in some medium other than words.

NOTE

1. "Ritual abuse" is a term employed for a spectrum of very serious maltreatment cases, usually involving sexual, physical, and psychological abuse, in the context of some kind of ritual. Although ritual abuse remains a very controversial form of abuse (Faller, 2003), surveys of child maltreatment professionals indicate that about 10% of professionals have encountered ritual abuse cases (Goodman, Bottoms, Qin, & Shaver, 1994).

FOURTEEN

False Allegations of Sexual Abuse

Kathleen Coulborn Faller

Nondisclosing children, the topic covered in chapter 13, and false allegations are in some respects two sides of the same coin. Professionals worry that too persistent probing of a child who does not disclose sexual abuse will result in a false allegation. Because of the relationship of these topics to one another, the research that informs professionals about nondisclosure also relates, in part, to the issue of false allegations.

Almost every allegation of sexual abuse raises a question about its veracity (e.g., Campbell, 1992; Lipian, Mills, & Brantman, 2004; Schudson, 1992). Although there has always been some skepticism about sexual abuse, many professionals working in this area perceive the current reaction as one of "backlash" (e.g., Hechler, 1988; Myers, 1994, 1995; Olafson, Corwin, & Summit, 1993). The truth of children's allegations of sexual abuse is being challenged; the techniques of professionals working in the sexual abuse field are being criticized; and the child protection system is being attacked for oversubstantiating sexual abuse, as well as for other types of alleged incompetence (e.g., Ceci & Bruck, 1995; Eberle & Eberle, 1986; Schultz, 1989; Wakefield & Underwager, 1988; Wexler, 1990).

Professionals involved in assessing children said to have been sexually abused, therefore, must understand what is known about false allegations. Five topics are discussed in this chapter: (1) the difference between an unsubstantiated case and a deliberate false case, (2) criteria for deciding that a case is false or true, (3) base rates for false allegations by adults and children, (4) situations where there is risk that an allegation by an adult is false, and (5) situations where there is risk that an allegation by a child is false.

DIFFERENTIATING AN UNSUBSTANTIATED CASE FROM A FALSE ALLEGATION

To give background for understanding the difference between cases that are not substantiated and false reports, some child protection contextual history is provided. Studies that try to categorize unsubstantiated cases of sexual abuse are then discussed. This discussion provides a basis for differentiating a deliberate false allegation from an unsubstantiated sexual abuse case.

How Reporting Requirements Impact Case Flow

In the United States, there are laws that mandate the reporting of suspected cases of child maltreatment, including suspected sexual abuse. State statutes require professionals (usually all persons in educational settings with children, all health care professionals, and all mental health personnel, and in some states everyone regardless of their roles) to report suspected abuse. Moreover, there are civil and criminal penalties for failure to report and protections from lawsuits for reporters (Myers, 1998; National Center for the Prosecution of Child Abuse, 1997).

Since the threshold for reporting is rather low ("reasonable cause to suspect maltreatment" or "reasonable cause to believe" the child has been maltreated), and there are legal protections and penalties related to reporting (National Center for the Prosecution of Child Abuse, 1997), it is to be expected that some reported cases will not be substantiated after investigation. From the time mandated reporting first became a federal statutory requirement in the Child Abuse Prevention and Treatment Act (1974) to the present, there has been a dramatic increase in the number of reports, from 670,000 in 1976 to more than 3 million cases involving 5.5 million children in 2003 (American Association for Protecting Children, 1988; National Child Abuse and Neglect Data System, 2005a&b). From 1994 onward, more than 3 million children have been reported annually (McCurdy & Daro, 1994; National Child Abuse and Neglect Data System, 2005a&b; Peddle & Wang, 2001). At the same time, the proportion of unsubstantiated cases has risen. In the mid-1970s, approximately 60% of cases were substantiated (American Association for Protecting Children, 1988), whereas by 2003, about a third of cases were (National Child Abuse and Neglect Data System, 2005a&b). There are several causes for the decrease in the proportion of cases substantiated.

First, in order to manage the overwhelming influx of cases, states developed screening measures. Using various criteria, states screen out approximately one-third of cases (National Child Abuse and Neglect Data System, 2005a&b). Cases are screened out because they do not involve maltreatment but involve some other problem (e.g., delinquency, a child mental health problem, a custody dispute, or, in some jurisdictions, a parental substance abuse problem that is not affecting the children). Because child protection laws only apply to caretakers, cases are also screened out because the abuser is not a caretaker. A substantial proportion of child sexual abuse is perpetrated by noncaretakers (e.g., Faller, 1994; Hershkowitz, Horowitz, & Lamb, 2005).

Turning to cases that are screened in, cases may not be substantiated after child protective services (CPS) investigation for a wide range of reasons. Most common, as reflected in national data, is the lack of sufficient information to make a determination about maltreatment (National Child Abuse and Neglect Data System, 2005a&b). Substantiation rates for sexual abuse and reasons for not substantiating are fairly consistent with those for other types of child maltreatment (National Child Abuse and Neglect Data System, 2005a&b).

Some states have been collecting data on the subcategory of unsubstantiated cases: deliberate false allegations of child maltreatment. Only seven states contribute false allegation data. The total number of cases so categorized in 2003 was 436 cases, 0.0% of the total number of investigations ($n=1,590,905$) (National Child Abuse and Neglect Data System, 2005a&b). These numbers are not broken down by type of maltreatment alleged.

Studies of Sexual Abuse Case Dispositions

There are a few studies that focus on reports and dispositions in sexual abuse cases. Two such studies were conducted by researchers at the Kempe National Center for the Prevention and Treatment of Child Abuse and Neglect (Jones & McGraw, 1987; Oates et al., 2000). Jones and McGraw (1987) studied the proportion of cases founded (substantiated) and reasons for failure to substantiate in a sample of 576 sexual abuse reports made to the Denver County Department of Social Services during 1983. In this sample, 53% of cases were founded, and the remaining 47% were not. The largest proportion were not founded because of insufficient information (24%). The next largest category of cases was unsubstantiated suspicion (17%). In the latter category, usually an adult reported suspicion of sexual abuse and accepted the disposition of unfounded when it was rendered. Only 6% of cases were classified as fictitious (false).

A decade later, Oates et al. (2000) replicated this study, using 551 sexual abuse reports (year 1993) to Denver County Department of Social Services. Although the classification system is somewhat different in the replication, the findings reflect the national trend of decreased rates of substantiation: 43% of cases were substantiated, 21% were inconclusive, 34% were classified as "not sexual abuse," and 2.5% "erroneous accounts by children." The findings of both of these studies are discussed in additional detail further below.

Deliberate False Allegations Versus Unsubstantiated Reports

Unfortunately, some authors (e.g., Besharov, 1990; Gardner, 1991, 1992, 1995; Wexler, 1990), referring to the proportion of cases that are not substantiated, imply that an unsubstantiated case is the equivalent of a deliberate false allegation. Based upon this distortion, these writers have asserted that there is an overwhelming flood of false, maliciously made reports of child maltreatment. The implication of this assertion is that at least a million calculated false reports are made every year. (For a careful review of the issue of overreporting of child abuse, see Finkelhor, 1990.) As noted above, based upon the 2003 official reports, which are limited by the number of states that report deliberate false reports, the actual number ($n = 436$) is 0.04% of the more than one million reports suggested by some writers (e.g., Besharov, 1990). To arrive at the 0.04% estimate, a number of assumptions were made, which potentially limit its accuracy. Nevertheless, existing data suggest that calculated false reports represent quite a small percentage of reports of child maltreatment.

Also, a number of authors have declared that there is an atmosphere of hysteria about allegations of sexual abuse (Gardner, 1991; Nathan, 2003; Nathan & Snedecker, 1995; Rabinowitz, 1990, 2003; Renshaw, 1987; Wexler, 1990) and have likened charges of sexual abuse to the Salem witch trials (Gardner, 1991; Nathan & Snedecker, 1995). (See Myers, 1995, for a discussion of the inappropriateness of this analogy.) No data, however, are provided to support these assertions. (See Finkelhor, 1994, for a discussion of data that refute the assertion that there is a hysteria related to sexual abuse.)

METHODOLOGY FOR DECIDING AN ALLEGATION IS FALSE OR TRUE

An index of the salience of the question of whether a sexual abuse allegation is false or true is its attention in the professional literature (e.g., Ceci & Bruck, 1995; Everson, Boat, Bourg, & Robertson, 1996; Ney, 1995). Criteria for false reports have received a great deal of attention (e.g., Lipian et al., 2004; Ney, 1995). They are the subject of literature reviews, practice-based observations, and incidence studies. Although clinical criteria in children's accounts for true allegations have been proposed (e.g., Corwin, 1988; Faller, 1988a), there are also some studies using criteria independent of children's statements. Issues related to determining if an allegation is either false or true are then discussed. In addition, there are instructive analogue studies that present professionals with children's true and false accounts of events and ask professionals to rate the account either true or false.

Criteria for False Allegations

A fundamental challenge in the study of false allegations of sexual abuse is knowing with certainty that the cases being studied are false, so that indeed the study is of the characteristics of false allegations. Practitioners and researchers have proposed or used a number of criteria that would indicate the case is false.

One of the dilemmas is that one professional's criterion for a false allegation may be regarded as insignificant or even indicative of a true account by another professional. For example, Green (1986, 1991) reported on 11 cases involving custody disputes he had seen in his psychiatric practice. He defined four of these accounts as false. From these four cases, Green derived characteristics of false allegations, which he asserted were especially prevalent in divorce. His article occasioned an article in response by a number of experts in sexual abuse (Corwin, Berliner, Goodman, Goodwin, & White, 1987) who challenged his list of characteristics of false allegations. Among other things, Corwin and colleagues pointed out that divorce was both a context in which ongoing sexual abuse might finally be reported and a situation that might precipitate sexual abuse.

Similarly, the practice of making inferences about the likelihood of sexual abuse from behaviors during interactions between the child and the accused parent (e.g., Haynes-Seman & Baumgarten, 1994) has been challenged (Faller, Froning, & Lipovsky, 1991). The research related to the capacity of professionals to discern whether a caretaker–child relationship is abusive is discussed in chapter 4.

Literature Reviews

Some writers have reviewed the literature on false sexual abuse allegations and argue that certain types of cases are likely to be false (Bernet, 1993; Mikkelsen, Guthiel, & Emens, 1992). Bernet (1993) provides a review of 40 works and suggests an array of child and adult variables that result in false sexual abuse reports: (1) indoctrination, (2) suggestion, (3) fantasy, (4) delusion, (5) misinterpretation, (6) miscommunication, (7) innocent lying, (8) deliberate lying, (9) confabulation, (10) pseudologia phantasia (fantasy or pathological lying without an evident motive), (11) overstimulation, (12) group contagion, and (13) perpetrator substitution (see also American Academic of Child and Adolescent Psychiatry, 1997b).

Mikkelsen et al. (1992) examined the false cases described in the literature and proposed four categories: (1) arising out of custody disputes (i.e., divorce), (2) stemming from the accuser's psychological disturbance, (3) resulting from conscious manipulation, and (4) being caused by iatrogenic elements.

Both of these categorizations take into account that false accusations may derive from children or adults. Although both articles appear in peer-reviewed journals, they are subject to the methodological limitation of knowing, with certainty, that allegations are true or false.

Practice-Derived Criteria and Advice

Arguably, the criterion that would ensure with certainty that no sexual abuse occurred is "no opportunity," that is, that the offender did not have access to the victim, or the victim was not exposed to the offender (American Academic of Child and Adolescent Psychiatry, 1997a&b). In individual cases encountered in practice, "no opportunity" can be useful, assuming that the source of the assertion that there has been no access is trustworthy. To use this criterion in research, a researcher would need to accumulate a body of such cases, study them, and determine what characteristics these cases have in common. Even then, it might be erroneous to assume that the identified characteristics usually are attributes of false allegations because such characteristics might also be found in true cases (Faller, 1988a, 1988b). In addition, the sample being studied might not represent the full spectrum of false allegation cases. However, because of the difficulty of finding a sample of "no opportunity" cases, no such research has been conducted.

Courts and child protection agencies often assume that retraction of an allegation is a signal that the original allegation is false (e.g., Jones & McGraw, 1987). Typically when the victim retracts, legal intervention is not pursued. To use this criterion in research, however, researchers would need to differentiate true retractions of false allegations from false retractions of true allegations (see chapter 13). Researchers have found that a proportion of children recant in actual cases of sexual abuse (e.g., Elliott & Briere, 1994; Goodwin, Sahd, & Rada, 1982; Malloy, Lyon, Quas, & Forman, 2005; T. Sorenson & Snow, 1991). In some of these studies, sexual abuse is documented by another indicator of abuse, such as medical evidence (S. Gordon & Jaudes, 1996) or offender confession (T. Sorenson & Snow, 1991). Because the absence of medical evidence and the failure to confess do not signal the absence of sexual abuse, no parallel research on false cases exists. Indeed, recantation of actual sexual abuse is one of the characteristics of the child sexual abuse accommodation syndrome (Lyon, 1996, 2002c; Olafson, 2002; Summit, 1983).

Polygraph results have been used as one of several measures by one team of practitioner/researchers (Raskin & Esplin, 1991a, 1991b), and the polygraph is often used by law enforcement to screen cases for criminal prosecution (e.g., Abrams & Abrams, 1993; Faller, Birdsall, Henry, Vandervort, & Silverschanz, 2001; Faller & Henry, 2000). If the suspect passes a polygraph, the veracity of the allegation is questioned. Conversely, if the suspect fails a polygraph, this failure adds credibility to the allegation. Although the polygraph has its proponents (e.g., Abrams & Abrams, 1993), the scientific validity and reliability of the polygraph have yet to be demonstrated. In a review conducted for the U.S. Office of Technology Instruction, the polygraph was found to have only a somewhat better than chance probability of differentiating true from false statements (Saxe, Doughtery, & Cross, 1985, 1987). Moreover, the properties of the polygraph, in that it measures autonomic nervous system response when responding to questions, make it particularly problematic in sexual abuse cases (Cross & Saxe, 1992, 2001). One study examined the relationship between polygraph findings and other indicia of likelihood (e.g., details from the child interview, medical evidence, CPS findings, law enforcement findings) in 42 sexual abuse allegations and found no relationship (Faller, 1997).

Schultz (1989) employed suspect denial as an indicator that the allegation was false. He gathered information while attending two meetings of Victims of Child Abuse Laws (VOCAL), an advocacy group for individuals who state they have been falsely accused of abuse. All 100 respondents completing questionnaires indicated they had been falsely accused of sexual abuse, and all stated they had been vindicated in court. No data were relied upon other than the participants' questionnaire responses. Schultz was studying the negative consequences of being accused of sexual abuse and making suggestions for systemic change. Raskin and Esplin (1991a, 1991b) included the persistent denial by the accused as one of their criteria indicating the accusation was untrue.

The most common sources of criteria for false allegations found in the literature on sexual abuse are as follows: (1) criteria that are consensually derived, (2) a disposition by a mandated professional or body (CPS, law enforcement, or court), or (3) the writer's clinical judgment. Although consensually derived criteria seem the most promising measure, experts can be in agreement and still be wrong (Conte, Sorenson, Fogarty, & Dalla Rosa, 1991; Faller & Corwin, 1995; Poole & Lamb, 1998). For example, for more than 50 years, based upon Freud's work, mental health professionals believed that the overwhelming majority of children's accusations of sexual abuse had their basis in fantasy (Faller & Corwin, 1995; Lipian et al., 2004; Masson, 1984; Olafson et al., 1993).

Large-Sample Studies

Several large-sample studies have addressed the issue of false allegations of sexual abuse, using varying criteria (Faller & DeVoe, 1995; Horowitz, Salt, & Gomez-Schwartz, 1984; Jones & McGraw, 1987; Oates et al., 2000; Thoennes & Tjaden, 1990; Trocme & Bala, 2005). The criteria employed and their findings are discussed in this section.

Although their methodologies are somewhat different, the two Kempe Center studies described above used criteria agreed upon by a group of sexual abuse experts to classify sexual abuse allegations (Jones & McGraw, 1987; Oates et al., 2000). Jones and McGraw (1987) first asked caseworkers to categorize cases (categories, as already noted, included fictitious allegation by child and fictitious allegation by adult). If there was a question about how to categorize the case, it was reviewed by the researchers and classified. However, Jones and McGraw also reviewed 10 randomly selected cases from each of the categories: (1) reliable accounts, (2) insufficient evidence, and (3) unsubstantiated suspicion. The researchers reported complete agreement between the caseworkers and themselves on the cases reviewed. It also appears that all cases where there were recantations, fictitious allegations by adults, or fictitious allegations by children were examined by the research team, and a number of the fictitious allegation cases were reclassified. In their study, Jones and McGraw classified 6% as fictitious allegations. The percentage rises to 8% when cases classified as insufficient information are eliminated from the analysis.

In the second Kempe Center study (Oates et al., 2000), the researchers relied primarily on the disposition of the protective services record. The exception was 2% of cases in which the researchers could not discern the disposition from reading the case record. In these cases, they asked the caseworker. In addition, every 20th case was independently coded by a member of the research team. Interrater reliability was 89.9%, suggesting that the consensually derived criteria can be applied to actual cases. As noted above, there were four general categories in the coding system: (1) sexual abuse, (2) not sexual abuse, (3) inconclusive cases (where there could be sexual abuse), and (4) erroneous allegations by children (14 cases, 2.5%). These include three allegations (0.5%) made in collusion with parents, three (0.5%) misinterpretations, and eight (1.5%) false reports by children.

In the pioneering assessment and treatment program at Tufts University Department of Psychiatry (Horowitz et al., 1984), referenced in chapter 4, researchers classified 181 cases as likely ($n=156$; 86%) and unconfirmed ($n=25$; 14%) based upon the assessment and treatment results. Within the unconfirmed cases were three subcategories: highly unlikely ($n=16$; 9%), uncertain ($n=9$; 5%), and false by child ($n=7$; 5%).

Graham and Watkeys (1991) reviewed 410 cases of sexual abuse allegations from one local authority in Wales (1986–1989), a jurisdiction without mandatory reporting. Of these, 197 (48%) were considered substantiated, and 90 (22%) were not substantiated but reflected well-intentioned family or professional concern. Seventy-four (18%) were classified as false allegations, half of which were characterized as malicious. Of the false cases, eight (2%) were made directly by children.

Thoennes and colleagues (Thoennes & Tjaden, 1990) studied allegations of sexual abuse in divorce, thus in a special circumstance. They employed the CPS worker's or domestic relations court expert's opinion to classify cases as (1) likely, (2) unlikely, or (3) uncertain. Examining 9,000 cases in family/divorce courts involving custody/visitation disputes from 12 jurisdictions, these researchers found 169 cases (<2%) with allegations of sexual abuse. Of these, 50% were classified likely, 33% unlikely, and 17% inconclusive. Cases where there was disagreement between the child protection worker and the court-appointed evaluator, as well as other cases without a definitive disposition, were classified as inconclusive.

More recently, Trocme and Bala (2005) examined data collected in the 1998 Canadian Incidence Study (Public Health Agency of Canada, 2000) ($n=7,672$) for false allegations of all types of maltreatment. Trocme and

Bala (2005) relied on CPS worker opinion, which was based upon the results of worker investigations. The overall false allegation rate was 4%, with neglect being the most common type of false allegation, but sexual abuse had a higher rate, 6% (weighted). Three percent of false allegations were made by children, but none of these involved sexual abuse.

Small-Sample Studies and Assertions Without Data

The remaining studies consist of small samples, mostly from the practices of the writers and many involving divorce. These small-sample studies either do not articulate the criteria employed or rely upon the clinical judgment of the writers (Benedek & Schetky, 1985; Goodwin, Sahd, & Rada, 1979; Green, 1986; Schuman, 1986). Generally, information relied upon includes not only the child's statements and behavior but also information related to the parents and the circumstances of the allegation. There are also writers who describe what they believe are the characteristics of false allegations but who provide no data (Blush & Ross, 1986; Gardner, 1989, 1992, 1995; Renshaw, 1987).

Criteria for True Allegations

In contrast to the almost insurmountable difficulty of determining for sure that an allegation is false, it *is* possible to know, in certain cases, that the allegation is true. For example, in instances where pornography involving the victim is found, where the offender's DNA-typed semen is detected, when the child is diagnosed with venereal disease, when the offender confesses, where there is a reliable eye witness, or when there is other compelling physical evidence, interviewers can be confident that sexual abuse occurred. However, the absence of such compelling findings does not mean that the accusation is false. In addition, with some of these criteria, positive findings will indicate sexual abuse, but not necessarily a specific offender (venereal disease, medical evidence). There is also a literature that describes characteristics in the child's account that are thought to be hallmarks of a true account. This literature is discussed in chapter 16.

There have been several studies of children's statements in cases substantiated by other means—audiovisual evidence (Bidrose & Goodman, 2000; Sjoberg & Lindblad, 2002), confessions (Faller, 1988b; T. Sorenson & Snow, 1991), criminal convictions (T. Sorenson & Snow, 1991), sexually transmitted disease (Lawson & Chaffin, 1992; Lyon, in press), and medical evidence (Muram, 1989; Muram, Speck, & Gold, 1991). These studies are described in chapter 13. These studies documented that children did not necessarily give complete and coherent accounts of their victimization, despite the veracity of the sexual victimization. Their accounts were characterized by false denial rates of 20–60%, and when they did report, they often minimized their sexual victimization. Thus, evidently interviews, even when conducted by sexual abuse experts, are likely to yield false negatives (i.e., a failure to disclose actual sexual abuse, or less than complete disclosure) in a substantial proportion of cases. This appears to be a problem of larger proportion than false positives (i.e., false accusations of sexual abuse by children) (Bidrose & Goodman, 2000; Faller, 1988b; Lawson & Chaffin, 1992; T. Sorenson & Snow, 1990).

Analogue Research

There are analogue studies that address the ability of professionals to determine whether a report of experience is true or false. Professionals are shown videotapes of children's accounts and asked to determine whether the child is lying or telling the truth. Thus, professionals appear to be judging the believability of the child's report.

Ceci and colleagues describe studies that illustrate the fallibility of clinical judgment (Ceci, Huffman, Smith, & Loftus, 1994; Ceci & Leichtman, 1995). In one study, they used videotapes of three children's responses in the Sam Stone analogue study (Ceci & Leichtman, 1995). Children in one condition received both preevent stereotyping information about Sam Stone and postevent leading questions in an attempt to get them to say that Sam Stone came to their classroom and ripped a book and soiled a teddy bear. Ceci and colleagues showed the videotapes to 119 researchers and practitioners at two conferences. These professionals scored at less than chance level in rating the veracity of children's accounts. Ceci and colleagues conducted a comparable study with five true and five false vignettes from the "mousetrap" study, in which children were programmed to state they had caught their finger in a mousetrap as well as relate true events in their lives. They showed these 10 videotapes to 109 professionals in psychology, law enforcement, social work, and psychiatry. The results again indicate that professionals scored at chance levels to differentiate false accounts and true ones. Interestingly, neither study of professionals has been published in its own right, but rather appeared in the discussion section of the study from which it derived. A weakness of both of them is that the vignettes were not representative of the full spectrum of children's accounts but were chosen based upon criteria that were not clearly articulated.

Similar findings regarding human/professional inability to discern false and true accounts were reported by Dalenberg (1992). She had mothers assist 97 children in developing either a true or false account of physical punishment by another adult. Dalenberg then had the children's videotaped statements rated for veracity by graduate students, probation officers, social workers, and professional licensure applicants. The participants were able to classify correctly 52% of the accounts. Their assessments were compared to those of a computer program, using 31 objective criteria. The computer was correct 84% of the time.

These studies argue in favor of criteria that are applied systematically and against relying on subjective impressions of truthfulness and believability. This issue is addressed in depth in chapter 16.

BASE RATES FOR FALSE REPORTS BY ADULTS VERSUS CHILDREN

False accounts of sexual victimization may be made by adults or children or may involve adult–child collusion. In the 1985 Kempe Center study (Jones & McGraw, 1985), of all reports, 5% were fictitious allegations by adults and 1% fictitious allegations by children. When cases in which there was insufficient information are eliminated, the rates for fictitious allegations are 6% for adults and 2% for children.

In the more recent Kempe Center study (Oates et al., 2000), results were somewhat different. In the "not abuse" category are cases determined unlikely but no malicious intent was found ($n=114$; 21%), situations in which a parent or relative overreacted to signs and symptoms ($n=32$; 6%), and cases where a community professional made a report that was unfounded (e.g., a teacher reported a child who was masturbating in class) ($n=30$, 5%). There were 20 (3.6%) cases judged to be malicious false reports. These break down into nine (1.6%) cases made by adults, three (0.5%) cases of adult–child collusion, and eight (1.5%) false allegations by children.

As noted above, Graham and Watkeys (1991) documented 74 (18%) false cases from a Welsh sample. Of those regarded as malicious, 7% were made by adults and 2% by children.

Trocme and Bala (2005) provided data on the source of false reports of child maltreatment, including false reports of sexual abuse. Forty-three of 798 sexual abuse investigations in their study were deemed to be false (5% unweighted). None were made by children, but eight (19%) were made by custodial parents, seven (16%) by noncustodial parents, and six (14%) by relatives, neighbors, or acquaintances. The remaining 22 were made by "others" or the source could not be identified.

The findings from these four studies are not entirely consistent. They suggest, however, that professionals should be more worried about false reports emanating from adults than from children.

RISK SITUATIONS FOR FALSE ALLEGATIONS BY ADULTS

Adults in certain contexts are reported to be more likely to make false allegations of sexual abuse. The context cited most frequently is divorce (Benedek & Schetky, 1985; Bresee, Stearns, Bess, & Packer, 1986; Faller, 1991a; Faller & DeVoe, 1995a; Gardner, 1989, 1991; Graham & Watkeys, 1991; Jones & McGraw, 1987; Klajner-Diamond, Wehrspann, &

Steinhauer, 1987; Mikkelsen et al., 1992). However, there is disagreement regarding the motivations for making false allegations. Benedek and Schetky (1985) and Gardner (1989) found these parents, almost all of whom they said were mothers, make calculated false reports. Gardner described these women as wanting to "wreak vengeance" upon their ex-spouses. Benedek and Schetky also diagnosed many of these mothers with paranoid personality disorder.

Other researchers have found few consciously made false allegations. Jones and McGraw (1987) noted that a substantial number of adults making fictitious allegations in custody disputes were suffering post-traumatic stress disorder (PTSD) and that a number were otherwise psychiatrically disturbed. In these cases, untrue reports were not conniving but a consequence of psychiatric illness. Thoennes and Tjaden (1990), who studied allegations in divorce, had data on motivation of only half of the accusers in their 169 cases, but found only eight cases where the report appeared to be a calculated false accusation and five where the charge appeared to arise from parental emotional disturbance. In only half of their cases was the accusation of sexual abuse made by the mother. In a study of 215 cases with sexual abuse allegations in divorce, Faller and DeVoe (1995a) found that 21% of cases appeared to be false, but most wrongly accusing parents seemed genuinely to believe the child had been victimized. Only 10 cases involved parents who knew they made false charges.

Emotional disturbance, other than in divorce cases, appears to cause some adults to believe incorrectly that a child has been sexually abused. Goodwin et al. (1979), Klajner-Diamond et al. (1987), and Faller (1988a) found that sometimes psychotic adults have delusions that children are being sexually abused. Although providing no data, Lipian et al. (2004) also note adult and parental delusions as a source of false abuse allegations. Some of the adults in Jones and McGraw's (1987) sample were not involved in divorces but suffered PTSD and other psychiatric disturbance. Interestingly, two of Jones and McGraw's nine fictitious accusers were emotionally disturbed professionals. Klajner-Diamond et al. (1987) reported PTSD in some mothers who made false allegations, although they also describe mothers with PTSD whose children had, in fact, been sexually abused.

Gardner (1991, 1992, 1995) wrote that 95% of allegations are true, yet he declared that the overwhelming majority of cases in daycare, nursery schools, and divorces are false. Gardner faulted parents, "validators," and "therapists" (his quotes). He attributed the "deluge" of false accusations essentially to the wish of parents and professionals themselves to be involved in sexual activities with children. According to Gardner, making false allegations of sexual abuse and viewing sexual abuse as rampant satisfy the perverse needs of the accuser. Every time the adult makes an accusation, he/she imagines the sexual activity and is sexually gratified by this fantasy. Also, Gardner asserted that the overwhelming majority of persons conducting evaluations for sexual abuse and providing sexual abuse treatment are incompetent.

RISK SITUATIONS FOR FALSE ALLEGATIONS BY CHILDREN

As noted above, false accusations of sexual abuse by children are uncommon (e.g., Everson & Boat, 1989; Gomez-Schwartz, Horowitz, & Cardinelli, 1990; Jones & McGraw, 1987; Leventhal, Bentovim, Elton, Tranter, & Read, 1987; Lyon, 1995; Oates et al., 2000). In the first Kempe Center study (Jones & McGraw, 1987) such allegations comprised 1% of all reports (and 2% when insufficient information cases are eliminated). In the second Kempe Center study (Oates et al., 2000), erroneous allegations by children consisted of 14 cases (2.5%) and involved three subcategories: (1) collusion with an adult (3 cases; 0.5%), (2) child confused/m istaken (3 cases; 0.5%), and (3) fabricated allegations by child (8 cases; 1.5%). Faller (1988a) believed that 3% of her clinical sample of 194 cases were false accounts by children. Goodwin et al. (1982) found one false account by a child in the 46 cases they reviewed. Horowitz et al. (1984), whose project at Tufts University is mentioned above, involved extensive assessment. They found fewer than 5% of 181 consecutive referrals to be false allegations by children.

In their study of 212 sexual abuse experts, Conte et al. (1991) found that respondents noted false allegations of sexual abuse by children occurred "seldom" but noted them in several contexts: being involved in a custody battle, psychological disturbance of the child, being exposed to a sexually overstimulating but nonabusive atmosphere, wanting to punish a hated parent, having no sense of obligation to tell the truth, and being too young to distinguish fact from fantasy.

Children whose parents are involved in divorce with custody or visitation disputes have been described by a number of authors as making false accusations (Benedek & Schetky, 1987a&b; Gardner, 1989; Green, 1986; Jones & McGraw, 1987; Jones & Seig, 1988; Levanthal et al., 1987; Renshaw, 1987). In Conte et al.'s (1991) survey of sexual abuse professionals, 90% of respondents thought that being involved in a custody battle "occasionally" resulted in distortions of the child's report. Jones and McGraw (1987) describe nine cases seen at the Kempe Center, all involving custody disputes, where both parent and child made a false allegation. They noted enmeshed relationships between these parents and children and, as cited above, psychiatric disturbance in the parents. Faller and De-Voe (1995a) reported nine cases (2.5%) that involved fused adult–child or child false allegations in the study of 215 cases in divorce described above.

Reports indicate that false accusations are more likely to be made by older children, usually adolescents (Faller, 1988a; Jones & McGraw,

1987; Tufts New England Medical Center, 1984). Jones and McGraw (1987) identified eight allegations made by five children, four of whom were female adolescents who had been sexually abused in the past and had symptoms of PTSD. These researchers concluded that the PTSD resulted in distortions leading to the false allegations. Faller (1988a) identified adolescents as making the majority of false allegations. These children had histories of prior sexual abuse but appeared to make the allegations for instrumental reasons, for example, to cover up their con-sensual sexual activity or to effect removal from the home. Similarly, Graham and Watkeys (1991) found that some children making false allegations did so to extricate themselves from unsatisfactory living sit-uations. Benedek and Schetky (1987a&b) similarly report false accusa-tions made by adolescents for secondary gain. The American Academic of Child and Adolescent Psychiatry (AACAP) guidelines (American Academic of Child and Adolescent Psychiatry, 1990) and AACAP prac-tice parameters (American Academic of Child and Adolescent Psychia-try, 1997a&b) also caution evaluators that adolescents may make false reports because of vindictiveness or to cover their own sexuality. The majority of the false reports in Horowitz et al. (1984) sample were from adolescents, as well. Reasons Horowitz and colleagues noted were anger at the accused, an attempt to influence the living situation, and emotional disturbance. Eight of the 14 (57%) false allegations in the sec-ond Kempe Center study were made by adolescents (Oates et al., 2000).

Emotional disturbance on the part of the child has been suggested as a source of false allegations (American Academic of Child and Adolescent Psychiatry, 1997b; Bernet, 1993; Conte et al., 1991; Jones & McGraw, 1987; Mikkelsen et al., 1992). A range of possible diagnoses have been pro-posed, including PTSD (Jones & McGraw, 1987), delusions (Bernet, 1993), pseudologia phantastica (Bernet, 1993), and severe mental illness.

Infrequently children have been found to identify the wrong abuser (American Academic of Child and Adolescent Psychiatry, 1997b; Ber-net, 1993). Faller (1988a) observed that some children cite someone who is less feared or less loved than the actual offender, and Faller reported four children in 136 divorce cases who accused their biological fathers when in fact someone else committed the abuse (Faller, 1991a). Simi-larly, Graham and Watkeys (1991) found that children making false re-ports had been sexually abused but did not correctly identify the abuser. However, De Young (1986) is of the opinion that the evidence is against the child implicating a convenient rather than the actual perpetrator. Bernet (1993) cited several mechanisms reported to be related to perpe-trator substitution, including fantasy, psychosis, confabulation, and Oedipal wishes, as well as simply lying.

Young children may also be the source of false or possibly ficti-tious allegations (Conte et al., 1991; Levanthal et al., 1987; Lipian et al., 2004). Faller (1988a, 1993) has identified social desirability responses as a category of false allegation by young children. Young children may not understand the question, may not know the answer, or may merely wish to please the evaluator and respond affirmatively to yes/no questions (e.g., "Did Uncle Joe put his finger in your peepee?"). As noted in chapter 8, these possibilities are the reason for limiting the use of yes/no questions. Numerous experts (e.g., Boat & Everson, 1989; Lamb & Sternberg, 1999; Merchant & Toth, 2001; Poole & Lamb, 1998; Reed, 1996; White & Quinn, 1988) express strong reservations regarding these sorts of questions. However, as noted in chapters 8 and 10, the findings from analogue studies are mixed regarding the risk of yes/no questions. In some studies, they only rarely produce false positives (Goodman & Clarke-Stewart, 1991), but in research involving very young children, such questions produced false positives more frequently (Bruck, Ceci, Francoeur, & Renick, 1995; Gordon et al., 1993).

Gardner (1991) cites the following factors as leading to false allegations of sexual abuse by children: their polymorphous perversity and consequent penchant to fantasize about sexual activity, including such activity with adults; children's exposure to sexual abuse prevention programs, which cause them to confuse appropriate touch with sexual abuse and stimulate their sexual fantasies; and the "ubiquity of environmental sexual stimuli," such as MTV and pornographic videos. His criteria for deciding the likelihood of sexual abuse are discussed in chapter 16.

Two individual cases are described in the literature as detailed false allegations by children (Bernet, 1997; Hershkowitz, 2001). Bernet's case derived from an audiotaped "interrogation" of 5-year-old girl by her babysitter. The allegation arose when the child evidenced fear of a broom because she said her parents played a game called "sweep your bootie." Bernet (1997) quoted examples of coercive questioning techniques that ultimately resulted in the 5-year-old making allegations of severe abuse against both her parents.

The second example in the literature (Hershkowitz, 2001) involved a 10-year-old girl who walked through the woods on her way home from school, an activity she was forbidden to do. A man exposed himself and forced her to look at his penis. She ran away. Initially she failed to report the event but later, upon the advice of friends, decided to report it to her mother. In order to avoid problems because of her delay, she took the same route through the woods and arrived home crying. Her mother asked her a series of direct questions including whether someone had touched her private parts, which she affirmed. When interviewed, the girl stated that she had been forcibly thrown down and raped. However, the forensic medical exam revealed no evidence of rape or penetration. Eventually she recanted and gave a statement about the man exposing himself to her several days earlier. Hershkowitz subjected both accounts to criteria-based content analysis, which is described in chapter 15, and concluded that the exposure account contained criteria of a true allegation, and the rape account did not. Of note is that, in both of these case examples, questioning techniques by nonprofessionals appeared to have played a role in the false accusations.

SUMMARY AND CONCLUSIONS

The issue of false allegations of sexual abuse has received a great deal of attention in the professional literature. It is important to appreciate, however, that it is quite difficult to be sure that allegations are false. Although a number of criteria have been proposed for false allegations, most research relies on consensually derived opinion that an allegation is false or the disposition by a mandated professional. Studies using these criteria suggest that deliberate false allegations of sexual abuse are uncommon, although a substantial proportion of sexual abuse cases are not substantiated.

In contrast, some allegations of sexual abuse can be documented as true because there is a positive indicator independent of the sexual abuse report, for example, sexually transmitted disease or other physical evidence, audiovisual evidence, or offender confession. Research examining cases with an independent indicator of likelihood found false denial rates ranging from 20% to 60% and minimization of the sexual abuse by some children. The cases in these studies, however, may not be representative of the full spectrum of true sexual abuse cases.

When deliberate false allegations are made, they appear to more likely to come from adults than from children. Risk situations noted in the literature for adults making false allegations include divorce/custody disputes and adults with mental health problems. In the very small number of cases in which children make false allegations, they are likely to be adolescents, children with mental health problems, and children making false allegations to get themselves out of difficult situations. Very young children may also be the source of fictitious reports, but these usually derive from inappropriate questioning techniques.

Nevertheless, the accumulated research and knowledge indicate that children's failure to report actual sexual abuse constitutes a greater challenge for professionals than false allegations of sexual abuse.

FIFTEEN

Standardized Tests and Measures

William N. Friedrich, Erna Olafson, &
Kathleen Coulborn Faller

The majority of professionals who interview and assess sexually abused children are not specifically trained in and do not use standardized measures. For example, Conte et al. (1991) found that only 28% of the experts in their study employed psychological tests during the course of evaluations. Indeed, most current forensic interview protocols do not incorporate testing (e.g., Bourg et al., 1999; Lamb & Sternberg, 1999; Merchant & Toth, 2001; Poole & Lamb, 1998), even though many of the protocols have been developed by professionals trained in psychological testing. Presently, most professionals agree that psychological tests are neither necessary nor sufficient for deciding whether or not a child has been sexually abused (American Academy of Child and Adolescent Psychiatry, 1997b; American Professional Society on the Abuse of Children, 1997, 2002).

Testing, however, can be extremely helpful as one component of information gathering about the possibly sexually abused child (American Academy of Child and Adolescent Psychiatry, 1990; American Professional Society on the Abuse of Children, 1990; Carnes, Wilson, & Nelson-Gardell, 1999). First, psychological testing can be helpful in understanding the overall functioning of the child being evaluated for possible sexual abuse (Faller, 1996a). These test findings may be important in interpreting the child's behavior and statements during the interview and in other contexts. In addition, alleged victims may be administered intelligence tests, not because of any relationship between intelligence and risk, but to assess some aspects of competency (Faller, 2003).

Second, certain standardized measures specifically test for the effects of sexual abuse (Elliott & Briere, 1994; Kuehnle, 1996, 1998). Although the focus of this book is on interviewing to determine whether a child has been sexually abused, symptoms or effects of sexual abuse can be indicators of the probability of sexual abuse. For example, the Child Sexual Behavior Inventory (CSBI) (e.g., Friedrich, 2002) (described further below) gathers data on children's sexualized behavior. Comparative research on this instrument shows that certain sexualized behaviors by sexually abused children are rarely reported for children who have no sexual victimization history.

Third, there are abuse-specific screening measures that can be administered and scored by almost all professionals interviewing for child sexual abuse. Depending upon the measure, they are completed by the parent, the child, or another professional, such as a teacher, who has considerable contact with the child. Findings from these screening instruments can be integrated with interview and other information to strengthen the data used for deciding about the probability of sexual abuse.

Test findings are also invaluable in alerting parents to their children's problems (Friedrich, 1990), treatment planning (Friedrich, 1990, 2002), measuring treatment progress (Friedrich, 2002), and even policy development (Sebre et al., 2004),[1] but these four functions are not addressed in this chapter.

This chapter covers the strengths and limitations of psychological tests, descriptions of commonly used trauma-specific measures, their integration into interview formats, sequelae of sexual abuse that can be measured with standardized measures, and a summary of the findings from research on sexually abused children using these and other measures.

STRENGTHS AND LIMITATIONS OF PSYCHOLOGICAL TESTS

Standardized tests with sexually abused children were initially embraced by child abuse professionals because of their diagnostic potential. Tests also had an appeal in court because their findings were "objective." These responses led to the overinterpretation of single "diagnostic" markers such as whether or not a child drew genitals on a human figure drawing (Hibbard, Roghmann, & Hoekelman, 1987; Veltman & Browne, 2002; Yates, Beutler, & Crago, 1985) or how the child positioned anatomical dolls (Friedrich, 2002). Because the impact of sexual abuse is so variable, reliance on a single behavior or symptom is inappropriate. At the same time, there are strong rationales for the utilization of valid and reliable empirical measures. These measures include both psychological tests that require advanced training for administration and interpretation and screening checklists that can be used by a greater variety of professionals.

Strengths of Test Findings

Testing has several advantages over relying solely on interview findings.

Testing Yields Normative Data

Systematic assessment of individuals using standardized measures yields group or actuarial data that have better predictive validity than does clinical assessment of an individual case (Meehl, 1954). When clinicians balance their interview findings with actuarial data, this can add to the predictive validity of their clinical assessment of individual cases.

Data From Standardized Measures Have Validity

Standardized measurements are also reliable and valid (Meyer et al., 2001). In Meyer and colleagues' review, data from more than 125 meta-analyses on test validity showed not only that psychological test validity is strong and compelling but also that it is comparable to medical test validity. Further, they concluded that clinicians who rely exclusively on interviews are prone to incomplete understanding of their clients (Meyer et al., 2001).

Testing Can Be Cost-Effective

Screening measures take 5–20 minutes, with most in the 5–10 minute range. Screening measures provide unique sources of information and inexpensively expand the utility of the interview.

*Standardized Measures Can Mediate Against the Emotionality
of Sexual Abuse Cases*

Given the variability in presentation and the heightened emotionality that often accompanies allegations of sexual abuse; standardized measures can present a template that can allow for a more objective evaluation process in these complex situations. This template can generate hypotheses about the likelihood of sexual abuse, the possible impact of abuse, and optimal treatment formats.

Standardized Measures Assure Systematic Data Collection

Standardized measures also assure the collection of information about a spectrum of relevant factors. Interviewers may overlook some areas and concentrate on others, thus missing important information and sometimes biasing assessment results. For example, sexual behavior in younger children is a charged topic that covers many different types of behaviors, including self-stimulation, boundary problems, sexual knowledge, and intrusive sexual behavior with children and adults. Interviewers typically cover this topic in a relatively cursory manner, for example, "Have you noticed any increase in sexual behaviors since your child told you about what happened?" A more thorough assessment is possible via several parent-completed checklists.

Limitations of Psychological Testing

Standardized instruments also have limitations in shedding new and valid light on the particular child in question.

Sometimes Adult Report Is Biased

Many standardized measures employed with preschool and young school-age children rely on caretaker report. Although caretakers are feasible and useful sources of information, especially with children too young to self-report, caretakers may lack objectivity and either over-report or underreport the child's behaviors and symptoms. Caretakers may also have a skewed view of the child for a variety of personal and/or cultural reasons.

Illustrative of absence of objectivity are scores on the CSBI in custody and visitation disputes between separated parents. Some of the highest scores obtained on the CSBI came from parents who were accusing their ex-spouse of sexual abuse (Friedrich, Talley, Panser, Fett, & Zins-meister, 1997). In these situations, obtaining data from at least one other source is recommended. Moreover, research using the CSBI with parents and preschool teachers or nurses documents that these adults may make discrepant observations because they see the child at different times; for example, parents see children at bath and bedtime whereas teachers do not (Friedrich & Trane, 2002; Larsson & Svedin, 2002).

In Using Behavior Rating Scales, Use More Than One Data Source

A rule of thumb with the use of standardized measures is to use more than one reporter and to assess at least two behavioral outcomes. This is more difficult with very young children, who cannot self-report. When children are between 8 and 10 years of age, their capacity for self-perception and perspective taking has improved, and their ability to read questions is reasonably advanced. Children this age can add useful information to the assessment process. Completing a checklist gives many children an opportunity not only to talk about how they are feeling, but also about any abuse.

Interpretation of Findings Can Be Inappropriate

The interpretation of the data by an interviewer or evaluator may be naive or overly inclusive. For example, as the developer of the CSBI, the first author of this chapter, the late William Friedrich, reported regularly hearing from attorneys and psychologists how a child's score on this scale was used to "diagnose" sexual abuse. This happened despite repeated warnings in the manual that this is inappropriate and no single behavior or combination of behaviors can prove that abuse occurred. The same is true for the use of the Trauma Symptom Checklist for Children (TSCC) to diagnose posttraumatic stress disorder (PTSD) when, in actuality, the TSCC assesses PTSD-related symptoms.

Developmental Issues

For a variety of personal and cultural reasons, many children are poor reporters about their internal states, especially those children with trauma histories who employ avoidance, denial, and numbing to cope with their pain (Olafson, 1999). Perhaps for neurological as well as psychological reasons, children with extensive maltreatment histories are less accurate at identifying their own emotions and those of people around them than nonmaltreated children (Putnam, 2006). Cognitive development also plays a role; in average children, it usually matures between ages 8 and 9, when the child's affective self-understanding comes to be based on internal, mental cues (La Greca, 1990). Before this age, young children are likely to rely on situational or body cues to identify their feelings. Brighter children with a larger vocabulary for feelings may provide reasonably valid reports by 8 years, but disadvantaged children may not be able to give valid reports until older. For example, it is around the age of 8 years that children move from all-or-none thinking about their traits and begin to see themselves more selectively, for example, good in one area and not as good in another. Interview and self-report measures with preschool and young elementary-age children should employ concrete and action-oriented questions, for example, "Do you cry?" versus "Are you sad?"

Contextual Impact

Finally, younger children take their cues from the context, including their perceived support from a parent. This is certainly true of interview reports but can also apply to standardized measures. When there is a threat to safety, as in homes where there is ongoing battering or child maltreatment, there is a likelihood of underreporting by children and, indeed, by all parties (Bancroft & Silverman, 2002; Carnes et al., 1999).

Behavior Rating Scales Do Not Yield a Diagnosis

No behavior rating scales have proven to have the discriminative ability necessary to be deemed diagnostic tests. The quality of the information professionals obtain will depend in part on the measure used. For example, results of a self-esteem scale are less directly related to the likelihood of sexual abuse than the results of PTSD screening or measures of sexualized behaviors. Sexual abuse is not a condition such as depression, and as noted above, there is no standard list of symptoms that are assessed to yield a diagnosis (Friedrich, 2002).

BRIEF OVERVIEW OF MEASURES

In this section, standardized measures that may be employed in sexual abuse assessments are described. These include instruments completed by the child's caretaker, instruments completed by the child, and projective measures sometimes employed with children to gather information indirectly.

Behavior Checklists Completed by Parents

A number of behavior checklists that assess overall functioning and specific symptoms have been employed with maltreated children (e.g., the Louisville Behavior Checklist: Tufts New England Medical Center, 1984; Chantler, Pelco, & Mertin, 1993; Achenbach Child Behavior Checklist [CBCL]: Friedrich, 1990; J. Waterman & Lusk, 1993). Chantler et al. (1993) found limited support for the utility of the Louisville Behavior Checklist in differentiating a sexually abused sample, a clinical sample, and a community sample.

The 113-item Achenbach CBCL is the most widely used with maltreated children (Achenbach, 1991a). The CBCL taps competencies and problem behaviors for children ages 4–18 and has a separate version for 2- to 3-year-olds (Achenbach, Edelbrock, & Howell, 1987). The most widely used version is completed by the caretaker, but there are is also a Teacher Report Form and a Youth Self-Report Form for older children (Achenbach, 1991b). The CBCL has a clinical cutoff and yields a total problems score, internalizing and externalizing scores, and a competency score. Scores are also provided along a number of subscales, for example, anxiety/depression, withdrawal, and aggression.

When traumatic effects are assessed in children who are too young to self-report, parents can complete the Trauma Symptom Checklist for Young Children (TSCYC) (Briere et al., 2001). This 90-item symptom checklist is intended for children ages 3–12. The TSCYC has eight clinical scales: posttraumatic stress—intrusion, posttraumatic stress—avoidance, posttraumatic stress—arousal, posttraumatic stress—total, sexual concerns, dissociation, anxiety, depression, and anger/aggression. Preliminary data on 219 caretakers indicate that the TSCYC has good reliability, and its clinical scales differentiated children with histories of sexual abuse, physical abuse, and witnessing domestic violence from children without such histories (Briere et al., 2001).

Although a key marker of sexually abused children is sexualized behavior; the CBCL and comparable instruments have only a small number of items related to sexualized behavior (Friedrich, 1990). Because of the need for a more thorough assessment of sexual behavior, Friedrich spent more than 20 years developing a standardized measure, the CSBI for measuring symptoms that tend to be specific to sexually victimized children. The current version has 38 items and is used for caretaker report on children ages 2–12. The CSBI has a clinical cutoff and yields a total score and two subscale scores: a developmentally related behaviors score and sexual-abuse–specific items score.

However, because many child sexual abuse victims are nonsymptomatic, the absence of a pathological level of sexualized behavior does not mean the child has not been sexually abused. One study found that severe sexual abuse is associated with victims becoming either avoidant of sexuality, and presumably exhibiting fewer sexual behaviors, or hypersexual (Merrill, Guimond, Thomsen, & Milner, 2003). Sexualized behavior is the most frequently found symptom specific to a history of child sexual abuse, but it is nevertheless present in only about 40% of children believed to have been sexually abused (Friedrich, 1994).

The CSBI has also been used internationally. Comparisons of responses of U.S. parents and parents from Sweden and the Netherlands show differences in children's sexualized behavior by culture (Friedrich, Sandfort, Osstveen, & Cohen-Kettenis, 2000; Larsson, Svedin, & Friedrich, 2000). Parents in both Sweden and the Netherlands endorse higher rates of sexual behavior by their children than do American parents. In Sweden, higher rates were more pronounced among boys.

If dissociation is suspected, parent input can be obtained via the Child Dissociative Checklist (CDC) for children of 12 or younger. This 20-item screening measure is a public domain document freely available for reproduction and use. There are no valid self-report measures about dissociation for younger children (Putnam, Helmers, & Trickett, 1993; Putnam, 1997). This measure is not diagnostic of sexual abuse or of dissociation, but it can alert evaluators to recommend children for the structured clinical interviews by skilled clinicians that are necessary for formal diagnosis.

Behavior Checklists Completed by Children/Teens

Yet another checklist that is intended to address the dearth of instruments specific to sexually abused (and other traumatized) children is the TSCC (Briere, 1996; Briere & Lanktree, 1992). The TSCC is 54-item rating scale designed for children 8 and older and has six subscales (anxiety, depression, posttraumatic stress, sexual concerns, dissociation, and anger). It has been shown to be psychometrically reliable and to have predictive validity (Sadowski & Friedrich, 2000). Older adolescents are better served by a similar, but longer measure, the Trauma Symptom Inventory (Briere, 1996). As noted above, the CBCL has a child/teen form, the Youth Report Survey.

If anxiety is suspected, the Multidimensional Anxiety Scale of Children, a 39-item self-report measure, is much more complete than the less inclusive anxiety component of the TSCC (March, 1997). It is intended for children ages 8–19. To screen for anxiety, this measure has shown good reliability as well as discriminate validity.

The Adolescent Dissociative Experiences Scale (ADES) is a useful self-report dissociative screening measure for older children (Armstrong, Putnam, Carlson, Libero, & Smith, 1997; Friedrich, Olafson, & Connelly, 2004). Like the CDC, it is a freely available public domain document. Because of its obvious face validity, results from this test depend on the willingness of adolescents to report unusual feelings and internal states.

Depression is strongly correlated with child sexual abuse and other child maltreatment histories although specific to neither; two brief self-report measures have good reliability and validity for adolescent self-report of depressive symptoms. The Beck Depression Inventory is a 21-item, self-report measure intended for adolescents and adults ages 13–80 (Beck, 1996). The Children's Depression Inventory is a 27-item self-report scale for children and adolescents ages 6–17. It is written at a first-grade reading level. Although not specific to child sexual abuse, depression is one of its most common outcomes; in addition, the poverty of thought and affect that characterizes severe depression may affect children's witness capacity (Putnam, 2003, 2006). Like the ADES, the validity of both depression inventories depends on the ability and the willingness of children and adolescents to disclose their internal states; in cases where avoidance, minimization and denial appear to be prominent, projective tests or structured interviews may provide more information (Friedrich et al., 2004)

Projective Tests

Clinicians and researchers have employed projective measures with the belief that victims may provide content in response to these instruments related to their sexual experiences. Such sources of data may be useful with children who are avoidant of abuse-related questions in the interview. However, findings from projective measures should be used with caution and should not be a basis, by themselves, for a conclusion about sexual abuse.

Human figure drawings are some of the oldest projective measures and more recently have been offered as a diagnostic tool for sexual abuse (L. W. Peterson & Hardin, 1997). Regrettably, Peterson and Hardin's scoring system has never been independently validated regarding its ability to distinguish sexually abused children from comparison children. Hibbard et al. (1987) examined the drawing of genitalia on children with and without a history of sexual abuse. Although children with a history were more likely to draw genitals, the proportion of children producing genitals in the abused group was small (see also Veltman & Browne, 2002; Yates et al., 1985).

The Rorschach, the Children's Apperception Test, the Thematic Apperception Test, and the Roberts Apperception Test have all been used do differentiate themes in children's stories in response to pictures (Friedrich, 2002; Friedrich & Share, 1997). Special mention of the Roberts Apperception Test is appropriate since the drawings are more active and realistic; furthermore, Cards 5 and 15 pull specifically for sexual themes (Friedrich, 1990). Sexual content has also been shown to discriminate between sexually abused and nonabused children on the Rorschach (Friedrich, Einbender, & McCarty, 1999).

In addition, pictures intended to elicit content from children about physical abuse, sexual abuse, neglect, and interpersonal violence have been developed, specifically the Projective Story Telling Cards (PST Cards) (Caruso, 1988). Eight PST Cards are focused specifically on possible sexual abuse. This instrument is the work of a clinical psychologist and an artist colleague. The manual offers no details about the validation of these cards, and the representation of them in the manual as a diagnostic test is one of the ways that testing can be abused.

Moreover, Friedrich (1994) used two of the PST Cards with children having a history of possible sexual abuse and those with no such history. He found that the explicit nature of the cards elicited stories involving sexual themes from the vast majority of respondents, and there was no significant difference in the proportion producing such stories between the two groups. In addition, although the children in the cards are drawn so that they could be of either gender, making the cards appropriate for both male and female victims, there are few pictures suggesting female sex offenders. Thus, interviewers are cautioned about the utility of these cards, and they are not recommended for forensic interviews or assessment. They may be more useful in treatment.

Even more concerning is a later series of PST Cards produced by Casebeer (1989), which depict sexual exploitation and ritual abuse of children. These cards are much more explicit than the earlier cards. For example, several persons in the exploitation cards are partially naked, and ritual abuse cards have graphic representations of satanic acts and artifacts. Although it can be argued that children without histories of exploitive and ritual abuse will not recognize what is in these pictures, these cards are not recommended, except perhaps in treatment of children with known exploitive and ritual abuse histories.

INCORPORATING TESTING INTO INTERVIEWING FOR SEXUAL ABUSE

General psychological testing of the child, trauma-specific measures, and abuse screening instruments can be used in a single child-interview format, but all types of psychological testing integrate better in a two to three interview format (Briere et al., 2001; Faller, 2003), extended assessment formats (Carnes, Wilson, Nelson-Gardell, 2000; Friedrich, 2002), and the total family assessments that are generally conducted when intrafamilial sexual abuse is alleged (Faller, 2003; Kuehnle, 1996).

Some child advocacy centers have the child's caretaker complete the CSBI (e.g., Friedrich, 2002). After providing relevant child history, the caretaker completes the instrument while the child is being interviewed.

Kuehnle (1996) advises the use of standardized measures for assessing trauma (e.g., TSCC; Briere, 1996) and abuse-specific behaviors (e.g., CSBI, Friedrich, 2002) along with an interview of the child.

The National Children's Advocacy Center incorporates screening measures into an extended assessment (Carnes et al., 1999). This program utilizes two checklists from parents, the CBCL (Achenbach, 1991a) and the CSBI (Friedrich, 1997), and one self-report measure for older children, the TSCC (Briere, 1996). The data from the checklists, as well as screening completed regarding the child's developmental level, the child's view of their family/support system, and other findings are incorporated into the results of the interviews to make a decision regarding the credibility of the child's report. This approach couches the child's statements into a broader view of the child and is also used in subsequent treatment planning.

As part of a comprehensive family assessment, which relies on two child interviews or a six-interview extended assessment, the University of Michigan Family Assessment Clinic uses three screening checklists, the CBCL (Achenbach, 1991a), the CSBI (Friedrich, 2002), and the TSCYC (Briere et al., 2001; Faller, 2003). Children 10 and older may be asked to complete the TSCC (Briere, 1996).

Friedrich (1995, 2002) suggests a template for determining the likelihood of sexual abuse, sexual abuse impact, and appropriate treatment. This framework involves the assessment of the presence of behavior problems reflecting difficulties in self-regulation, including sexualized behavior and PTSD and issues that are more specific to the individual, including shame and guilt and problematic parent–child relationships. If the professional adheres to this template, standardized assessment measures to evaluate PTSD, sexual behavior problems, and shame and guilt in children who are old enough to validly self-report, should be employed. The quality of the parent–child relationship should also be assessed. The framework involves a well-articulated and structured approach incorporating the use of standardized measures (CSBI, CBCL, Adolescent Sexual Behavior Inventory [ASBI] [Friedrich, Lysne, & Sim, 2004]) and a number of other checklists. In addition, outlines for components of the interview and suggested questions are included (Friedrich, 2002).

Interviewers are hard-pressed to cover not only the event(s) that brought the child to the assessment but also to assess the range of possible outcomes without an extended format. In response to a question, "How well do you believe your child is functioning relative to his peers?" the parent's response may be widely divergent from that of their spouse or from such people as daycare providers and teachers. Clinicians always struggle to separate the noise from the substance of the situation, and standardized tests, when used appropriately, can assist in this process. A model that involves several interviews and testing is desirable, although not feasible in every case, given the current structure of child welfare and child advocacy center services. When a caretaker is the alleged abuser or is nonprotective, a multiple interview model that incorporates screening measures should be strongly considered.

COMMON SYMPTOMS AND INDICATORS OF SEXUAL VICTIMIZATION

Although sexually abused children experience a wide range of symptoms that may be indicators of sexual victimization, there are domains of functioning that are more specific to sexual abuse. It is advisable when assessing for possible sexual abuse to concentrate on these domains. Support for this strategy comes as well from data suggesting that more generic constructs such as self-esteem issues, depression, and anxiety are less specific to sexual abuse than are other domains, such as sexual behavior and attitudes, PTSD, and dissociation (Kendall-Tackett, Williams, & Finkelhor, 1993). In addition, abuse specific cognitions such as shame and guilt related to the abuse have been increasingly researched and shown to predict response to treatment (Feiring, Taska, & Lewis, 2002).

However, it is also useful to put these sexual-abuse–specific symptoms in perspective with data from a more broad-based behavior rating scale completed by the parent, for example, the CBCL, as well as a determination of a younger child's developmental level, for example, by having the parent complete the Child Development Inventory (Ireton, 1992).

Sexualized Behavior

Sexualized behavior is the most common marker of sexual victimization, although only about 40% of children with a history of sexual abuse engage in such behavior and sexualized behavior can be related to other experiences (Friedrich, 2002; Friedrich & Trane, 2002). There are also data that indicate that sexual behavior can be a function of family and child factors other than sexual abuse (Friedrich, 1997). Measures that can be employed to assess for sexualized behavior include the CSBI (Friedrich, 1997, 2002) and the Sexual Abuse Symptom Checklist (Kolko, Moser, & Weldy, 1988), which also holds promise but has been less extensively tested than the CSBI. The interviewer may also review the results from these sexual behavior checklists with the caretaker to obtain more detailed information or clarification. For teenagers, self-report measures such as the TSCC (Briere, 1996) and the teen and parent versions of the ASBI are recommended (Friedrich, Lysne, & Sim, 2004). The domains of sexual risk-taking and behaviors that open up a teen to being victimized should also be assessed.

Dissociation

Dissociation is not common but has been reliably reported in children and teens, particularly those with histories of severe, prolonged maltreatment. Children who are dissociative often are unaware that they dissociate, and they are likely to have a slower developing vocabulary for emotions and self-understanding. In addition, children who grow up in families where abuse is rampant often have caregivers who are poor reporters of their child's behavior. All of these factors make assessment more difficult (Putnam, 1997). The CDC and the ADES or quick screening measures for dissociation as described above.

Posttraumatic Stress

PTSD is more common in sexually abused children than is dissociation, but perhaps a majority of sexually abused children will have neither disorder. In addition, symptoms vary depending upon the child's age. For example, a reexperiencing phenomenon in younger traumatized children can manifest as stereotypic and numbly repetitive play. PTSD-related behaviors include self-injurious behaviors, which may represent flashbacks, hyperarousal, or numbness and also somatic symptoms, which can be a manifestation of hyperarousal (Kendall-Tackett, 2003). The irritable reactivity of children who have PTSD is often misdiagnosed as attention deficit hyperactivity disorder (Friedrich et al., 2004).

If a diagnosis is not needed, and the clinician is simply wanting to look at PTSD-related symptoms, the TSCC (Briere, 1996) or TSCYC (Briere, Johnson, Bissada, Damon, Crouch et al., 2001) can be quite helpful. Subscales from the CBCL have also been developed to assess for PTSD-related symptoms (Wolfe, Gentile, & Wolfe, 1989). The TSCC is a self-report measure; the TSCYC is a parent report measure, and the CBCL has parent and teacher report versions and a self-report version for adolescents. Other measures not reviewed in detail here for child and adolescent PTSD are the Children's PTSD Reaction Index, the Children's Impact of Events Scale–Revised, the Impact of Events Scale, and the Children's Reaction to Traumatic Events Scale (Friedrich et al., 2004).

Shame and Responsibility

Shame and attributions of responsibility for the abuse are clearly abuse and trauma related. Although shame and feelings of responsibility have been identified as consequences of sexual abuse for more than two decades (e.g., Faller, 1988a; Sgroi, 1982), only recently have these effects have begun to be studied systematically (Feiring & Taska, 2005; Feiring et al., 1998, 2002; Negrao, Bonano, Noll, Putnam, & Trickett, 2005). Shame is related both to the persistence of depression (Feiring et al., 1998) and to the increased risk for sexual aggression (Hall, Mathews, & Pearce, 1998). Presently, however, there is no standardized measure for attributions of shame in sexual abuse victims.

OVERVIEW OF FINDINGS FROM RESEARCH ON STANDARDIZED MEASURES

Testing, especially comparisons of children with and without a history of sexual abuse, can be used by professionals to inform them about the presentation of children who have been sexually abused. Three types of tests are covered in this section: findings from testing not specifically for sexual abused children, findings from testing that taps sexual concerns, including sexualized behavior, and findings from tests that assess the impact of sexual abuse on functioning.

Findings From Generic Testing

Data are available from assessments that compare the overall function-ing of children with a history of sexual abuse to children without a history, although the findings are mixed. Research examining the cogni-tive functioning of sexually abused children fails to find global deficits (J. Waterman & Lusk, 1993). However, several studies do suggest that sexually abused children may have more academic problems than their nonabused counterparts (Boney-McCoy & Finkelhor, 1996; Einbender & Friedrich, 1989; Lyon & Saywitz, 1999). Similarly, based upon a hypoth-esis that sexual abuse has a negative impact on self-esteem, researchers have employed the Piers Harris Self-Concept Scale (Cohen & Mannarino, 1988; Gomez-Schwartz, Horowitz, & Cardinelli, 1990; Tufts New England Medical Center, 1984). A comparable hypothesis has led to the use of the Children's Depression Inventory with sexually abused children (Cohen & Mannarino, 1988; Lipovsky, Saunders, Murphy, & Shane, 1989).

J. Waterman and Lusk (1993) report 11 studies in which sexually abused and nonabused children were compared, using results from the CBCL. These studies suggest that sexually abused children have more behavior problems than do nonabused children but, as a group, are typ-ically not more disturbed than other clinical samples. In addition, sexu-ally abused children score significantly higher on the sexual problems subscale of the CBCL (J. Waterman & Lusk, 1993). Two slightly different PTSD-related subscales have been empirically developed and extend the utility of the CBCL with sexually abused children (Friedrich, Beilke, & Urquiza, 1988; Wolfe et al., 1989).

Sexual Concerns

There have been a number of excellent comparison studies related to sex-ualized behavior, facilitated in large part to develop specific instruments to assess sexual behavior in children. For example, researchers have uti-lized parent report on the six sexual behavior items from the CBCL (Achenbach, 1991a) or the 38-item CSBI (Friedrich, 1997). Adolescent self-report can be obtained from either the Adolescent Sexual Concerns Questionnaire (Hussey & Singer, 1993) or the ASBI (Friedrich, Lysne, &

Sim, 2004). Self-report of this important dimension is now available for both children and teens with the TSCC (Briere, 1996). The majority of studies published since the Kendall-Tackett et al. (1993) review that have examined sexual behavior found that sexually abused children exhibit increases in sexualized behavior relative to comparison groups. These results are true for both children and teenagers.

Children

Among children, for example, total sexual behavior as measured by the CSBI differed significantly between sexually abused girls and two comparable groups of 6- to 12-year-old girls (Cosentino, Meyer-Bahlburg, Alpert, Weinberg, & Gaines, 1995). The CSBI also discriminated between sexually abused children and nonabused children from two psychiatric programs, as did the sexual behavior items from the CBCL (Friedrich, Jaworski, Huxsahl, & Bengston, 1997).

The CSBI was also utilized in a large-scale study of 2- to 12-year-old children (Friedrich et al., 2001). In this study were 1,114 nonabused normative children, 620 sexually abused children, and 577 psychiatric outpatients. Given the demographic differences of the samples, age, sex, maternal education, and family income were controlled for in the between-groups analyses. Sexually abused children exhibited a greater frequency of sexual behaviors than did either the normative or the psychiatric outpatient samples. Sexual behavior was more common in the psychiatric sample than the normative sample, and it was noted that sexualized behavior was related to behavior problems measured by the CBCL (Achenbach, 1991a). In addition, both life stress and family sexuality accounted for significant variance in total sexual behavior for the combined samples.

Sexual abuse was related to significantly elevated sexual behavior on the CSBI in 43–67% of sexually abused children in a sample from Quebec (Wright et al., 1998). These findings are consistent with earlier research on asymptomatic children.

There is one study conducted in a medical clinic that did not find the CSBI had diagnostic utility because some children who did not report sexual abuse or have medical evidence had high scores on the CSBI (Drach, Wientzen, & Ricci, 2001). Friedrich, Trane, and Gully (2005), while commending these clinicians for employing standardized measures, raise questions about Drach and colleagues' methodology and conclusions.

Other research has focused on why it is that some children who are sexually abused develop sexual behavior problems and others do not. This line of research is quite important not only because it illuminates the presence of moderator variables but also because sexual abuse is a potential risk factor for future sexual victimization and sexual offending. Hall, Mathews, and Pearce (1998) studied 100 children ages 3–7.

All had been seen in two programs for sexually abused children. The extensive treatment files of these children were coded, and all but one were sorted into three groups: those who exhibited developmentally expected sexual behavior ($n=22$), developmentally problematic sexual behavior ($n=15$), and interpersonal problematic sexual behavior ($n=62$). They found 20 variables that best distinguished between children with and without problems. These fell into five categories: sexual abuse experience of the child, features of the child, the child's history, parent–child relationship quality, and caregiver characteristics. Examples of these variables include sexual arousal of the child during the abuse, excessive masturbation by the child, a physical abuse history for the child, role reversal with the parent, and maternal history of PTSD.

The summary finding was that sexual abuse, in combination with a variety of additional features, is related to increasingly problematic sexual behavior problems. These problems can be interpersonal and include children exhibiting sexual behavior with other children.

However, sexual abuse also seems to be associated with a more sexualized view of interpersonal relationships in general. For example, sexually abused children provided the largest number of stories that had a sexualized theme in response to a stimulus picture card (Friedrich & Share, 1997). Similarly, Gully (2000) has found that sexually abused children respond to ambiguous stimulus pictures with stories that reflect increased negative feelings and also expectations of sexual abuse.

It makes sense that sexually abused children would exhibit more concern about their safety, particularly the safety of their genitals. This would be more likely if there were a history of anogenital penetration. In fact, children with possible sexual abuse who were referred for a pediatric examination and who had positive medical findings exhibited elevated distress (Gully, Britton, Hansen, Goodwill, & Nope, 1999).

Adolescents

Significantly higher rates of sexual risk-taking behaviors were noted in adolescents with a history of sexual abuse relative to the nonabused members of a longitudinal cohort from New Zealand (Fergusson, Horwood, & Lynskey, 1997). Subjects whose sexual abuse involved intercourse (either attempted or completed) had the highest rates of early-onset sexual activity, teenage pregnancy, unprotected intercourse, and sexually transmitted diseases. They were also the most likely to be victims of later sexual assault, attempted rape, or rape. These findings are supported by a study of 125 sexually abused adolescent girls (Cinq-Mars, Wright, Cyr, McDuff, & Friedrich, 2005). Girls who had experienced penetration became pregnant sooner than girls who had not experienced penetration. The adverse nature of the impact was associated with the presence of family violence as well as several other family risk factors.

Two different self-report scales have been developed specifically to examine sexual behavior in teenagers, and both have been used with sexually abused samples. The Adolescent Sexual Concerns Questionnaire was used to assess the sexual concerns and behaviors of teenagers in an inpatient setting (Hussey & Singer, 1993). Six of the sexual items demonstrated discriminative validity, with more problematic concerns and behaviors reported by the sexually abused group. The longer ASBI was used in a study of teenagers who were either sexually abused or psychiatric patients (Friedrich, Lysne, & Sim, 2004). The ASBI has both a self-report and parent-report version and similar factors are measured on each version. They are sexual distress and anxiety, sexual interest, sexual risk-taking, disturbed body image, and also intrusive and rule-violating behavior. Parent and self-reports correlated significantly, and a strong relationship between maltreatment, particularly sexual abuse, and disturbed sexual behavior in adolescents was noted. However, physical abuse, life stress, and impaired family relationships are also significant correlates of sexual behavior in adolescents.

Sexually abused teenagers, particularly older ones, are also more likely to report sexual concerns on the TSCC (Friedrich et al., 1997). Sexually abused 15- to 18-year-olds reported significantly more sexual preoccupation and more sexual distress than their nonabused psychiatric counterparts. The same but not as marked differences were not noted for the 12- to 14-year-old groups. Possible contributors to this absence of differences for the younger group could derive from the greater problems with self-report at this age in younger children.

Disturbed sexual behavior in teenagers is even more concerning given the riskier outcomes, including pregnancy, chronic health problems, particularly chronic genitourinary and gynecologic symptoms, and even severe illness and death (Springs & Friedrich, 1992). For example, the high-risk sexual behaviors that can lead to infection by sexually transmitted diseases, including HIV/AIDS, are strongly correlated with histories of child sexual abuse (Putnam, 2006). Consequently, while this review is focusing on short-term effects, the long-term outcomes of a number of sexually abused children and teenagers will forever be altered by their earlier experiences.

Posttraumatic Stress

Research on PTSD and related disorders in sexual abuse victims has been complicated by the appreciation that a number of the adult criteria for PTSD are not applicable to children. For example, it is impossible for preschoolers to describe their defensive avoidance or inner states (Scheeringa, Peebles, Cook, & Zeanah, 2001). At the same time, research has expanded because of the development of more specific devices to assess for PTSD. A comprehensive listing of these measures is contained in a supplement published by the American Academy of

Child and Adolescent Psychiatry (1998). Finally, clinicians have a developing awareness that PTSD victims may also experience developmental interference or episodic or persistent symptomatology throughout their lives. Work groups made up of experts from the National Child Traumatic Stress Network are working to create and validate new diagnoses such as complex posttraumatic stress disorder or developmental trauma disorder for children whose biological and physical development has been affected by chronic, severe early trauma and maltreatment (Briere & Spinazzola, 2005; Cook et al., 2005; Spinazzola, Blaustein, & van der Kolk, 2005; van der Kolk, Roth, Pelcovitz, Sunday, & Spinazzola, 2005).

The incidence of PTSD in sexually abused children varies widely. One study found that a significant proportion of sexually abused children (43.9%) referred for mental health services suffered full-blown PTSD, and the vast majority of the others exhibited partial PTSD symptoms (McLeer, Deblinger, Henry, & Orvaschel, 1992). This percentage was even higher (71%) in a subsequent study of treatment for PTSD in sexually abused children (Deblinger, Lippmann, & Steer, 1996).

The specificity of PTSD to sexual abuse has also been studied. For example, sexually abused teenagers reported significantly more symptoms on the posttraumatic stress scale of the TSCC than did their non-abused psychiatric counterparts (Sadowski & Friedrich, 2000). PTSD was diagnosed in 36.3% of sexually abused children and only 1.3% of clinically referred, nonabused children (McLeer, Deblinger, Henry, & Orvaschel, 1992). It is important to note that none of the sexually abused children in this study had been referred for treatment, and so it is possible that this frequency represents a baseline rate of PTSD in nonreferred sexually abused children between the ages of 6 and 16.

In a study conducted by Elliott and Briere (1994), 336 children 8–15 years old who presented for assessment of possible sexual abuse were compared on a number of measures, including the TSCC. Based upon all measures, children were classified according to the likelihood of sexual abuse. Children, who disclosed some or all of their sexual abuse and who were classified as credible, scored the highest overall (most symptomatic) and highest on the six subscales of the TSCC. Children thought not to have been sexually victimized scored next highest on the TSCC, and those who were thought to have been sexually abused, but who were either not disclosing or recanting, scored the lowest on symptoms.

A review of 25 studies of PTSD in children indicates that three factors have been found to consistently mediate the development of PTSD in children: the severity of the trauma exposure, trauma-related parental distress, and temporal proximity to the traumatic event (American Academy of Child and Adolescent Psychiatry, 1998). These relationships have been found to be specifically true for sexual abuse (Cohen & Mannarino,

1996). Cohen and Mannarino's study also found that parental support mitigated the development of PTSD.

Dissociation

Dissociation is thought to be a function of more chronic and severe trauma exposure and thus is related to PTSD (American Academy of Child and Adolescent Psychiatry, 1998). In fact, research with the TSCC found that significantly higher levels of overt dissociation in sexually abused 12- to 14-year-olds and 15- to 18-year-olds relative to a comparison group of psychiatric patients (Friedrich et al., 1997). Several studies have shown that sexually abused children score significantly higher on the CDC than nonabused comparison children (Friedrich et al., 2004). More recently, it was found that sexual abuse was significantly associated with dissociation, as well as other mental health problems, including risk-taking behavior, self-mutilation, and sexual aggression. Dissociation seemed to have an important mediating role between sexual abuse and psychiatric disturbance (Kisiel & Lyons, 2001).

Sexual-Abuse–Related Cognitions

Previous research has focused on the overt behavior of sexually abused children. As more of these children are being treated for the effects of abuse, interest has developed in how these children think about themselves and their abuse, and whether these appraisals are related to the development and persistence of symptoms. Shame has emerged as a constellation of feelings that is more specifically related to sexual abuse than a related, but more generic construct, that is, self-esteem. Sexual abuse victims often express the desire to avoid exposure and hide themselves when talking about their abuse (Feiring, Taska, & Lewis, 1998). This appears to be related to shame as well as the PTSD construct of avoidance.

In addition to shame, the victim may report self-blame and view himself or herself as helpless. For example, Spacarelli (1995) found that the combination of negative self-appraisals and negative life events are related to internalizing symptoms in sexually abused girls. In addition, more negative appraisals were directly related to the number of types of sexual abuse the child experienced.

Feiring et al. (1998, 2002) studied the role of shame and attributional style in the adaptation of children and teens. Their first study found that shame and self-blaming attributions were strongly related to depression, self-esteem, and posttraumatic-type symptoms measured at 8 weeks of discovery of abuse. Shame and attribution style, particularly pessimism, mediated the relation between number of abusive events and internalizing symptoms.

Feiring et al.'s sample was reexamined 1 year later, and once adjustment at abuse discovery was accounted for, shame and attribution style explained additional variation in subsequent adjustment, whereas abuse severity did not (Feiring et al., 2002). A pessimistic attribution style at abuse discovery moderated the relation between severity of abuse and subsequent depressive symptoms and self-esteem. The patterns of change in shame and attribution predicted which children remained at risk or improved in adjustment.

CONCLUDING COMMENTS

While this chapter has not addressed the broad issue of a more comprehensive psychological assessment of sexually abused children, it has identified a number of instruments that can be used to assess abuse-specific outcomes and their moderators. These tests can be used in forensic settings to supplement information obtained in the interview and thus help arrive at a determination about the likelihood of child sexual abuse. They can also be employed to assist clinicians to assess children as they enter therapy and then to monitor children's therapeutic progress. However, none of the measures described is diagnostic. A number of limitations were identified, including children's ability to self-report and caretakers' willingness to respond in an accurate and honest manner. Because of these limitations, it is recommend that evaluators obtain test results from several informants across several behavioral and symptom domains.

NOTE

1. For example, a valid symptom checklist was utilized to screen children in Eastern European countries. Data from that epidemiological study were used to influence policy makers in one of these countries, Latvia, to provide reimbursement to clinicians who were treating sexually abused children.

SIXTEEN

Criteria for Deciding About the Likelihood of Sexual Abuse

Kathleen Coulborn Faller

A major clinical and forensic challenge in the sexual abuse field is how to make a decision about the likelihood of abuse. The field, however, has progressed from a time when interviewers and other practitioners used intuition or their own personal criteria, to the use of guidelines or frameworks to determine probability of sexual abuse. Many of the frameworks were developed about 10 years ago. These earlier frameworks are based primarily upon practice. More recent frameworks attempt to be data driven. These frameworks are described in this chapter, and commonalities among them are discussed and critiqued. In addition, the Sexual Abuse Legitimacy Scale (SALS) is reviewed and critiqued. Following that, a procedure that takes into account some of the guideline shortcomings is presented.

GUIDELINES FOR DECIDING ABOUT THE LIKELIHOOD OF SEXUAL ABUSE

Sixteen guidelines or frameworks are found in the literature and are described below. Any research that is relevant to the particular framework is also discussed. Table 16.1 organizes and lists the criteria found in the individual frameworks. Commonalties and differences in these criteria are charted, and the criteria and shortcomings are discussed.

1. Sgroi, Porter, and Blick

Sgroi, Porter, and Blick (1982) were among the first to offer guidance about deciding if children have been sexually abused. They focus on child behavioral indicators, of both a sexual and nonsexual nature. They list 20 such indicators: (1) overly compliant behavior; (2) acting-out, aggressive behavior; (3) pseudomature behavior; (4) hints about sexual activity; (5) persistent and inappropriate sexual play with peers, toys, or with themselves, or sexually aggressive behavior with others; (6) detailed and

Table 16.1 Criteria Included in Frameworks and Guidelines for Substantiating Sexual Abuse

Criterion	Number	Guidelines
A. Child Interview Information		
1. Sexual abuse description	4	6, 11, 14, 15
a. Detail	11	1, 2, 3, 4, 5, 7, 10, 11, 12, 13, 14
b. Child's perspective	6	2, 5, 7, 9 (2), 10, 12 (3)
c. Advanced sexual knowledge	9	1, 2, 6 (5), 7, 8, 9 (2), 11, 12, 14
d. Other		3, 8
2. Offender behavior	2	
a. Use of inducements to participate	2	2, 9
b. Admonitions not to tell	7	2, 3, 4, 9, 11, 12, 14
c. Progression of abuse	3	8, 9, 12 (2)
3. Contextual information	4	3, 5 (2), 9, 11
a. Idiosyncratic event	6	2, 3, 7, 8, 11, 12
b. Where	3	2, 3, 4
c. When	2	2, 3
d. Where others were	2	2, 4
e. Clothing	1	2 (2)
f. Whether told	2	2 (2), 9
g. Other	2	11 (5), 12
4. Emotional reaction of the child	1	11
a. Affect consistent abuse description	10	2 (6), 3, 5, 6 (2), 7, 8, 9, 10, 11, 14
b. Affect related to the offender	3	3, 6, 11
c. Recall of affect during event	5	2, 3, 7, 11, 12
d. Reluctance to disclose	6	2, 3, 6 (–), 8, 10 (–), 11 (–)
e. Other	3	3, 4, 11
5. Child functioning		
a Competency		
1. Recall of past	2	9, 11
2. Truth from lie	1	11
3. Fact from fantasy	3	8, 9, 11
4. Not suggestible	1	12
b. Psychological testing	4	5, 8, 14, 15
c. Motivation to tell the truth	5	3, 8, 9, 10, 11,
d. Consistency of accounts	7	3 (4, –), 7, 8, 10 (2), 11, 12, 14
e. Feasibility	4	8, 10, 11, 14
6. Structural qualities of the child's account	4	9, 10, 11 (4), 12

continued

Table 16.1 continued

Criterion	Number	Guidelines
B. Information From Other Sources		
1. Child behavior in other contexts		
a. Statements to others	6	1, 2, 7, 9, 12, 14
b. Nonsexual symptoms	9	1 (16), 2 (6), 5 (3), 6 (15), 7, 8 (5), 12 10, (12), 13
c. Sexualized behavior	10	1 (3), 5, 6 (3), 7, 8 (4), 9 (2), 10, 12, 14, 15
d. Other	3	5, 9 (2), 12 (2)
2. Offender		
a. Overall functioning	1	7
b. Results of polygraph	1	7 (–)
c. Results of plethysmograph		
d. Psychological test results		
e. Other victims	3	7, 10 (2), 12
f. Confession/admission	1	6, 14
3. Family		
a. Information related to nonoffending parent		
b. Marital functioning		
c. Family functioning	3	7, 10 (2), 12
d. Family history of abuse	2	2, 12
4. Medical findings	11	3 (3), 4, 5, 7, 8, 9 (5), 10, 11, 12, 13, 14 (3), 15
5. Police evidence	2	2, 12
6. Witnesses	3	2 (2), 12, 14

Numbers in parentheses indicate the number of indicators the author provided in that general category. A minus (–) indicates that the absence of that particular characteristic would indicate child sexual abuse. Key for frameworks and guidelines:

1. Sgroi, Porter, and Blick (1982).
2. Faller (1984, 1988b, 1990, 1993).
3. DeYoung (1986).
4. Leventhal et al. (1987).
5. Sink (1988).
6. Corwin (1988).
7. Jones and McGraw (1987).
8. Conte et al. (1991).
9. Benedek and Schetky (1987a, 1987b).
10. Wehrspann et al. (1987).
11. SVA and CBCA (Raskin & Esplin, 1991b; Stellar & Boychuk, 1992; Yuille 1988).
12. Heiman (1992).
13. Haskett et al. (1995).
14. Wharff (1998).
15. Dammeyer (1998).
16. Peters (2000).

age-inappropriate understanding of sexual behavior (especially by young children); (7) arriving early at school and leaving late; (8) poor peer relationships or inability to make friends; (9) lack of trust; (10) non-participation in school or social activities; (11) inability to concentrate in school; (12) sudden drop in school performance; (13) extraordinary fears of males; (14) seductive behavior with males; (15) running away from home; (16) sleep disturbances; (17) regressive behavior; (18) withdrawal; (19) clinical depression; and (20) suicidal feelings.

Theirs is a pioneering effort to identify characteristics of sexually abused children that might be noted during the course of evaluation and used to make a decision about likelihood of abuse. Today, clinicians would regard the sexual indicators as more likely to be associated with sexual abuse (Faller, 1993; Friedrich, 1993, 1996) and would recognize that nonsexual indicators could be related to a wide range of trauma, including sexual abuse.

2. Faller

Faller (1984, 1988b, 1990, 1993) has addressed criteria for decision-making in several writings. Her protocol includes interview data and corroborating information. Interview data are subsumed under three general categories: (1) statements and/or behavior regarding the sexual acts, which are explicit, told from a child's viewpoint, and demonstrate advanced sexual knowledge; (2) information regarding the context of the abuse, such as when, where, and under what circumstances the abuse occurred; and (3) an emotional reaction consistent with the account given, for example reluctance to disclose, fear, anxiety, or anger. Corroborating evidence includes the following: (1) confessions, (2) medical findings, (3) physical evidence, and (4) eye witnesses. The clinical protocol was applied to 103 confessed cases (Faller, 1988b). As noted in chapter 13, each of the three categories from children's reports were found in about 80% of reports, but only 68% of cases had all three.

3. De Young

De Young (1986) observed that it is rare for a young child's account of sexual abuse to be characterized by four aspects, clarity, celerity, certainty, and consistency, and cites the reasons for the absence of such findings. She then sets out criteria for judging the truthfulness of an allegation. First, she states the evaluator should probe for elaborated details, which should include (1) a description of a specific action (sexual abuse), (2) the context of the abuse, (3) secrecy details, and (4) affective details, that is, how the child felt at the time of the abuse. Second, she sees sexual and nonsexual behavioral indicators as important but notes that lists of such indicators are taken from a variety of contexts and are a "melange." She suggests using the four categories of effects of sexual abuse developed by Finkelhor (1986), which are (1) traumatic sexualization, (2) betrayal, (3) disempowerment, and (4) stigmatization. She then instructs the evaluator to assess the vulnerability of the child to sexual abuse, and finally any motivation for lying.

4. Leventhal, Bentovim, Elton, Tranter, and Read

Leventhal collaborated with British colleagues Bentovim, Elton, Tranter, and Read (1987) in developing a framework for use in medical settings. Having noted that false allegations by children are rare, they set forth the following criteria for substantiation: (1) the child's attitude during disclosure, (2) detail related to both the sexual abuse and context, (3) a description of any threats regarding secrecy, and (4) the child's response to telling the doctor.

5. Sink

Sink (1988a) proposed a hierarchical model for evaluation of possible sexual abuse with four levels. She differentiated between legal criteria and psychosocial criteria for validating an allegation. Level 1 satisfies legal requirements, is labeled "direct communication," and is defined as verbal disclosure, demonstrations with anatomical dolls, and physical corroboration. Level 2 consists of indirect communication, such as ambiguous statements, sexualized play, behavior, content in response to projective measures, and reactions to sexual stimuli, or retraction of prior disclosure. Level 3 is acute traumatic symptomatology, which lacks sexualized content, found in the child's play or functioning (e.g., sleep disturbances, toileting problems). Level 4 is cumulative stress symptomatology, which is manifested in chronic behavioral maladaptation, such as phobias, depression, or conduct disorder.

6. Corwin

Corwin (1988) centered his discussion on the child's emotional and behavioral indicators, categorized into three levels of specificity or likelihood that the criteria indicate sexual abuse. These indicators vary somewhat by the child's developmental stage (i.e., whether the child is a preschooler, school age, or adolescent). The general indicator categories most specific to sexual abuse for all developmental stages are (1) nightmares about the sexual abuse; (2) premature eroticization; (3) fearfulness related to sexuality, the sexual abuse situation, or the alleged offender; (4) an age-appropriate, circumstantially congruent description of being sexually abused; and (5) dissociative phenomena. These indicators were developed and refined by a group of experts in clinical evaluation of sexual abuse.

7. Jones and McGraw

Jones and McGraw (1987) developed a list of attributes of the child's statement indicating a true allegation: (1) explicit detail, (2) unique or distinguishing detail, (3) child's language, (4) child's perspective, and (5) emotion expressed. Other information from the child is also important: (1) the child's psychological response to the abuse, (2) the pattern of abuse, (3) an element of secrecy, and, (4) in some cases, pornography, sadism, and ritualism. They also include "supporting features" in their criteria: (1) a family history that includes problems that are correlated with sexual abuse, such as spouse abuse, substance abuse, or criminal activity; (2) symptomatic behavior of the child during the time of the abuse; (3) the pattern of disclosure; (4) the child's statements to other people; (5) consistency in the child's account; (6) expression of sexual themes play or drawings; (7) advanced sexual knowledge; and (8) other victims within the household. Physical or physiological evidence is an additional criterion.

8. Conte, Sorenson, Fogarty, and Dalla Rosa

Conte, Sorenson, Fogarty, and Dalla Rosa (1991), in their survey of 212 sexual abuse experts from 44 states, inquired, among other things, about criteria used in substantiating a report and the level of importance of each criterion. The highest ranked criterion was compelling medical evidence, followed by several attributes related to sexuality and characteristics of the child's statement. Those related to sexuality were (1) age-inappropriate sexual knowledge, (2) sexualized play during the interview, (3) precocious or apparently seductive behavior, (4) response to the anatomical dolls consistent with that of a sexually abused child, (5) excessive masturbation, and (6) preoccupation with the genitals. The highly rated characteristics of the child's account were (1) consistency over time, (2) idiosyncratic details surrounding the abuse, (3) a progression of sexual activity, (4) elements of pressure or coercion, (5) a logical account, and (6) the ability to distinguish fact from fantasy. Conte and colleagues noted that some of these criteria are not supported by empirical studies.

9. Benedek and Schetky

Benedek and Schetky (1987a, 1987b) list the following findings related to the child that enhance and detract from the credibility of an allegation: (1) language, (2) spontaneous play/drawings, (3) affect, (4) behavior, (5) motives, (6) memory, (7) cognitive development, (8) credibility history, (9) physical exam, and (10) relationship with parents.

10. Wehrspann, Steinhauer, and Klajner-Diamond

Wehrspann, Steinhauer, and Klajner-Diamond (1987) divide confirming findings into two general categories: medical indicators and criteria from the child's presentation. The latter may include information from the child interview and information provided by others who have contact with the child. The criteria are (1) spontaneity, (2) repetition over time,

(3) internal consistency, (4) external consistency, (5) embedded responses (remarks, usually made in the context of conversation about something else, which indicate advanced sexual knowledge, memories of sexual abuse, or affect arising from the sexual abuse), (6) amount/quality of details, (7) story told from a child's viewpoint, (8) evidence of the (child sexual abuse) accommodation syndrome, (9) or, conversely, consistency in the face of challenge, and (10) sexually specific symptoms.

Wehrspann et al. (1987) also attempt to compare their criteria to those advanced by others, especially the German experts on statement validity analysis (SVA) and criterion-based content analysis (CBCA) (e.g., Undeutch, 1989), whose work guided that of Raskin and Esplin (1991b), and Yuille (1988), described below. Although they generally find agreement about criteria, their work preceded much of the current writing on SVA and CBCA that are described next.

11. Statement Validity Analysis and Criterion-Based Content Analysis

Raskin and Esplin (1991b), Stellar and Boychuk (1992), and Yuille (1988) have advocated a method of evaluating the truthfulness of children's statements about their sexual abuse called SVA and CBCA, which has its origins in Germany (Undeutch, 1989). Indeed, SVA and CBCA have fairly wide acceptance in Europe (e.g., Lamers-Winkelman & Buffing, 1996a&b; Stellar & Boychuk, 1992; Stellar & Kohnken, 1989) and are employed to evaluate reports of a range of experiences, not merely sexual abuse. Bradford (1994) describes SVA as holding promise as an objective approach for joint law enforcement–social work investigative teams in Great Britain, but G. M. Davies (1994) advises caution.

SVA refers to the overall schema for evaluating the report (the interview quality, the CBCA rating, and the completion of a validity checklist). This checklist includes 13 characteristics from four domains: (1) background characteristics (does the child possess any characteristics that might indicate the allegation is false?), (2) interview characteristics (quality of the interview and absence of interviewer attempts to influence the child), (3) motivational factors (has the child been influenced to make a false report?), and (4) investigative questions (are the offense characteristics implausible or inconsistent with one another or with a typical sexual abuse situation?) (Lamb, Sternberg, Esplin, Hershkowitz, & Orbach, 1997).

CBCA requires a careful examination of the child's spontaneous statement, either using a videotape of the child interview or a transcript. CBCA analyzes 19 content areas which are organized into five general categories. The categories and content areas are as follows: (1) general characteristics (logical structure, unstructured production, and quantity of details), (2) specific contents (contextual embedding, descriptions of interactions, reproduction of conversation, and unexpected complications), (3) peculiarities of content (unusual details, superfluous details, accurately reported details misunderstood, related external associations, accounts of subjective mental state, and attribution of perpetrator's mental state), (4) motivation (spontaneous corrections, admitting lack of memory, raising doubts about one's testimony, self-deprecation, and pardoning the perpetrator), and (5) offense-specific elements (details characteristic of the offense) (e.g., Anson, Golding, & Gully, 1993; Raskin & Esplin, 1991b). The content areas suggest this methodology is potentially more useful with older than younger children (Anson et al., 1993; Craig, Scheibe, Raskin, Kircher, & Dodd, 1999). In addition, unlike the other guidelines, this one does not have criteria specific to sexual abuse.

Raskin and Esplin (1991b) and Stellar and Boychuk (1992) report on research using CBCA in an analogue study in Germany. In addition, Raskin and Esplin describe a study involving children seen by themselves, 20 of whom CBCA found to be sexually abused and 20 of whom CBCA found not, that is whose statements were doubtful. Similarly, Craig et al. (1999) describe findings using CBCA on 48 cases. They report CBCA was used to classify 35 cases as "confirmed" and 13 cases as "highly doubtful." Evidently no cases were uncertain, using this methodology.

Other research has been less supportive of the efficacy of CBCA. Anson et al. (1993) used CBCA to code information from 23 cases from the State of Utah with both a videotape of the child's statement and a full confession of the offender. The interviewers were either master's level social workers or doctoral level psychologists. Each videotape was rated by two researchers specifically trained in CBCA. Problems were found in interrater reliability, with higher reliabilities on low-frequency criteria. In addition, the 19 criteria were not consistently found in these interviews, the average rate being 0.41 and ranging from 0 (not present in any interview) to 0.91 (present in almost all interviews). Thus, none of the criteria was present in every interview.

Using CBCA, Ceci, Huffman, Smith, & Loftus (1994) rated true and false accounts from the "mousetrap study," in which preschoolers were programmed over time to visualize paired true and false (e.g., finger caught in a mousetrap) events. These researchers did not find that CBCA differentiated true from false reports. However, they interpret these findings as not necessarily being a fair test of CBCA, saying CBCA is supposed to detect lying. (Supporters of CBCA would probably not agree that it is a lie detector.) Ceci and colleagues think they created false memories in their preschoolers; thus their subjects were not lying but really believed their false memories (Ceci, Huffman, et al. 1994; Ceci & Leichtman, 1995; Ceci, Loftus, et al., 1994).

Similarly, Lamb and colleagues employed CBCA on 98 videotaped interviews. Although more CBCA criteria were found on cases independently rated as "likely" and "very likely" than on cases rated "unlikely" and "very unlikely," these differences were less striking than in other studies (Hershkowitz, Lamb, Sternberg, & Esplin, 1997; Lamb, Sternberg, Esplin, & Hershkowitz, 1997). In addition, Lamb and colleagues advise caution in using CBCA to make decisions about likelihood of sexual abuse (Lamb et al., 1997).

Finally, Rugby and Brigham (1998) found in a study of 169 white and African-American undergraduates that CBCA failed to differentiate between truth tellers and liars, with very high rates of false positives. Since this was a study of young adults, and CBCA scores are based upon linguistic productivity, this finding is not unexpected. The researchers also found differences in the presence and patterns of the CBCA criteria by race, suggesting it is geared to white linguistic conventions (Ruby & Brigham, 1998).

There is another concern about SVA and CBCA. They have often been used by their proponents not as a method for substantiating an allegation of sexual abuse but as a strategy to challenge the conclusions of other mental health professionals. When SVA and CBCA are used in this way, the methodology employed by the "adverse" mental health expert is challenged and a conclusion of abuse is disputed.

12. Heiman

Heiman (1992) reviewed past attempts to develop frameworks for decision-making about sexual abuse. Her goal was to present a methodology that could assist the clinician in organizing the assessment process and in decision-making. She divides the areas for data gathering into five domains: (1) history of symptoms, both sexual (inappropriate or precocious sexual behavior, intrusive recollections of the abuse) and nonsexual (e.g., sleep disturbance, aggressive behavior, clinging behavior, exaggerated fears, somatic complaints, dissociation); (2) (child's) verbal report (explicit details, details beyond the child's developmental stage, a progression of activities, secrecy, threats, bribes, contextual information, affective details, and idiosyncratic details); (3) phenomenological experience of abuse (as stated or evidenced in the form of sequelae, e.g., feelings of betrayal, powerlessness, stigmatization, and shame and guilt); (4) presentational style (e.g., affect, evidence of coaching); and (5) corroborating evidence (e.g., medical findings, police evidence, statements to others, other witnesses). For each area, she poses framing questions and lists indicators for positive findings. She argues for systematic consideration of findings in all five domains but, like other writers, does not offer any minimum criteria for a positive finding of sexual abuse.

13. Haskett, Wayland, Hutcheson, and Tavana

Haskett, Wayland, Hutcheson, and Tavana (1995) asked 20 child protection services workers about the criteria they used to determine likelihood of child sexual abuse, using a sample of 175 cases. These researchers found that the child's detailed statement, medical evidence, the child's affect and behavior during the interview, and the child's symptoms and behavior, particularly sexual behavior, as noted in other contexts, were criteria used to determine whether or not to substantiate sexual abuse. These caseworkers did not rely on offender characteristics to make their determinations, but offenders were interviewed by these caseworkers in fewer than a fifth of cases. False reports were thought to be associated with custody disputes and child secondary gain (Haskett et al., 1995).

14. Wharff

Wharff (1998) conducted a comparable study for her dissertation research with 16 evaluators and 67 cases from the Boston area. Approximately half the evaluators used a defined protocol, the APSAC *Guidelines for Psychosocial Evaluation of Suspected Sexual Abuse in Young Children* (1990). Wharff asked about 25 criteria found in the literature. She then conducted factor analysis which revealed three clusters of indicators related to likelihood: (1) characteristics of the child's disclosure, (2) the child's sexual awareness and behavior, and (3) physical findings.

15. Dammeyer

Dammeyer's (1998) article reviews past surveys of professionals regarding methods of data-collection and strategies for determining likelihood of sexual abuse. Unlike most other writers, he attempts to base his guidelines on research. He selects five criteria for determining likelihood and then examines each in terms of the amount of research support for it. The criteria are (1) medical findings, (2) child's report, (3) information gathered through the use of media (e.g., anatomical dolls, puppets), (4) age-inappropriate sexualized behavior, and (5) psychological test findings.

With regard to medical findings, Dammeyer (1998) notes that the presence of some types of findings (e.g., pregnancy, semen, or a sexually transmitted disease) represent strong evidence of sexual abuse, but that other medical findings are less conclusive, and that many types of sexual abuse, for example, fondling and exposure, leave no physical findings. Dammeyer notes that the child's report is generally recognized as a critical source of information. However, he also points out that there may be false reports, even though they are low frequency, that reports in divorce cases may be less reliable and that young children are suggestible.

Referring to data from the use of media, Dammeyer (1998) differentiates between findings from mere observation and findings when these media are used as a method for communication. He concludes, nevertheless, that data obtained from media must be viewed cautiously.

Next, Dammeyer (1998) notes the work of Friedrich (Friedrich, Beilke, & Urquiza, 1988) in the study of children's sexualized behavior, describing the Child Sexual Behavior Inventory (CSBI) as an instrument for collecting information about sexualized behavior. He notes the CSBI is particularly sensitive for children 2–6 years of age and less useful with 7- to 12-year-old girls. Because children can acquire sexual knowledge from sources other than sexual abuse, his advice is for evaluators to use sexualized behavior cautiously in decision-making.

Finally, Dammeyer takes up the issue of children's psychological test findings. He observes that instruments completed by parents (e.g., CSBI, Child Behavior Checklist) show greater differences between children with and without a history of sexual abuse, than those completed by children. He concludes that test findings provide modest to minimal information about whether or not a child has been sexually abused.

16. Peters

Peters (2000) conducted research in which she used six vignettes of possible sexual abuse. Criteria she examined were the child's verbal disclosure, the child's doll play, collateral information, and affect. She compared the responses to these vignettes from experts in the sexual abuse field (a sample from members of the American Professional Society on the Abuse of Children [APSAC] who conducted child abuse assessments) and college undergraduates. Both groups placed more weight on verbal disclosure and collateral information than on doll play and affect. The experts were more conservative in their ratings, more knowledgeable about the child abuse literature, and more believing of children than the undergraduates.

Commonalities and Differences Among Frameworks

There is considerable consistency in what these writers find important to consider. All guidelines include findings from the child interview, and there is general agreement in the field about the centrality of the child interview in sexual abuse evaluations (e.g., Corwin, 1988; Dammeyer, 1998; De Young, 1986; Faller, 1988b, 1990; Faller & Corwin, 1995; Levanthal et al., 1987; Risin & McNamara, 1989; Sink, 1988). The most frequently cited factors from the child interview are detail of the sexual abuse (11), affect consistent with the abuse description (10), and advanced sexual knowledge (9). Regarding information from other sources, 11 of the guidelines mention medical evidence, six note nonsexual symptoms, and nine note sexual symptoms observed in other settings as important. Only two specify physical evidence that might be gathered from the scene of the crime, for example, an instrument that might have been used or pornography. However, when such evidence is found, it is very important (Faller & Corwin, 1995).

Interestingly, none of the guidelines mention the plethysmograph, polygraph results (except Jones and McGraw, 1987, do not think these results should be considered), psychological testing results of the offender, nor information related to the nonoffending parent or the marriage. However, the lack of inclusion of these criteria may be because these guidelines focus on the probative value of the child interview. Among professionals who evaluate and treat sexual offenders there is increasing reliance on the plethysmograph and the polygraph, especially for screening to determine if the offender has disclosed all sexual acts and if the offender is reoffending (Salter, 2002).

Some authors emphasize factors that seem unimportant to others. For example, Corwin (1988) and Sgroi (1982) emphasize nonsexual symptoms of stress, citing many different ones as indicative of sexual abuse, and CBCA stresses structural aspects of the child's account and contextual factors. In the case of four criteria, authors may hold opposing views. For instance, some believe that a reluctance to disclose is characteristic of a true allegation, while others look for spontaneity in the child's disclosure as an index of veracity.

Most frameworks do not address the issues of how much information a child must produce or in how many areas confirming information must be found in order to substantiate a case. However, Jones and McGraw (1987) state that the major factor in their determination of sexual abuse is the child's statement that he/she has been sexually abused. Faller (1988a) says that behavior or statements about the sexual abuse are both necessary and sufficient for substantiation and discusses both research findings and clinical explanations for why confirming information may be absent in some types of cases. Sink (1988) notes that for a case to be substantiated in the legal arena, level 1 information must be elicited. However, information from levels 2–4 can be used by a mental health professional both to form an opinion about the likelihood of sexual abuse and to plan treatment. Dammeyer (1998) points out shortcomings in all domains of evidence he examines but notes that certain types of medical evidence are compelling. The general absence of guidance regarding how much of what kinds of information is necessary to substantiate leaves that decision up to the evaluator. The issue of forming conclusions about sexual abuse is taken up again in chapter 17.

SEXUAL ABUSE LEGITIMACY SCALE

Gardner (1987, 1989, 1992, 1995) has produced criteria for differentiating true and false allegations of sexual abuse that differ markedly from those proposed by other writers and therefore are addressed separately here. As the criteria reflect, these apply primarily to allegations of sexual abuse in divorce. Gardner has argued, however, that his criteria apply to a wide spectrum of cases and are not even exclusive to sexual abuse. Nevertheless, he calls his list the Sexual Abuse Legitimacy Scale (SALS). Altogether he proposes 84 factors. The factors derive from three general sources, the accusing parent, the child, and the male, who presumably is the accused. The 30 factors related to the accusing parent (usually the mother) include information about her early childhood, events that precede the evaluation, and information obtained during the evaluation. There are also 30 factors related to the child, which include characteristics of the child's account of the sexual abuse, the presence of a custody dispute, the child's affect associated with the abuse allegation, and more general emotional and behavioral problems. Twenty-four factors are related to the accused, the evidence of the presence of pedophilia. The factors in the SALS are marked to indicate whether positive findings are characteristic of true or false allegations.

Gardner (1995) had a practice of interviewing the mother, the child, and the father, in various combinations. Gardner also advised that others be interviewed, for example, relatives, friends, and therapists. Through this process, he said he collected confirming and disconfirming data and rated each of the 84 factors in the SALS.

Some factors Gardner included are found in other frameworks, for example, under child factors, the degree of specificity of the details of the sexual abuse and advanced sexual knowledge for age. The factors in the SALS, however, vary considerably in their relevance to allegations of sexual abuse and the degree of subjective judgment they require. Some are quite subjective, for example, "the litany" as a child factor and moralism as a mother factor. Others are more objective, for example, child school attendance and performance, but its relevance to an allegation of sexual abuse is not clear. Professionals may find many indicators open to a variety of interpretations, depending upon the particular case. For example, a child may be reluctant to disclose sexual abuse if his/her caretaker is unsupportive but may disclose readily if the caretaker is supportive. Similarly, interviewers might question a conclusion that an allegation is false based upon the fact the accusing parent reports to authorities before informing the accused or the accusing parent admonishes the child to tell the truth.

When Gardner rates these factors, the absence of findings leads to F rating. For example, if a 6-year-old has no history of running away, this is rated as disconfirming of a true allegation. If the child does not feel guilty over participation in the abuse, this is supportive of a false allegation. Likewise, if the father reports no child pornography and no history of substance abuse, these findings are recorded as disconfirming of the abuse accusation (Faller, 1998).

Also of note is that the offender criteria assume that all sex offenders are pedophiles, when current knowledge suggests a minority of offenders are pedophiles—that is, individuals whose primary sexual orientation is to children (e.g., Barbaree & Seto, 1997; Marshall, 1997). By screening only for criteria of pedophilia, Gardner has structured the SALS to disconfirm sexual abuse.

Finally, underlying the SALS is a belief that children have a high level of sexual awareness and engage in repeated sexual fantasies, including ones involving adults. This awareness and their basic cruelty often cause children to make false allegations of sexual abuse (Gardner, 1991, 1992, 2001). Hence, Gardner argued that other evaluators are wrong when they assume that advanced sexual knowledge is a marker for sexual abuse (Gardner, 2001). Moreover, he believed that adults (interviewers and accusing parents) are sexually gratified every time they contemplate the accused having sexual contact with the alleged victim (Gardner, 1992).

SUGGESTED PROCEDURE FOR COLLECTING DATA FOR DECISION-MAKING

Berliner and Conte (1993) raise important questions about an "indicators" approach in making decisions about whether children have been sexually abused. Examples of an indicators approach are the frameworks described in this chapter and the SALS. Berliner and Conte cite the subjectivity in choices of criteria, discuss certain indicators about which clinicians disagree, and state that the absence of positive indicators does not mean the child has not been sexually abused. They review a number of the decision-making frameworks described in this chapter and are particularly critical of criteria-based context analysis and the SALS. They recommend, instead of an "indicators" approach, reliance on following consensually derived procedures for good practice, for example, as to number of interviews, questioning techniques, and use of media to communicate with the child. Heiman's (1992) framework, which specifies domains to be explored systematically, is an effort in this direction.

Faller (2003) attempts to incorporate both indicators and process in a methodology for decision-making that requires the professional to document (1) what information the professional has obtained, (2) what the range of possible interpretations is for each piece of information (an aspect of assessment discussed in greater detail in the next chapter), (3) what the professional believes is the most likely interpretation, and (4) how much weight the professional places on that piece of information. This documentation also allows the professional to specify the medium employed to obtain information from the child. Although this methodology can be used by a single professional, it can also be employed by a team or by several professionals who may have different views. Table 16.2 was used to record the information.

Table 16.2 Data for Assessing the Likelihood of Sexual Abuse (Faller, 2003)

Child's name   Child's age   Date   Clinician(s)

Alleged event or events covered (e.g., last incident, most serious incident)

I. Child Interview Data		Possible Interpretations	Most Likely	Importance
A. The sexual behavior				
1. Types of sexual acts	Frequency/ duration			
a.				
b.				
c.				
d.				
2. Verbal description	Y N			
Specify				
a. Child's perspective	Y N			
Specify				
b. Explicit sexual acts	Y N			
Specify				
3. Demonstrations	Y N			
a. Medium (e.g., dolls, drawings)				
b. Explicit demonstrations	Y N			
4. Advanced sexual knowledge	Y N			
Specify				

B. Context of the Sexual Abuse		Possible Interpretations	Likely	Imp.
1. Where it happened	Y N NA*			
Specify				
2. When it happened	Y N NA*			
Specify				
3. Grooming or inducements	Y N NA*			
Specify				

Table 16.2 continued

B. Context of the Sexual Abuse				Possible Interpretations	Likely	Imp.
4. Whereabouts of others	Y	N	NA*			
Specify						
5. Child's clothing	Y	N	NA*			
Specify						
6. Suspect's clothing	Y	N	NA*			
Specify						
7. Idiosyncratic event	Y	N	NA*			
Specify						
8. Child's emotional state	Y	N	NA*			
Specify						
9. Strategies to discourage telling	Y	N	NA*			
Specify						
10. Disclosures by child	Y	N	NA*			
Specify						
11. Reactions of persons told	Y	N	NA*			
Specify						
12. Other						
Specify						

C. Recantations	Y	N
Specify		

D. Child's affect during direct inquiry/disclosure			Possible Interpretations	Likely	Imp.
1. Reluctance to disclose	Y	N			
Specify					

continued

Table 16.2 continued

D. Child's affect during direct inquiry/disclosure			Possible Interpretations	Likely	Imp.
2. Other affects (e.g., embarrass-ment, guilt, anxiety, disgust, anger, fear)	Y	N			
Specify					

E. Child's functioning					
1. Child's sexualized behavior	Y	N			
Specify					
2. Child's externalizing behavior	Y	N			
Specify					
3. Child's internalizing behavior	Y	N			
Specify					
4. Child's competence	Y	N			
Specify					
5. Child's developmental level	Y	N			
Specify					
6. Cultural issues	Y	N			
Specify					
7. Other	Y	N			

II. Information From Other Sources			Possible Interpretations	Likely	Imp.
A. Medical findings	Y	N			
Specify					
B. Police evidence	Y	N			
Specify					
C. Explanation of suspect	Y	N			
D. Any witnesses	Y	N			
Specify					

II. Information From Other Sources			Possible Interpretations	Likely	Imp.
E. Other alleged victims	Y	N			
Specify					
F. Child's statements in other contexts	Y	N			
Specify					
G. Relevant observations by others (e.g., parents)	Y	N			
Specify					
H. Evidence from other professionals	Y	N			
Specify					
I. Other information	Y	N			
Specify					

Instructions

1. Complete protocol using information from all sources (background material, testing, interviews, collateral contacts, standardized measures). For each type of information, consider alternative explanations for its presence, absence, and/or significance. If the child describes multiple incidents of sexual abuse, focus on most recent or best remembered.
2. Findings related to sexual abuse allegations can be open to a variety of interpretations, for example:
   A. Misinterpretation of benign activity (e.g., childcare)
   B. Communication problem
   C. Coaching/programming by others
   D. Sexual knowledge for other source
   E. Different offender
   F. Lying
   G. Fantasizing by child
   H. Sexual abuse
   I. Exaggeration
   J. Minimization
3. Select the interpretation that seems most likely and indicate in the appropriate column.
4. Indicate on a 5-point scale how important the particular piece of information is to the decision about the likelihood of sexual abuse in the appropriate column: 1, very important; 2, important; 3, slightly important; 4, unimportant; 5, very unimportant.

*NA, not asked.

Although Faller's (2003) methodology is useful, it derives from practice experience. It also focuses most attention on the child interview and other information derived from the child. It has been used with success on actual cases and outlines a process for professionals. However, it has not been widely used or evaluated rigorously.

Its advantages are that it incorporates most of the criteria recommended by writers about decision-making, and it documents in one place, with specific descriptions, all the information that might be drawn upon in decisions about the likelihood of sexual abuse. Once the information is documented, the possible interpretations, most likely interpretation, and the weight can be systematically considered for each piece of information. The completed document can be the basis of the discussion of the decision by a team of professionals.

SUMMARY AND CONCLUSIONS

Practitioners and researchers have developed a variety of criteria for deciding about the probability of sexual abuse. There is some degree of consensus among the 16 frameworks discussed in this chapter, specifically about the importance of details in the child's statement, medical evidence (although the consensus of medical professionals is that medical findings are only found in a minority of cases; Bays & Chadwick, 1993), and the child's sexualized behavior in other contexts. The one framework that has been the subject of research is CBCA, but the findings are mixed. Because of the lack of evidence-based indicators of likelihood, interviewers and other professionals who must determine the probability of sexual abuse are advised to rely upon a process for data collection, following the suggestions of Berliner and Conte (1993) and adapting or adopting the framework developed by Faller and included in this chapter. The SALS, because of its underlying assumptions and narrowness of focus, is not advised (Faller, 1998).

SEVENTEEN

Formulating Conclusions About Sexual Abuse

Kathleen Coulborn Faller

Once all the data on criteria for decision-making have been collected, interviewers typically form some conclusions. Although conclusions may be formed about a number of issues, the one addressed in this chapter is whether or not the professional thinks the child has been sexually abused. This chapter addresses several issues related to conclusions from an interview or assessment for sexual abuse. First, the issue of types of conclusions that interviewers and other professionals may state is discussed. Second, potential errors in opinion formation are covered. This discussion leads into the third topic, alternative explanations for concerns about sexual victimization. Finally, the concept of a continuum of certainty is described.

TYPES OF CONCLUSIONS ARTICULATED BY PROFESSIONALS

An area of some controversy is what sort of conclusions professionals are able to draw based upon interview and other data. Although there are a range of conclusions that interviewers might reach, the central issue in interviewing for sexual abuse is whether or not the child has been sexually abused. Some believe it is appropriate and ethical for professionals to reach a conclusion about sexual abuse (American Academy of Child and Adolescent Psychiatry, 1990, 1997b; American Professional Society on the Abuse of Children, 1990, 1997), and others do not (Melton & Limber, 1989). There are two reasons why there is controversy about concluding sexual abuse did or did not happen. First, mental health professionals, who conduct many of the child interviews, are not trained in determining whether an event took place (i.e., sexual abuse), although in practice, they often make such determinations. Second, some sexual abuse cases are litigated in either child protection or criminal court, where a judge, jury, or other court official determines the relative credibility of witnesses and whether sufficient evidence for sexual abuse has been presented. As discussed below, the issue of witness credibility is indirectly related to the likelihood of sexual abuse.

Professionals who interview children about possible sexual abuse usually produce a written report that includes some conclusions. However, not all reports include conclusions regarding the likelihood of sexual abuse. Some investigative reports, for example, those produced by the Chadwick Center for Child Protection in San Diego (Davies, Cole, Albertella, McCulloch, Allen, & Kekevian, 1996) and some written by law enforcement, do not offer a conclusion regarding the likelihood of sexual abuse. For example, the Chadwick Center for Child Protection Protocol (D. Davies et al., 1996) instructs the interviewer to cite information obtained during the assessment that is supportive or not supportive of sexual abuse but not to state directly whether or not the interviewer believes the child has been sexually abused.

In contrast, several guidelines state that professionals can draw a conclusion about whether or not the child has been sexually abused (American Academy of Child and Adolescent Psychiatry, 1990, 1997b; American Professional Society on the Abuse of Children, 1990, 1997). That the professional can do so is, at this point, the majority opinion (Myers, 1992, 1998); however, Melton and Limber (1989) disagree. Melton's position appears to have moderated somewhat (Melton, 1994), but he remains convinced that mental health professionals should not testify that a particular child has been sexually abused. He focuses on the role of mental health professionals and might hold a different view about the role of child protection workers or law enforcement professionals.

Because the interviewer's conclusions may become part of the court process, exactly how these conclusions are stated is important (American Academy of Child and Adolescent Psychiatry, 1997b). The American Professional Society on the Abuse of Children (1990, 1997) guidelines provide alternative ways of expressing this conclusion. The guidelines state that the professional may assert either that he/she believes the abuse did or did not occur, that the child's statement or behavior is consistent or inconsistent with abuse, or the findings reflect a history or the absence of a history of sexual abuse.

Although professionals may form conclusions about the likelihood of sexual abuse, courts do not allow professionals to testify whether they believe the child or whether the child is telling the truth (Melton, 1994; Melton & Limber, 1989; Myers, 1992, 1998). Moreover, the American Professional Society on the Abuse of Children (1990, 1997) guidelines advise the professionals to communicate that mental health professionals have no special ability to determine when people are telling the truth. This advice is consistent with Melton's opinion.

Of course, the reality is that the criteria discussed in chapter 16 lead to a conclusion about the likelihood of an allegation of sexual abuse, and thereby indirectly to a conclusion about the truthfulness of the child. Moreover, if the interviewer concludes that the child has been abused and that the child has named an offender, but the offender denies, then the evaluator has formed a conclusion indirectly about the truth of the suspect's assertions. Indeed, it is quite difficult to form conclusions about other issues, such as whether the child is safe and what type of treatment or intervention is indicated, without first forming a conclusion about the likelihood of sexual abuse.

Nevertheless, professionals are advised not to include in written reports an opinion regarding the truthfulness of either the child or the alleged offender. Similarly, professionals should avoid assertions about the truthfulness of child or suspect when on the witness stand.

PROFESSIONALS NEED TO BE AWARE OF POTENTIAL ERRORS IN DECISION-MAKING

Although professionals attempt to form accurate conclusions about the likelihood of sexual abuse, they may be prone to errors in their decision-making processes. Potential errors have been addressed by several writings (American Academy of Child and Adolescent Psychiatry, 1997b; American Professional Society on the Abuse of Children, 1997, 2002; Poole & Lamb, 1998). Poole and Lamb (1998) describe several types of errors, based upon research on issues other that sexual abuse decision-making, and illustrate how these can affect conclusions in sexual abuse cases. Some of these errors relate to a misperception of the meaning of symptoms and behaviors: (1) the problem of reversed conditional probabilities, (2) the error in the representativeness heuristic, (3) ignoring base rates (e.g., the percentage of children who are sexually abused in a particular population), and (4) illusory correlations.

These errors generally derive from the narrowness of the professional's knowledge, specifically knowing a lot about sexual abuse victims but not knowing how prevalent victims' symptoms and behaviors are in other populations or in the general population. To illustrate, sexualized behavior is the most common marker for sexual abuse, being found in about 40% of children with a history of sexual abuse, but sexualized behavior is also correlated with domestic violence and family nudity (Friedrich, 1997, 2002).

Although knowing that the base rate of a problem is either high or low affects the risk for false positives (when the base rate is low), the sexual abuse base rate is difficult to determine. There is research on the lifetime prevalence of sexual abuse, which is quite high, 30–40% for women and at least half that for men (Bolen & Scannapieco, 1999). There is research on the number of cases each year that are reported (~300,000) and substantiated (~100,000) (National Child Abuse and Neglect Data

System, 2005), but it is difficult to determine how many sexual abuse cases go unreported.

Poole and Lamb (1998) cite an article by Wood (1996) that applies Bayes's theorem to decision-making about the likelihood of sexual abuse. This theorem begins with base rates, for example, the rate of sexual abuse in the population being examined. It then takes a particular symptom (e.g., imitating sexual intercourse), and its prevalence among victims of sexual abuse versus nonvictims. The base rate is multiplied by the proportion of victims with the symptom divided by the proportion of nonvictims with the symptom to determine the posterior odds that the child has been sexually abused. Thinking about abuse probability in terms of Bayes's theorem is useful for professionals because this helps them consider both the proportion of the population that experiences sexual abuse and that nonvictims may also have symptoms considered related to sexual abuse. Nevertheless, actually applying Bayes's theorem to case decision-making is not that feasible. First, in most cases the professional has to consider multiple signs and symptoms derived from various sources. Second, many of the signs and symptoms have not or cannot be subjected to scientific study in order to determine proportional probabilities. Finally, as noted above, the base rate of sexual abuse is elusive.

Another group of errors described by Poole and Lamb (1998) relate to various biases: (1) confirmation bias (i.e., only seeking information to support sexual abuse and either not seeking or ignoring information that disconfirms it), (2) the availability heuristic (e.g., relying on data that are highly salient or easily obtained), (3) anchoring and adjustment (e.g., filtering new knowledge through the lens of existing knowledge), and (4) estimating event frequencies. The third type of bias is highly relevant to sexual abuse interviewers. Often judgments about the importance or probability of incoming information related to the allegation are influenced by whom the interviewer talked to first or what the interviewer judges to be in the child's best interest.

Finally, Poole and Lamb (1998) note that research does not support a conclusion that there is a relationship between the level of certainty, amount of experience, and accuracy of opinion. Another piece of work that addresses these issues is a study by Horner, Guyer, and Kalter (1993a, 1993b). In their study, they asked respondents to rate the likelihood of sexual abuse and their degree of certainty on a single case involving a 3-year-old child and a situation of divorce. These authors report a wide range of opinion and of certainty among the persons involved in the study. However, the original data were collected at the clinic where the case was evaluated, and additional data were derived from later presentations where the authors withheld some of the facts (P. Ludolph, personal communication, November 1996). Moreover, Horner and colleagues characterize the respondents as experts in clinical evaluation of child sexual abuse. Some were, yet others were students in field placements and internships. As a consequence, respondents likely varied in their expertise in determining the likelihood of sexual abuse. The issue of the professional's degree of certainty is discussed further below.

PROFESSIONALS SHOULD CONSIDER ALTERNATIVE EXPLANATIONS FOR ALLEGATIONS OF SEXUAL ABUSE

In the last 15 years, there has been heightened concern about confirmatory bias among interviewers for sexual abuse (e.g., American Academy of Child and Adolescent Psychiatry, 1997b; Poole & Lamb, 1998). As noted above, confirmatory bias involves seeking only information that supports sexual abuse and interpreting information obtained in a way supportive of sexual abuse, and not considering alternative explanations.

Some possible alternative explanations are discussed in chapter 16 (see table 16.2):

A. Actual report of sexual abuse
B. Misinterpretation of benign activity by the child
C. Misinterpretation of benign activity by the adult
D. Communication problems
E. Coaching/programming of the child
F. Sexual knowledge from another source
G. A different offender
H. Lying by the child
I. Fantasizing by the child
J. Attention seeking by the child
K. Exaggeration by the child or an adult
L. Minimization of actual sexual abuse

These alternative explanations can be employed in considering an allegation as a whole as well as individual pieces of information gathered during the assessment process.

The American Academy of Child and Adolescent Psychiatry (1997b) practice parameters elaborate these explanations further, citing possible explanations for denials of sexual abuse and for assertions of sexual abuse. The explanations for denials are as follows:

A. The alleged abuse did not occur
B. The child was pressured by the perpetrator or family members to recant
C. The child is protecting the perpetrator or family members without being pressured directly
D. The child is frightened or distressed by the investigation process
E. The child does not want to testify because of shame or guilt

F. The child assumes she/he is responsible for the abuse
G. The child consciously or unconsciously is "accommodating" the abuser (Summit, 1983)
H. The interviewer triggered false denial by having the perpetrator in the room

Despite the evident focus of the American Academy of Child and Adolescent Psychiatry (1997b) practice parameters on false allegations, its list of causes of false allegations is prefaced by a statement that most allegations are true. The practice parameters also state that an allegation may be partly true and partly false or may have a "nidus" of truth but be mostly false because of repetitive questioning. Possible explanations for assertions of abuse offered in the practice parameters are as follows:

A. The allegation is false
1. Parental misinterpretations and suggestion
2. Misinterpretation of the child's physical condition
3. Parental delusion
4. Parental indoctrination of the child
5. Interviewer's suggestion
6. Misinterpretation by the child of parental behavior (as abusive)
7. Group contagion (hysteria regarding sexual abuse; Gardner, 1991)
B. The (false) allegation is produced by unconscious mental mechanisms in the child
1. Fantasy
2. Delusion
3. Misinterpretation
4. Miscommunication
5. Confabulation
C. The (false) allegation is produced by conscious and purposeful mental mechanisms in the child
1. Fantasy lying
2. Innocent lying
3. Deliberate lying
D. Perpetrator substitution, that is, someone other than whom the child accuses is the offender

RATIONALE FOR CONSIDERING ALTERNATIVE EXPLANATIONS

Even though research to date indicates that false allegations are uncommon (e.g., Oates et al., 2000; Trocme & Bala, 2005), it is important to consider alternative explanations. Several societal factors increase the likelihood of explanations other than actual sexual abuse. Some of these are described in chapter 4. First, in the late 1970s, when sexual abuse was "rediscovered," there was little awareness of sexual abuse as a possible explanation for symptoms and findings. Professionals were not very knowledgeable, and caretakers and their children had not been educated about sexual abuse.

Since that time, professionals have received specific training, the public has learned about sexual abuse through news about specific cases and more general educational materials, and children have been exposed to sexual abuse prevention materials in educational and recreational settings. Although this increased information has likely played a role in discovering actual cases of sexual abuse, it also has the potential of increasing false reports and misconceptions. Professionals and caretakers may misinterpret certain signs and symptoms as indicating sexual abuse when they are actually caused by something else. Similarly, this knowledge may increase the risk of both adults and children misinterpreting a benign activity, such as bathing a child's genitals or applying medication to them, as sexual abuse. (Of course, sometimes sex offenders disguise their abuse as childcare behavior.) In addition, it is also possible that knowledge of sexual abuse and societal response to it may cause some persons to make calculated false reports.

Knowledge about sexual abuse is not the only societal change that should enhance consideration of alternative explanations. Another is increased access to knowledge about sex and sexual activity. Evidence of advanced sexual knowledge is usually considered a red flag for possible sexual abuse. However, children may learn about sexual activity from sexually explicit videos and the Internet. These means of knowledge acquisition were nonexistent in the 1970s, although videos may have been accessible in the 1980s. So, professionals need to rule out the possibility that advanced sexual knowledge came from these sources or from observing sexual activity.

LEVEL OF CERTAINTY THAT SEXUAL ABUSE HAS OCCURRED

An important issue is the degree of certainty the professional has about the conclusions. There are a number of writings that address this issue (American Academy of Child and Adolescent Psychiatry, 1997b; American Professional Society on the Abuse of Children, 1997; Faller, 2003; Jones & McGraw, 1987). The American Academy of Child and Adolescent Psychiatry (1997b) practice parameters use the standards of proof in legal proceedings to anchor their discussion, noting that these range from probable cause (~25%; the standard for making a child protective services [CPS] report), to preponderance of the evidence (~51%; the standard in civil litigation), to clear and convincing evidence (~75%; the standard for termination of parental rights), and finally beyond a reasonable doubt (~95%; the standard for criminal conviction). These guidelines also suggest that professionals borrow from the medical profession the standard "reasonable degree of medical certainty." The American Professional Society on the Abuse of Children's *Guidelines for Psychosocial Evaluation of Suspected Sexual Abuse in Young Children* (1997) focus merely on the fact that some evaluations are inconclusive.

Jones and McGraw (1987) have developed a useful framework for addressing this issue. They speak of a continuum of certainty (see also Faller, 2003).

In table 17.1, levels of certainty are juxtaposed to the standards for action by CPS, the child protection court jurisdiction, and criminal prosecution. One reason for presenting this continuum is to emphasize the point that, indeed, there will be degrees of certainty. Professionals who interview for sexual abuse, however, should not regard their activities as similar to or supplanting those of the courts.

In very few cases will the professional be absolutely certain sexual abuse did or did not occur; it is probably inadvisable to make an absolute statement in most cases. The language employed by the professional should reflect the degree of certainty about the likelihood of sexual abuse in the instant case (Faller, 1993, 2003). Moreover, given the

Table 17.1 Continuum of Certainty About Sexual Abuse (adapted from Jones & McGraw, 1987)

100% certain the child was sexually abused				100% certain the child was not sexually abused
Very Likely	Likely	50–50	Unlikely	Very unlikely
	CPS substantiation		CPS denial	
95% probability— beyond a reasonable doubt; criminal conviction standard		51% probability— preponderance of the evidence; standard for court jurisdiction to protect the child		

research demonstrating the substantial proportion of false negatives (Faller, 1988b; Lawson & Chaffin, 1992; Lyon, in press; Saywitz, Goodman, Nicholas, & Moan, 1989; T. Sorenson & Snow, 1991) described in chapter 13 and the cautionary comments of Conte, Sorenson, Fogarty, and Dalla Rosa (1991) regarding indicators of sexual abuse, professionals are advised to use language such as "sexual abuse could not be substantiated" rather than "sexual abuse did not occur."

SUPPORTING CONCLUSIONS

It is important for interviewers to support their conclusions with the evidence employed in reaching them (American Academy of Child and Adolescent Psychiatry, 1990; American Professional Society on the Abuse of Children, 1990, 1997; Faller, 1993, 2003). The evidence can consist of information from all sources, not merely the child interview(s). Child interview data should include verbatim statements and behavioral observations (American Professional Society on the Abuse of Children, 1990, 1997; Bourg et al., 1999). Good documentation of the interview (e.g., a video or audiotape) can be used to ensure that statements are verbatim and observations are accurate. It is useful to chronicle the information gathered and then separately state the conclusions or opinion, referring back to supporting evidence.

INCONCLUSIVE ASSESSMENTS

Sometimes the evaluation is inconclusive. Both the American Professional Society on the Abuse of Children and American Academy of Child and Adolescent Psychiatry (1997b, 2002) guidelines point out that the professional may not be able to form a conclusion and should so state and document the reasons why. A number of professionals (Faller, 1993; James, Everson, & Friedrich, n.d.) recommend an extended evaluation in such circumstances. (See the discussion of extended evaluations in chapter 5, which addresses number of interviews.)

Professionals face significant dilemmas regarding protection of children when the assessment of the allegation is inconclusive. The need to foster attachment between parent and child may be in conflict with the issue of safety.

Hewitt (1991) proposed a sensible case management strategy, which she implemented in seven inconclusive cases of sexual abuse allegations in divorce with young children. She conducted interviews with the child, each parent, and each parent–child dyad. In the dyadic sessions, she had each parent communicate to the child what parts of the body should not be touched and had the accused parent give the child permission to tell if he engaged in sexually inappropriate behavior with the child. The nonaccused parent was instructed, when indicated, in how to listen to the child and ask questions in a nonleading manner. Initially, visits with the child and accused parent were supervised. Then the child was monitored for at least one year with unsupervised visits. In a 5-year follow-up, there were no complaints of subsequent abuse in six cases, and questionable but not clearly abusive behavior in one. Although Hewitt's strategy does not speak to all cases where children are at risk, this practice innovation can serve as a model.

SUMMARY

Most of the advice to professionals has been on how to conduct the child interview, and little attention has been given to forming and formulating conclusions about sexual abuse (e.g., Bourg et al., 1999; Lamb & Sternberg, 1999; Poole & Lamb, 1998). Indeed, although the majority opinion is that interviewers can form conclusions about the likelihood of sexual abuse (e.g., Faller, 2003; Myers, 1998), distinctions should be made between this opinion and whether the professional believes the child or whether or not the child is truthful. Even though conclusions about these issues may be logical extensions of a conclusion about sexual abuse, professionals are advised not to include them in written reports or court testimony.

Professionals need to consider a range of explanations for a sexual abuse allegation and not merely attend to information that supports abuse. Because sexual abuse usually is without witnesses and its substantiation rests primarily on children's statements and behavior, interviewers will rarely have the highest confidence in their conclusions. This is true both for ruling in and for ruling out sexual abuse. Interviewers' conclusions should be stated in such a way as to reflect their degree of certainty about the presence or absence of sexual abuse and the basis of conclusions.

References

Abrams, S., & Abrams, J. B. (1993). *Polygraph testing of the pedophile.* Portland, OR: Gwinner Press.

Achenbach, T. M. (1991a). *Manual for the Child Behavior Checklist/4-18 and 1991 Profile.* Burlington, VT: University of Vermont Department of Psychiatry.

Achenbach, T. M. (1991b). *Manual for the Teacher's Report Form and the 1991 profile.* Burlington, VT: University of Vermont Department of Psychiatry.

Achenbach, T., Edelbrock, C., & Howell, C. (1987). Empirically-based assessment of behavioral/emotional problems of 2–3 year old children. *Journal of Abnormal Child Psychology, 15,* 629–650.

Achenbach, T., & Rescorla, L. (2000). *Child Behavior Checklist for Ages 1.5–5, and Caregiver-Teacher Report Form for Ages 1.5–5 (CBCL 1.5–5, C-TRF).* Orlando, FL: Psychological Assessment Resources.

Ahlquist, A. (2002). *Child maltreatment and domestic violence: Cognitive graphic interviewing.* (Available from Ann Ahlquist, 11975 45th Avenue, N. Minneapolis, MN, 55442)

Akehurst, L., Milne, R., & Kohnken, G. (2003). The effects of children's age and delay on recall in a cognitive or structured interview. *Psychology, Crime, and the Law, 9*(1), 97–107.

Aldridge, J., Lamb, M., Sternberg, K., Orbach, Y., Esplin, P., & Bowler, L. (2004). Using human figure drawing to elicit information from alleged sexual abuse victims. *Journal of Consulting and Clinical Psychology, 72*(2), 304–316.

Aldridge, M., & Wood, J. (1988). *Interviewing children: A guide for child care and forensic practitioners.* New York: Wiley.

Aldridge, N. (1998). Strengths and limitations of forensic child sexual abuse interviews with anatomical dolls: An empirical review. *Journal of Psychopathology and Behavioral Assessment, 20*(1), 1–41.

Aman, C., & Goodman, G. (1990). Children's use of anatomically detailed dolls to recount an event. *Child Development, 61,* 1859–1871.

American Academy of Child and Adolescent Psychiatry. (1990). *Guidelines for the evaluation of child and adolescent sexual abuse.* (Available from AACAP, 3615 Wisconsin Avenue NW, Washington, DC, 20016)

American Academy of Child and Adolescent Psychiatry. (1997a). Practice parameters for child custody evaluations. *Journal of the American Academy of Child and Adolescent Psychiatry, 36,* 57S–68S.

American Academy of Child and Adolescent Psychiatry. (1997b). Practice parameters for the forensic evaluation of children and adolescents who may have been physically or sexually abused. *Journal of the American Academy of Child and Adolescent Psychiatry, 36,* 37S–56S.

American Academy of Child and Adolescent Psychiatry. (1998). Children and adolescents with posttraumatic stress disorder. *Journal of the American Academy of Child and Adolescent Psychiatry, 37*(10, Suppl.), 46S–62S.

American Association for Protecting Children. (1988). *Highlights of official child neglect and abuse reporting.* Denver, CO: American Humane Association.

American Association on Mental Retardation. (1992). *Mental retardation: Definition, classification, and system of supports.* Washington, DC: Author.

American Bar Association, Criminal Justice Section. (1985). *Recommendations regarding guidelines for fair treatment of child witnesses in cases where child abuse is alleged.* Washington, DC: American Bar Association.

American Professional Society on the Abuse of Children. (1990). *Guidelines for psychosocial evaluation of suspected sexual abuse in young children.* (Available from APSAC National Operations Manager, Daphne Wright & Associates, Management Group, P.O. Box 30669, Charleston, SC 29417)

American Professional Society on the Abuse of Children. (1995). *Guidelines for the use of anatomical dolls.* (Available from APSAC National Operations Manager, Daphne Wright & Associates, Management Group, P.O. Box 30669, Charleston, SC 29417)

American Professional Society on the Abuse of Children. (1997). *Guidelines for psychosocial evaluation of suspected sexual abuse in children* (2nd ed.). (Available from APSAC National Operations Manager, Daphne Wright & Associates, Management Group, P.O. Box 30669, Charleston, SC 29417)

American Professional Society on the Abuse of Children. (2000). *Guidelines from the APSAC Videotape Task Force.* (Available from APSAC National Operations Manager, Daphne Wright & Associates, Management Group, P.O. Box 30669, Charleston, SC 29417)

American Professional Society on the Abuse of Children. (2002). *Guidelines on investigative interviewing in cases of alleged child abuse.* (Available from APSAC National Operations Manager, Daphne Wright & Associates, Management Group, P.O. Box 30669, Charleston, SC 29417)

American Psychiatric Association. (2000). *Diagnostic and statistical manual of mental disorders* (4th ed.). Washington, DC: Author.

American Psychological Association. (1994). Guidelines for child custody evaluations in divorce proceedings. *American Psychologist, 49*(7), 677–680.

Anson, D., Golding, S., & Gully, K. (1993). Child sexual abuse allegations: Reliability of criteria-based content analysis. *Law and Human Behavior, 17*(3), 331–341.

Arata, C. M. (1998). To tell or not to tell: Current functioning of child sexual abuse survivors who disclosed their victimization. *Child Maltreatment, 3,* 63–71.

Ards, S., Chung, C., & Myers, S. (1998). The effects of sample selection bias on racial differences in child abuse reporting. *Child Abuse and Neglect, 22*(2), 103–115.

Armstrong, J. G., Putnam, F. W., Carlson, E. B., Libero, D. Z., & Smith, S. R. (1997). Development and validation of a measure of adolescent dissociation:

The Adolescent Dissociative Experiences Scale. *Journal of Nervous Mental Disorders, 185,* 491–497.

August, R., & Foreman, B. (1989). A comparison of sexually abused and non-sexually abused children's behavioral responses to anatomically correct dolls. *Child Psychiatry and Human Development, 20*(1), 39–47.

Bagley, C., & Ramsey, R. (1986). Sexual abuse in childhood: Psychosocial outcomes and implications for social work practice. *Journal of Social Work and Human Sexuality, 4,* 33–47.

Baladerian, N. (1991). Sexual abuse of people with developmental disabilities. *Sexuality and Disability, 9*(4), 323–335.

Baladerian, N. (1994). Abuse and neglect of children with disabilities. *ARCA Factsheet,* no. 36. Retrieved November 27, 2003, from http://www.archrespite.org/archfs36.htm.

Baladerian, N. (1997). *Forensic Interviewers Guidebook to Use with Suspected Assault Victims with Cognitive and/or Communication Impairments.* Washington, D.C.: National Aging Resource Center on Elder Abuse.

Balogh, R., Bretherton, K., Whibley, S., Berney, T., Graham, S., Richold, P., et al. (2001). Sexual abuse in children and adolescents with intellectual disability. *Journal of Intellectual Disability Research, 45*(3), 194–201.

Bancroft, L., & Silverman, J. G. (2002). *The batterer as parent: Addressing the impact of domestic violence on family dynamics.* Thousand Oaks, CA: Sage Publications.

Barbaree, H., & Seto, M. (1997). Pedophilia: Assessment and treatment. In D. R. Laws & W. O'Donohue (Eds.), *Sexual deviance* (pp. 175–193). New York: Guilford Press.

Barth, R. P. (2004). Child welfare and race: Models of disproportionality. In D. M. Derezotes, J. Poertner, & M. F. Testa (Eds.), *Race matters in child welfare* (pp. 25–46). Washington, DC: Child Welfare League of America Press.

Bartlett-Simpson, B., Kneeshaw, S., & Schaffer, D. (1993). The use of anatomical dolls to assess child sexual abuse. *International Journal of Play Therapy, 2*(2), 35–51.

Bauer, E. (1994). Diagnostic validity of the use of an instrument for assessing behaviors of children with anatomical dolls. *Dissertation Abstracts International, 54*(12-B), 6441. (UMI No. 19961201)

Bauer, P. J. (2002). Building toward a past: Construction of a reliable long-term recall memory system. In N. Stein & P. J. Bauer (Eds.), *Representation, memory, and development: Essays in honor of Jean Mandler* (pp. 17–42). Mahwah, NJ: Lawrence Erlbaum Associates.

Bauer, P., Hertsgaard, L. A., & Dow, G. A. (1994). After 8 months have passed: Long-term recall of events by 1- to 2-year-old children. *Memory, 2,* 353–382.

Bauer, P. J., & Wewerka, S. (1995). One- to two-year-olds' recall of events: The more expressed, the more impressed. *Journal of Experimental Child Psychology, 59,* 475–496.

Bays, J. (1990). Are the genitalia of anatomical dolls distorted? *Child Abuse and Neglect, 14,* 171–175.

Bays, J., & Chadwick, D. (1993). Medical diagnosis of the sexually abused child. *Child Abuse and Neglect, 17*(1), 91–110.

Beck, A. T. (1996). *Beck Depression Inventory–II.* San Antonio, TX: Psychological Corporation.

Benedek, E., & Schetky, D. (1985). Allegations of child sexual abuse in custody cases. In E. Benedek & D. Schetky (Eds.), *Advances in child psychiatry and the law.* (pp145-156). New York: Brunner/Mazel.

Benedek, E., & Schetky, D. (1987a). Problems in validating allegations of sexual abuse. Part 1: Factors affecting perception and recall of events. *Journal of the American Academy of Child and Adolescent Psychiatry, 26*(6), 912–915.

Benedek, E., & Schetky, D. (1987b). Problems in validating allegations of sexual abuse. Part 2: Clinical evaluation. *Journal of the American Academy of Child and Adolescent Psychiatry, 26*(6), 916–921.

Bergman, M. (2003, October 8). *Nearly 1-in-5 speak a foreign language at home; most also speak English "very well," Census Bureau reports.* Retrieved October 19, 2003, from http://www.census.gov/PresRelease/www/releases/archives/census_2000/001406.html.

Berliner, L. (1988). Deciding whether or not the child has been sexually abused. In B. Nicholson & J. Bulkley (Eds.), *Allegations of sexual abuse in divorce and custody disputes* (pp. 12-27). Washington, DC: American Bar Association.

Berliner, L. (1991). Clinical work with sexually abused children. In C. Hollin & K. Howells (Eds.), *Clinical approaches to sex offenders and their victims* (pp. 209–228). New York: John Wiley & Sons.

Berliner, L. (1997a). Intervention with children who experience trauma. In D. Chicchetti & S. Toth (Eds.), *Developmental perspective on trauma: Theory, research, and intervention* (pp. 491–514). Rochester, NY: University of Rochester Press.

Berliner, L. (1997b). Research findings on child sexual abuse investigations. In R. Lieb, L. Berliner, & P. Toth (Eds.), *Protocols and training standards: Investigating allegations of child sexual abuse* (pp. 5–23). Olympia, WA: Evergreen State College, Washington State Institute for Public Policy.

Berliner, L. (2000, January). *Taping versus note-taking by forensic interviewers.* San Diego, CA: San Diego Conference on Child Maltreatment, Children's Hospital and Health Center.

Berliner, L., & Conte, J. (1993). Sexual abuse evaluations: Conceptual and empirical obstacles. *Child Abuse and Neglect, 16*(1), 111–125.

Berliner, L., & Conte, J. (1995). The effects of disclosure and intervention on sexually abused children. *Child Abuse and Neglect, 19*(3), 371–384.

Berliner, L. (with Lieb, R.). (2001, January). *Child sexual abuse investigations: Testing documentation methods* (Document No. 01-01-4102). Olympia, WA: Washington State Institute for Public Policy.

Berliner, L., Stern, P., & Stephenson, C. (1992). Should investigative interviews of children be recorded? *Journal of Interpersonal Violence, 7,* 278–284.

Bernet, W. (1993). False statements and differential diagnosis of abuse allegations. *Journal of the American Academy of Child and Adolescent Psychiatry, 32*(5), 903–910.

Bernet, W. (1997). Case study: Allegations of abuse created in a single interview. *Journal of the America Academy of Child and Adolescent Psychiatry, 36*(7), 966–970.

Besharov, D. (1990). Gaining control over child abuse reports. *Public Welfare, 2,* Spring, 34–47.

Bidrose, S., & Goodman, G. (2000). Testimony and evidence: A scientific case study of memory for child sexual abuse. *Applied Cognitive Psychology, 14,* 197–213.

Blush, G., & Ross, K. (1986). *SAID Syndrome: Sexual allegations in divorce.* Unpublished manuscript. (Available from G. Blush, Macomb County Psychodiagnostic Clinic, 40 N. Main Street, Court Building, Mt. Clemens, MI 48043-8606)

Boat, B., & Everson, M. (1988a). Interviewing young children with anatomical dolls. *Child Welfare, 67*(4), 336–352.

Boat, B., & Everson, M. (1988b). The use of anatomical dolls among professionals in sexual abuse evaluations. *Child Abuse and Neglect, 12,* 171–179.

Boat, B., & Everson, M. (1989). False allegations of sexual abuse by children and adolescents. *Journal of the American Academy of Child and Adolescent Psychiatry, 28,* 230–235.

Boat, B., & Everson, M. (1993). The use of anatomical dolls in sexual abuse evaluations: Current research and practice. In G. Goodman & B. Bottoms (Eds.), *Child victims, child witnesses* (pp. 47–70). New York: Guilford Press.

Boat, B., & Everson, M. (1994). Exploration of anatomical dolls by non-referred pre-school-aged children: Comparisons by age, gender, race, and socioeconomic status. *Child Abuse and Neglect, 18*(2), 139–154.

Boat, B., & Everson, M. (1996). Concerning practices using anatomical dolls. *Child Maltreatment, 2*(1), 96–104.

Boat, B., Everson, M., & Amaya-Jackson, L. (1996). Consistency of children's sexualized or avoidant reactions to anatomical dolls: A pilot study. *Journal of Child Sexual Abuse, 5*(10), 89–104.

Boat, B., Everson, M., & Holland, J. (1990). Maternal perceptions of nonabused children's behaviors after the children's exposure to anatomical dolls. *Child Welfare, 69*(5), 389–400.

Bolen, R., & Lamb, L. (2002). Guardian support of sexually abused children: A study of its predictors. *Journal of Interpersonal Violence, 7*(3), 265–276.

Bolen, R., & Scannapieco, M. (1999). Prevalence of child sexual abuse: A corrective meta-analysis. *Social Services Review, 73*(3), 281–313.

Boney-McCoy, S., & Finkelhor, D. (1996). Is youth victimization related to trauma symptoms and depression after controlling for prior symptoms and family relationships? A longitudinal, prospective study. *Journal of Consulting and Clinical Psychology, 64*(6): 1406–1416.

Booth, A., & Crouter, A. C. (Eds.). (2001). *Does it take a village? Community effects on children, adolescents, and families.* Mahwah, NJ: Lawrence Erlbaum Associates.

Bottoms, B., Goodman, G., Schwartz-Kennedy, B., Sachsenmeier, T., & Thomas, S. (1990, June). *Keeping secrets: Implications for child testimony.* Paper presented at the biennial meeting of the American Psychology and Law Society, Williamsburg, VA.

Bourg, W., Broderick, R., Flagor, R., Kelly, D., Ervin, D., & Butler, J. (1998). *Oregon interviewing guidelines for center based interviewers.* Salem, OR: State Office of Services to Children and Families.

Bourg, W., Broderick, R., Flagor, R., Kelly, D., Ervin, D., & Butler, J. (1999). *A child interviewer's guidebook.* Thousand Oaks, CA: Sage Publications.

Bowen, C., & Howie, P. (2002). Context and cue cards in young children's testimony: A comparison of brief narrative elaboration and context reinstatement. *Journal of Applied Psychology, 87*(6), 1077–1085.

Boychuk, T., & Stellar, M. (1992). *Videotaped forensic interview of the school age child.* Unpublished manuscript. (Available from Tascha Boychuk, Center for Child Protection, St. Joseph's Hospital, 350 W. Thomas Rd., Phoenix, AZ)

Bradford, R. (1994). Developing an objective approach to assessing allegations of sexual abuse. *Child Abuse Review, 3*(2), 93–101.

Bradley, A., & Wood, J. (1996). How do children tell? The disclosure process in child sexual abuse. *Child Abuse and Neglect, 20*(9), 881–891.

Brainerd, C., & Ornstein, P. (1991). Children's memory for witnessed events: The developmental backdrop. In J. Doris (Ed.), *The suggestibility of children's recollections* (pp. 10–20). New York: American Psychological Association.

Bresee, P., Stearns, G., Bess, B., & Packer, L. (1986). Allegations of child sexual abuse in child custody disputes. *American Journal of Orthopsychiatry, 56*(4), 560–569.

Bricklin, B. (1995). *The custody evaluation handbook: Research-based solutions and applications.* New York: Brunner-Mazel.

Briere, J. (1996). *Professional manual for the Trauma Symptom Checklist.* Odessa, FL: Psychological Assessment Resources.

Briere, J. (1999). *Trauma Symptom Checklist for Young Children (TSCYC).* (Available from John Briere, Department of Psychiatry, Emergency Medicine, University of Southern California, 2020 Zonal Avenue, Los Angeles, CA 90033)

Briere, J., Johnson, K., Bissada, A., Damon, L., Crouch, J., Gil, E., et al. (2001). The trauma symptom checklist for young children (TSCYC): Reliability and association with abuse exposure in a multi-site study. *Child Abuse and Neglect, 25*(8), 1001–1014.

Briere, J., & Lanktree, C. (1992, January). *Further data on the Trauma Symptom Checklist for Children: Reliability, validity, and sensitivity to treatment.* Paper presented at the Responding to Child Maltreatment conference, San Diego.

Briere, J., & Spinazzola, J. (2005). Phenomenology and psychological assessment of complex posttraumatic states. *Journal of Traumatic Stress, 18*(5), 401–412.

Brigham, J. C. (1998). Adults' evaluations of characteristics of children's memory. *Journal of Applied Developmental Psychology, 19*(1), 15–39.

Britton, H., & O'Keefe, M. A. (1991). Use of nonanatomical dolls in the sexual abuse interview. *Child Abuse and Neglect, 15,* 567–573.

Brown, D., Lamb, M., Pipe, M.-E., Orbach, Y., & Lewis, C. (2005, January). *Using drawings with children to elicit reports of touch after short and long delays.* Paper presented at the Society for Applied Research in Memory, Victoria, NZ.

Brown, D., & Pipe, M. E. (2003). Individual differences in children's event memory reports and the narrative elaboration technique. *Journal of Applied Psychology, 88*(2), 195–206.

Brown, D., Scheflin, A., & Hammond, C. (1998). *Memory, trauma, treatment, and the law.* New York: W.W. Norton.

Bruck, M., Ceci, S., & Francoeur, E. (2000). Children's use of anatomically detailed dolls to report genital touching in a medical examination: Developmental and gender comparisons. *Journal of Applied Experimental Psychology, 6*(1), 74–83.

Bruck, M., Ceci, S., Francoeur, E., & Renick, A. (1995). Anatomically detailed dolls do not facilitate preschoolers' reports of a pediatric examination involving genital touching. *Journal of Experimental Psychology: Applied, 1*(2), 95–109.

Bruck, M. Ceci, S., & Hembrooke, H. (1998). Reliability and credibility of young children's reports: From research to policy to practice. *American Psychologist, 53,* 136–151.

Bruck, M., Ceci, S., & Hembrooke, H. (2002). The nature of children's true and false narratives. *Developmental Review, 22*, 520–554.

Bruck, M., Ceci, S., & Melnyk, L. (1997). External and internal sources of variation in the creation of false repots in children. *Learning and Individual Differences, 9*, 289–316.

Bruck, M., Ceci, S., & Rosenthal, R. (1995). Children's allegations of sexual abuse: A reply to commentators. *Psychology, Public Policy, and Law, 1*(2), 494–520.

Bruck, M., & Melnyk, L. (2004). Individual differences in children suggestibility: A review and synthesis. *Applied Cognitive Psychology, 18*, 947–996.

Bruck, M., Melnyk, L., & Ceci, S. (2000). Draw it again Sam: The effect of drawing on children's suggestibility and source monitoring ability. *Journal of Experimental Child Psychology, 77*, 169–196.

Bull, R. (1995). Innovative techniques for the questioning of child witnesses, especially those who are young and those with learning disability. In M. Zaragoza, J. Graham, G. Hall, R. Hirschman, & Y. Ben-Porath (Eds.), *Memory and testimony in the child witness* (pp. 179–194). Thousand Oaks, CA: Sage Publications.

Burgess, A., & Hartman, C. (1993). Children's drawings. *Child Abuse and Neglect, 17*(1), 161–168.

Burgess, A., Hartman, C., Wolbert, W., & Grant, C. (1987). Child molestation: Assessing impact in multiple victims. *Archives in Psychiatric Nursing, 1*(1), 33–39.

Burgess, A., McCausland, M., & Wolbert, W. (1981). Children's drawings as indicators of sexual trauma. *Perspectives in Psychiatric Care, 14*, 50–58.

Burgess, E. (1988). Sexually abused children and their drawings. *Archives of Psychiatric Nursing, 2*(2), 65–73.

Butler, E., Fukurai, H., Dimitrius, J., & Krooth, R. (2001). *Anatomy of the McMartin child molestation case.* Lanham, MD: University of America Press.

Butler, S., Gross, J., & Haynie, H. (1995). The effect of drawing on memory performance in young children. *Developmental Psychology, 31*, 597–608.

California Attorney General's Office. (1994, July). *Child victim witness investigative pilot projects: Research and evaluation final report.* Sacramento, CA: Author.

California Institute on Human Services. (2004). *Guide for forensic interviewing of Spanish-speaking children.* Sonoma, CA: Sonoma State University, 1801 E. Cotati Avenue, Rohnert Park, CA 94928.

Camparo, L., Wagner, J., & Saywitz, K. (2001). Interviewing children about real and fictitious events: Revisiting the narrative elaboration procedure. *Law and Human Behavior, 25*(1), 63–60.

Campbell, T. (1992). False allegations of sexual abuse and their apparent credibility. *American Journal of Forensic Psychology, 10*(4), 21–35.

Campis, L. B., Hebden-Curtis, J., & Demaso, D. R. (1993). Developmental differences in detection and disclosure of sexual abuse. *Journal of the American Academy of Child and Adolescent Psychiatry, 32*(5), 920–924.

Cantlon, J., Payne, G., & Erbaugh, C. (1996). Outcome based practice: Disclosure rates of child sexual abuse comparing allegation blind and allegation informed structured interviews. *Child Abuse and Neglect, 20*(11), 1113–1120.

Carlson, R. (1995). A critical analysis of the use of anatomically detailed dolls in the assessment of child sexual abuse. *Dissertation Abstracts International, 55*(12-B), 5561. (UMI No. 19970101)

Carnes, C., & LeDuc, D. (1998). *Forensic evaluation of children.* Huntsville, AL: National Children's Advocacy Center. (Available from the National Children's Advocacy Center, 200 Westside Square, Suite 700, Huntsville, AL 35801)

Carnes, C., Nelson-Gardell, D., Wilson, C., & Orgassa, U. (2001). Extended forensic evaluation when sexual abuse is suspected: A multi-site study. *Child Maltreatment, 6*(3), 230–242.

Carnes, C., Wilson, C., & Nelson-Gardell, D. (1999). Extended forensic evaluation when child abuse is suspected: A model and preliminary data. *Child Maltreatment, 4,* 242–254.

Carnes, C., Wilson, C., & Nelson-Gardell, D. (2000). Addressing the challenges and controversies in child sexual abuse interviewing: The forensic evaluation protocol and research project. In K. C. Faller (Ed.), *Maltreatment in early childhood: Tools for research-based intervention* (pp. 83–104). New York: Haworth Press.

Carter, C., Bottoms, B., & Levine, M. (1996). Linguistic and socioemotional influences on the accuracy of children's reports. *Law and Human Behavior, 20*(3), 335–358.

Carter, I., & Parker, L. (1991). Intrafamilial sexual abuse in American Indian families. In M. Q. Patton (Ed.), *Family sexual abuse: Frontline research an evaluation* (pp. 106–117). Thousand Oaks, CA: Sage Publications.

Carter, M. (1995). Effects of rater knowledge of children's and adolescents' presenting problem on scores for draw-a-person: Screening procedure for emotional disturbance. *Dissertation Abstracts International, 55*(11-B). (UMI No. 970101)

Caruso, K. (1988). *Basic users manual to accompany Projective Story Telling Cards.* Redding, CA: Northwest Psychological Publishers.

Casebeer, M. (1989). *Projective Story Telling Cards.* Redding, CA: Northwest Psychological Publishers.

Ceci, S. J., & Bruck, M. (1993). The suggestibility of the child witness: A historical review and synthesis. *Psychological Bulletin, 113,* 403–439.

Ceci, S. J., & Bruck, M. (1995). *Jeopardy in the courtroom: A scientific analysis of children's testimony.* Washington, DC: American Psychological Association.

Ceci, S., Bruck, M., & Francoeur, E. (2000). Children's use of anatomically detailed dolls to report genital touching in a medical examination: Developmental and gender comparisons. *Journal of Experimental Psychology: Applied, 6*(1), 74–83.

Ceci, S., Bruck, M., & Rosenthal, R. (1995). Children's allegations of sexual abuse: Forensic and scientific issues: A reply to commentators. *Psychology, Public Policy, and Law, 1*(2), 494–520.

Ceci, S. J., Crossman, A. M., Scullin, M. H., Gilstrap, L., & Huffman, M. L. (2002). Children's suggestibility research: Implications for the courtroom and the forensic interview. In H. L. Westcott, G. M. Davies, & R. H. C. Bull (Eds.), *Children's testimony: A handbook of psychological research and forensic practice* (pp. 117–130). West Sussex, UK: John Wiley & Sons.

Ceci, S. J., Huffman, M. L. C., Smith, E., & Loftus, E. F. (1994). Repeatedly thinking about a non-event: Source misattributions among preschoolers. *Consciousness and Cognition, 3,* 388–407.

Ceci, S., & Leichtman, M. (1995). The effects of stereotypes and suggestions on preschoolers' reports. *Developmental Psychology, 31*(4), 568–578.

Ceci, S., Loftus, E., Leichtman, M., & Bruck, M. (1994). The role of source mis-attributions in the creation of false beliefs among preschoolers. *International Journal of Clinical and Experimental Hypnosis, 62,* 304–320.

Cederborg, A.-C., & Lamb, M. (2006). How does the legal system respond when children with learning difficulties are victimized? *Child Abuse and Neglect, 30*(5), 537–547.

Cederborg, A.-C., Orbach, Y., & Sternberg, K. (2000). Investigative interviews of child witnesses in Sweden. *Child Abuse and Neglect, 24*(10), 1355–1361.

Center for Child Protection. (1992). *Sexual abuse evidentiary interview protocol.* (Available from the Center for Child Protection, Children's Hospital and Health Center, 3020 Children's Way MC 5016, San Diego, CA 92123)

Cerezo, A., & D'Ocon, A. (1999). Sequential analysis in coercive mother-child interaction: The predictability hypothesis in abusive dyads. *Child Abuse and Neglect, 23*(2), 99–113.

Cerezo, A., D'Ocon, A., & Dolz, L. (1996). Mother-child interactive patterns in abusive families versus nonabusive families: An observational study. *Child Abuse and Neglect, 20*(7), 573–587.

Chae, Y., & Ceci, S. J. (2005). Individual differences in children's recall and suggestibility: The effect of intelligence, temperament, and self-perceptions. *Applied Cognitive Psychology, 19,* 383–407.

Chaffin, M., Lawson, L., Selby, A., & Wherry, J. (1997). False negatives in sexual abuse interviews: Preliminary investigation of a relationship to dissociation. *Journal of Child Sexual Abuse, 6*(3), 15–29.

Chantler, L., Pelco, L., & Mertin, P. (1993). The psychological evaluation of child sexual abuse using the Louisville Behavior Checklist and Human Figure Drawing. *Child Abuse and Neglect, 17*(2), 271–280.

Child Abuse Prevention and Treatment Act (CAPTA) (1974), Pub. L. No. 93-247, U.S.C. TITLE 42 Chapter 67 SECTION 5101–5107.

Child Trends Databank. (2002). *Family structure.* Retrieved October 27, 2003, from http://www.childtrendsdatabank.org/indicators/59FamilyStructure.cfm.

Child Welfare League of America. (2002, September). *Research roundup: Child welfare workforce.* Washington, DC: Child Welfare League of America.

Chipungu, S. S., & Bent-Goodley, T. B. (2003). Race, poverty and child maltreatment. *APSAC Advisor, 15*(2), 9–10.

Chong, I., Yu, D., Martin, G., Harapiak, S., & Garinger, J. (2000). Response switching to repeated questions by individuals with developmental disabilities. *Developmental Disabilities Bulletin, 28*(1), 56–66.

Cinq-Mars, M., Wright, J., Cyr, M., McDuff, P., & Friedrich, W. N. (2005). Sexual at-risk behaviors and violence in dating relationships of sexually abused adolescent girls. *Journal of Child Sexual Abuse, 14*(2), 49–68.

Clarke-Stewart, A., Malloy, L., & Allhusen, V. (2004). Verbal ability, self-control, and close relationships with parents protect children against misleading suggestions. *Applied Cognitive Psychology, 18,* 107–1058.

Clarke-Stewart, A., Thompson, W., & Lepore, S. (1989, August). Manipulating children's interpretations through interrogation. In G. Goodman (Chair), *Can children provide accurate eyewitness reports?* Symposium conducted at the meeting of the Society for Research on Child Development, Kansas City, MO.

Cohen, J. A., Deblinger, E., Mannarino, A. P., & de Arellano, M. A. (2001). The importance of culture in treating abused and neglected children: An empirical review. *Child Maltreatment, 6,* 148–157.

Cohen, J., & Mannarino, A. (1988). Psychological symptoms of sexually abused girls. *Child Abuse and Neglect, 12,* 571–577.

Cohen, J. A., & Mannarino, A. P. (1996). Factors that mediate treatment outcome in sexually abused preschoolers. *Journal of the American Academy of Child and Adolescent Psychiatry, 35,* 1402–1410.

Cohen-Lieberman, M. S. (1999). Draw and tell: Drawings within the context of child sexual abuse investigations. *Art of Psychotherapy, 26*(3), 185–194.

Cohen-Lieberman, M. S. (2003). Drawing in forensic investigations of child sexual abuse. In C. Malchiodi (Ed.), *Handbook of art therapy* (pp. 167–180). New York: Guilford Press.

Cohn, D. (1991). Anatomical doll play of preschoolers referred for sexual abuse and those not referred. *Child Abuse and Neglect, 15*(4), 455–466.

Colby, I., & Colby, D. (1987a). Videotaped interviews in child sexual abuse cases: The Texas example. *Child Welfare, 66*(1), 25–34.

Colby, I., & Colby, D. (1987b). Videotaping the child sexual-abuse victim. *Social Casework, 68*(2), 117–121.

Cole, C. B., & Loftus, E. F. (1987). The memory of children. In S. J. Ceci, M. P. Toglia, & D. F. Ross (Eds.), *Children's eyewitness memory* (pp. 178–208). New York: Springer-Verlag.

Conte, J. (2002). *Critical issues in child sexual abuse.* Thousand Oaks, CA: Sage Publications.

Conte, J., Sorenson, E., Fogarty, L., & Dalla Rosa, J. (1991). Evaluating children's reports of sexual abuse: Results from a survey of professionals. *American Journal of Orthopsychiatry, 61*(3), 428–437.

Cook, A., Spinazzola, J., Ford, J., Lanktree, C., Blaustein, M., Cloitre, M., et al. (2005). Complex trauma in children and adolescents. *Psychiatric Annals, 35*(5), 390–398.

Cordon, I., Saetermoe, C., & Goodman, G. (2005). Facilitating children's accurate responses: Conversational rules and interview style. *Applied Cognitive Psychology, 19,* 249–266.

Corwin, D. (1988). Early diagnosis of child sexual abuse: Diminishing the lasting effects. In G. Wyatt & G. Powell (Eds.), *The lasting effects of child sexual abuse* (pp. 251–270). Newbury Park, CA: Sage Publications.

Corwin, D., Berliner, L., Goodman, G., Goodwin, J., & White, S. (1987). Child sexual abuse in custody disputes: No easy answers. *Journal of Interpersonal Violence, 2*(1), 91–105.

Cosentino, C. E., Meyer-Bahlburg, H. F. L., Alpert, J. L., Weinberg, S. L., & Gaines, R. (1995). Sexual behavior problems and psychopathology symptoms in sexually abused girls. *Journal of the American Academy of Child and Adolescent Psychiatry, 34,* 1033–1042.

Cowling, A. (2006). *Anatomically correct dolls in false allegation cases.* Retrieved February 26, 2006, from http://www.allencowling.com/false15.htm.

Craig, R., Scheibe, R., Raskin, D., Kircher, J., & Dodd, D. (1999). Interviewer questions and content analysis of children's statements of sexual abuse. *Applied Developmental Science, 3*(2), 77–85.

Crawford v. Washington. (2004). Retrieved September 2, 2006, from http://www.supremecourtus.gov/opinions/03pdf/029410.pdf#search=%22Crawford%20supreme%20court%20decision%22.

Cross, T., & Saxe, L. (1992). A critique of the validity of polygraph testing in child sexual abuse cases. *Journal of Child Sexual Abuse, 1*(4), 19–33.

Cross, T., & Saxe, L. (2001). The polygraph: The lure of the magic lasso. *Child Maltreatment, 6*(3), 195–206.

Crosse, S. B., Kaye, E., & Ratnofsky, A. C. (1993). *A report on the maltreatment of children with disabilities.* Washington, DC: National Center on Child Abuse and Neglect, Department of Health and Human Services.

Cruz, V. (2000). *Interviewing children with disabilities.* Retrieved November 27, 2003, from http://www.developmentaldisability.org/Abused.pdf.

Dalenberg, C. (1992, January). *True and false allegations of physical abuse: The role of the mother in constructing a believable story.* Paper presented at the San Diego Conference on Responding to Child Maltreatment, San Diego, CA.

Dalenberg, C. J. (1996). Fantastic elements in child disclosure of abuse. *APSAC Advisor, 9*(2), 1, 5–10.

Dalenberg, C. J., Hyland, K. Z., & Cuevas, C. A. (2002). Sources of fantastic elements in allegations of abuse by adults and children. In M. Eisen, J. Quas, & G. Goodman (Eds.), *Memory and suggestibility in the forensic interview* (pp. 185–204). Mahwah, NJ: Lawrence Erlbaum.

Dammeyer, M. (1998). The assessment of child sexual abuse allegations: Using research to guide clinical decision making. *Behavioral Sciences and the Law, 16*, 21–34.

Davey, R., & Hill J. (1999). The variability of practice in interviews used by professionals to investigate child sexual abuse. *Child Abuse and Neglect, 23*(6), 571–578.

Davies, D. (2002). *Interviewing children with disabilities; curriculum for the APSAC forensic interview clinic.* American Professional Society on the Abuse of Children, http://apsac.fmhi.usf.edu/.

Davies, D., Cole, J., Albertella, G., McCulloch, L., Allen, K., & Kekevian, L. (1996). A model for conducting forensic interviews with child victims of abuse. *Child Maltreatment, 1*(2), 189–199.

Davies, D., & Lyon, T. (2006, January 26). *Getting more (and more accurate) information in your forensic interview: What the research and experience has taught us.* Workshop presented at the 20th International San Diego Conference on Child and Family Maltreatment, San Diego, CA.

Davies, G. M. (1991). Research on children's testimony: Implications for interview practice. In C. R. Rollin & K. Howells (Eds.), *Clinical approaches to sex offenders and their victims* (pp. 93–115). Chichester, UK: Wiley.

Davies, G. M. (1994). Statement validity analysis: An art or a science? Commentary on Bradford. *Child Abuse Review, 3*(2), 104–106.

Davis, S. L., & Bottoms, B. L. (2002). The effects of social support on the accuracy of children's reports: Implications for the forensic interview. In M. Eisen, J. Quas, & G. Goodman (Eds.), *Memory and suggestibility in the forensic interview* (pp. 437–458). Mahwah, NJ: Lawrence Erlbaum.

Dawson, B., Vaughan, A., & Wagner, W. (1992). Normal responses to sexually anatomically detailed dolls. *Journal of Family Violence, 7*(2), 135–152.

de Arellano, M., Waldrop, A., Deblinger, E., Cohen, J., Danielson, C., & Mannarino, A. (2005). Community outreach program for child victims of traumatic events. *Behavior Modification, 29*(1), 130–155.

Deblinger, E., Lippman, J. T., & Steer, R. (1996). Sexually abused children suffering post-traumatic stress symptoms: Initial treatment outcome findings. *Child Maltreatment, 1,* 310–321.

Deitrich-MacLean, G., & Walden, T. (1988). Distinguishing teaching interactions of physically abusive from nonabusive parent-child dyads. *Child Abuse and Neglect, 12*(4), 469–480.

DeLipsey, J. M., & James, S. (1988). Videotaping the sexually abused child: The Texas experience. In S. Sgroi (Ed.), *Vulnerable populations: Vol. 1. Evaluation and treatment of sexual abused children and adult survivors* (pp. 229–264). Lexington, MA: Lexington Books.

DeLoache, J. (1995). The use of dolls in interviewing young children. In M. Zaragoza, J. Graham, G. Hall, R. Hirschman, & Y. Ben-Porath (Eds.), *Memory and testimony in the child witness* (pp. 160–178). Newbury Park, CA: Sage Publications.

DeLoache, J., & Marzolf, D. (1995). The use of dolls to interview young children: Issues of symbolic representation. *Journal of Experimental Clinical Psychology, 60*(1), 155–173.

De Marneff, D. (1994). Gender recognition and gender labeling: An empirical study of toddlers. *Dissertation Abstracts International, 54*(11-B), 5959. (UMI No. 19961101)

De Marneff, D. (1997). Bodies and words: A study of young children's genital and gender knowledge. *Gender and Psychoanalysis, 2*(1), 3–33.

Dent, H. (1986). Experimental study of the effectiveness of different techniques of questioning mentally handicapped child witnesses. *British Journal of Clinical Psychology, 27,* 13–17.

Dent, H. (1992). The effects of age and intelligence on eyewitnessing ability. In H. Dent & R. Flin (Eds.), *Children as witnesses* (pp. 1–13). Oxford, England: John Wiley.

DeVoe, E., & Faller, K. C. (1999). Characteristics of disclosure of children who may have been sexually abused. *Child Maltreatment, 4*(3), 217–227.

DeVoe, E., & Faller, K. C. (2002). Questioning strategies in interviews with children who may have been sexually abused. *Child Welfare, 81*(1), 5–32.

De Young, M. (1986). A conceptual model for judging the truthfulness of a young child's allegation of sexual abuse. *American Journal of Orthopsychiatry, 56*(4), 550–559.

DiPietro, E., Runyon, D., & Fredrickson, D. (1997). Predictors of disclosure during medical evaluation for suspected sexual abuse. *Journal of Child Sexual Abuse, 6*(1), 133–142.

Dorado, J., & Saywitz, K. (2001). Interviewing preschoolers from low- and middle-SES communities: A test of the narrative elaboration recall improvement technique. *Journal of Clinical Child Psychology, 30*(4), 568–580.

Drach, K., Wientzen, J., & Ricci, L. (2001). The diagnostic utility of sexual behavior problems in diagnosing sexual abuse evaluation clinic. *Child Abuse and Neglect, 25*(4), 289–503.

Drucker, P. M., Grego-Vigorito, C., Moore-Russell, M., Alvaltroni, P., & Ryan, E. (1997, April). *Drawing facilitates recall of traumatic past events in young chil-*

dren of substance abusers. Paper presented at the Biennial Conference of the Society for Research in Child Development, Washington, DC.

Dubowitz, H., Black, M., & Harrington, D. (1992). The diagnosis of child sexual abuse. *American Journal of Diseases of Children, 146*, 688–693.

Dunkerley, G., & Dalenberg, C. (2000). Secret-keeping in black and white children as a function of interviewer race, racial identify, and risk for abuse. In K. C. Faller (Ed.), *Maltreatment in early childhood: Tools for research-based intervention* (pp. 13–36). New York: Haworth Press.

Eagleson, K. (2002, December). *Interviewing reluctant children*. Paper presented at the American Professional Society on the Abuse of Children Forensic Interview Clinic, Bowling Green, KY.

Earle, K. A., & Cross, A. (2001). *Child abuse and neglect among American Indian/Alaska Native children: An analysis of existing data*. Portland, ME: University of Southern Maine, Muskie School of Public Service, Institute for Child and Family Policy.

Eberle, P., & Eberle, S. (1986). *The politics of child abuse*. Secaucus, NJ: Lyle Stuart.

Einbender, A., & Friedrich, W. (1989). Psychological functioning and behavior of sexually abused girls. *Journal of Consulting and Clinical Psychology, 57*, 155–157.

Eisen, M., & Goodman, G. (1998). Trauma, memory, and suggestibility in children. *Development and Psychopathology, 10*(4), 717–738.

Eisen, M., Goodman, G., Qin, J., & Davis, S. (1998). Memory and suggestibility in maltreated children: New research relevant to evaluating allegations of abuse. In S. Lynn & K. McConkey (Eds.), *Truth in memory* (pp. 163–189). New York: Guilford Press.

Ellefson, J. (2006, January 26). *Forensic use of anatomical dolls*. Workshop presented at the San Diego International Conference on Child and Family Maltreatment, San Diego, CA.

Elliott, A., O'Donohue, W., & Nickerson, M. (1993). The use of sexually anatomically detailed dolls in the assessment of sexual abuse. *Clinical Psychology Review, 13*(3), 207–221.

Elliott, D., & Briere, J. (1994). Forensic sexual abuse evaluations of older children: Disclosures and symptomatology. *Behavioral Science and the Law, 12*, 261–277.

Ellis, N., McCartney, J., Ferretti, R., & Cavalier, A. (1977). Recognition memory in mentally retarded persons. *Intelligence, 3*, 310–317.

End Child Prostitution, Child Pornography, and Trafficking of Children for Sexual Purposes (ECPAT). (2005). *Updates*. Retrieved on March 6, 2006, from http://www.ecpat.net/eng/index.asp.

Engelberg, E., & Christianson, S. (2002). Stress, trauma, and memory. In M. Eisen, J. Quas, & G. Goodman (Eds.), *Memory and suggestibility in the forensic interview* (pp. 143–164). Mahwah, NJ: Lawrence Erlbaum.

Everson, M. (1991, January). *Evaluating young children for possible sexual abuse*. Presentation given at the San Diego Conference on Responding to Child Sexual Maltreatment, San Diego, CA.

Everson, M. (1992a). *Guidelines for assessing the very young child*. (Available from M. Everson, Department of Psychiatry, Program on Child Trauma and Maltreatment CB #7160, University of North Carolina–Chapel Hill, Chapel Hill, NC 27599-7160.)

Everson, M. (1992b, January). *Models of sexual abuse evaluations.* Presentation given at the Evaluating Young Children for Possible Sexual Abuse APSAC Training Institute, Health Science Response to Child Maltreatment, San Diego, CA.

Everson, M. (1996, January). *The art and science of forensic interviewing: Models for forensic assessment.* Paper presented at National Conference on Responding to Child Maltreatment, San Diego, CA.

Everson, M. (1997). Understanding bizarre, improbable, and fantastic elements in children's accounts of abuse. *Child Maltreatment, 2*(2), 134–149.

Everson, M. (1999). *Leading and suggestive questions in the child forensic interview.* Unpublished manuscript. (Available from Mark Everson, Program on Child Trauma and Maltreatment CB #7160, University of North Carolina–Chapel Hill, Chapel Hill, NC 27599-7160.)

Everson, M., & Boat, B. (1989). False allegations of sexual abuse by children and adolescents. *Journal of the American Academy of Child and Adolescent Psychiatry, 28*(2), 230–235.

Everson, M., & Boat, B. (1990). Sexualized doll play among young children: Implications for the use of anatomical dolls in sexual abuse evaluations. *Journal of the American Academy of Child and Adolescent Psychiatry, 29*(5), 736–742.

Everson, M., & Boat, B. (1994). Putting the anatomical doll controversy in perspective: An examination of the major doll uses and related criticisms. *Child Abuse and Neglect, 18*(2), 113–130.

Everson, M., & Boat, B. (1997). Anatomical dolls in child sexual abuse assessments: A call for forensically relevant research. *Applied Cognitive Psychology, 11,* S55–S74.

Everson, M., & Boat, B. (2002). The utility of anatomical dolls and drawings in child forensic interviews. In M. Eisen, J. Quas, & G. Goodman (Eds.), *Memory and suggestibility in the forensic interview* (pp. 383–408). Mahwah, NJ: Laurence Erlbaum.

Everson, M., Boat, B., Bourg, S., & Robertson, K. (1996). Beliefs among professionals about the rates of false allegations of child sexual abuse. *Journal of Interpersonal Violence, 11*(4), 541–553.

Everson, M., Boat, B., & Robertson, K. (1992). *Beliefs about the frequency of false allegations of child sexual abuse: Where you stand depends on where you sit.* Paper given at the San Diego Conference on Responding to Child Maltreatment. (Available from Mark Everson, Department of Psychiatry, CB 7160, University of North Carolina–Chapel Hill, Chapel Hill, NC 27599-7160)

Everson, M., & Faller, K. C. (1999, June). *The art and science of forensic interviewing.* Paper presented at the APSAC Colloquium on Child Maltreatment, San Antonio, TX.

Everson, M., & McKnight, E. (2002). *Screener for Adolescent Maltreatment (SAM): A pilot study.* (Available from Mark Everson, Program on Child Trauma and Maltreatment CB #7160, University of North Carolina–Chapel Hill, Chapel Hill, NC 27599-7160.)

Faller, K. C. (1984). Is the child victim of sexual abuse telling the truth? *Child Abuse and Neglect, 8,* 473–481.

Faller, K. C. (1988a). *Child sexual abuse: An interdisciplinary manual for diagnosis, case management, and treatment.* New York: Columbia University Press.

Faller, K. C. (1988b). Criteria for judging the credibility of children's statements about their sexual abuse. *Child Welfare, 67*(5), 389–401.

Faller, K. C. (1990a). Sexual abuse by paternal caretakers: A comparison of abusers who are biological fathers in intact families, stepfathers, and non-custodial fathers. In A. Horton, B. Johnson, L. Roundy, & D. Williams (Eds.), *The Incest Perpetrator: A Family Member No One Wants to Treat* (pp. 44–65). Newbury Park, CA: Sage Publications.

Faller, K. C. (1990b). *Understanding child sexual maltreatment.* Newbury Park, CA: Sage Publications.

Faller, K. C. (1991a). Possible explanations for child sexual abuse allegations in divorce. *American Journal of Orthopsychiatry, 61*(1), 86–91.

Faller, K. C. (1991b). Types of questions for assessing allegation of sexual abuse. *APSAC Advisor, 3*(1), 3–5.

Faller, K. C. (1993). *Child sexual abuse: Assessment and intervention.* Washington, DC: National Center on Child Abuse and Neglect, U.S. Department of Health and Human Services.

Faller, K. C. (1994). Extrafamilial sexual abuse. In S. Kaplan & D. Pelcovitz (Eds.), *Child and adolescent clinics of North America* (pp. 713–727). New York: W.B. Saunders & Co.

Faller, K. C. (1996a). *Evaluating children suspected of having been sexually abused: The APSAC study guides 2.* Thousand Oaks, CA: Sage Publications.

Faller, K. C. (1996b). Interviewing children who may have been abused: A historical perspective and overview of controversies. *Child Maltreatment, 1*(2), 4–18.

Faller, K. C. (1997). The polygraph, its use in decision-making about child sexual abuse: An exploratory study. *Child Abuse and Neglect, The International Journal, 21*(10), 993–1008.

Faller, K. C. (1998). The parental alienation syndrome: What is it and what data support it? *Child Maltreatment, 3*(2), 100–115.

Faller, K. C. (2000a). Child maltreatment and protection in the United States. *Journal of Aggression, Trauma, and Maltreatment, 2*(4), 1–12.

Faller, K. C. (2000b). Individual change in children and direct social work practice. In P. Allen-Meares & C. Garvin (Eds.), *Handbook on direct social work practice* (pp. 161–180). Newbury Park, CA: Sage Publications.

Faller, K. C. (2000c). Questioning children who may have been sexually abused: A synthesis of research and practice. *Journal of Aggression, Trauma, and Maltreatment, 2*(4), 37–56.

Faller, K. C. (2003). *Understanding and assessing child sexual maltreatment* (2nd ed.). Newbury Park, CA: Sage Publications.

Faller, K. C. (2005). Anatomical dolls: Their use in assessment of children who may have been sexually abused. *Journal of Child Sexual Abuse, 14*(3), 1–21.

Faller, K. C., Birdsall, W. C., Henry, J., Vandervort, F., & Silverschanz, P. (2001). What makes sex offenders confess? An exploratory study. *Journal of Child Sexual Abuse, 10*(4), 31–49.

Faller, K. C., & Corwin, D. (1995). Children's interview statements and behaviors: Role in identifying sexually abused children. *Child Abuse and Neglect, 19*(1), 71–82.

Faller, K. C., & DeVoe, E. R. (1995a). Allegations of sexual abuse in divorce. *Journal of Child Sexual Abuse, 4*(4), 1–25.

Faller, K. C., & DeVoe, E. R. (1995b, December). *Final report: Computer-assisted interviewing of children who may have been sexually abused.* National Institute of Mental Health, Small Business Innovation Research Program (R44 MH 47624-02). Ann Arbor, MI: University of Michigan School of Social Work.

Faller, K. C., & Everson, M. (2003). *Forensic and clinical issues with children who may have been sexually abused: Potential conflict between the child's best interest and the legal system.* Unpublished manuscript, University of Michigan School of Social Work.

Faller, K. C., Froning, M., & Lipovsky, J. (1991). The parent-child interview: Use in evaluating child allegations of sexual abuse by a parent. *American Journal of Orthopsychiatry, 61*(4), 552–557.

Faller, K. C., & Henry, J. (2000). Child sexual abuse: A case study in community collaboration. *Child Abuse and Neglect, 24*(9), 1215–1225.

Faller, K. C., & Plummer, C. (1996). Multi-offender/multi-victim cases of sexual abuse: The impact of acquittal. *Children's Legal Rights Journal, 16*(2), 23–30.

Feiring, C., & Taska, L. (2005). The persistence of shame following sexual abuse: A longitudinal look at risk and recovery. *Child Maltreatment, 10*(4), 337–349.

Feiring, C., Taska, L., & Lewis, M. (1998). The role of shame and attributional style in children's and adolescents adaptation to sexual abuse. *Child Maltreatment, 3,* 129–142.

Feiring, C., Taska, L., & Lewis, M. (2002). Adjustment following sexual abuse discovery: The role of shame and attributional style. *Developmental Psychology, 38,* 79–92.

Fergusson, D. M., Horwood, L. J., & Lynskey, M. T. (1997). Childhood sexual abuse, adolescent sexual behaviors and sexual revictimization. *Child Abuse and Neglect, 21,* 789–803.

Fergusson, D. M., Horwood, L. J., & Woodward, L. J. (2000). The stability of child abuse reports: A longitudinal study of reporting behavior of young adults. *Psychological Medicine, 30,* 529–544.

Finkelhor, D. (1979). *Sexually victimized children.* New York: Free Press.

Finkelhor, D. (1986). *Sourcebook on child sexual abuse.* Newbury Park, CA: Sage Publications.

Finkelhor, D. (1990). Is child abuse overreported? *Public Welfare, 1,* (Winter), 23–29.

Finkelhor, D. (1994). Current information about the scope and nature of child sexual abuse. *The Future of Children: Sexual Abuse of Children, 4*(2), 31–53.

Finkelhor, D., & Baron, L. (1986). High risk children. In D. Finkelhor (Ed.), *Sourcebook on child sexual abuse* (pp. 60–88). Thousand Oaks, CA: Sage Publications.

Finkelhor, D., Hotaling, G., Lewis, I., & Smith, C. (1990). Sexual abuse in a national survey of adult men and women. *Child Abuse and Neglect, 14,* 19–28.

Finkelhor, D., Mitchell, K., & Wolak, J. (2000). *Online victimization: A report on the Nation's youth.* Washington, DC: Department of Justice, National Center for Missing and Exploited Children.

Finnila, K., Mahlberg, N., Santtila, P., Sandnabba, K., & Niemi, P. (2003). Validity of a test of children's suggestibility for predicting responses to two interview situations differing in their degree of suggestiveness. *Journal of Experimental Child Psychology, 85,* 32–49.

Fisher, R., Brennan, K., & McCauley, M. (2002). The cognitive interview method to enhance eyewitness recall. In M. Eisen, J. Quas, & G. Goodman (Eds.), *Memory and suggestibility in the forensic interview* (pp. 265–286). Mahwah, NJ: Lawrence Erlbaum.

Fisher, R., & Geiselman, R. E. (1992). *Memory-enhancing techniques for investigative interviewing: The cognitive interview.* Springfield, IL: Charles Thomas.

Fivush, R., & Hammond, N. R. (1990). Autobiographical memory across pre-school years: Towards reconceptualizing childhood amnesia. In R. Fivush & J. A. Hudson (Eds.), *Knowing and remembering in young children* (pp. 223–248). New York: Cambridge University Press.

Fivush, R., Peterson, C., & Schwarzmueller, A. (2002). Questions and answers: The credibility of child witnesses in the context of specific questioning techniques. In M. Eisen, J. A. Quas, & G. S. Goodman (Eds.), *Memory and suggestibility in the forensic interview* (pp. 331–355). Mahwah, NJ: Lawrence Erlbaum.

Foa, E., Steketee, G., & Rothbaum, B. (1989). Behavioral/cognitive conceptualization of post-traumatic stress disorder. *Behavior Therapy, 20,* 155–176.

Fontes, L. A. (1993). Disclosures of sexual abuse by Puerto Rican children: Oppression and cultural barriers. *Journal of Child Sexual Abuse, 2*(3), 21–35.

Fontes, L. A. (1995). *Sexual abuse in nine North American cultures.* Thousand Oaks, CA: Sage Publications.

Fontes, L. A. (1997). Conducting ethical cross-cultural research on family violence. In G. K. Kantor & J. L. Jasinski (Eds.), *Out of the darkness: Contemporary research perspectives on family violence* (pp. 296–312). Thousand Oaks, CA: Sage Publications.

Fontes, L. A. (2000). *Interviewing children from immigrant families about maltreatment* [Audiotape]. Newbury Park, CA: Sage Publications.

Fontes, L. A. (2005a). *Child abuse and culture: Working with diverse families.* New York: Guilford Press.

Fontes, L. A. (2005b). Interviewing diverse children and families about maltreatment. *Child abuse and culture: Working with diverse families* (pp. 83–107). New York: Guilford Press.

Fontes, L. A. (2005c). Interviewing immigrant children and families about child maltreatment: Setting the stage. *Protecting Children, 20*(1), 37–46.

Fontes, L. A., Cruz, M., & Tabachnick, J. (2001). Views of child sexual abuse in two cultural communities: An exploratory study with Latinos and African Americans. *Child Maltreatment, 6,* 103–117.

Freeman, K., & Morris, T. (1999). Investigative interviewing with children: Evaluation of the effectiveness of the training program for child protective workers. *Child Abuse and Neglect, 25*(7), 701–713.

Friedrich, W. (1990). *Psychotherapy of sexually abused children and their families.* New York: W.W. Norton.

Friedrich, W. (1993). Sexual victimization and sexual behavior in children: A review of recent literature. *Child Abuse and Neglect, 17*(1), 59–66.

Friedrich, W. (1994, January). *APSAC Institute: Treatment outcomes in child sexual abuse.* Paper presented at the San Diego Conference of Responding to Child Maltreatment, Center for Child Protection, Children's Hospital and Health Center, San Diego, CA.

Friedrich, W. N. (1995). *Psychotherapy with sexually abused boys.* Thousand Oaks, CA: Sage Publications.

Friedrich, W. (1997). *Child sexual behavior inventory*. Odessa, FL: Psychological Assessment Resources.

Friedrich, W. N. (2002). *Psychological assessment of sexually abused children and their families*. Thousand Oaks, CA: Sage Publications.

Friedrich, W., Beilke, R., & Urquiza, A. (1988). Behavior problems in young sexually abused boys: A comparison study. *Journal of Interpersonal Violence, 3*, 21–28.

Freidrich, W. N., Einbender, A., & McCarty, P. (1999). Sexually abused girls and their Rorschach responses. *Psychological Reports, 85*(2), 355–362.

Friedrich, W. N., Fisher, J., Dittner, C., Acton, R., Berliner, L., Butler, J., et al. (2001). Child Sexual Behavior Inventory: Normative, psychiatric and sexual abuse comparisons. *Child Maltreatment, 6*, 37–49.

Friedrich, W. N., Jaworski, T. M., Huxsahl, J., & Bengston, B. (1997). Dissociative and sexual behaviors in children and adolescents with sexual abuse and psychiatric histories. *Journal of Interpersonal Violence, 12*, 155–171.

Friedrich, W. N., Lysne, M., & Sim, L. (2004). Assessing Sexual Behavior in High-Risk Adolescents with the Adolescent Clinical Sexual Behavior Inventory (ACSBI). *Child Maltreatment, 9*(3), 239–250.

Friedrich, W. N., Olafson, E., & Connelly, L. (2004). Child abuse and family assessment. In L. Sperry (Ed.), *Assessment of couples and families* (pp. 207–247). New York: Brunner-Routledge.

Friedrich, W. N., Sandfort, T., Osstveen, J., & Cohen-Kettenis, P. (2000). Cultural differences in sexual behavior: 2–6 year old Dutch and American children. *Journal of Psychology and Human Sexuality, 12*(1–2), 117–129.

Friedrich, W. N., & Share, M. C. (1997). The Roberts Apperception Test for Children: An exploratory study of its use with sexually abused children. *Journal of Child Sexual Abuse, 6*, 83–91.

Friedrich, W., Talley, N., Panser, L., Fett, S., & Zinsmeister, A. (1997). Concordance of reports of childhood abuse by adults. *Child Maltreatment: Journal of the American Professional Society on the Abuse of Children, 2*(2), 164–171.

Friedrich, W. N., & Trane, S. (2002). Sexual behaviors across multiple settings. *Child Abuse and Neglect, 26*(3), 243–246.

Friedrich, W. N., Trane, S., & Gully, K. (2005). It is a mistake to conclude that sexual abuse and sexualized behavior are not related: A reply to Drach, Wientzen, and Ricci (2001). *Child Abuse and Neglect, 29*, 297–302.

Gardner, R. (1987). *The parental alienation syndrome and the differentiation between fabricated and genuine child sexual abuse*. Cresskill, NJ: Creative Therapeutics.

Gardner, R. (1989). Differentiating between *bona fide* and fabricated allegations of sexual abuse of children. *Journal of the American Academy of Matrimonial Lawyers, 5*, 1–25.

Gardner, R. (1991). *The sex abuse hysteria: The Salem witch trials revisited*. Cresskill, NJ: Creative Therapeutics.

Gardner, R. (1992). *True and false accusations of child sex abuse*. Cresskill, NJ: Creative Therapeutics.

Gardner, R. (1995). *Protocols for sex abuse evaluation*. Cresskill, NJ: Creative Therapeutics.

Gardner, R. (1998). *The parental alienation syndrome* (2nd ed.). Cresskill, NJ: Creative Therapeutics.

Gardner, R. (2001). The normal-sexual-fantasy consideration in sex-abuse evaluations. *American Journal of Play Therapy, 29*(2), 83–94.

Garven, S., Wood, J., & Malpass, R. (2000). Allegations of wrongdoing: The effects of reinforcement on children's mundane and fantastic claims. *Journal of Applied Psychology, 85*(1), 38–49.

Geddie, L. (1994). SES and ethnic differences in nonabused preschoolers' interactions with anatomically detailed dolls. *Dissertation abstracts international, 55*(2-B), 590. (UMI No. 19970201)

Geiselman, R., & Padilla, J. (1988). Cognitive interviewing with child witnesses. *Journal of Police Science and Administration, 16*, 236–242.

Geiselman, R., Saywitz, K., & Bornstein, G. (1993). Effects of cognitive questioning techniques on children's recall performance. In G. S. Goodman & B. Bottoms (Eds.), *Child victims, child witnesses: Understanding and improving testimony* (pp. 71–93). New York: Guildford.

General Accounting Office. (2003). *Child welfare: HHS could play a greater role in helping child welfare agencies recruit and retain staff* (GAO 03-357). Washington, DC: Author.

Ginsburg, H. (1997). *Entering the child's world: The clinical interview in psychological research and practice.* New York: Cambridge University Press.

Glaser, D., & Collins, C. (1988). The response of young, non-sexually abused children to anatomically correct dolls. *Journal of Child Psychology and Psychiatry, 30*(4), 547–560.

Goldson, E. (2001). Maltreatment among children with disabilities. *Infants and Young Children, 13*(4), 44–54.

Gomez-Schwartz, B., Horowitz, J., & Cardinelli, A. (1990). *Child sexual abuse: Initial effects.* Newbury Park, CA: Sage Publications.

Goodman, G., & Aman, C. (1990). Children's use of anatomically detailed dolls to recount an event. *Child Development, 61*, 1859–1871.

Goodman, G., Aman, C., & Hirschman, J. (1987). Child sexual and physical abuse: Children's testimony. In S. J. Ceci, M. Toglia, & D. Ross (Eds.), *Children's eyewitness testimony* (pp. 1–23). New York: Springer-Verlag.

Goodman, G., Bottoms, B., Qin, J., & Shaver, P. (1994). *Characteristics and sources of allegations of ritualistic child abuse* (Grant # 90CA1405, Final Report to the National Center on Child Abuse and Neglect). Washington, DC: National Clearinghouse on Child Abuse and Neglect.

Goodman, G., Bottoms, B., Schwartz-Kennedy, B., & Rudy, L. (1991). Children's memory for a stressful event: Improving children's reports. *Journal of Narrative and Life History, 1*, 9–99.

Goodman, G. S., & Clarke-Stewart, A. (1991). Suggestibility of children's testimony: Implications for sexual abuse investigations. In J. Doris (Ed.), *The suggestibility of children's recollections* (pp. 92–105). Washington, DC: American Psychological Association.

Goodman, G., Quas, J., Batterman-Faunce, J., Riddelsberger, M., & Kuhn, J. (1994). Predictors of accurate and inaccurate memories of traumatic events experienced in childhood. *Consciousness and Cognition, 3*, 269–294.

Goodman, G., Quas, J., Batterman-Faunce, J., Riddelsberger, M., & Kuhn, J. (1997). Children's reaction to and memory of a stressful event: Influences of age, anatomical dolls, knowledge, and parental attachment. *Applied Developmental Sciences, 1*(2), 54–75.

Goodman, G. S., & Reed, R. S. (1986). Age differences in eye witness testimony. *Law and Human Behavior, 10*, 317–332.

Goodman, G. S., Rudy, L., Bottoms, B. L., & Aman, C. (1990). Children's concerns and memory: Issues of ecological validity on the study of children's eye witness testimony. In R. Fivush & J. Hudson (Eds.), *Knowing and remembering in young children* (pp. 249–284). New York: Cambridge University Press.

Goodman-Brown, T., Edelstein, R., Goodman, G., Jones, D., & Gordon, D. (2003). Why children tell: A model of children's disclosures of sexual abuse. *Child Abuse and Neglect, 27*(5), 525–541.

Goodwin, J., Sahd, D., & Rada, R. (1979). Incest hoax. In W. Holder (Ed.), *Sexual abuse of children* (pp. 37–46). Englewood, CO: American Humane Association.

Goodwin, J., Sahd, D., & Rada, R. (1982). False accusations and false denials of incest: Clinical myths and clinical realities. In J. Goodwin (Ed.), *Sexual abuse: Incest victims and their families* (pp. 17–26). Boston: John Wright.

Gopnik, A., & Graf, P. (1988). Knowing how you know: Young children's ability to identify and remember the sources of their beliefs. *Child Development, 59*, 1366–1371.

Gordon, B., Ornstein, P., Nida, R., Follmer, A., Crenshaw, C., & Albert, G. (1993). Does the use of dolls facilitate children's memories of visits to the doctor? *Applied Cognitive Psychology, 7*, 459–474.

Gordon, S., & Jaudes, P. (1996). Sexual abuse evaluations in the emergency department: Is history reliable? *Child Abuse and Neglect, 20*, 315–322.

Gorman-Smith, D., & Matson, J. (1992). Sexual abuse and persons with mental retardation. In W. O'Donohue & J. Greer (Eds.), *The sexual abuse of children: Theory and research* (Vol. 1, pp. 285–306). Hillsdale, NJ: Laurence Erlbaum Associates.

Graham A., & Watkeys, J. (1991). False allegations in child sexual abuse: The pattern of referral in an area where reporting is not mandatory. *Children and Society, 5*(2), 111–122.

Green, A. (1986). True and false allegations of sexual abuse in child custody disputes. *Journal of the American Academy of Child Psychiatry, 25*(4), 449–456.

Green, A. (1991). Factors contributing to false allegation of child sexual abuse in custody disputes. *Children and Youth Services Review, 15*(2), 177–189.

Gries, L., Goh, D., & Cavanaugh, J. (1996). Factors associated with disclosure during child sexual abuse assessment. *Journal of Child Sexual Abuse, 5*(3), 1–19.

Grobstein, G. (1997). Human figure drawings and the identification of child sexual abuse. *Dissertation Abstracts International, 57*(8-A), 3391. (UMI # 9701497)

Gross, J., & Haynie, H. (1998). Drawing facilitates children's verbal reports of emotionally laden events. *Journal of Experimental Psychology: Applied, 4*, 163–179.

Gross, J., & Haynie, H. (1999). Drawing facilitates children's verbal reports after long delays. *Journal of Experimental Psychology: Applied, 5*(3), 265–283.

Groth, N., & Stevenson, T. (1990). *Anatomical drawings for use in the investigation and intervention of child sexual abuse.* Dunedin, FL: Forensic Mental Health Associates.

Gudjonsson, G. H. (1984). A new scale of interrogative suggestibility. *Personality and Individual Differences, 5*, 303–314.

Gudjonsson, G. H. (1987). A parallel form of the Gudjonsson Suggestibility Scale. *British Journal of Clinical Psychology, 26*, 215–221.

Gudjonsson, G. H. (1992). *The psychology of interrogations, confessions, and testimony.* Chichester, UK: Wiley.

Gudjonsson, G., & Henry, L. (2003). Child and adult witnesses with developmental disability. *Legal and Criminological Psychology, 8*(2), 241–252.

Guidelines for the Social Work Interview. (n.d.). CARES Program, Emanuel Hospital, Portland, OR.

Gully, K. J. (2000). Initial development of the Expectations Test for Children: A tool to investigate social information processing. *Journal of Clinical Psychology, 56,* 1551–1563.

Gully, K. J., Britton, H., Hansen, K., Goodwill, K., & Nope, J. L. (1999). A new measure for distress during child sexual abuse examinations: The genital examination distress scale. *Child Abuse and Neglect, 23,* 61–70.

Hagood, M. (1992). Diagnosis or dilemma: Drawings of sexually abused children. *British Journal of Projective Psychology, 37*(1), 22–33.

Hagood, M. (1999). The development of children's drawings with reference to possible indicators of sexual abuse. *Dissertation Abstracts International, 60*(4-B), 1852. (UMI # 9922274)

Hall, D. K., Mathews, F., & Pearce, J. (1998). Factors associated with sexual behavior problems in young sexually abused children. *Child Abuse and Neglect, 22,* 1045–1063.

Haskett, M., Wayland, K., Hutcheson, J., & Tavana, T. (1995). Substantiation of sexual abuse allegations: Factors involved in the decision-making process. *Journal of Child Sexual Abuse, 4*(2), 19–47.

Haynes-Seman, C. (1991, October). *Assessment of allegations of sexual abuse in divorce.* Presentation given at the National Conference on Child Abuse and Neglect, Denver, CO.

Haynes-Seman, C., & Baumgarten, D. (1994). *Children speak for themselves.* New York: Brunner/Mazel.

Haynes-Seman, C., & Hart, J. S. (1988). Interactional assessment: Evaluation of parent-child relationships in abuse and neglect. In D. Bross, R. Krugman, M. Lenherr, D. A. Rosenberg, & B. Schmitt (Eds.), *The new child protection team handbook* (pp. 181–198). New York: Garland Publishing.

Haynes-Seman, C., & Krugman, R. (1989). Sexualized attention: Normal interaction or precursor to sexual abuse? *American Journal of Orthopsychiatry, 59*(2), 238–245.

Hechler, D. (1988). *The battle and the backlash: The child sexual abuse war.* Lexington, MA: Lexington Books.

Heiman, M. (1992). Annotation: Putting the puzzle together: Validating allegations of child sexual abuse. *Journal of Child Psychology and Psychiatry, 33*(2), 311–329.

Henry, J. (1999). Videotaping child disclosure interviews: Exploratory study of children's experiences and perceptions. *Journal of Child Sexual Abuse, 8*(4), 35–49.

Henry, L., & Gudjonsson, G. (1999). Eyewitness memory and suggestibility in children with mental retardation. *American Journal of Mental Retardation, 104*(6), 491–508.

Henry, L., & Gudjonsson, G. (2003). Eyewitness memory, suggestibility, and repeated recall sessions in children with mild and moderate intellectual disabilities. *Law and Human Behavior, 27*(5), 481–505.

Henry, L., & Gudjonsson, G. (2004). The effects of memory trace strength on eyewitness recall in children with and without intellectual disabilities. *Journal of Experimental Child Psychology, 89,* 53–71.

Herman, J. (1981). *Father-daughter incest.* Cambridge, MA: Harvard University Press.

Herman, J. (2000). *Father-daughter incest, with a new afterword.* Cambridge, MA: Harvard University Press.

Hershkowitz, I. (2001). A case study of child sexual abuse false allegation. *Child Abuse and Neglect, 25,* 1397–1411.

Hershkowitz, I., Horowitz, D., & Lamb, M. (2005). Trends in children's disclosure of abuse in Israel: A national study. *Child Abuse and Neglect, 29*(11), 1203–1214.

Hershkowitz, I., Lamb, M., Sternberg, K., & Esplin, P. (1997). The relationships among interviewer utterance type, CBCA scores, and the richness of children's responses. *Legal and Criminological Psychology, 2*(2), 169–176.

Hershkowitz, I., Lamb, M., Sternberg, K., & Horowitz, D. (2002). A comparison of mental and physical context reinstatement in forensic interviews with alleged victims of sexual abuse. *Appplied Cognitive Psychology, 16*(4), 429–441.

Hershkowitz, I., Orbach, Y., Lamb, M., Sternberg, K., Pipe, M., & Horowitz, D. (2006). Dynamics of forensic interviews with suspected abuse victims who do not disclose. *Child Abuse and Neglect, 30*(7), 753–770.

Hewitt, S. (1991). Therapeutic management of preschool cases of alleged but unsubstantiated sexual abuse. *Child Welfare, 70*(1), 59–67.

Hewitt, S. (1993, January). *Assessment of very young children.* Presentation given at the San Diego Conference on Responding to Child Maltreatment, San Diego, CA.

Hewitt, S. (1994). Preverbal sexual abuse: What two children report in later years. *Child Abuse and Neglect, 18*(10), 821–826.

Hewitt, S. (1999). *Assessing allegations of sexual abuse in preschool children: Listening to small voices.* Thousand Oaks, CA: Sage Publications.

Hewitt, S., & Arrowood, A. (1994). Systematic touch exploration as a screening procedure for child abuse: A pilot study. *Journal of Child Sexual Abuse, 3*(2), 31–43.

Hewitt, S., & Friedrich, W. (1991a). *Assessing sexual abuse in very young children.* Unpublished manuscript. (Available from S. Hewitt, 3300 Edinborough Way, Suite 418, Edina, MN 55435)

Hewitt, S., & Friedrich, W. (1991b). Effects of probable sexual abuse on preschool children. In M. Q. Patton (Ed.), *Family sexual abuse* (pp. 32–43). Newbury Park, CA: Sage Publications.

Hewitt, S. K., Friedrich, W. N., & Allen, J. (1994). *Factors in assessing sexual abuse allegations in a sample of two-year-old children.* Presentation at Responding to Child Maltreatment Conference, Center for Child Protection, Children's Hospital and Health Center, San Diego, CA.

Hibbard, R. A., & Hartmann, G. A. (1990). Emotional indicators in human figure drawings of sexually victimized and nonabused children. *Journal of Clinical Psychology, 46,* 211–219.

Hibbard, R. A., & Hartmann, G. A. (1993). Components of child and parent interviews in cases of alleged sexual abuse. *Child Abuse and Neglect, 17,* 495–500.

Hibbard, R. A., Roghmann, K., & Hoekelman, R. A. (1987). Genitalia in children's drawings: An association with sexual abuse. *Pediatrics, 79,* 129–137.

Hindman, J. (1987). *Step by step: Sixteen steps toward legally sound sexual abuse investigations.* Ontario, OR: AlexAndria Associates.

Holliday, R. (2003a). The effect of a prior cognitive interview on children's acceptance of misinformation. *Applied Cognitive Psychology, 17*(4), 443–457.

Holliday, R. (2003b). Reducing misinformation effects in children with cognitive interviews: Dissociating recollection and familiarity. *Child Development, 74*(3), 728–751.

Holmes, L., & Veith, V. (2003). Finding words/Half a nation: Forensic interview training programs of CornerHouse and APRI's National Center for the Prosecution of Child Abuse. *APSAC Advisor, 15*(1), 4–8.

Home Office. (1992). *Memorandum of good practice on video recorded interviews with child witnesses in criminal proceedings.* London, UK: Her Majesty's Stationery Office.

Home Office. (2002). *Achieving the best evidence in criminal proceedings: Guidance for vulnerable and intimidated witnesses, including children.* London, UK: Her Majesty's Stationery Office.

Hoorwitz, A. N. (1992). *The clinical detective.* New York: W.W. Norton.

Horner, T., Guyer, M., & Kalter, N. (1993a). The biases of child abuse experts. *Bulletin of the American Academy of Psychiatry and the Law, 21*(3), 261–292.

Horner, T., Guyer, M., & Kalter, N. (1993b). Clinical expertise and the assessment of child sexual abuse. *Journal of the American Academy of Child and Adolescent Psychiatry, 32*(5), 925–931.

Horowitz, J., Salt, P., & Gomez-Schwartz, B. (1984). Unconfirmed cases of sexual abuse. In Tufts New England Medical Center Department of Psychiatry, *Sexually exploited children: Service and research* (pp. 11-20). Unpublished final report for the U.S. Office of Juvenile Justice and Delinquency Prevention. (Available from Department of Psychiatry, Tufts New England Medical Center, 171 Harrison Avenue, Boston, MA 02111)

Howe, J., Burgess, A., & McCormack, A. (1987). Adolescent runaways and their drawings. *Arts in Psychotherapy, 14,* 35–40.

Howe, M. L., Cicchetti, D., Toth, S. L., & Cerrito, B. M. (2004). True and false memories in maltreated children. *Child Development, 75*(5), 1402–1417.

Huffman, M. L., Crossman, A. M., & Ceci, S. J. (1997). "Are false memories permanent?": An investigation of the long-term effects of source misattributions. *Consciousness and Cognition, 6,* 482–490.

Humphrey, H., III. (1985). *Report on Scott County Investigations.* Minneapolis, MN: Office of the Attorney General, State of Minnesota.

Hungerford, A. (2005). The use of anatomically detailed dolls in forensic investigations: Developmental considerations. *Journal of Forensic Psychology Practice, 5*(1), 75–87.

Hussey, D., & Singer, M. (1993). Sexual and physical abuse: The adolescent sexual Concerns questionnaire (ASCQ). In M. I. Singer, L. T. Singer, & T. M. Anglin (Eds.), *Handbook for screening adolescents at psychosocial risk* (pp. 131–163). New York: Lexington Books.

Inbau, F. (2001). *Criminal interrogation and confessions* (4th ed.). Philadelphia: Lipppincott Williams & Wilkins.

Ireton, H. (1992). *Child Development Inventory.* Minneapolis, MN: Behavior Science Systems, Inc.

Jackson, H., & Nuttal, B. (1993). Clinicians' bias in evaluating allegations of sexual abuse. *Child Abuse and Neglect, 17*(1), 127–144.

James, B. (1989). *Treating traumatized children.* Lexington, MA: Lexington Books.

James, B., Everson, M., & Friedrich, W. (n.d.). *Extended evaluations of allegations of child sexual abuse.* (Available from Mark Everson, Program on Child Trauma and Maltreatment CB #7160, University of North Carolina–Chapel Hill, Chapel Hill, NC 27599-7160.)

Jampole, L., & Webber, M. (1987). An assessment of the behavior of sexually abuse and non-sexually abused children with anatomically correct dolls. *Child Abuse and Neglect, 11,* 187–192.

Jedel, R. (1994). The clinical assessment of child sexual abuse of preschool children using anatomically detailed dolls. *Dissertation Abstracts International, 55*(3-B), 1186. (UMI No. 19970401)

Johnson, R., & Shrier, D. (1985). Sexual victimization of boys: Experience at an adolescent medicine clinic. *Journal of Adolescent Medicine, 6*(5), 372–376.

Jones, D. P. H. (1992). *Interviewing the sexually abused child* (4th ed.). London: Gaskell.

Jones, D. P. H., & McGraw, E. M. (1987). Reliable and fictitious accounts of sexual abuse to children. *Journal of Interpersonal Violence, 2*(1), 27–45.

Jones, D. P. H., & Seig, A. (1988). Child sexual abuse allegations in custody and visitation cases: A report of 20 cases. In B. Nicholson & J. Bulkley (Eds.), *Sexual abuse allegations in custody and visitation cases* (pp. 22-36). Washington, DC: American Bar Association.

Kadushin, A., & Kadushin, G. (1997). *The social work interview: A guide for human service professionals.* New York: Columbia University Press.

Kaplan, S., & Kaplan, S. (1981). The child's accusation of sexual abuse during a divorce and custody struggle. *Hillside Journal of Clinical Psychiatry, 3*(1), 81–95.

Katz, S., Schoenfeld, D., Levanthal, J., & Cicchetti, D. (1995). The accuracy of children's reports with anatomically correct dolls. *Developmental and Behavioral Pediatrics, 16*(2), 71–76.

Kaufman, B., & Wohl, A. (1992). *Casualties of childhood: A developmental perspective on sexual abuse using projective drawings.* New York: Brunner/Mazel.

Kaufman, J., Jones, B., Steiglitz, E., Vitulano, L., & Mannarino, A. (1994). The use of multiple informants to assess children's maltreatment experiences. *Journal of Family Violence, 9*(3), 227–248.

Keary, K., & Fitzpatrick, C. (1994). Children's disclosure of sexual abuse during formal investigation. *Child Abuse and Neglect, 18*(7), 543–548.

Kendall-Tackett, K. (1992). Beyond anatomical dolls: Professionals' use of other play therapy techniques. *Child Abuse and Neglect, 16*(1), 139–142.

Kendall-Tackett, K. (2003). *Treating the lifetime health effects of childhood victimization.* Kingston, NJ: Civic Research Institute.

Kendall-Tackett, K., & Watson, M. (1991). Factors that influence professionals' perceptions of behavioral indicators of child sexual abuse. *Journal of Interpersonal Violence, 6*(3), 385–395.

Kendall-Tackett, K. A., Williams, L. M., & Finkelhor, D. (1993). Impact of sexual abuse on children: A review and synthesis of recent empirical studies. *Psychological Bulletin, 113,* 164–180.

Kenyon-Jump, R., Burnette, M., & Robertson, M. (1991). Comparison of behaviors of suspected sexually abused and nonabused preschool children using anatomical dolls. *Journal of Psychopathology and Behavioral Assessment, 13*(3), 225–240.

Kisiel, C. L., & Lyons, J. S. (2001). Dissociation as a mediator of psychopathology among sexually abused children and adolescents. *American Journal of Psychiatry, 158,* 1034–1039.

Klajner-Diamond, H., Wehrspann, W., & Steinhauer, P. (1987). Assessing the credibility of young children's allegations of sexual abuse: Clinical issues. *Canadian Journal of Psychiatry, 32*(7), 610–614.

Kolko, D., Moser, J., & Weldy, S. (1988). Behavioral/emotional indicators of sexual abuse in child psychiatric inpatients: A controlled comparison with physical abuse. *Child Abuse and Neglect, 12,* 529–541.

Koocher, G., Goodman, G., White, S., & Friedrich, W. (1995). Psychological science and the use of anatomically detailed dolls. *Psychological Bulletin, 118*(2), 199–222.

Koppitz, E. (1983). Projective drawings with children and adolescents. *School Psychology Review, 12*(4), 421–427.

Kuehnle, K. (1996). *Assessing allegations of child sexual abuse.* Sarasota, FL: Professional Resource Exchange.

Kuehnle, K. (1998). Child sexual abuse evaluations: A scientist-practitioner model. *Behavioral Sciences and the Law, 16*(1), 5–20.

Kvam, M. H. (2000). Is sexual abuse of children with disabilities disclosed? A retrospective analysis of child disability and the likelihood of sexual abuse among those attending Norwegian hospitals. *Child Abuse and Neglect, 24*(8), 1073–1084.

La Greca, A. (1990). *Through the eyes of the child: Obtaining self-reports from children and adolescents.* Needham Heights, MA: Allyn & Bacon.

Lamb, M. (1994). The investigation of child sexual abuse: An interdisciplinary consensus statement. *Child Abuse and Neglect, 18,* 1021–1028.

Lamb, M., & Garretson, M. (2003). The effects of interviewer gender and child gender on the informativeness of alleged child sexual abuse victims in forensic interviews. *Law and Human Behavior, 27*(2), 157–171.

Lamb, M., Hershkowitz, I., Sternberg, K., Boat, B., & Everson, M. (1996). Investigative interviews of alleged sexual abuse victims with and without anatomical dolls. *Child Abuse and Neglect, 20,* 1251–1259.

Lamb, M., Orbach, Y., Sternberg, K., Hershkowitz, I., & Horowitz, D. (2000). Accuracy of investigators' verbatim notes of their forensic interviews with alleged child abuse victims. *Law and Human Behavior, 24*(6), 699–708.

Lamb, M., & Sternberg, K. (1999, March). *Eliciting accurate investigative statements from children.* Presentation given at the 15th National Symposium on Child Sexual Abuse, Huntsville, AL.

Lamb, M., Sternberg, K., Esplin, P., Hershkowitz, I., & Orbach, Y. (1997). Criterion-based content analysis: A field validation study. *Child Abuse and Neglect, 21*(3), 255–264.

Lamb, M., Sternberg, K., Orbach, Y., Esplin, P., Stewart, H., & Mitchell, S. (2003). Age differences in young children's responses to open-ended invitations in forensic interviews. *Journal of Consulting and Clinical Psychology, 71*(5), 926–934.

Lamb, M., Sternberg, K., Orbach, Y., Hershkowitz, I., Horowitz, D., & Esplin, P. (2002). The effects of intensive training and ongoing supervision on the quality of investigative interviews with alleged sex abuse victims. *Applied Developmental Science, 6*(3), 114–125.

Lamb, M. E., & Thierry, K. L. (2005). Understanding children's testimony regarding their alleged abuse: Contributions of field and laboratory analog research. In D. M. Teti (Ed.), *Handbook of research methods in developmental science* (pp. 489–508). Malden, MA: Blackwell Publishing.

Lamers-Winkelman, F., & Buffing, F. (1996a). Children's testimony in the Netherlands: A study of statement validity analysis. *Criminal Justice and Behavior, 23*(2), 304–321.

Lamers-Winkelman, F., & Buffing, F. (1996b). Children's testimony in the Netherlands: A study of statement validity analysis. In B. L. Bottoms & G. S. Goodman (Eds.), *International perspectives on child abuse and children's testimony: Psychological research and law* (pp. 45–61). Thousand Oaks, CA: Sage Publications.

Larsson, I., & Svedin, C. G. (2002). Teachers' and parents' reports on 3- to 6-year-old children's sexual behavior—a comparison. *Child Abuse and Neglect, 26*(3), 247–266.

Larsson, I., Svedin, C. G., & Friedrich, W. N. (2000). Differences and similarities in sexual behaviour among pre-schoolers in Sweden and USA. *Nordic Journal of Psychiatry, 54*(4), 251–257.

Lawson, L., & Chaffin, M. (1992). False negatives in sexual abuse disclosure interviews *Journal of Interpersonal Violence, 7*(4), 532–542.

Leichtman, M., & Ceci, S. (1995). The effects of stereotypes and suggestions on preschoolers' reports. *Developmental Psychology, 31*(4), 568–578.

Leichtman, M. D., Morse, M. B., Dixon, A., & Wilch-Ross, M. (2000). Source monitoring and suggestibility: An individual differences approach. In K. P. Roberts & M. Blades (Eds.), *Children's source monitoring* (pp. 257–288). Mahwah, NJ: Lawrence Erlbaum Associates.

Lepore, S., & Sesco, B. (1994). Distorting children's reports and interpretations of events through suggestion. *Journal of Applied Psychology, 79*, 108–120.

Leventhal, J., Bentovim, A., Elton, A., Tranter, M., & Read, L. (1987). What to ask when sexual abuse is suspected. *Archives of Disease in Childhood, 62*, 1188–1195.

Leventhal, J., Hamilton, J., Rekedal, S., Tebano-Micci, A., & Eyster, C. (1989). Anatomically correct dolls used in interviews of young children suspected of having been sexually abused. *Pediatrics, 84*(5), 900–906.

Levy, H., Markovic, J., Kalinowski, M. N., & Ahart, S. (1995). Child sexual abuse interviews: The use of anatomic dolls and the reliability of information. *Journal of Interpersonal Violence, 10*(3), 334–353.

Lie, G.-Y., & Inman, A. (1991). The use of anatomical dolls as assessment and evidentiary tools. *Social Work, 36*(5), 396–398.

Lipian, M., Mills, M., & Brantman, A. (2004). Assessing the verity of children's allegations of abuse: A psychiatric overview. *International Journal of Law and Psychiatry, 27*, 249–263.

Lipovsky, J., Saunders, B., & Murphy, S. (1989). Depression, anxiety, and behavior problems among victims of father-child sexual assault and nonabused siblings. *Journal of Interpersonal Violence, 4*(4), 452–468.

Loftus, E. F., & Pickrell, J. E. (1995). The formation of false memories. *Psychiatric Annals, 25*, 720–725.

London, K., Bruck, M., Ceci, S., & Shuman, D. (2005). Disclosure of child sexual abuse: What does the research tell us about how children tell? *Psychology, Public Policy, and the Law, 11,* 194–226.

Luna, C., & Wang, A. (2005, May 17). Samantha Runyon's killer to die, jury says. *Los Angeles Times, Section: California, Metro Desk, Part B,* p. 1.

Lyon, T. D. (1995). False allegations and false denials in child sexual abuse. *Psychology, Public Policy, and Law, 1*(2), 429–437.

Lyon, T. D. (1996). Assessing children's competency to take the oath. *APSAC Advisor, 1,* 4–8.

Lyon, T. D. (1999a). The new wave in children's suggestibility research: A critique. *Cornell Law Review, 84,* 1004–1087.

Lyon, T. D. (1999b). *Questioning children: The effects of suggestive and repeated questioning.* Retrieved January 26, 2006, from C:USC\ARTICLES\guide\rethinkrev.wpd.

Lyon, T. D. (2001). Speaking with children: Advice from investigative interviewers. In F. Talley & A. Urquiza (Eds.), *Handbook for the treatment of abused and neglected children* (pp. 65-81). Needham Heights, MA: Allyn & Bacon.

Lyon, T. D. (2002a, August). *Child maltreatment and the law: Avila's acquittal.* Paper presented at the American Psychological Association Annual Convention, Chicago, IL.

Lyon, T. D. (2002b, May). *Minimizing suggestibility and maximizing competency through structured interviewing.* Presentation at the 10th Annual Colloquium of the American Professional Society on the Abuse of Children, New Orleans, LA.

Lyon, T. D. (2002c). Scientific support for expert testimony on child sexual abuse accommodation. In J. Conte (Ed.), *Critical issues in child sexual abuse* (pp. 107–138). Thousand Oaks, CA: Sage Publications.

Lyon, T. D. (in press). False denials: Overcoming methodological biases in abuse disclosure research. In M. E. Pipe, M. Lamb, Y. Orbach, & A. Cederborg (Eds.), *Disclosing abuse: Delays, denials, retractions, and incomplete accounts.* Mahway, NJ: Earlbaum

Lyon, T. D., & Saywitz, K. (1999). Reducing maltreated children's reluctance to answer hypothetical oath-taking questions. *Law and Human Behavior, 25,* 81–92.

Lyon, T. D., & Saywitz, K. (2000). *Qualifying children to take the oath: Materials for interviewing professionals.* Retrieved January 26, 2006, from http://awweb.usc.edu/users/tlyon/.

Lyon, T., Saywitz, K., Kaplan, D., & Dorado, J. (2001). Reducing maltreated children's reluctance to answer hypothetical oath-taking competency questions. *Law and Human Behavior, 25*(1), 81–92.

Maan, C. (1991). Assessment of sexually abused children with anatomically detailed dolls: A critical review. *Behavioral Sciences and the Law, 9,* 43–51.

Madonna, P., Van Scoyk, S., & Jones, D. P. H. (1991). Family interactions within incest and nonincest families. *American Journal of Psychiatry, 128*(1), 46–49.

Malloy, L., Lyon, T., Quas, J., & Forman, J. (2005, January). *Factors affecting children's sexual abuse disclosure patterns in a social services sample.* Paper presented at the San Diego Conference on Child and Family Maltreatment, San Diego, CA.

Mansell, L. (1990). *Naptime.* New York: William Morrow.

Mansell, S., Sobsey, D., & Moskal, R. (1998). Clinical findings among sexually abused children with and without developmental disabilities. *Mental Retardation, 36,* 12–22.

March, J. (1997). *Multidimensional anxiety scale for children: Technical manual.* North Tonawanda, NY: MultiHealth Systems, Inc.

Marchetti, A., & McCartney, J. (1990). Abuse of persons with mental retardation: Characteristics of the abused, the abusers, and the informers. *Mental Retardation, 28*(6), 367–371.

Marshall, W. (1997). Pedophilia: Psychopathology and theory. In D. R. Laws & W. O'Donohue (Eds.), *Sexual deviance* (pp. 152–174). New York: Guilford Press.

Marxsen, D., Yuille, J. C., & Nisbet, M. (1995). The complexities of eliciting and assessing children's statements. *Psychology, Public Policy, and Law, 1*(2), 450–460.

Masson, J. (1984). *Assault on the truth.* New York: Farrar, Straus, Giroux.

McCann, J., Voris, J., & Simon, M. (1992). Genital injuries resulting from sexual abuse: A longitudinal study. *Pediatrics, 89,* 307–317.

McCartney, J. (1987). Mentally retarded and nonretarded subjects' long-term recognition memory. *American Journal of Mental Retardation, 92*(3), 312–317.

McCarty, L. (1981). Investigation of incest: Opportunity to motivate families to seek help. *Child Welfare, 10,* 679–689.

McCurdy, K., & Daro, D. (1994). *Current trends in child abuse reporting and fatalities: Results of the 1993 Annual Fifty State Survey.* Chicago: National Committee for the Prevention of Child Abuse.

McDermott-Steinmetz-Lane, M. (1997). *Interviewing for child sexual abuse: Strategies for balancing forensic and therapeutic factors.* Notre Dame, IN: Jalice.

McGoldrick, M., Giordano, J., Garcia-Preto, N. (Eds.). (2005). *Ethnicity and family therapy.* New York: Guilford Press.

McGoldrick, M., Pearce, J. K., & Giordano, J. (Eds.). (1996). *Ethnicity and family therapy* (2nd ed.). New York: Guilford Press.

McLeer, S. V., Deblinger, E., Henry, D., & Orvaschel, H. C. (1992). Sexually abused children at high risk for posttraumatic stress disorder. *Journal of the American Academy of Child and Adolescent Psychiatry, 31,* 875–879.

Meehl, P. E. (1954). *Clinical vs. actuarial prediction.* Minneapolis, MN: University of Minnesota Press.

Melton, G. (1994). Doing justice and doing good: Conflicts for mental health professionals. *The Future of Children: Sexual Abuse of Children, 4*(2), 102–118.

Melton, G., & Limber, S. (1989). Psychologists' involvement in cases of child maltreatment. *American Psychologist, 44*(9), 1225–1233.

Merchant, L., & Toth, P. (2001). *Child interview guide.* Seattle, WA: Harborview Center for Sexual Assault and Traumatic Stress.

Merriam-Webster Online Dictionary. (2006a). Forensic. Retrieved January 30, 2006, from http://www.m-w.com/dictionary/clinical.

Merriam-Webster Online Dictionary. (2006b). Clinical. Retrieved January 30, 2006, from http://www.m-w.com/dictionary/forensic.

Merrill, L. L., Guimond, J. M., Thomsen, C. J., & Milner, J. S. (2003). Child sexual abuse and number of sexual partners in young women: The role of abuse severity, coping style, and sexual functioning. *Journal of Consulting and Clinical Psychology, 71,* 987–996.

Merritt, K. A., Ornstein, P. A., & Spicker, B. (1994). Children's memory for a salient medical procedure: Implications for testimony. *Pediatrics, 94,* 17–23.

Meyer, G. J., Finn, S. E., Eyde, L. D., Kay, G. G., Moreland, K. L, Dies, et al. (2001). Psychological testing and psychological assessment: A review of evidence and issues. *American Psychologist, 56,* 128–165.

Mikkelsen, E., Gutheil, T., & Emens, M. (1992). False sexual-abuse allegations: Contextual factors and clinical subtypes. *American Journal of Psychotherapy, 46*(4), 556–570.

Mildred, J. (2003). Claims-makers in the child sexual abuse "wars": Who are they and what do they want? *Social Work, 48*(4), 492–504.

Miller, T., Veltkamp, L., & Janson, D. (1987). Projective measures in the clinical evaluation of sexually abused children. *Child Psychiatry and Human Development, 18*(1), 47–57.

Milne, R., & Bull, R. (2003). Does the cognitive interview help children to resist the effects of suggestive questioning? *Legal and Criminological Psychology, 8*(1), 21–38.

Milne, R., Bull, R., Koehnken, G., & Memon, A. (1995). The cognitive interview and suggestibility. *Issues in Criminological and Legal Psychology, 22*, 21–27.

Morgan, M. (with contributions from Virginia Edwards). (1995). *How to interview sexual abuse victims, including the use of anatomical dolls.* Newbury Park, CA: Sage Publications.

Moyer, B. (1994). The suggestiveness of children's behaviors and verbalizations in anatomical doll interviews. *Dissertation Abstracts International, 54*(10-B), 5398. (UMI No. 19960901)

Muram, D. (1989). Child sexual abuse: Relationship between sexual acts and genital findings. *Child Abuse and Neglect, 13*(2), 211–216.

Muram, D., Speck, P., & Gold, S. (1991). Genital abnormalities in female siblings and friends of child victims of sexual abuse. *Child Abuse and Neglect, 15*(1–2), 1991, 105–110.

Myers, J. E. B. (1992). *Legal issues in child abuse and neglect practice.* Newbury Park, CA: Sage Publications.

Myers, J. E. B. (1993). Adjudication of child sexual abuse cases. *The Future of Children, 4*(2), 86–119.

Myers, J. E. B. (1994). *The backlash: Child protection under fire.* Thousand Oaks, CA: Sage Publications.

Myers, J. E. B. (1995). New era of skepticism regarding children's credibility. *Psychology, Public Policy, and Law, 1*(2), 387–398.

Myers, J. E. B. (1998). *Legal issues in child abuse and neglect practice* (2nd ed.). Newbury Park, CA: Sage Publications.

Myers, J. E. B. (2004). *A history of child protection in America.* Philadelphia: Xlibris.

Myers, J. E. B., Goodman, G., & Saywitz, K. (1996). Psychological research in children as witnesses: Practical applications fro forensic interviews and courtroom testimony. *Pacific Law Journal, 27*, 1–82.

Nathan, D. (2003, May 4). The exorcists. *Washington Post Sunday*, Book World, p. T04.

Nathan, D., & Snedecker, M. (1995). *Satan's silence: Ritual abuse and the making of a modern American witchhunt.* New York: Basic Books.

National Center for the Prosecution of Child Abuse. (1997). *Child abuse and neglect state statute series Vol. 3.* Washington, DC: National Center on Child Abuse and Neglect Clearinghouse.

National Center on Health Statistics. (2002). *Advance report on final divorce statistics for 1989–1990.* Retrieved October 27, 2003, from http://www.cdc.gov/nchs/products/pubs/pubd/mvsr/supp/44-43/mvs43_9s.htm.

National Child Abuse and Neglect Data System. (2005a). *Child maltreatment, 2003.* Washington, DC: U.S. Department of Health and Human Services, Administration on Children, Youth, and Families (Government Printing Office).

National Child Abuse and Neglect Data System. (2005b). *Summary of key findings from calendar year 2003.* Washington, DC: National Clearinghouse on Child Abuse and Neglect. Retrieved October 15, 2005, from http://nccanch.acf.hhs .gov/pubs/factsheets/canstats.cfm.

National Children's Advocacy Center (Producer). (1985). *Sanctuary.* (Available from the National Children's Advocacy Center, 210 Pratt Avenue, Huntsville, AL 35801)

National Children's Advocacy Center. (2005). Spanish Speaking Forensic Interviewing. Retrieved September 1, 2006, from Traininghttp://www.nationalcac .org/professionals/trainings/courses/spanish_forensic_interview.html.

National Children's Alliance. (2006). *History of NCA and CAC movement.* Retrieved February 2, 2006, from http://www.nca-online.org/pages/page .asp?page_id=4021.

National Clearinghouse on Child Abuse and Neglect Information. (2003, February). Maltreatment of children with disabilities training and prevention program resources. Retrieved November 27, 2003, from http://nccanch.acf.hhs .gov/pubs/reslist/maldis.cfm.

National Data Archive on Child Abuse and Neglect. (2003). *Adoption and Foster Care Analysis and Reporting System (AFCARS).* Retrieved September 1, 2006, from http://www.ndacan.cornell.edu/NDACAN/Datasets/Abstracts/ DatasetAbstract_AFCARS_General.html.

National Institute of Child Health and Human Development. (1999). *NICHD forensic interview protocol.* (Available from Michael Lamb, National Institute of Child Health and Human Development, P.O. Box 3006, Rockville, MD 20847)

Naumann, R. (1985). *The case of the indecent dolls or can voodoo be professional?* Unpublished manuscript.

Negrao, C., Bonano, G., Noll, J., Putnam, F., & Trickett, P. (2005). Shame, humiliation, and childhood sexual abuse: Distinct contribution and emotional coherence. *Child Maltreatment, 10*(4), 350–363.

Nelson, K. (1986). *Event memory.* Hillsdale, NJ: Erlbaum.

Ney, T. (Ed.). (1995). *True and false allegations of child sexual abuse: Assessment and Case management.* New York: Brunner-Mazel.

Oates, R. K., Jones, D. P. H., Denson, A., Sirotnak, A., Gary, N., & Krugman, R. (2000). Erroneous concerns about child sexual abuse. *Child Abuse and Neglect, 24*(1), 149–157.

Olafson, E. (1999). Using testing when family violence and child abuse are issues. In A. R. Nurse (Ed.), *Family Assessment: Effective uses of personality tests with couples and families* (pp. 230–256). New York: John Wiley & Sons, Inc.

Olafson, E. (2002). When paradigms collide: Roland Summit and the rediscovery of child sexual abuse. In J. Conte (Ed.), *Critical issues in child sexual abuse* (pp. 71–106). Thousand Oaks, CA: Sage Publications.

Olafson, E., Corwin, D. L., & Summit, R. C. (1993). Modern history of child sexual abuse awareness: Cycles of discovery and suppression. *Child Abuse and Neglect, 17*(1), 7–24.

Olafson, E., & Fitch, S. (2001). *Children's memory and suggestibility: A training outline*. Columbus, OH: Institute for Human Services, for the Pennsylvania Child Welfare Competency-Based Training and Certification Program.

Olafson, E., Kenniston, J., & Boat, B. (2003). *Forensic interviewer training manual*. Cincinnati, OH: Childhood Trust.

Olafson, E., & Lederman, C. (2006). The state of the debate about children's disclosure patterns of child sexual abuse. *Juvenile and Family Court Journal, 57*(1), 27-40.

Orbach, Y., Hershkowitz, I., Lamb, M., Esplin, P., & Horowitz, D. (2000). Assessing the value of structured protocols for forensic interviews of alleged child abuse victims. *Child Abuse and Neglect, 24*(6), 733–752.

Orbach, Y., & Lamb, M. (1999). Assessing the accuracy of a child's account of sexual abuse: A case study. *Child Abuse and Neglect, 23*(1), 91–98.

Ornstein, P. A., & Hadden, C. A. (2002). The development of memory: Toward an understanding of children's testimony. In M. Eisen, J. Quas, & G. Goodman (Eds.), *Memory and suggestibility in the forensic interview* (pp. 29–62). Mahwah, NJ: Lawrence Erlbaum.

Paine, M. L., & Hansen, D. (2002). Factors influencing children to self-disclose sexual abuse. *Clinical Psychology Review, 22*, 271–295.

Palmer, S. E., Brown, R., Rae-Grant, N., & Loughlin, M. J. (1999). Responding to children's disclosures of familial abuse: What survivors tell us. *Child Welfare, 78*(2), 259–282.

Peddle, N., & Wang, C-T. (2001). *Current trends in child abuse reporting and fatalities. The 1999 fifty state survey*. Chicago: Prevent Child Abuse America.

Pence, D., & Wilson, C. (1994). *Team investigation of child sexual abuse*. Thousand Oaks, CA: Sage Publications.

Perlman, N., & Ericson, K. (1992). Issues related to sexual abuse of persons with developmental disabilities: An overview. *Journal of Developmental Disabilities, 1*(1), 19–23.

Peters, D. F. (1991). The influence of stress and arousal on the child witness. In J. Doris (Ed.), *The suggestibility of children's recollections* (pp. 86–91). Washington, DC: American Psychological Association.

Peters, D. F. (2000). Examining child sexual abuse evaluations: The types of information affecting expert judgment. *Child Abuse and Neglect, 25*(1), 149–178.

Peterson, C., & Bell, M. (1996). Children's memory for traumatic injury. *Child Development, 67*, 3045–3070.

Peterson, C., & Biggs, M. (1997). Interviewing children about trauma: Problems with "specific" questions. *Journal of Traumatic Stress, 10*, 279–290.

Peterson, C., Dowden, C., & Tobin, J. (1999). Interviewing preschoolers: Comparison of yes/no and wh-questions. *Law and human Behavior, 23*(5), 539–555.

Peterson, L. W., & Hardin, M. E. (1997). *Children in distress: A system for screening children's art*. New York: W.W. Norton.

Pezdek, K., Finger, K., & Hodge, D. (1997). Planting false childhood memories: The role of event plausibility. *Psychological Science, 8*, 437–441.

Pezdek, K., & Hinz, T. (2002). The construction of false events in memory. In H. L. Westcott, G. M. Davies, & R. H. C. Bull (Eds.), *Children's testimony: A handbook of psychological research and forensic practice* (pp. 99–116). West Sussex, UK: John Wiley & Sons.

Pezdek, K., & Hodge, D. (1999). Planting false childhood memories in children: The role of event plausibility. *Child Development, 70,* 887–895.

Pezdek, K., & Taylor, J. (2002). Memory for traumatic events in children and adults. In M. Eisen, J. Quas, & G. Goodman (Eds.), *Memory and suggestibility in the forensic interview* (pp. 165–184). Mahwah, NJ: Lawrence Erlbaum.

Pierce, L., & Pierce, R. (1984). Race as a factor in the sexual abuse of children. *Social Work Research and Abstracts, 20,* 9–14.

Pipe, M. E., Goodman, G. S., Quas, J., Bidrose, S., Ablin, D., & Craw, S. (1997). Remembering early experiences during childhood. In J. D. Read & D. S. Lindsay (Eds.), *Recollections of trauma: Scientific evidence and clinical practice* (pp. 417–423). New York: Plenum Press.

Pipe, M. E., Lamb, M. E., Orbach, Y., & Esplin, P. W. (2004). Recent research on children's testimony about experienced and witnessed events. *Developmental Review, 24,* 440–468.

Pipe, M. E., & Salmon, K. (2002). What children bring to the interview context: Individual differences in children's event reports. In M. Eisen, J. Quas, & G. Goodman (Eds.), *Memory and suggestibility in the forensic interview* (pp. 235–264). Mahwah, NJ: Laurence Erlbaum Associates.

Poole D. A., & Dickinson, J. (2005). The future of the protocol movement: Commentary on Hershkowitz, Horowitz and Lamb (2005). *Child Abuse and Neglect, 29*(11), 1197–1202.

Poole, D. A., & Lamb, M. (1998). *Investigative interviews of children.* Washington, DC: American Psychological Association.

Poole, D. A., & Lindsay, D. S. (1996). *Effects of parents' suggestions, interviewing techniques, and age on young children's event reports.* Paper presented at the NATO Advanced Study Institute on Recollection of Trauma: Scientific Research Clinic Practice, Port de Bourgenay, France.

Poole, D. A., & Lindsay, D. S. (2002). Children's suggestibility in the forensic context. In M. Eisen, J. Quas, & G. Goodman (Eds.), *Memory and suggestibility in the forensic interview* (pp. 355–381). Mahwah, NJ: Lawrence Erlbaum.

Poole, D. A., & White, L. (1991). Effects of question repetition on the eyewitness testimony of children and adults. *Developmental Psychology, 27,* 975–986.

Poole, D. A., & White, L. (1993). Two years later: Effects of question repetition on the eyewitness testimony of children and adults. *Developmental Psychology, 29,* 844–853.

Poole, D. A., & White, L. (1995). Tell me again and again: Stabilities and change in the repeated testimonies of children and adults. In M. Zaragoza, J. Graham, G. Hall, R. Hirschman, & Y. Ben-Porath (Eds.), *Memory and testimony in the child witness* (pp. 24–40). Newbury Park, CA: Sage Publications.

Powell, M. B., & Thomson, D. M. (1997). Contrasting memory for temporal-source and memory for content in children's discrimination of repeated events. *Applied Cognitive Psychology, 11,* 339–360.

Public Health Agency of Canada. (June, 2000). *Canadian Incidence Study of Reported Child Abuse and Neglect Final Report.* Prepared by Nico Trocmé, Bruce MacLaurin, Barbara Fallon, Joanne Daciuk, Diane Billingsley, Marc Tourigny, Micheline Mayer, John Wright, Ken Barter, Gale Burford, Joe Hornick, Richard Sullivan, Brad McKenzie. Ottawa, CA: Author.

Putnam, F. W. (1997). *Dissociation in children and adolescents: A developmental perspective.* New York: Guilford Press.

Putnam, F. W. (2003). Ten-year research review update: Child sexual abuse. *Journal of the American Academy of Child and Adolescent Psychiatry, 42*(3), 269–278.

Putnam, F. W. (2006). The impact of trauma on child development. *Juvenile and Family Court Journal, 56*(1), 1–11.

Putnam, F. W., Helmers, K., & Trickett, P. K. (1993). Development, reliability, and validity of a child dissociation scale. *Child Abuse and Neglect, 17,* 731–742.

Quas, J., Goodman, G., Bidrose, S., Pipe, M., Craw, S., & Ablin, D. (1999). Emotion and memory: Children's long-term remembering, forgetting, and suggestibility. *Journal of Experimental Child Psychology, 72,* 235–270.

Quas, J. A., Qin, J., Schaaf, J. M., & Goodman, G. S. (1997). Individual differences in children's and adults' suggestibility and false event memory. *Learning and Individual Differences, 9,* 359–390.

Quas, J. A., Schaaf, J. M., Alexander, K. W., & Goodman, G. S. (2000). Do you really remember it happening or do you only remember being asked about it happening? Children's source monitoring in forensic contexts. In K. P. Roberts & M. Blades (Eds.), *Children's source monitoring* (pp. 197–226). Mahwah, NJ: Lawrence Erlbaum Associates.

Rabinowitz, D. (1990, May). Out of the mouth of babes to a jail cell: Child abuse and the abuse of justice: A case study. *Harper's Magazine,* 52–63.

Rabinowitz, D. (2003). *No crueler tyrannies: Accusation, false witness, and other terrors of our times.* New York: Free Press.

Rappaport, S. R., Burkhardt, S. A., & Rotatori, A. F. (1997). *Child sexual abuse curriculum for the developmentally disabled.* Springfield, IL: Charles Thomas.

Raskin, D., & Esplin, P. (1991a). Assessment of children's statements of sexual abuse. In J. Doris (Ed.), *The suggestibility of children's recollections* (pp. 153–165). Washington, DC: American Psychological Association.

Raskin, D., & Esplin, P. (1991b). Statement validity analysis: Interview procedures and content analysis of children's statements of sexual abuse. *Behavioral Assessment, 13*(30), 265–291.

Realmuto, G., Jensen, J., & Wescoe, S. (1990). Specificity and sensitivity of sexually anatomically correct dolls in substantiating abuse: A pilot study. *Journal of the American Academy of Child & Adolescent Psychiatry, 29*(5), 743–746.

Realmuto, G., & Wescoe, S. (1992). Agreement among professionals about a child's sexual abuse status: Interviews with sexually anatomically correct dolls as indicators of abuse. *Child Abuse and Neglect, 16*(5), 719–725.

Redlich, A., Myers, J. E. B., & Goodman, G. (2002). A comparison of two forms of hearsay in child sexual abuse cases. *Child Maltreatment, 7*(4), 312–328.

Reed, L. D. (1996). Findings from research on children's suggestibility and implications for conducting child interviews. *Child Maltreatment, 1*(2), 105–120.

Renshaw, D. (1987). Child sexual abuse: When wrongly charged. In *Encyclopaedia Britannica medical and mental health annual* (pp. 301–303). Chicago: Encyclopedia Britannica, Inc.

Reynolds, L. A. (1997). *People with mental retardation and sexual abuse.* Silver Spring, MD: Association for Retarded Citizens.

Richards, D., Watson, S., & Bleich, R. (2000). Reporting a sexual assault for people who have a developmental disability: Guidelines and practices. *Journal of Developmental Disabilities, 7*(1), 130–141.

Riordan, R., & Verdel, A. (1991). Evidence of sexual abuse in children's art products. *School Counselor, 39*(2), 116–121.

Risin, L., & McNamara, R. (1989). Validation of child sexual abuse: The psychologist's role. *Journal of Clinical Psychology, 45*(1), 175–184.

Roberts, D. (2002). *Shattered bonds: The color of child welfare.* New York: Basic Books.

Roberts, K. P. (2002). Children's ability to distinguish between memories from multiple sources: Implications for the quality and accuracy of eyewitness statements. *Developmental Review, 22,* 403–435.

Roberts, K. P., & Blades, M. (2000). *Children's source monitoring.* Mahwah, NJ: Erlbaum.

Roberts, K. P., & Lamb, M. (1999). Children's responses when interviewers distort details during investigative interviews. *Legal and Criminological Psychology, 4*(2), 23–31.

Roberts, K., Lamb, M., & Sternberg, K. (2004). The effects of rapport-building style on children's reports of a staged event. *Applied Cognitive Psychology, 18*(2), 189–202.

Roberts, K., & Powell, M. (2006). The consistency of false suggestions moderates children's reports of a single instance of a repeated event: Predicting increases and decreases in suggestibility. *Journal of Experimental Child Psychology, 94*(1), 68–89.

Rosenberg, D., & Gary, N. (1988). Diagnostic teams of team members and consultants: Sexual abuse of children. In D. Bross, R. Krugman, M. Lenherr, D. Rosenberg, & B. Schmitt (Eds.), *The new child protection team handbook* (pp. 66–81). New York: Garland Publishing.

Ruby, C., & Brigham, J. (1998). Can criteria-based content analysis distinguish between true and false statements of African-American speakers? *Law and Human Behavior, 22*(4), 369–388.

Rudy, L., & Goodman, G. S. (1991). Effects of participation on children's reports: Implications for children's testimony. *Developmental Psychology, 27,* 1–26.

Rush, F. (1980). *The best kept secret: Sexual abuse of children.* Englewood Cliffs, NJ: Prentice Hall.

Russell, D. E. H. (1986). *Incest in the lives of girls and women.* New York: Basic Books.

Russell, D. E. H., & Bolen, R. (2000). *The epidemic of rape and child sexual abuse in the United States.* Thousand Oaks, CA: Sage Publications.

Russell, D. E. H., Schurman, R., & Trocki, K. (1988). Long-term effects of incestuous abuse: A comparison of Afro-American and white American women. In G. Wyatt (Ed.), *The lasting effects of child sexual abuse* (pp. 119–134). Thousand Oaks, CA: Sage Publications.

Sadowski, C. M., & Friedrich, W. N. (2000). Psychometric properties of the Trauma Symptom Checklist for Children (TSCC) with psychiatrically hospitalized adolescents. *Child Maltreatment, 5,* 364–372.

Sadowski, P., & Loesch, L. (1993). Using children's drawings to detect potential child sexual abuse. *Elementary School Guidance and Counseling, 28*(2), 115–123.

Salmon, K., Bidrose, S., & Pipe, M. (1995). Providing props to facilitate children's even reports: A comparison of toys with real items. *Journal of Experimental Child Psychology, 60,* 174–194.

Salmon, K., & Pipe, M. (1997). Props and children's event reports: The impact of a 1-year delay. *Journal of Experimental Child Psychology, 65,* 261–292.

Salter, A. (2002, October 7). *What makes an effective sex offender treatment program?* Preconference workshop presented at the 18th Annual Midwest Conference on Child Sexual Abuse, Middleton, WI.

Samra, J., & Yuille, J. (1996). Anatomically neutral dolls: Their effects in the memory and suggestibility of 4- to 6-year old eyewitnesses. *Child Abuse and Neglect, 20*(12), 1261–1272.

Sas, L., & Cunningham, A. (1995). *Tipping the balance to tell the secret: The public discovery of child sexual abuse.* (Available from the London Court Clinic, 254 Pall Mall Street, London N6A 5P6)

Sattler, J. (1998). *Clinical and forensic interviewing of children and families.* San Diego: Author.

Sauzier, M. (1989). Disclosure of sexual abuse: For better or for worse. *Pediatric Clinics of North America, 12,* 455–469.

Saxe, L., Doughtery, D., & Cross, T. (1985). The validity of polygraph testing: Scientific analysis and public controversy. *American Psychologist, 38*(3), 355–356.

Saxe, L., Doughtery, D., & Cross, T. (1987). The validity of polygraph testing: Scientific analysis and public controversy. In L. Wrightsman, C. Willis, & S. Kassin (Eds.), *On the witness stand* (pp. 14–36). Thousand Oaks, CA: Sage Publications.

Saywitz, K. (1995). Improving children's testimony: The question, the answer, the environment. In M. Zaragoza, J. Graham, G. Hall, R. Hirschman, & Y. Ben-Porath (Eds.), *Memory and testimony in the child witness* (pp. 113–140). Thousand Oaks, CA: Sage Publications.

Saywitz, K., & Geiselman, R. E. (1998). Interviewing the child witness: Maximizing completeness and minimizing error. In S. Lynn & K. McConkey (Eds.), *Truth in memory* (pp. 190-223). New York: Guilford Press.

Saywitz, K., Geiselman, R., & Bornstein, G. (1992). The effects of cognitive interviewing and practice on children's recall performance. *Journal of Applied Psychology, 77*(5), 744–756.

Saywitz, K., Goodman, G., & Lyon, T. (2002). Interviewing children in and out of court. In J. Myers, L. Berliner, J. Briere, C. Hendrix, C. Jenny, & T. Reid (Eds.), *The APSAC handbook on child maltreatment* (2nd ed., pp. 349–377). Thousand Oaks, CA: Sage Publications.

Saywitz, K., Goodman, G., Nicholas, E., & Moan, S. (1989, April). *Children's memories of genital examinations: Implications for cases of child sexual assault.* Paper presented at the biennial meeting of the Society for Research on Child Development, Kansas City, MO.

Saywitz, K., Goodman, G., Nicholas, E., & Moan, S. (1991). Children's memory for a genital examination: Implications for child sexual abuse cases. *Journal of Consulting and Clinical Psychology, 59,* 682–691.

Saywitz, K. J., & Lyon, T. D. (2002). Coming to grips with children's suggestibility. In M. L. Eisen, G. S. Goodman, & J. A. Quas (Eds.), *Memory and suggestibility in the forensic interview* (pp. 85–113). Hillsdale, NJ: Erlbaum.

Saywitz, K., & Nathanson, R. (1993). Children's testimony and their perceptions of stress in and out of the courtroom. *Child Abuse and Neglect, 17*(5), 613–622.

Saywitz, K., Nathanson, R., Snyder, L., & Lamphear, V. (1993). *Preparing children for the investigative and judicial process: Improving communication, memory, and emotional resiliency. Final report to the National Center on Child Abuse and Neglect.* (Available from Karen Saywitz, UCLA School of Medicine, Department of Psychiatry, 1000 West Carson Street, Torrance, CA 90509)

Saywitz, K., & Snyder, L. (1993). Improving children's testimony with preparation. In G. Goodman & B. Bottoms (Eds.), *Child victims, child witnesses: Understanding and improving testimony* (pp. 117–146). New York: Guilford Press.

Scheeringa, M. S., Peebles, C. D., Cook, C. A., & Zeanah, C. H. (2001). Toward establishing procedural, criterion, and discriminant validity for PTSD in early childhood. *Journal of the American Academy of Child and Adolescent Psychiatry, 40,* 52–60.

Schudson, C. (1992). Antagonistic parents in family courts: False allegations or false assumptions about true allegations of child sexual abuse? *Journal of Child Sexual Abuse, 1*(2), 113–116.

Schultz, L. (1989). One hundred cases of unfounded child sexual abuse: A survey and recommendations. *Issues in Child Abuse Accusations, 1*(1), 29–38.

Schuman, D. (1986). True and false allegations of sexual abuse in child custody disputes. *Journal of the American Academy of Child Psychiatry, 4,* 449–456.

Scullin, M. H., & Ceci, S. J. (2001). A suggestibility scale for children. *Personality and Individual Differences, 30,* 843–856.

Scullin, M. H., Kanaya, T., & Ceci, S. J. (2002). Measurement of individual differences in children's suggestibility across situations. *Journal of Experimental Psychology: Applied, 8*(4), 233–246.

Sebre, S., Sprugevica, I., Novotni, A., Bonevski, D., Pakalniskiene, V., Popesku, D., et al. (2004). Incidence of child-reported emotional and physical abuse: Cross-cultural comparisons of rates, risk factors, and psychosocial symptoms. *Child Abuse and Neglect, 28*(1), 113–127.

Sgroi, S. (1980). Sexual molestation of children: The last frontier of child abuse. In L. Schultz (Ed.), *Sexual victimology of youth* (pp. 25–35). Springfield, IL: Charles Thomas.

Sgroi, S. (1982). *Handbook of clinical intervention in child sexual abuse.* Lexington, MA: Lexington Books.

Sgroi, S., Carey, J., & Wheaton, A. (1989). Sexual avoidance training for adults with mental retardation. In S. Sgroi (Ed.), *Vulnerable populations* (Vol. 2, pp. 203–216). Lexington, MA: Lexington Books.

Sgroi, S, Porter, F., & Blick, L. (1982). Validation of sexual abuse. In S. Sgroi (Ed.), *Handbook of clinical intervention in child sexual abuse* (pp. 39–81). Lexington, MA: Lexington Books.

Sidun, N., & Rosenthal, R. (1987). Graphic indicators of sexual abuse in Draw-A-Person Tests of psychiatrically hospitalized adolescents. *Arts in Psychotherapy, 14*(1), 25–33.

Siegel, D. J. (1999). *The developing mind: Toward a neurobiology of interpersonal experience.* New York: Guilford Press.

Sigelman, C., Budd, E., Spanhel, C., & Schoenbrock, C. (1981). Asking questions of retarded persons: A comparison of yes/no and either/or formats. *Applied Research in Mental Retardation, 5,* 347–357.

Simkins, L., & Renier, A. (1996). An analytical review of the empirical literature on children's play with anatomically detailed dolls. *Journal of Child Sexual Abuse, 5*(1), 21–45.

Sink, F. (1988). A hierarchical model for evaluation of child sexual abuse. *American Journal of Orthopsychiatry, 58*(1), 129–135.

Sivan, A., Schor, D., Koeppl, G., & Noble, L. (1988). Interaction of normal children with anatomical dolls. *Child Abuse and Neglect, 12,* 295–304.

Sjoberg, R., & Lindblad, F. (2002). Limited disclosure of sexual abuse in children whose experiences were documented by videotape. *American Journal of Psychiatry, 159*(2), 312–314.

Skinner, L. (1996). Assumptions and beliefs about the role of AD dolls in child sexual abuse validation interviews: Are they supported empirically? *Behavioral Sciences and the Law, 14*(2), 167–185.

Skinner, L., & Berry, K. (1993). Anatomically detailed dolls and the evaluation of child sexual abuse evaluations: Psychometric considerations. *Law and Human Behavior, 17*(4), 399–421.

Slicner, N. (1989). Guidelines for videotape interviews in child sexual abuse cases. *American Journal of Forensic Psychology, 7*(1), 61–74.

Smith, D., Letourneau, E., Saunders, B., Kilpatrick, D., Resnick, H., & Best, C. (2000). Delay in disclosure of childhood rape: Results from a national survey. *Child Abuse and Neglect, 24*(2), 273–287.

Snow, B., & Sorenson, T. (1990). Ritualistic child abuse in a neighborhood setting. *Journal of Interpersonal Violence, 5*(4), 474–487.

Sobsey, D. (1994). *Violence and abuse in the lives of people with disabilities: The end of silent acceptance?* Baltimore, MD: Paul H. Brookings Publishing.

Sorenson, E., Bottoms, B., & Perona, A. (1997). *Intake and forensic interviewing in the Children's Advocacy Center setting: A handbook* (1st ed.). Washington, DC: National Network of Children's Advocacy Centers and the Office of Juvenile Justice and Delinquency Prevention.

Sorenson, T., & Snow, B. (1991). How children tell: The process of disclosure of sexual abuse. *Child Welfare, 70*(1), 3–15.

Spacarelli, S. (1995). Measuring abuse stress and negative cognitive appraisals in child sexual abuse: Validity data on two new scales. *Journal of Abnormal Child Psychology, 23,* 703–727.

Spencer, N., Devereaux, E., Wallace, A., Sundrum, R., Shenoy, M., Bacchus, C., et al. (2004). Disabling conditions and registration for child abuse and neglect: QA population-based study. *Pediatrics, 116*(3), 609–613.

Spinazzola, J., Blaustein, M., & van der Kolk, B. A. (2005). Posttraumatic stress disorder treatment outcome research: The study of unrepresentative samples? *Journal of Traumatic Stress, 18*(5), 425–436.

Springs, F., & Friedrich, W. N. (1992). Health risk behavior and medical sequelae of child sexual abuse. *Mayo Clinic Proceedings, 67,* 527–532.

Stahl, P. (1994). *Conducting child custody evaluations: A comprehensive guide.* Thousand Oaks, CA: Sage Publications.

Starr, R. 1987. Clinical judgment of abuse-proneness based upon parent-child interactions. *Child Abuse and Neglect, 11,* 87–92.

State of Michigan. (1998, August). *Forensic interview protocol* (FIA Publ. No. 779). Lansing, MI: Governor's Task Force on Children's Justice and the Michigan Family Independence Agency.

State of Michigan. (2005, April). *Forensic interview protocol* (DHS Publ. No. 779, Rev.). Lansing, MI: Governor's Task Force on Children's Justice and the Michigan Department of Human Services.

Steele, B., & Pollock, C. (1974). A psychiatric study of parents who abuse infants and small children. In R. Helfer & C. H. Kempe (Eds.), *The battered child* (2nd ed., pp. 89–134). Chicago: University of Chicago Press.

Steinmetz, M. M. (1997). *Interviewing for child sexual abuse: Balancing forensic and therapeutic factors.* Notre Dame, IN: Jalice.

Stellar, M., & Boychuk, T. (1992). Children as witnesses in sexual abuse cases: Investigative interview and assessment techniques. In H. Dent & R. Flin (Eds.), *Children as witnesses* (pp. 47–72). Chichester, UK: J. Wiley.

Stellar, M., & Kohnken, G. (1989). Criteria-based statement analysis. In D. C. Raskin (Ed.), *Psychological methods in criminal investigation and evidence* (pp. 217–245). New York: Springer.

Sternberg, K. (2001, January). *Structured interview format for forensic interviewers.* Workshop presented at the 15th Annual San Diego Conference on Responding to Child Maltreatment, San Diego, CA.

Sternberg, K., Lamb, M., Davies, G., & Wescott, H. (2001). The memorandum of good practice: Theory versus application. *Child Abuse and Neglect, 25*(50), 669–681.

Sternberg, K., Lamb, M., Esplin, P., & Baradaran, L. (1999). Using a scripted protocol in investigative interviews: A pilot study. *Applied Developmental Science, 3*(2), 70–76.

Sternberg, K., Lamb, M., Hershkovitz, I., Yudilevitch, L., Orbach, Y., Esplin, P., et al. (1997). Effects of introductory style on children's abilities to describe experiences of sexual abuse. *Child Abuse and Neglect, 21*(11), 1133–1146.

Sternberg, K., Lamb, M., Orbach, Y., Esplin, P., & Mitchell, S. (2001). Use of a structured investigative protocol enhances young children's responses to free-recall prompts in the course of forensic interviews. *Journal of Applied Psychology, 86*(5), 997–1005.

Steward, M. (1989, November). *Final report of grant #90CA1332: The development of a model interview for young child victims of sexual abuse.* Davis, CA: University of California Department of Psychiatry.

Steward, M. S., Bussey, K., Goodman, G. S., & Saywitz, K. J. (1993). Implications of developmental research for interviewing children. *Child Abuse and Neglect, 17,* 25–37.

Steward, M. S., Steward, D. S., Farquhar, L., Myers, J., Welker, J., Joye, N., et al. (1996). *Interviewing young children about body touch and handling.* Monograph series of the Society for Research on Child Development. Chicago: University of Chicago Press.

Stogner v. California, 539 U.S. 607 (2003). Amici Curiae.

Strickler, H. (2001). Interaction between family violence and mental retardation. *Mental Retardation, 39*(6), 461–471.

Sugar, M. (1992). Toddler's traumatic memories. *Infant Mental Health Journal, 13*(3), 245–251.

Sullivan, P. M., & Knutson, J. F. (1994). *The relationship between child abuse and neglect and disabilities: Implications for research and practice.* Omaha, NE: Boys Town National Research Hospital.

Sullivan, P. M., & Knutson, J. F. (2000). Maltreatment and disabilities: A population-based epidemiological study. *Child Abuse and Neglect, 24*(10), 1257–1263.

Summit, R. (1983). The child sexual abuse accommodation syndrome. *Child Abuse and Neglect, 7,* 177–193.

Summit, R. (1992). Abuse of the child sexual abuse accommodation syndrome. *Journal of Child Sexual Abuse, 1,* 153–163.

Sutherland, B. (1994). The relationship between previous sexual behavior and nonabused children's behavior dining assessment using anatomically detailed dolls. *Dissertation Abstracts International, 55*(2-B), 608. (UMI No. 19970201)

Swim, J., Borgida, E., & McCoy, K. (1993). Videotaped versus in-court witness testimony: Does protecting the child witness jeopardize due process? *Journal of Applied Social Psychology, 23*(8), 603–631.

Tarte, R., Vernon, C., Luke, D., & Clark, H. (1982). Comparison of responses by normal and deviant populations to Louisville Behavior Checklist. *Psychological Reports, 50*(1), 99–106.

Taylor, C., & Fontes, L. (1995). Seventh Day Adventists and sexual child abuse. In L. A. Fontes (Ed.), *Sexual abuse in nine North American cultures: Treatment and prevention* (pp. 176–199). Thousand Oaks, CA: Sage Publications.

Terr, L. (1998). What happens to early memories of trauma? A study of twenty children under age five at the time of documented traumatic events. *Journal of the American Academy of Child and Adolescent Psychiatry, 27*(1), 96–104.

Terry, W. (1991, January). *Perpetrator and victim accounts of sexual abuse.* Paper presented at Health Science Response to Child Maltreatment, Center for Child Protection, San Diego. (Available from William Terry, 343 North Allumbaugh Street, Boise, ID 83704)

Tharinger, D., Horton, C., & Millea, S. (1990). Sexual abuse of the mentally retarded. *Child Abuse and Neglect, 14*(3), 301–312.

Thierry, K., Lamb, M., Orbach, Y., & Pipe, M.-E. (2005). Developmental differences in the function and use of anatomical dolls during interviews with alleged sexual abuse victims. *Journal of Consulting and Clinical Psychology, 73*(6), 1125–1134.

Thoennes, N., & Tjaden, P. (1990). The extent, nature, and validity of sexual abuse allegations in custody/visitation disputes. *Child Abuse and Neglect, 14,* 151–163.

Thompson, V., & Smith, S. (1993). Attitudes of African American adults toward treatment in cases of child sexual abuse. *Journal of Child Sexual Abuse, 2*(1), 5–19.

Thornton, C., & Carter, J. (1986). Treatment considerations with Black incestuous families. *Journal of the American Medical Association, 78*(1), 49–53.

Tjaden, P., & Thoennes, N. (1992). Predictors of legal intervention in child maltreatment cases. *Child Abuse and Neglect, 16*(6), 807–821.

Trocme, N., & Bala, N. (2005). False allegations of abuse and neglect when parents separate. *Child Abuse and Neglect, 29*(11), 1333–1346.

Tufts New England Medical Center, Division of Child Psychiatry. (1984). *Sexually exploited children: Service and research project* (Final Report for the Office of Juvenile Justice and Delinquency Prevention). Washington, DC: Department of Justice.

Tye, M., Amato, Honts, C., Devitt, M., & Peters, D. (1999). The willingness of children to lie and the assessment of credibility in an ecologically relevant laboratory setting. *Applied Developmental Science, 3*(2), 92–109.

Tylden, E. (1987). Child sexual abuse. *Lancet, 2,* 1017.

Ullman, S. (2003). Social reactions to child sexual abuse disclosures: A critical review. *Journal of Child Sexual Abuse, 12*(10), 89–122.

Undeutch, U. (1989). The development of statement reality analysis. In J. Yuille (Ed.), *Credibility assessment* (pp. 101–119). Dordrecht, The Netherlands: Kluwer.

U.S. Department of Health and Human Services. (2001). *Child maltreatment, 1999.* Washington, DC: U.S. Government Printing Office.

U.S. Department of Justice. (1993). *Joint investigations of child abuse: Report of a symposium* (NCJ142056). Washington, DC: U.S. Department of Justice, Office of Justice Programs, National Institute of Justice.

Valenti-Hein, D. (2002). Use of visual tools to report sexual abuse for adult with mental retardation. *Mental Retardation, 40*(4), 297–303.

van der Kolk, B. A. (1999). Trauma and memory. In B. A. van der Kolk, A. C McFarlane, & L. Weisaeth (Eds.), *Traumatic stress: The effects of overwhelming experience on mind, body, and society* (pp. 279–302). New York: Guilford Press.

van der Kolk, B. A., Crozier, J., & Hopper, J. (2001). Child abuse in America: Prevalence, costs, consequences and intervention. In K. Franey, R. Geffner, & R. Falconer (Eds.), *The cost of child maltreatment: Who pays? We all do* (pp. 223–242). San Diego, CA: Family Violence and Sexual Assault Institute.

van der Kolk, B. A., Roth, S., Pelcovitz, D., Sunday, S., & Spinazzola, J. (2005). Disorders of extreme stress: The empirical foundation of a complex adaptation to trauma. *Journal of Traumatic Stress, 18*(5), 389–399.

van der Kolk, B. A., van der Hart, O., & Marmar, C. R. (1996). Dissociation and information processing in posttraumatic stress disorder. In B. A. van der Kolk, A. C. McFarlane, & L. Weisaeth (Eds.), *Traumatic stress: The effects of overwhelming experience on mind, body, and society* (pp. 303–327). New York: Guilford Press.

Veith, V. I. (1999). When the cameras roll: The danger of videotaping child abuse victims before the legal system is competent to assess children's statements. *Journal of Child Sexual Abuse, 7*(4), 113–121.

Veith, V. I. (2002). *Memory and suggestibility research: Does the surreal world of the laboratory apply to the real world?* Finding Words: Interviewing Children and Preparing for Court, Sarasota, FL. November 14, 2002.

Veltman, M., & Browne, K. (2002). The assessment of drawings from children who have been maltreated: A systematic review. *Child Abuse Review, 11*(1), 19–37.

Verdun, M. (1988). Comparison of human figure drawings of sexually abused children, physically abused children, and children who have been both sexually and physically abused with drawings of clinical and normal controls. *Dissertation Abstracts International, 49*(4-B). (UMI No. 890601)

Virginia Commonwealth University Partnership for People With Disabilities. (2005). *Abuse and neglect of children and adults with developmental disabilities.* Retrieved April 1, 2006, from http://www.maltreatment.vcu.edu/info/.

Vizard, E. (1991). Interviewing children suspected of being sexually abused: A review of theory and practice. In. C. Hollin (Ed.), *Clinical approaches to sex offenders and their victims* (pp. 117–148). New York: John Wiley.

Vizard, E., & Trantner, M. (1988). Helping young children to describe experiences of child sexual abuse: General issue. In A. Bentovim, A. Alton, J.

Hildebrand, M. Trantner, & E. Vizard (Eds.), *Child sexual abuse within the family: Assessment and treatment* (pp. 84–104). Bristol, UK: John Wright.

Wakefield, H., & Underwager, R. (1988). *Accusations of child sex abuse.* Springfield, IL: Charles Thomas.

Walker, A. G. (1994). *Handbook on questioning children.* Washington, DC: American Bar Association Center on Children and the Law.

Walker, A. G. (1999). *Handbook on questioning children* (2nd ed.). Washington, DC: American Bar Association Center on Children and the Law.

Walker, A. G. (2001, April). *Forensic interviewing of children.* Huntsville, AL: Advanced Training Institute, American Professional Society on the Abuse of Children.

Walker, N. (1997). Should we question how we question children? In J. Read & D. Lindsay (Eds.), *Recollections of trauma: Scientific evidence and clinical practice* (pp. 517–521). New York: Plenum Press.

Wallen, V. (1998). *OFCO's 1998 investigation the Wenachee sexual abuse investigations.* Olympia, WA: State of Washington Office of the Family and Children's Ombudsman. Retrieved Febuary 6, 2006, from http://www.governor.wa.gov/ofco/wen/wentoc.htm.

Walters, S., Holmes, L., Bauer, G., & Veith, V. (June, 2003). *Finding words, a half a nation by 2010; Preparing children for court.* Retrieved September 6, 2006, from http://www.ndaa.org/pdf/finding_words_2003.pdf

Wang, P., & Baron, M. (1997). Language: A code for communicating. In M. Batshaw (Ed.), *Children with disabilities* (4th ed., pp. 275–292). Baltimore, MD: Paul H. Brookes Publishing.

Ward, E. (1985). *Father-daughter rape.* New York: Grove Press.

Warren, A. R., Hulse-Trotter, K., & Tubbs, E. (1991). Inducing resistance to suggestibility in children. *Law and Human Behavior, 15,* 273–285.

Warren, A. R., & Marsil, D. F. (2002). Why children's suggestibility remains a serious concern. *Law and Contemporary Problems, 65* 127–147.

Warren, A. R., & McCloskey, L. C. (1997). Language in social contexts. In S. Berko-Gleason (Ed.), *The development of language* (4th ed, pp. 210-258). Boston, MA: Allyn & Bacon Publishing.

Waterman, A. H., Blades, M., & Spencer, C. (2001). Interviewing children and adults: The effect of question format on the tendency to speculate. *Applied Cognitive Psychology, 15,* 521–531.

Waterman, J., & Lusk, R. (1993). Psychological testing in evaluation of child sexual abuse. *Child Abuse and Neglect, 17,* 145–159.

Wehrspann, W., Steinhauer, P., & Klajner-Diamond, H. (1987). Criteria and a methodology for assessing credibility of sexual abuse allegation. *Canadian Journal of Psychiatry, 32*(7), 615–623.

Weill, R., Dawson, B., & Range, L. (1999). Behavioral and verbal responses of unabused externalizing children to anatomically detailed dolls. *Journal of Family Violence, 14*(1), 61–70.

Weissman, H. N. (1991). Forensic psychological examination of the child witness in cases of alleged sexual abuse. *American Journal of Orthopsychiatry, 61,* 48–58.

Welbourne, P. (2002). *Videotaped evidence of children: Application and implications of the Memorandum of Good Practice.* (Available from Penelope Welbourne,

Department of Social Policy and Social Work, University of Plymouth, Devon PL4 8AA, United Kingdom)

Wescott, H. L., & Jones, D. P. (1999). Annotation: The abuse of disabled children. *Journal of Child Psychology and Psychiatry, 40*, 497–506.

Wexler, R. (1990). *Wounded innocents: The real victims of the war against child abuse.* Buffalo, NY: Prometheus Books.

Wharff, E. (1998). A study of decision-making criteria in child sexual abuse evaluations. *Dissertation Abstracts International, 59*(1-A), 0326. (UMI No. 0419-4209)

Whitcomb, D. (1993). *Child victims as witnesses: What the research says.* Newton, MA: Educational Development Center, Inc.

White, S. (1986). Uses and abuses of the sexually anatomically correct dolls. *APA Division of Child, Youth, and Family Services Newsletter, 9*(1), 3–4.

White, S., & Quinn, K. (1988). Investigatory independence in child sexual abuse evaluations: Conceptual considerations. *Bulletin of the American Academy of Psychiatry and the Law, 16*(3), 269–278.

White, S., Strom, G., & Quinn, K. (n.d.). *Guidelines for interviewing preschoolers with sexually anatomically detailed dolls.* Cleveland, OH: Case Western Reserve University School of Medicine.

White, S., Strom, G., Santilli, G., & Halpin, B. (1986). Interviewing young sexual abuse victims with anatomically correct dolls. *Child Abuse and Neglect, 10,* 510–519.

Wilkinson, T., & Rainey, J. (with staff writers). (1989, January 19). Tapes of the children decided the case for most jurors. *Los Angeles Times,* pp. A1, A22.

Willcock, E., Morgan, K., & Hayne, H. (2003, July 7). *Can children use anatomical drawings to indicate where they have been touched?* Poster session presented at Psychology and Law: International Conference, Edinburgh, Scotland.

Wilson, J., & Pipe, M. (1994). Cues and secrets: Influenced on children's event reports. *Developmental Psychology, 30*(4), 525–525.

Wilson, J., & Pipe, M. (1998). The effects of cues in young children's recall of real events. *New Zealand Journal of Psychology, 18,* 65–70.

Wilson, J., & Powell, M. (2001). *A guide to interviewing children: Essential skills for counselors, police, lawyers, and social workers.* London: Routledge.

Wolfe, V. V., Gentile, C., & Wolfe, D. A. (1989). The impact of sexual abuse on children: A PTSD formulation. *Behavior Therapy, 20,* 215–228.

Wolfner G., Faust, D., & Dawes, R. (1994). The use of anatomically detailed dolls in sexual abuse evaluations. *Applied and Preventative Psychology, 2*(1), 1–11.

Wood, J. (1996). Weighing evidence in sexual abuse evaluation: An introduction to Bayes theorem. *Child Maltreatment, 1,* 25–36.

Wood, K., & Garven, S. (2000). How sexual abuse interviews go astray: Implications for prosecutors, police, and child protection services. *Child Maltreatment, 5*(2), 109–118.

Wright, J., Friedrich, W. N., Cyr, M., Theriault, C., Perron, A., Lussier, Y., et al. (1998). The evaluation of Franco-Quebec victims of child sexual abuse and their mother: The implementation of a standard assessment protocol. *Child Abuse and Neglect, 22,* 9–24.

Wyatt, G. (1985). The sexual abuse of Afro-American and white-American women in childhood. *Child Abuse and Neglect, 9,* 507–518.

Wyatt, G., & Mickey, R. (1988). Support form parents and others as it mediates the effects of sexual abuse. In G. Wyatt (Ed.), *The lasting effects of child sexual abuse* (pp. 211–226). Thousand Oaks, CA: Sage Publications.

Yates, A., Beutler, L., & Crago, M. (1985). Drawings by child victims of abuse. *Child Abuse and Neglect, 9,* 183–189.

Yuille, J. (1988). The systematic assessment of children's testimony. *Canadian Psychology, 29*(3), 247–259.

Yuille, J. (2002, May). *The step-wise interview: Guidelines for interviewing children.* (Available from John C. Yuille, Department of Psychology, University of British Columbia, 2136 W. Mall, Vancouver, B.C. Canada V6T 1Z4)

Zweirs, M. (1999). *Effective interviews with children: A comprehensive guide for counselors and human services workers.* Philadelphia, PA: Accelerated Development.

Index

AACAP. *See* American Academy of Child and Adolescent Psychiatry
academics, 219
accuracy, 106, 114, 160
Achenbach Child Behavior Checklist, 146, 212, 216
ADES. *See* Adolescent Dissociative Experiences Scale
Adolescent Dissociative Experiences Scale (ADES), 213, 218
adolescents
  behavior checklists completed by, 213–14
  false allegations by, 204
  interviewing of, 83
  sexualized behavior in, 217, 221–22
  suggestibility of, 14, 15
Adolescent Sexual Concerns Questionnaire, 219, 222
adult reports, 175–76
African Americans, 84, 165, 166, 167, 169, 181
Alaskan Natives, 165
allegations, false. *See* false allegations
American Academy of Child and Adolescent Psychiatry (AACAP), 4, 5, 41, 46, 53, 59, 61, 62, 134, 204, 222–23, 252–54, 256
American Professional Society on the Abuse of Children (APSAC), 4, 41, 52, 58, 64, 101, 115, 134, 235, 236, 255, 256

American Psychological Association (APA), 4
amnesia, 29
analogue studies
  on anatomical dolls, 112, 119–22
  on drawing, 137–38
  on false allegations, 200–201
  on interviewing, 32
  on media, 112
  on misleading questions, 19, 108
  on private parts touch, 179–80
  on secret keeping, 180–82
  on special needs children, 159
  on young children, 150
anal touch, 121, 122, 179–80
anatomical dolls, 113–29
  analogue studies on, 112, 119–22
  challenges to, 110
  and children with no abuse history, 116–17
  as demonstration aid, 126–27, 140
  field studies, 122–24
  and focused questions, 96
  functions, 124–26
  genital size on, 118–19
  as memory stimulus, 126
  objections to, 113
  research and guidelines on, 114–16
  responses of children with and without history of sexual abuse, 117–18
  scenarios for use, 127
  in stepwise interview, 67

analogue studies on *(continued)*
  strategies for use, 126–28
  value added from use of, 119–24
anatomical drawings, 129–33, 140,
    141n.1
Anatomical Sex Abuse Indicators, 135
anxiety, 82, 213, 217, 222
APA. *See* American Psychological As-
    sociation
APSAC. *See* American Professional
    Society on the Abuse of Children
Asian Americans, 165
Asperger's syndrome, 152
audiotaping, 60, 63
audiovisual evidence, 177–78, 199
autism, 152
Avila, Alejandro, 31–32
avoidance, 211

backlash, 191
base rate, 201, 250–51
battered child syndrome, 38, 39
Bayes's theorem, 251
Beavers-Timberlawn Family Evalua-
    tion Scale, 40
Beck Depression Inventory, 214
behavior checklists, 212–14
believing stance, 45–46, 47
bias, 44, 172, 210, 251, 252
bilingual interviewer, 171–72
blacks. *See* African Americans
blind interview, 46
body parts inventory, 125
breasts, 119
Bruck, Maggie, 11
bug-in-the-ear, 38, 43n.2
Burgess's drawing tasks, 136–37

California, 51
California Institute on Human Ser-
    vices, 166
CARES Program, 53
caretakers
  behavioral and affective observa-
      tions, 146
  critical assessment of information,
      147
  history from, 147

information from, 145–46, 210, 215
  and nondisclosure, 182–83
case-based differences, 83–85
case dispositions, 193
case flow, 192–94
Caucasians, 165, 166
CBCA. *See* criterion-based content
    analysis
CBCL. *See* Child Behavior Checklist
CDC. *See* Child Dissociative Checklist
Ceci, Stephen J., 11, 21–23, 31, 102,
    200
cerebral palsy, 152
Chadwick Center for Child Protec-
    tion, 53, 100, 249
challenges, 82–83, 106, 110
child advocacy centers, 51, 166, 215
Child Behavior Checklist (CBCL),
    146, 212, 213, 217, 218, 219, 220
Child Development Inventory, 146,
    217
Child Dissociative Checklist (CDC),
    213, 218, 224
child protective services (CPS), 8,
    35–38, 47, 81–82
children
  dependence, 14
  developmentally disabled, 152–63
  maltreatment, 38, 153, 154, 165, 192,
      198, 211, 214, 218
  memory and suggestibility, 10–34
  nondisclosing, 96, 175–90
  parent-child interaction model,
      38–39
  planting of false beliefs in, 21–23
  questioning strategies for, 19,
      90–109
  responses to anatomical dolls,
      116–18
  risk situations for false allegations,
      203–6
  sexualized behavior, 220–21
  standardized testing, 146, 207–25
  in welfare system, 165–66
  as witnesses, 10, 11–12
  See also child sexual abuse;
      preschoolers; young children
Children's Apperception Test, 214

Children's Depression Inventory, 214, 219
Children's Hospital and Health Center (San Diego, Calif.), 53
child sexual abuse
    accommodation syndrome, 183, 189
    alternative explanations for allegations of, 252–54
    barriers to identification in special needs children, 154–62
    common symptoms and indicators of, 217–18, 254
    criteria for deciding likelihood of, 226–47
    and cultural differences, 164–74
    false allegations of, 191–206, 237
    forensic and clinical interviewer roles in, 3–9
    formulating conclusions about, 248–57
    high-certainty cases, 15–16, 176–79
    interviewer objectivity and allegations of, 44–49
    level of certainty of occurrence, 254–56
    models for assessing, 35–43
    nondisclosure of, 96, 175–90
    penetrating, 28, 29, 221
    related cognitions, 224–25
    reported by adults, 175–76
    risk for special needs children, 153–54
    See also interviews
Child Sexual Abuse Accommodation Syndrome, 46
"Child Sexual Abuse Accommodation Syndrome, The" (Summit), 183
Child Sexual Behavior Inventory (CSBI), 134, 146, 207–8, 210, 212–13, 215, 216, 217, 219, 220, 236
Christianity, 171
clinical, definition of, 4, 9n.1
clinical interviewing, 3–9
close-ended questions, 91–92, 98, 109n.1

closure, 79, 80, 82
coercive questions, 103–5
cognitive development, 211
cognitive interview, 68, 74, 78–80
commands, 105
communication
    of children with special needs, 156, 157, 161, 163
    in developmental assessment, 73
    direct and indirect, 230
    media for, 110, 111, 161
    potential impediments to, 167–71
competency assessment, 68, 70–71, 83, 207
comprehensive assessment model, 41–43
conclusions, 248–57
concurrent validity, 33n.1
confessions. See offender confessions
confidentiality, 173
confirmatory bias, 44, 251, 252
consistency, 52, 106
contact information, 80
context, 78, 211
cooperation, 73
Corner House, 53, 83
cost effectiveness, 209
co-witness information, 104
CPS. See child protective services
criminal prosecution, 64
criterion-based content analysis (CBCA), 163n.1, 232–34, 237, 243
CSBI. See Child Sexual Behavior Inventory
cued invitations, 97
cued recall, 13, 114, 149–50
culture, 164–74, 213
    diverse backgrounds in child welfare system, 165–66
    learning about child's, 172
    potential impediments to communication and disclosure, 169–70
    and sexual abuse, 166–67
    strategies for achieving cultural competence, 171–73
    subcultures, 170
custody disputes, 39, 195, 198, 202, 203, 210

Dalenberg, Constance J., 30, 200
databases, 86
data-gathering, 159–63, 209, 235,
    242–43, 244–47
data sources, 210
Davies, D., 156
daycare, 202
decision-making, 226–47, 250–52
delusions, 202, 204
demographics, 83, 117
denial, 184, 211
dependence, 14
depression, 214, 217, 218, 224
details, 77–78
developmental assessment, 73
developmental issues, 211
developmentally disabled, 152–63
developmental stages, 143–44, 230
diagnostic overshadowing, 155
direct communication, 230
directive question, 95
direct question, 100
disabled, 152–63
disclosure, 85, 91, 167–71, 183–86
dissociation, 213, 217, 218, 224
divorce, 4, 39, 40, 167, 198, 202,
    203
doctor toys, 112
documentation
    audiotaping, 60, 63
    informing child about, 65
    of interview, 58–65, 256
    method of, 7, 58–62
    note taking, 6, 58, 59, 63
    research on, 63–64
    videotaping, 6, 59, 60–62, 63–65
dolls. *See* anatomical dolls
drawing, 129–39
    analogue studies, 137–38
    anatomical, 129–33, 141n.1
    Burgess's tasks, 136–37
    as communication aid, 137–39
    free, 134
    human figure, 214
    picture, 133–39, 141n.2
    practice, 138–39
    as screening tool, 134
    stick figures, 149

traditional tasks, 135–36
    by young children, 149
DUR-X questions, 105–6

early childhood memory, 144
ecological validity, 17, 18, 23, 33n.1
embarrassment, 30
Emmanuel Hospital (Portland, Ore.),
    53
emotional disturbance, 202, 204
emotions, 80, 209
ethnically diverse agencies, 171
ethnicity, 84, 164–74
event frequency, 251
event plausibility, 23–24
explicit memory, 11–12, 144
exposure, genital, 205–6
externalizing behaviors, 117
externally derived questions, 106
eye witness, 199

failure to thrive, 38–39
false affirmatives, 102, 103
false allegations
    analogue research on, 200–201
    base rates for, adults versus
        children, 201
    criteria for, 194–97
    deliberate, 193–94
    differentiating unsubstantiated
        case from, 191–94
    and interview structure, 86
    large-sample studies, 197–99
    and leading questions, 178
    literature reviews, 195
    methodology for determining
        veracity of allegation, 194–201
    practice parameters on, 253
    proportion of cases involving, 47,
        48
    risk situations for, adults, 201–
        3
    risk situations for, children,
        203–6
    of sexual abuse, 191–206, 237
    Sexual Abuse Legitimacy Scale,
        237–42, 247
    and skeptical stance, 46, 49

small-sample studies and assertions without data, 199
false beliefs, 20–23
false negatives, 86, 99, 121, 175
false positives, 102, 103, 107, 115, 120, 121, 160, 205
false statements, 14, 15
family structure, 167–68
fantasy, 11, 112, 205
fears, 146
females, 10, 45, 47, 176, 224
Fivush, Robyn, 18
flashbacks, 29, 218
focused questions, 96, 97, 100, 109n.1
following child's lead, 85
forensic, definition of, 4
forensic interviewing, 3–9
foster care, 165
free drawings, 134
free recall, 13, 31, 120, 128, 149, 163, 181
Friedrich, William, 210, 212, 216, 236
functional assessment, 73–80
funnel approach, 92

gender, 47
generic testing, 219
genitals, 30, 118–22, 134, 135, 179–80, 214, 221
gonorrhea, 177
Goodman, Gail, 11
ground truth, 47
Gudjonsson Suggestibility Scale, 15
Guide for Forensic Interviewing of Spanish-Speaking Children, 166
"Guidelines for Child Custody Evaluations in Divorce Proceedings," 4
Guidelines for Psychosocial Evaluation of Suspected Sexual Abuse in Children, 4
Guidelines for Psychosocial Evaluation of Suspected Sexual Abuse in Young Children, 235, 255
guilt, 216

habit memory, 12
Handbook on Questioning Children (Walker), 83

Harbor-UCLA Sexual Abuse Crisis Center, 184
health care professionals, 3, 81
Hewitt, Sandra, 12
high-certainty cases, 15–16, 176–79
Hispanics, 165, 169
history, 147, 173, 175
hourglass approach, 92
human figure drawings, 214
hyperamnesia, 29
hyperarousal, 218

immigrants, 167, 169
implicit memory, 12
incest, 40
inconclusive assessments, 256–57
indirect communication, 230
infants, 12, 143
intelligence, 25
intercourse, 221
interpretation of findings, 210
interpreters, 171–72
interrater reliability, 34n.1
interview aids. *See* media
interviews
    child interview model, 36–37
    cognitive, 68, 74, 78–80
    culturally competent, 164–74
    with developmentally disabled, 157–63
    documentation of, 58–65, 256
    forensic versus clinical, 3–9
    incorporating testing into, 215–17
    informing child about, 65, 70, 173
    introducing topic of concern, 75–76
    media for, 110–41
    with nondisclosing children, 187–88
    number of, 50–57
    objectivity of, 44–49
    one versus several by same person, 51–53
    practice observations on interviewer/professional stance, 48–49
    research on interviewer/professional stance, 47–48

interviews *(continued)*
  single versus multiple interviewers,
    50–51
  structure, protocols, and guide-
    lines, 66–89
  See also questioning techniques
intrafamilial sexual abuse, 84, 182–83,
  184
invitational probe, 100
Islam, 171

joint investigation model, 37–38
Jordan (Minn.), case, 53, 57n.1
Judaism, 171

Kempe National Center for the Pre-
  vention and Treatment of Child
  Abuse, 193, 197–98, 201, 203, 204
Kinetic Family Drawing, 135, 136, 138

Lamb, Michael, 88n.2, 91, 98, 100, 122,
  130
language, 111, 156, 161, 165, 166, 170,
  171–72
Latinos. *See* Hispanics
Latvia, 225n.1
law enforcement personnel, 35–38,
  47–48, 81–82
leading questions, 6, 68, 86, 98, 99,
  101–3, 178
learning disabilities, 152, 153, 159
least preferred questions/probes, 92,
  94, 101–6
legal professionals, 47–48
less preferred questions/probes, 92,
  94, 98–101
lies, 68, 70–71
linear structure, of interview, 87
logistics, 52
Louisville Behavior Checklist, 135,
  212
Lyon, Thomas D., 11, 53, 72, 102

males, 176, 184
maltreatment, 38, 153, 154, 165, 192,
  198, 211, 214, 218, 222
Mansell, S., 155
mass media, 32, 45
masturbation, 221, 230

maternal skepticism, 16
maternal support, 16
McMartin preschool case, 53
media
  advantages of, 111–12
  anatomical drawings, 129–33,
    141n.1
  data obtained from, 235
  for developmentally disabled,
    160–61
  disadvantages of, 112–13
  helpful with young children,
    148–49, 189
  for interviewing children, 67,
    110–41
  for nondisclosing children, 188–89
  picture drawing, 133–39, 141n.2
  See also anatomical dolls
medical evidence, 177, 196, 199, 230,
  235
medical examinations, 36, 42, 107–8,
  120–21, 154
Memorandum of Good Practice, 77,
  85, 88n.1, 102, 108
memory
  age-related differences in, 19–20
  circumstances and characteristics
    that affect, 25–26
  definition of, 11
  early childhood, 144
  explicit versus implicit, 11–13
  free recall, cued recall, and recogni-
    tion, 13, 31
  inaccurate, 14
  for repeated events, 26–27
  retrieval, 13
  sources of knowledge about chil-
    dren's, 15–18
  and stress, 28–30
  traces versus constructions, 13
  traumatic, 144–45
  of very young children, 18–19
mental health professionals, 47–48,
  248
mental retardation, 152–53, 156, 158,
  159, 161
misleading questions, 19, 108
modesty, 30
Mormonism, 171

"mousetrap" study, 21–22, 200
Multidimensional Anxiety Scale of
    Children, 213
multiple choice questions, 98, 99, 100,
    101
Muslims, 171

narrative account, 77
narrative cues, 97
narrative elaboration, 77–78
National Center for the Prosecution
    of Child Abuse, 35, 83
National Children's Advocacy Center
    (NCAC), 18, 51, 55–56, 166, 216
National Child Traumatic Stress Net-
    work, 223
National Institute of Child Health
    and Human Development
    (NICHD), 76, 88–89n.2, 91,
    130–31, 187
Native Americans, 84, 165
NCAC. See National Children's Ad-
    vocacy Center
Netherlands, 213
neutrality, 6, 44, 45, 46, 47
neutral topic, 80
NICHD. See National Institute of
    Child Health and Human Devel-
    opment
nightmares, 29
nondisclosing children, 96, 175–90
    audiovisual evidence research,
        177–78
    delay in reporting, 184–85
    disclosure as process, 183–86
    in high-certainty cases, 176–79
    interviewing of, 187–88
    medical evidence studies, 177
    offender confession studies, 178–79
    practice techniques used with,
        186–89
    predictors of, 182–83
    research on disclosure failures,
        175–82
    strategies to assist, 187
nonverbal memory, 144
"no opportunity" cases, 195–96
normalizing strategies, 188
normative data, 209

note taking, 6, 58, 59, 63
numbing, 211, 218
nursery school, 202

oath, 71
objectivity, 44–49, 208, 210
observation, 148
offender confessions, 178–79, 196, 199
omission errors, 30
open-ended questions/probes, 72, 75,
    82, 91–92, 93, 95, 96, 97, 122, 149
option-posing questions, 98

paired questions, 92
paranoid personality disorder, 202
parental figures, 182–83
parent-child interaction model, 38–41
parent-child relationship, 216
Peabody Picture Vocabulary Test-
    Revised, 154
pedophilia, 238, 241–42
penis, 113, 119
perpetrator proximity, 182–83
person-focused questions, 96
Pezdek, Kathy, 23, 24
phased interview, 66–67
phobia, 146
picture drawing, 133–39, 141n.2
play, 112
plethysmograph, 237
police. See law enforcement person-
    nel
polygraph, 196, 237
pornography, 199, 205
positive topic, 80
posttraumatic stress disorder (PTSD),
    202, 204, 210, 211, 216–18, 221–24
posttraumatic symptoms, 29
poverty, 164, 165
practice interview, 74–75
predictive validity, 33n.1
preferred questions/probes, 92, 93,
    95–98
pregnancy, 235
preschoolers
    analogue studies, 17
    implicit memory, 12
    interviewing of, 68, 83, 102
    memory of, 18–19

preschoolers *(continued)*
  planting of false beliefs in, 20, 21
  special consideration for, 142–51
  standardized testing, 210
  suggestibility of, 20
  testimony of, 20
prior disclosure, 182
private parts, 113, 114, 119–22, 127,
  129, 179–80
probability, 251
procedural memory, 144
professional training, 81
Projective Story Telling Cards (PST
  Cards), 215
projective tests, 214–15
pronouns, 161
props. *See* media
Protocol of Evidentiary Interviews,
  100
protocols, interview, 66–89
PST Cards. *See* Projective Story
  Telling Cards
psychiatric illness, 202
psychological testing, 207–25
  completed by children/teens,
    213–14
  completed by parents, 212–13, 236
  incorporated into interviewing,
    215–17
  overview of measures, 211–15
  research on, 219–25
  strengths and limitations of, 208–11
  See also specific measures and tests
PTSD. *See* posttraumatic stress
  disorder

questioning techniques, 90–109
  bases of advice about, 90–91
  close-ended, 91–92, 98, 109n.1
  coercive, 103–5
  externally derived, 106
  leading, 6, 68, 86, 98, 99, 101–3, 178
  least preferred, 92, 94, 101–6
  less preferred, 92, 94, 98–101
  misleading, 19, 108
  open-ended, 72, 75, 82, 91–92, 93,
    95, 97, 149
  preferred, 92, 93, 95–98
  repeated questions, 106–8

structure of, 105–6
use of continuum for, 91–105
"wh" questions, 77, 94, 97, 98, 100,
  105, 109n.1, 159, 163
yes/no questions, 98, 99–100, 105,
  107, 109n.1, 160, 205

race, 84, 164–74, 181
rape, 221
rapport building, 71–73, 75, 82, 87,
  105, 138, 158, 187
reaffirmation, 184
recantation, 184, 185–86, 196, 197
recapitulation, 79
recognition, 13
reestablishing equilibrium, 80
reinforcement, 104
reliability, 33n.1, 34n.1
religion, 171
repeated questions, 106–8, 161
reporting requirements, 192–94
responsibility, 218
retraction, 185–86, 196
risk-taking behaviors, 221, 222
ritual abuse, 190n.1, 215
Roberts Apperception Test, 214
Rorschach Test, 214, 215
rules, 68, 74–75
Runnion, Samantha, 31

SALS. *See* Sexual Abuse Legitimacy
  Scale
scaffolding, 149–50
screening, 192, 196, 208, 209, 215,
  216
scripted protocols, 69, 72
script memory, 26–27
secrets, 180–82
segmentation, 77
self-blame, 224
self-esteem, 217, 219, 224
self-injurious behavior, 155
semen, 199, 235
sensory impairments, 152
sentence structure, 92, 101
Seventh Day Adventism, 171
sexual abuse. *See* child sexual abuse
Sexual Abuse Legitimacy Scale
  (SALS), 237–42, 247

Sexual Abuse Symptom Checklist,
      217
sexualized behavior, 96, 116–18, 125,
      147, 211–13, 217, 219–22, 250
sexual knowledge, 44, 116–17, 147,
      155, 236, 254
sexually transmitted disease, 16, 49,
      177, 199, 221, 222, 235
shame, 216, 218, 224
siblings, 42
Siegel, Daniel, 11, 32
Sixth Amendment, 65n.1
skeptical stance, 46, 47
slang, 170
sleep, 146
social isolation, 156, 159
socioeconomic status, 25, 164–74
somatic memory, 12
Sorenson, T., 178, 183–84, 185
source misattribution errors, 21–23
source monitoring, 15, 20
Spanish language, 166–67
special needs
      barriers to identification of abuse in
         children with, 154–62
      definitions of, 152–53
      interviewing children with, 152–63
      media for children with, 160–61
      risk of sexual abuse for children
         with, 153–54
specific questions, 159
standard measures and tests, 146,
      207–25
      behavior checklists completed by
         children/teens, 213–14
      behavior checklists completed by
         parents, 212–13
      incorporating into interviewing,
         215–17
      overview of, 211–15
      projective, 214–15
      research on, 219–25
      See also specific measures and tests
statement validity analysis (SVA),
      163n.1, 232–34
stepfamilies, 167
Stepwise Interview, 67–68, 74
Sternberg, Kathleen, 88n.2, 91, 98, 100
stick figures, 149

story models, 95
Stossel, John, 21, 31
stress, 28–30, 187, 230
structure, of interview, 66–89
subcultures, 170
suggestibility
      of abused versus nonabused
         children, 27–28
      of adolescents, 14, 15
      of children, 18–24
      circumstances and characteristics
         that affect, 25–26
      definition of, 13–15
      of developmentally disabled, 161,
         163
      Gudjonsson Suggestibility Scale, 15
      and intelligence, 25
      sources of knowledge about
         children's, 15–18
      testing, 75
      Video Suggestibility Scale for
         Children, 15, 24
Summit, Roland, 183
suspect denial, 197
SVA. See statement validity analysis
Sweden, 213

tag questions, 101–2
Teach-A-Bodies, 113
tentative disclosure, 184
tests. See standard measures and
      tests; specific tests
Texas, 64
Thematic Apperception Test, 214
tools. See media
topic-focused questions, 96
touch, 30, 120–21, 131, 133, 156,
      179–80
Touch Continuum, 76, 149
trauma, 28–30, 51, 111, 144–45, 211,
      215, 224
Trauma Symptom Checklist for
      Children (TSCC), 33n.1, 210, 216,
      217, 218, 220, 222, 223
Trauma Symptom Checklist for
      Young Children (TSCYC), 146,
      212, 216, 218
Trauma Symptom Inventory, 213
truth, 68, 70–71, 194–201

TSCC. *See* Trauma Symptom Checklist for Children
TSCYC. *See* Trauma Symptom Checklist for Young Children
Tufts New England Medical Center, 184, 198

unconscious memory, 12
University of Michigan Family Assessment Clinic, 216
unsubstantiated case, 191–94

validity, 33n.1, 209, 232–34
VCUG. *See* voiding cystoureothrogram fluoroscopy
venereal disease. *See* sexually transmitted disease
Victims of Child Abuse Laws, 197
Video Suggestibility Scale for Children (VSSC), 15, 24
videotaping, 6, 59, 60–62, 63–65, 70, 177, 200
visitation disputes, 39, 198, 203, 210
voiding cystoureothrogram fluoroscopy (VCUG), 17, 28–29, 30, 120
VSSC. *See* Video Suggestibility Scale for Children

Walker, Anne Graffam, 12, 70, 71, 74, 83, 95, 99, 101–2, 105
Washington State, 80
Waterman, J., 219
welfare system, 165–66
"wh" questions, 77, 94, 97, 98, 100, 105, 109n.1, 159, 163
willingness to talk, 86
witnesses, 10, 11–12, 20, 199, 249

yes/no questions, 98, 99–100, 105, 107, 109n.1, 160, 205
young children
    assessment format for, 147–48
    cuing, 149–50
    definitions of, 143–44
    developmental stages, 143–44
    false allegations by, 205
    integration of information from several sources, 150–51
    interviewing, 144
    media helpful with, 148–49, 189
    observation of, 148
    practice recommendations, 145–51
    research findings on, 144–45
    special consideration for, 142–51
    standardized testing, 210
    See also preschoolers